Ancestry of Christian Thought:

Egyptian, Hebrew, Greek

Ancestry of Christian Thought:

Egyptian-Hebrew-Greek

The 2021 Re-Visitation of
Egyptian Light and Hebrew Fire: Theological and Philosophical Roots of Christendom in Evolutionary Perspective,
published in 1991

Karl W. Luckert

Published by Triplehood, 2021
Distributed byLightning Source—Ingram

Triplehood.com

Ancestry of Christian Thought: Egyptian-Hebrew-Greek.
Library of Congress Cataloging-in-Publication Data
Luckert, Karl W., 1934–

The 2021 Re-visitation of *Egyptian Light and Hebrew Fire: Theological and Philosophical Roots of Christendom in Evolutionary Perspective.* Karl W. Luckert—SUNY Press, 1991.
Out of print. The present revised 2021 Triplehood edition features:
454 Pages, 19 Illustrations, Bibliography, and Index.

ISBN 978-0-9839072-7-5

Introduction to Culture, Religion, and Evolution.

Ancient Egyptian civilization, culture, and religion.

Ancient Hebrew tradition and Judaism, presented as a reaction to Egyptian and Mesopotamian hyper-domestication.

Greek philosophy, indebted to ancient Egyptian ontology and soteriology.

Neo-Platonism and Gnosticism derived from Neo-Egyptian ontology and theology. A study based primarily on ancient Egyptian Pyramid Texts and Coffin Texts.

Theological and philosophical roots of Christian thought, as found in Egyptian, Hebrew, and Graeco-Roman texts.

Constantine the Great: His politics of Christianization.

Contents

List of Illustrations

Preface

Why this book?

Imbalances in learning—of what soldiers could not learn in World War II trenches and what victory-impaired veterans were unable to teach their offspring, and what their offspring assumed they knew better than their parents by virtue of having been born later—and what they intuited additionally in kindergartens, grade-schools, and at universities—all these together have created our present culture of messianic capitalism and exceptionalism. All these gains were won by sacrificing our culture's knowledge about history and about the finitude of human time—a flaw of learning, generated by the death-wishes of many progressive ancestral generations. Were our violent propagandists and heroes really what we think they have been? Or, were they bungling simpletons, accidentally in tune with the incidental levels of ignorance of those who revere them now?

This, on which America's Serpent of Culture has been feeding during the Nineteen-Sixties—when this author began teaching at university level—is still winding itself through the alimentary tract of Time and is, in our days, just now getting expelled into the realm of humus and fresh hope. Immune responses to save American democracy are fully stressed right now (November 2020).

Why did this book on the Ancestry of Christian Thought need to be written in the first place? Now that it has been written—why should anyone want to read it? Why would the New Testament not contain all there is to know about Christian Thought? Why should we even reach back into stories of the Hebrew Bible which Christians early on have accepted as their *Old* Testament? And why should anyone want to reach back still farther into ancient Egyptian funerary literature—into cults that three thousand years ago Levites and Israelites wanted to escape from forever?

The answer to these questions is surprisingly simple. Books written in any period of time, do not answer only questions that were asked in those periods; rather, they also have tried to solve puzzles that were left over from earlier epochs. Key teachings that in some form are contained in New Testament stories also answered questions that were raised over twice as long ago, in Egyptian Pyramid Texts and

Coffin Texts. This includes Christian key concepts like Reign of God, Savior, Son of God, Emperor worship, Transformation, Resurrection, Breath of Life, Second Birth, Heaven, Enthronement, divinely justified government and the general status of humankind.

Difficult concepts within the stream of Christian Thought, for following the Christian religion, may not have been made intentionally difficult to tighten discipline. Some opaque centralities of the Christian faith could just as easily have gotten centrally placed to improve on the solution of an older weighty problem. For instance, a commoner summoned to answer an ancient deified king, who sat in judgment, would understandably have found it necessary to rationalize his socially absurd predicament with utilizing religious logic, proportions, and demeanors that were survivable.

Yes, historians who study ancient Egypt are well served if they distinguish Egyptian materials that subsequently got modified by Persian, Greek and Roman conquerors or that got dragged away to different regions of the globe—to be caricatured there, or idolized by foreign habits of thinking.

Many answers to questions in human history have reached us with millennia and centuries of delay. Historical facts remain frozen in time, while words which are used to describe them often get modified before an awareness of facts catches up. And why is this point important? Imagine for a moment, listening to a series of questions and answers exchanged in conversation between two persons over the telephone. Then also imagine that someone along the trek of time has cut the outward-bound cable that leads from the person who is asking the questions to you. You can hear only the answers. If you never heard the question to which an answer was given, how many of these answers could you fully understand, or could relay to others correctly? Indeed, this is the befuddled state of affairs in the processes of much historical learning, about which Christian learners expect to be satisfied.

This is not all. After you verify all possible meanings and misunderstandings that you have been absorbing about ancient situations—an impossibility in itself—you discover that central points from the history of Christian Thought will rarely get cleared up by literal translation. Words in every language are getting utilized by people who do not know their language well enough to teach words by speaking, while you are listening.

The causes of possible misunderstanding are so numerous that we will never know them all—we will also never catch up with the speed at which words are changing their meanings while we try to use them precisely. But we can attempt honest beginnings, at least with regard to our most important beliefs. We at least can focus on the changing meanings of God, Father, Mother, Death, Resurrection, Transformation, Second Birth, Enthronement, Atonement, Salvation and then consider the fact that at the time when our religion was founded, few people bothered yet to distinguish religion from politics, distinguish chance from fate, or notice a difference between angels and natural forces. God the Father—Yahweh, the God who during earlier millennia still lived in the Sinai area alongside an Asherah-Spouse or All-Mother—the God of Israel, who desired to keep his name unspoken, has become squeamish about revealing his name at some point in human history. He did so, clearly in competition with the top-most Egyptian Hidden deity, Amun, to whom such behavior was ascribed several centuries earlier. Already Atum, earlier still, at Heliopolis, is mentioned occasionally as having not revealed his real name.

Christianity's most central message was taught by John the Baptizer and Jesus of Nazareth, concerning the "Kingdom of Heaven" or the "Empire or Reign of God" being at hand. These concepts combined are an allegory of the All-God's antithesis, explained by Jesus of Nazareth in opposition to the actual kingdoms and empires which, over the duration of several thousand years, had come to infest our planet. Imperially deified "Sons of God" have established and ruled these hyper-domestication establishments—which is—the same schemes that meanwhile, as historians, we have learned to appreciate as "civilizations."

The Triple-Ancestry of Christian Thought

Christianity is one of several large-scale religions. It is universalistic in outlook and today counts approximately 2.2 billion souls within its sphere of influence. All are milling about along the furrows of their own wake. The title of this book, *Ancestry of Christian Thought,* refers to the mental and linguistic umbrella that Christians, within their sphere of influence and during the past two thousand years, have constructed and adjusted. In all realms of life, in physical as well as in conceptual realms, entities are either forming, growing, changing, withering, or dying. And in this world all things are kept on track in an interplay with greater-than-human realities and their intermediaries.

The ancestry of Christian thought comprises world perspectives and religious fascinations that historically have preceded the Christian religion. We do not know all the clouds of thought which during two thousand years have been gathering and affecting the ways in which Christians were enabled to ask and to answer their questions. But with some help from archaeology and other human studies, we can discern three major ancestral patterns in Christian culture and religion—that is, to the extent to which their respective languages have left footprints of them along the inherited trails of observation.

This author grew up within the bounds of a Christianized culture. The culture was heated up to boiling ferment during World War II, and thereby he became acquainted early on, intensely, with the root of Christian thought that lies within the pattern of Judaic-Hebrew monotheism—of reckoning with a single greater-than-human source and center of reality.

Approximately a quarter century along the road of his life he noticed the contours of a slightly younger, philosophical Ionian-Greek ancestry as a next ancient root that has helped provoke Christian thought. Then thirdly and belatedly he became aware of the "ontology" that formerly was the ancient Egyptian world-view. And with this awareness, finally, he could discern the combined political and theological notion of an All-God's emanation known long ago.

This thought began to dawn after I had been teaching history of religions courses for more than two decades at university level. It happened as I was also searching among several other archaic patterns of religion comparatively—such as Navajo Indian and Olmec religion, and Daoist shamanism later. Pre-Pottery Neolithic monuments were found at Göbekli Tepe in 1995; they came to my attention in 2011.

Bible stories rested far too deeply embedded in the soul of this writer, for them to have enabled him to maintain an all-around historical objectivity toward ancient Egypt. For a while, these stories even proved to be an impediment to understanding foreign and ancient religions. The English language itself presented a formidable challenge. For example, its rules of capitalization tend to force any reader or writer to pretend that they can differentiate clearly among things, persons, gods, God, or idols. Thus, the simplest feat of religious enlightenment can, in English, be certified and distorted linguistically with the trick of capitalization.

A **poly**theist can become a **mono**theist by writing **God** instead of **gods**. A person who sees a little light can enlarge his "enlightenment" by that same magic into a historical "**P**eriod of **E**nlightenment." Reducing a goddess, such as **M**other **N**ature, to sheer natural forces for science, can be done by lowering "M...**N**" to "**n**ature."

The Judaic-Hebrew Ancestry: Like everyone around me, in my youth I became aware of only one major pre-Christian root of thought. It was the ancient Judaic-Hebrew tradition that historically, had begun to take shape perhaps during the reign of King David, about a thousand years before the Christian era. According to Hebrew scripture, which Christianity has adopted as Old Testament, ancient people of the Judaic-Hebrew orientation understood themselves as a people who have suffered under the powerful imperial civilization of ancient Egypt. Judaism remembers its Levitic priestly origins in a narrative about an escape of slaves from Egypt. According to that story, imperial Egypt at one time was Israel's slave-master or "hyper-domesticator"—a term that will be explained in Chapters 1 and 2.

As a later echo in biblical salvation history, Christians remember the birth trauma of their religion in a similar manner—not vis-à-vis a deified oppressive Egyptian pharaoh, but rather as subjects rising up to face the deified tyranny of Roman civilization. The crucifixion of Jesus of Nazareth by the Roman Empire became a turning point for Western history. The Founder-Messiah became the nemesis of all past, present and future Sons of God. He was born under, and thereby was instantly identified as an apparent subject of, Caesar Augustus. But the Christian story tells more. From the outset, it introduces this Jesus as the "Son of God" challenger, a very foil to the Emperor Augustus Octavius, who also presented himself, officially, as the son of a deity. Jesus was a commoner Jew who, later under Caesar Tiberius, was executed by crucifixion. Already in his birth story Jesus was positioned as challenger of deified Roman emperors—who had gotten mandated as ancient Egypt's theo-political imitators.

Judaic stories, fragments of which may be three thousand years old, tell of antecedent Hebrew patriarchs living in circumstances that predated the stories by approximately eight centuries. Later stories about Levitic Hebrews, about having escaped from Egypt as slaves, have added to the tradition of Judaic and Israelite religious thought an "Unnameable God Almighty." He became known by the acronym "Yahweh"—"I Am" in English. According to the Sinai archaeological evidence, this singular deity at some point in his history was associated with an Ashera wife. In Hebrew tradition, Yahweh is said to have commissioned Moses, utilizing him as leader who was to facilitate the Exodus escape of a group of chosen Levitic Israelites. The story content refers to conditions two or three centuries before scribes, employed by David's dynasty, could have collected some of the story events and brought them into the daylight of their political propaganda, of their history and religion. Still later, in *Second Isaiah*, Yahweh was credited also with having freed Judaic and Benjamite exiles, from Babylon, where God has utilized an "Anointed Savior," there identified as "Cyrus the Great of Persia," to allow these people to return home to Judah.

The Greek Philosophical-Scientific Ancestry: Some writings of Greek philosophers were repeatedly copied and were studied in Christian monasteries during the Middle Ages, in both the Eastern and Western regions. Books of Plato and Plotinus, and of Ante-Nicene Egyptian church fathers that did not conflict head-on with Nicene Christian orthodoxy, were also available. These sources contained allusions to ontology. They supported the Christian faith and were consulted to synthesize and systematize Christianity's God-story. They also were utilized to hone and to enrich the Greek and Latin languages which were being expanded to help manage an increasingly organized and imperially certified Christian liturgy. Christian skills were engaged politically to help transform the empire into something that would be Roman, and holy in a different way—and also would be congenial to emperors who were friendly toward Christianity.

Nevertheless, beginning with the Renaissance (ca. 1300-1700), new insights were won within Christian thought from reading early Greek philosophical and scientific texts. These older texts were utilized to speculate on fresh scientific insights. Older Platonic and so-called "Neo-Platonic" materials, which had proven useful to Saint Augustine (354-430), have later on been reshaped into Christian systematic theology. They were used to interpret reasons and assumptions of the early Church Councils—and they promoted an appetite for additional philosophical and scientific materials of Athenian and Alexandrian vintage. During the Renaissance, fragmented writings of Ionian pioneers in philosophy and science, additional writings of Plato and the later Physics of Aristotle, were also carried west. The enthusiasm caused by fresh textual supplies of ancient literatures also brought snippets of archaic mythology and religion that meanwhile, along the eastern Mediterranean, had been replaced with the Christian story. Thus, during the Renaissance, in the West, the entire Greek philosophical/scientific and pagan mythological mixture began to ferment politically—first in the monastery schools of Christianized Spain and France.

It was the theologian Thomas Aquinas (1225-1274) who in his theology opened up fresh breathing space for ferment and learning. He did this more than four centuries before other thinkers would be mature enough to utilize the breach that he has cut for them. When the "Enlightenment" generations (1685-1815) were born and schooled to study Nature "herself" or "itself," they found that Thomas Aquinas had already conceptually divided the field into "revealed" and "natural/rational" realms of knowledge—realms that grew from pre-Christian aggravations: from philosophy, science, and political theory. Soon after the Hellenic wave of philosophical and scientific speculations arrived in the West, some of its seed ideas began to germinate. Of course, fresh revolutionary notions have arrived in the West already in association with Christianity's first dogmas, embodied in orthodox Christian formulas. Younger generations of learners who never quite understood Saint Augustine's innovations as adaptation of the Christian faith to the larger context of "Hellenistic" ontology—as that world-view was exemplified best in the thought structure of Plotinus —congratulated themselves and celebrated their own foot-prints in history. They named their own period of learning after their personal estimate—the "Enlightenment."

In the rustic Christian enclave into which this author was born, very few people knew anything about the Enlightenment Period (*die Aufklärungszeit*) beyond its name. Moreover, at the time when I began asking children's questions about history, such curiosities were either ignored or eclipsed by ideological fad. Boys just four years older than I were issued rifles and sent to fight. When at last I awoke from childhood dreams and from the nightmares of World War II, my first longings were not in the direction of general learning, but for a state of awareness that permitted me to think about thinking for the sake of understanding the world and humankind. At the University of Kansas, gradually, I became interested in ancient philosophy, in comparative religions and a few other subjects that appeared relevant. There I became aware of the Greek philosophical root that has become important in Western intellectual history since the Renaissance and the Enlightenment. Both periods have drawn meaning and orientation from the prehistory and history of Greek philosophy, and most students of the two periods still acquired their basic learning skills in Christian monastery schools. The Greek philosophical root emerged into visibility later during the Enlightenment, as an intellectual alternative to the slightly older Judaic-Hebrew root which happens to represent the most obvious portion of Christianity's ancestral narrative.

Alongside the still living Hebrew root, scholars never finished their task of laying bare the Greek ancestral heritage of Christian thought. Archaeologically speaking, the enlightened philosopher-excavators scraped from the top layer of Western Civilization the overhead soil and shoveled it westward. There it was used to obliterate almost completely the distinction which Thomas Aquinas has managed to argue between "Revealed" and the newly available category of "Natural" knowledge. The latter could be acquired legitimately in a less intimate dependence on God or on the clergy, by "natural" common sense and reason. So the wielders of shovels, while trying to excavate pre-Christian Hellenic light from under their own dark piles of overhead scrapings, took advantage of their opportunity to misunderstand and to ignore the theological language of Christianity which, for them, had thereby gone out of focus. They never found the time to evaluate functionally, contrastingly and historically, the basic concepts of Greek philosophy which ostensibly have sparked their own personal Enlightenment.

All the while, scientific mathematical formulas were a slim diet for starved minds and for undernourished human souls. Indeed, Enlightenment excavators at some depth, and insufficiently back along the trail of their excavations, found not as much Hellenic light as they hoped. The darkest most mysterious data, down there, they discounted as ancient superstitions. Their knowledge of the Christian faith, of the Middle Ages seemed getting darker all the while. In getting their so-called "Long Eighteenth Century" (1688-1832) to appear brighter, illuminati in the West insisted on imagining the "Dark Middle Ages" as having been darker than they could imagine Islam to be—perhaps to make their own post-Christian Enlightenment appear brighter still, in comparison to either. After all, there was at least one Muslim scholar among those who carried copies of books westward from Byzantium's imperial (Christian) library!

The Ionian-Greek vein of golden wisdom turned out to be not entirely what Enlightenment scholars expected it to be. It held more vagaries than specific scientific insights, facts, or solutions. After all, the Ionian and early Greek philosophers had arrived at their "scientific" inferences while they were still rummaging about, trying to overcome Egyptian hyper-domestication "superstitions" of an earlier dispensation. Later Enlightenment thinkers, as they contemplated rational government, were unable to escape entirely the ancient Egyptian quandary—of seeing "political" and "religious" authorities behave very much alike. Culture and religion always have confounded each other's rationalities and faith assumptions. Still today, while trying to develop their purely utilitarian and atheistic theory for the proper governance of humankind, modern thinkers appear to be demonstrating that their "Political Science," by itself, is better suited to teach procedural tricks that enable greed for power, rather than to create societal harmonies.

The political strategy of separating religion from the state—of governing without appealing to de facto "religiosity"—remains the still unfulfilled dream of America's Founding Fathers. Jurisprudence in America still slithers along, without defining "religion" legally or more precisely. Our courts of law have not yet faced up to the task of properly identifying "religion" as a subject matter. Political power, authority and the rule of law, as well as mandates to govern by, have so far still been based on tautologies and hypothetical assumptions. With too little value-awareness, the United States Government, with its momentary occupant in the Oval Office, appears to understand just enough religion to generate chaos. No lasting ethics or laws can thrive on mere scientific or populist consent—or on the analytic debris that a majority of people are hoarding blindly.

As far as scribal skills and narratives are concerned, Enlightenment thoughts often do remain focused on narrow points of theory, severed from the practicalities of life. They remain fragments for which useful scientific solutions are unattainable or are too weak to be relevant. Narrow scientific solutions, in the longer run, tend to create more scars than they can heal along the peripheries of their problem areas. Modern politicians demonstrate effectively, that they are unable to communicate at the level of human souls where political behaviors are being managed actually and religiously. For example, they have been unable to create a folk literature which, without arcane enforcements, could teach some of the values or mores that, once upon a time, our ancestors have learned from old Bible stories—that is, have learned from the Hebrew prophetic experience while resisting the excesses that theocratic monarchies and empires have introduced.

In the camp of Christian education, learning appears to happen in the opposite direction. In order to compete with Enlightenment platitudes, many orthodox carriers of the Christian gospel, have deemed it necessary to toe the dogmatic lines of new illuminati. To survive in an Enlightenment environment, Christian apologists have labored to reinforce their historicized narratives with scientifically procured fragments of archaeological data. The Judaic-Hebrew ancestral root is being analyzed overly apologetic and is torn from the native soil by its own admirers. All the while, a thorough analysis of the Enlightenment's own Greek and Egyptian roots, together, was never begun in earnest. Not many people along both ancient roots, the Judaic-Hebrew and Ionian-Greek, are today aware that both of them have suckled their first common sense from imperial Egyptian statecraft and religion. The mythology of ancient Egypt's solar cult has provided starting points for subsequent Judaism, for Christendom, as it also has for Greek philosophical and subsequent secular scientific reasoning.

The Imperial-Egyptian Ancestral Root: It is known that the imperial tradition of ancient Egypt has begun a few centuries earlier than five thousand years ago. Egypt's beginning, alongside the first strata of so-called Mesopotamian "Civilization" also marks the beginnings of what has come to be named Western Civilization. In this book, oriented toward the history of religions, we are discounting much of the imperial Egyptian architecture and frills of "civilization." Instead, we choose to contemplate the religious leanings of slaves who were subjected to "hyper-domestication" tyranny. This means subjected to the "systematic enslavement" of fellow humankind.

In 1952 I, this writer, whose mind was still steeped in youthful bravado and ignorance, won an argument with one of my industrial arts masters concerning the unimportance of Egyptian civilization for the Christian West. I should not have come out ahead in this argument. There indeed was more to Egyptian civilization —more than a German lad relying on biblical narratives of Levitic slaves escaping the stranglehold of their Egyptian owners, and more than a teacher in industrial arts, in Stuttgart, could have known in 1952.

At that time, the ancient root meanings of the Pyramid and Coffin Texts lay still hidden in unpublished manuscripts. Translations became available in German a full ten years later (Sethe 1962) and in English an additional few years later (Faulkner 1969-73). No one can expect, even now, that suddenly there will be a rush regarding my revised exposition. Moreover, children of the Enlightenment, at this moment in time, are not very eager to view positively what they have rejected all along as primitive religious superstition. But this something, that four or five thousand years ago gave meaning to imperial strategy and religious acquiescence, entailed back then a quite brilliant ontology that still now begs to be better explained theologically, philosophically, humanistic-ally, and above all politically.

Amongst the skeptical spokesmen for modernity, some numbers of apologists and defenders of Graeco-Roman, of continental European as well as British-American Christianity, still seem to prevail. These people are not yet prepared to grant to ancients the ability of having had reasonable religious thoughts. All along they have been writing off their own distant ancestors as irrational primitive pagan polytheists. All the while, the function of countless "idols" in ancient Egypt can be seen, evolution-wise, comparable to hosts of angels, or to saintly personages in subsequent Jewish, Christian, or even Islamic congregations of faith—not to forget comparing them also to the throngs of *bodhisattvas* in Mahayana Buddhism, or to the heavenly generals in Chinese Daoism.

Even while representing a single Godhead, the Christian Trinity appears no more "spiritual" than was deemed the ancient Ninefoldness ("Ennead," or "Trinity Squared") of the nine gods at Heliopolis. The un-nameable Yahweh of Jewish theology appears to have been not any more exclusive or "spiritual" regarding his holy nature or name than a little earlier had been the Egyptian All-God "Amun" (Ammon). He was the Hidden One—who kept his name hidden even from his nearest divine underlings.

Acknowledgment

Sincere words of appreciation shall be appended here. The readability of our 2021 *Re-Visitation of Egyptian Light and Hebrew Fire,* 1991, in English, has been helped significantly during our editorial process in the Summer of 2018. Elizabeth Walters, is a native English speaker and a writer. Her assistance is greatly appreciated.

Numerous self-willed editorial changes, during an additional thirty months of revision, remain the author's own responsibility, and embarrassment perhaps. Having never in his life finished writing a book to its ultimate completion, so also this Revisitation will roll from the press leaving a fair share of work to be done by others in the future. Mortals speak and write only for a little while.

Almost a year before printing, Jason McCormick has kindly agreed to give the galleys a last quick reading. The author also acknowledges his help with sincere appreciation. But even his round of proof-reading has gotten disturbed with several more rounds of editing by the author.

Portland, Oregon
February 2021

Introduction:
Religion and Culture

Preview on Culture and Religion--an Allegory from Technology

If one were to explain Culture or Religion by comparing them to the functions of an automobile, then a full tank or battery, a combustion engine or electric motor, forward gears, and anything suitable for sustaining forward movement could be compared with the general functions and aspirations of "Culture."

By contrast, "Religion" can be explained as serving the function of balance, safety, and retreat. This includes half of the steering mechanism, all brakes, the gear for backing up and speed controls, thus, all levers that enable drivers to avoid running against hard obstacles, or to avoid areas that are too soft to support weight. Failure of controlling any of these situations could, instantly, reveal them as greater-than-human conditions that threaten the driver, passengers, and the vehicle itself.

All functions of limiting speed, of adjusting direction or of enabling moderation and retreat, represent situations that in human life correspond to the dimension of "Religion."

Measured by standards of life-sustaining results, both Culture and Religion are necessary. Depending on contexts, they both can be equally rational. Both are improvable; and both remain corruptible.

1

What is Culture? What is Religion?

Religions are torchlights, emitting light and smoke. They are carried by people on treks through darkness and gloom. Over the years, religious patterns of thought and behavior have been recorded by Western scholars in many ways. Most of their definitions are still useful to readers who take the time to immerse themselves in the broader ontological contexts in which the defining visionaries understood and wrote about them. Various aims and methodologies, among different minds, imply diverse interests and foci. Diverse emphases imply different "theories of being"—ontologies. Unique ontologies facilitate perspectives by which additional aspects of human life come into better focus.[1]

Every shape and characteristic of any entity or subject, or first impression remembered by a human mind, may over time be discovered as having been mislabeled or mistaken.

A historian, philosopher, psychologist, sociologist, anthropologist or theologian—all begin their train of specialized reasoning with a preferred ontological alignment. Suitable methodologies are devised to highlight subject matter in specified contexts. Our choice for this book is to pay attention to human relationships and to interactions with greater-than-human realities. In like manner, historians value events that can be arranged along the flow of time, in linear reckoning. Philosophers consider axioms and propositions to be fundamental. Psychologists traditionally have focused on "psyche" or "soul" as representing the essence of human life. More recently they have shifted instead to more easily observable "behavior." Sociologists study societal groupings on a wider scope; they observe how people interrelate and function. Anthropologists concern themselves with larger societal configu-

[1] Ontology is the branch of philosophical theory that concerns itself with the nature of "being." It is an attempt to define Being—Reality as it is.

rations and culture. Finally, to the chagrin of people who recognize nothing greater than themselves, theologians begin their work by focusing on what appears to be a greater-than-human configuration of reality, gods or God, or some other focal point of collective fascination.

In Western languages, collections of concepts that were bundled under the label "religion" have, in the domain of academe, been examined by scholars with varying degrees of erudition. Inasmuch as religion seems peripheral to the conquest of material things, for superficial living, it can be easily ignored or be banished from view. For instance, viewed from the perspective of philosophy, some types of religious thought tend to be judged crudely as "irrationalities." And frequently, in psychological perspective, religion tends to be reduced to emotionality or some type of abnormal, substandard behavior. Within Freudian psychology, a theistic religion may be seen as having originated with the "projection" of a human Father image. Sociologists of the Émile Dürkheim persuasion regard gods and totems as "collective elaborations," or "social representations"—thus as symbolic conceptualizations of concrete social togetherness. Marxists have defined religion by its role in the class struggle, as opium or tranquilizer utilized by capitalists in their exploitation of working people.

On the other hand, theologians who are committed to the ontology of a specific theistic tradition will focus first on the dimensions of an acknowledged God, or on a plurality of gods. They proceed to measure the gods of other people by their own standards. Theologians, as do other scholars who explicitly or implicitly operate on the basis of their personal ontology, tend to explain the wider world of religions as piecemeal phenomena, reflecting only fragments of the larger world that they themselves deem to be able to conceptualize more clearly than others.

Some theological systems have been moved as far as to depreciate the category of "religion" itself, as "other peoples' superstitions." For instance, the theology of Karl Barth or so-called "philosophies" held forth by certain Hindu gurus reserve the label "religion" to refer to weaknesses or superstitions that they detect in other people's outlook and behavior. Meanwhile, Barthian theologians and Hindu gurus classify their own ever-so-religious views as respectable "non-religious" ontologies or philosophies. Their points of view work as long as "non-religious" scientists or philosophers can establish reputations that keep them distinguished from ordinary superstitious folk. To accomplish this feat in the natural sciences, scientists conceptualize most of their objects, subject matter, and piecemeal data within an all-encompassing and fragment-able realm of Nature.

We therefore define Religion briefly, for use in this book, as "the response of humankind to so-experienced or to so-perceived greater-than-human configurations of reality."

This definition is relational in that it focuses on religious *Homo sapiens* as they experience and relate to the physical as well as to the socio-cultural environment. A religious person who becomes a historian's subject matter may or may not perceive the surrounding world in the same manner as an academic observer does. Nevertheless, religion is always linked to a person's own perception of the larger surrounding reality, thus to ontology. The larger ontology unmasks and categorizes one human activity as aggressive and identifies another experience as religious and still another as egalitarian or social. A neutral observer, therefore, can do no better than to observe how one religious behavior differs from another, in other societal contexts, or in how a person's religious behavior differs from aggressive behavior in contrast to quests for cultural survival.

All the while, all persons, whether they acknowledge their religiosity or not, do encounter greater-than-human configurations of reality "religiously."

Only persons who in their surroundings recognize nothing greater can attempt to begin thinking of themselves as being non-religious. By the very fact that any greater reality configuration is superior, it can never be fully comprehended or explained—neither by subjective experience nor by objective observation. All the while, with the same humility that a person acknowledges, religiously, his or her relational inferiority toward greater realities, a historian of religions may recognize instances of humble or pious styles of behavior thereby, as the presence of religious data.

Some historians of religions may object to our quantified delineation of the subject matter "religion." They may raise the objection that elves and dwarfs are less-than-human beings, and that human responses toward them would anciently have been classified as religious phenomena. A historian of religions must answer that, indeed, sincere responses to elves and dwarfs are still today religious behavior, as in the tradition of northern European peasants who, though surrounded by Christianized or modern secular culture, occasionally still pray for blessings and extra protection from these unseen divine earth-dwellers. Although, admittedly, the recipients of such prayers are regarded as being less than human nowadays by world-wise historians, they definitely are deemed greater by those people who today still offer them prayers and gifts—at least for the duration of their entreaties and their prayers.

The duration of how long persons retain their religious posture does not affect the basic proportionality of our observation. Not even the mightiest among deities is approached religiously by everyone, or all the time, as someone unquestionably greater. This is to say that a *Homo religiosus* practices religion neither one hundred percent nor all the time—just as a scientist is unable to practice science all the time. Every living Homo religiosus is always more than just that. He or she is also a *Homo ludens* and is, as such, a bundle of playfulness, oscillating between being a *Homo sapiens* aggressor or experimenter and a Homo religiosus engaged in common-sense religious retreats. I am prepared to classify a human response to reality as "religious" whenever there are behavioral indications that a responding person acknowledges, or defers to greater reality.

It is possible to observe and detect a person's religious responses even at the mild intensity level of "Fascination." Expressions of Fascination are religious behavior, because during a person's initial encounter, the object that fascinates is, ontologically speaking, not a less-than-human simple thing. Rather, its effects are inflicted from the outside onto the human who experiences—possibly to loom only momentarily as a potentially greater reality.

But being only a mild borderline religious response, a state of simple Fascination cannot be permanent and may quickly be transmuted in one of two opposing dimensions. An experience of Fascination may, by the defensive ego of an experiencing individual be dragged down the scale toward greater egalitarian Familiarity. From there it may slide further, past the point of "Hypothetical Re-arrangement" and prepare to inflict experimental control. However, flinching back it may repent by redefining itself as a victim and return religiously toward a tenaciously fascinating configuration of reality. An experiencing ego may as well retreat further. In retreat it may allow itself to sink into a more intense mode of religious experiencing and passive surrender. Inasmuch as a gradation of intensity is possible, the entire range of experiences and responses between total Control and total Surrender may be plotted quantitatively, along a graduated scale that scores degrees of experiential intensity and surrender.

The Teeter-Totter Scale (Figure 1)

Any subject matter that human minds wish to subject to academic scrutiny must be capable of delimitation. Thus, religion as a subject matter must be definable not only in terms of its content but also in contrast to what is not religion. This is to say that such general designations of religion as a "lifestyle" or a "way of life," although these may be broad enough to embrace all religious behavior, do not delimit sufficiently. To conceptualize a contrast between what is and what is not religion, it is necessary to begin with the simplest and most concrete ontological pattern imaginable—with a threefold ranking of creatures and entities relative to ourselves. It is necessary to perceive one another as being participants in the same larger environmental process or food chain. This threefold ranking begins at the central humanistic perspective, starting at the midpoint of human self-awareness and looking from there, both ways, in the two opposite directions.

All living beings on earth survive by feeding on lesser, conquerable substances. However, for security and comfort, for procreation and the nurture of offspring, they socialize with potential equals. At some level along the larger hierarchy, or "food chain," by which organisms on this planet are bound into a single fabric of life, everything and everyone eventually surrenders to a complexity of realities that together are greater. Thus, a fully conscious creature not only moves about to survive between Earth and Sky, but also discovers itself as being caught up in threefold proportional ontology and competition. This ontology includes the entire known dimension of a creature's realm of all possible experiences. Categories such as the greater Food Chain, Environment, or the Fabric of Life have all been referred to, in recent anthropological literature, rather "religiously" as greater-than-human realities.

Of course, in the case of a superior species (the members of which are capable of extensive mental reflection) the superiority that humankind recognizes in itself—alongside everything contained within its objectified all-embracing food chain or environment—does not necessarily also lead to subjective religious reckoning with one's own finitude. The activity of aggressive scientific wresting, with modern larger reality configurations, tends to be at least as serious as in ancient mythological contexts heroic bouts with gods, angels, devils, demons, or dragons were. Ontologically, our scientific challenges, and our quests, are not much better explained than the struggles of our heroic ancestors who acted within earlier world perspectives. We do not know, yet, what the objects or situations that we deem to control scientifically really are. How much greater or dangerous will they turn out to be after we completed our scientific aggregations.

The multitude of causes in nature that together determine our lives, and that eventually will do us in, can be approached in different ways. They can be accepted religiously, as divinities, or after analyzing them into smaller quanta, they can be diminished or hidden under heaps of soft word symbols and abstract philosophical principles—that is, under the mental excrement that remains, after analytic hunting, butchering, and mental "digestion" have occurred. If all of Nature together appears threatening and hostile, then a composite of many lesser natural forces, or even a chaotic array of such, may for a playful primate mind appear less intimidating. The human penchant for analysis makes it possible to kill, dissect, digest or to recast larger ontological threats, to make larger things appear smaller. It enables us to dispose of threatening entities in the abstract, as smaller epistemological puzzles, rather than as substantial real dangers.

The penchant for achieving physical as well as mental victories—the analytic breakdown of realities into smaller digestible or manageable portions—still empowers most human endeavors, theologies, philosophies, and especially the sciences. Some human groups have identified knowledge so won as natural or original attributes, as the condition of having eaten from a "tree of knowledge," as human original sin or evil, or as primates evolving into a species capable of predation. It is obvious that large gods are more fearsome than small ones. It is also obvious that gods of whatever size, who can be *analyzed* into smaller "aspects," will be less frightening than those who are still looming over humankind as virile and whole personages.

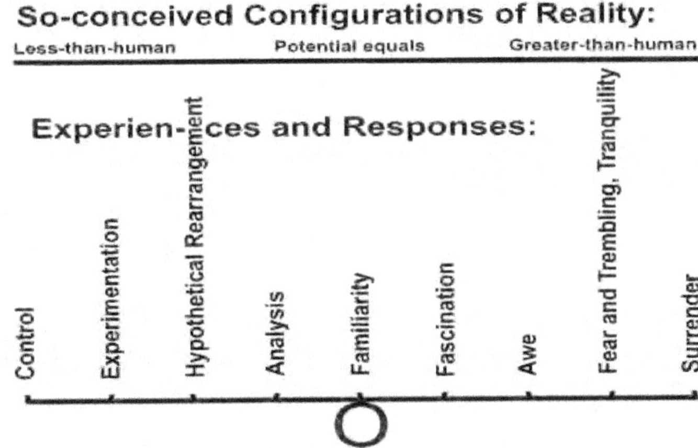

Figure 1. The Teeter-Totter: Human Experiences of, and Responses to, So-conceived Configurations of Reality

Systematic theologies accomplish theoretical victories with the abstract treatment of their relevant God or gods. Accordingly, our Teeter-Totter Scale of experiential intensities (Figure 1) is threefold. From left to right, it plots human responses to so-perceived reality configurations of increasing sizes or greatness. Thereby it measures degrees of religiosity, or intensities of religious experience. Human behavior toward less-than-human realities is not only not religious behavior, it also differs from behavior that is adjusted around the midpoint of the scale in relation to interactions with potential equals.

Less-than-Human Realities

Lesser realities are perceived by analysis and are re-evaluated or re-arranged hypothetically; they also can be manipulated, experimented with, conquered and controlled. The quest for food, aggression and progress, the sciences, technology and commercialized arts, all score heavily in this dimension among typical responses to so-perceived less-than-human realities.

The first step of the scientific approach is "Analysis." Starting at a neutral midpoint—it initially breaks down targeted "familiar" reality configurations into smaller, more manageable portions. Less-than-human realities can subsequently be rearranged, first hypothetically, and then by way of experimentation, manipulation, and control.

When potential equals are targeted as food or scientific variables, they either will put up a fight or compromise and submit less essential portions of themselves for analysis and for experimental modification. For example, a patient may permit a surgeon to operate within a clearly defined trouble area, such as the vicinity of a hernia. What the patient surrenders is not the entire being.

There is nothing particularly new or modern about our celebrated modern "scientific" experimental method. It is the same method by which all creatures with alimentary tracts eat and survive. It also is the same method by which many an ancient greater-than-human or potentially equal configuration of reality—such as a formidable animal, a god, or a fellow humanoid—has been confronted, captured, killed, reduced, or consumed. All latter-day mental, physical, or chemical analyses have already been anticipated as activities at the level of animals. They have been anticipated by the basic achievements of claws, teeth, and digestive juices, as well as by the mental reflections that hominids have applied during their still simple tasks of hunting, toolmaking, butchering, and eating. Latter-day scientific analysis by the hominid offspring of hunters—namely, the systematic breakdown of reality configurations into smaller portions—represents essentially an intellectual elaboration on such simple and primitive activities as tearing, biting, chewing, swallowing, and digesting. Initially, all rational creatures in the animal kingdom are caught up in the pursuit of such basic activities.

It follows that an excessive glorification of analysis, of teeth and biting, scores heavily among the engagements of advanced humanoid scientific "brain-tipped teeth." Such one-sidedness, sooner or later, will leave us marooned in a world littered by our own chewed-dry cut. In the end; it will leave everything downgraded to excrement, destined to go to humus. Termites that have reduced their woody residences to sawdust are, by their natural method of physical breakdown and analysis, compelled to move on. Where, with their mentally advanced termite skills, will humanoids hope to go? To some other planet? Or to some nirvana or heaven—after all their religious skepticism! Or, perchance, to that other more progressive place of eternal purging and analysis by fire? After all our scientific insights and discoveries, these mythic prospects persist. They appear to have become endemic aspects that continue to haunt human scientific minds and living souls.

Potential Equals

The central issue for the limited survival of mortal life appear to be moderation and goals of "balance." At the midpoint of the spectrum of Experiences and Responses, at the point of Familiarity, potential equals share and provide nurture; they communicate or compete with one another. Social co-operation and humanistic learning thrive best while they are focusing on balance points of equality. There they can thrive in accordance with the Golden Rule.

Inasmuch as one recognizes that a *Homo sapiens* and a *Homo religiosus* together add up to a *Homo ludens,* the metaphor of a teeter-totter beam seems to be appropriate. This analogy emphasizes the point that, all along, the biological and social playground dynamic has enticed human minds to identify the subject matter of "religion," as well as all commentary thereupon, to stream alongside the additional plethora of life, space, and time.

Encounters with potential equals are appreciated as oscillations around the middle of our spectrum and in relation to either end on the scale. Over the sequence of a day, between rising, eating, and falling asleep—and certainly over the course of a year—all living creatures on earth oscillate from one extremity on the scale toward the other. Inasmuch as hominids on the teeter-totter plank apply their intellect in their quest for nourishment and survival, analytically, they are *Homines sapientes.* But they also retain this ability of being analytic whenever they move in the other direction—while, religiously, they retreat from aggression. This happens when they are at rest or allow themselves to fall asleep. In fact, they are generally involved around the middle of the spectrum, tending toward both sides, alternating. Over the course of a lifetime, the experiential positions of hominids become stable and come to rest, willingly or unwillingly at the extreme point of Surrender at the right side of the spectrum. Willingly or unwillingly, every creature's existential teeter-totter balances the totality of aggressive behavior, religiously in the end, to fully endorse the creature's inherent vulnerability, mortality, and surrender.

A humane balance is necessary for coexistence, even in science laboratories and in technological workshops. Experiences of Fascination, i.e. mild religious experiences, are welcome even at academic ceremonies, to entice newcomers into the cultures of business, management, technology, scientific experimentation, and even militarism. Students who find Fascination in a certain subject are invited by professors to make it their major field of study. Yet the masters appreciate this mild degree of religious devotion only up to a point. No sooner has an excess of Fascination been sensed by those who preside over organizations of science, industrial production or educational achievements, than all available didactic knowhow is mobilized to bring a fascinating subject matter again within the range of Familiarity, common knowledge, and to get it under Control.

Fascination is thereby eclipsed; the targeted familiarized subject matter is reduced further by systematic Analysis, down to the level of incidents and fragments. Less-than-human objects are more likely than greater subjects to be subjected to hypothetical Rearrangement and Experimentation, and thereafter to full human Control. A satiated creature that intermittently has been a *Homo religiosus* on retreat does become hungry again. So he or she relapses into becoming a full-fledged *Homo sapiens necans*—someone who reasons and kills, butchers and dissects analytically. Of course, not only harmless or inferior species are victimized and endangered by the wide swings of human pendulums and temper tantrums upon their teeter-totters. The human species itself, with its collective visions of egalitarian coexistence and self-realization, has worked itself into many troubles by causing less-than-human imbalances. Or, should we regard them as being rationally legitimated imbalances?

Greater-than-Human Realities

By so-conceived greater-than-human configurations of reality, a human being is fascinated, awed, frightened, experimented with or dealt with in some other fashion, tranquilized, and eventually done in. Moving toward the right along our graduated experience-response spectrum, mild religious Fascination registers more intensely after it has advanced to a state of Awe. Enraptured in a state of Awe, the human being, as a *Homo religiosus,* rests poised at a temporary equilibrium. The human creature stands frozen, perhaps after the manner of the prophet Muhammad when he saw the angel Gabriel appear to him everywhere along the horizon. He could "move neither backward nor forward." In a similar situation, the three disciples of Jesus, who accompanied their master to his Mountain of Transfiguration, insisted on prolonging a stabilized sense of Awe—a kind of sustained equilibrium.

Much of religious ceremonialism aims at achieving and stabilizing the level of temporarily feasible bliss, as close as possible to the scale point of Awe. All the fine and not-so-fine arts of humankind, at various points in their history, have attempted to concretize, organize, and stabilize some fleeting scents, sounds or glimpses of paradisiac Awe. The music of Bach, Händel, and Mozart, among others, along with pipe organs in cathedrals and harps still waiting to be invented, plus orchestras and large brass ensembles, and the work of painters such as Michelangelo, Rembrandt and Dürer, have accomplished this feat to some degree for this writer. We conceptualize Awe on our teeter-totter scale as a midpoint along the right half of the dimension of possible religious experiences.

Nevertheless, ego-driven attempts to create actively structured and stabilized experiential states of Awe inevitably damage the quality of passive serenity that constitutes the essence of religious experiencing. Artificially mediated ecstasies compare to pure ones as canned edibles compare to fresh food. No denigration is intended. Canned rations for human nourishment certainly are preferable to the alternative of starvation or of chasing raw foods. Nevertheless, the next degree of interfering with ecstatic experiences, an addiction to intoxicants and mind-altering drugs, empties the experience of religious meaning—thus, removes it from its larger ontological context. After the chemical highs wear off, only raw emptiness yawns. It is not logical to subject a human mind to less-than-human chemical compounds and then expect from this induced imbalance a reward of genuine balanced greater-than-human bliss.

Leaning from the point of Awe still farther in the direction of passive experience, Fear and Trembling (a term borrowed from Kierkegaard) becomes the defining mode. In some religions, the ontological *mysterium tremendum* (a term from Rudolf Otto, *Das Heilige)* has been scaled down or circumvented. To surrender and to face death with poetry on one's lips may be the most rational behavior under slightly more severe or culturally sublimated conditions. Religious behavior is irrational only when it is expressed in relation to less-than-human things or idols, or toward pompous fellow potential equals.

All the while, meeting potential equals and discovering ways to coexist with them, in accordance with the Golden Rule, counts among the most rational lessons a human mind can learn. Acts of idolizing fellow human beings are, from the perspective of the Golden Rule, "religious" irrationalities and acts of manipulating fellow human beings, from that same middle vantage point, are "aggressive" cultural or scientific irrationalities. Either extremity threatens a balance and endangers humane existence.

In Buddhism, this point of fear and trembling might better be described as a state of transitional "serenity" or "tranquility." Had this book been written primarily for Buddhist monks, the right half of our teeter-totter spectrum could have been marked off with the eight steps from the Buddha's Eightfold or Middle Path. Discourse within less devout philosophical schools, methods for "knowing oneself"—that is, ritualized introspection and self-criticism—may as well serve the goal of achieving a meeker retreat toward balance and tranquility. All the while, even in the pursuit of sheer philosophical introspection, the presence of a greater-than-human standard of truth motivates the human ego to shrink, for contrast.

The endpoint to which all life on earth moves, in a variety of ever changing combinations of aggressive and retreat responses, is ultimate surrender in death. Over the course of most organisms' lives, death is prefigured by cycles of fatigue, by need for rest, or by falling asleep. Ritualized and organized religious paths often recommend to their members states of submission or surrender, to be attained, essentially while living, or soon to be realized more fully.

All organized religious paths of humankind, in one form or other, recognize degrees of surrender or levels of seeing or knowing. They distinguish carefully between preliminary less intense surrenders and states of awareness, on one hand, and the intensity of surrendering one's ego with the finality of death, on the other. The baptism of Christians means initiation into preliminary dying and rising with Christ (as in *Romans* 6:3–4), whereas for Buddhists the nirvana experience, or *moksha*, is the prefiguration of *pari-nirvana* (of *nirvana* having become more permanent).

Religious responses are gestures and patterns of retreat behavior—mental and physical—evoked always by the experienced presence of greater-than-human configurations of reality. Such retreat behavior affects modes of conscious activity as it also evokes tremors of emotion. These delimit the scope of perception while they also help estimate the range of subject matter that is deemed safe for objective thinking, for killing and eating, or for scientific takeover. On the other hand, acknowledging the presence of greater realities enables an aggressor, who suddenly finds himself up against insurmountable obstacles, to retreat honorably. This means that one may be enabled, religiously, to explain one's retreats as actions that are reasonable—that is, "reasonable" in communication with rational people who exercise their "will to live" likewise, by way of compromising. Religious behavior, in context, may be explained as an effort of showing honorable and rational deference—showing an ability to retreat from greater-than-human odds.

Ranging from Fascination, the mildest form of religious experience, toward mystic Surrender in death, which is the ultimate religious orientation, religion ranges over half the spectrum of rational human experiences and responses, that is, over half of the available range of ontological reckoning. By contrast, the left half on the total spectrum, ranging between Analysis and Control, is defined by demeanors of aggression.

Social balance among potential equals, near the middle of the spectrum, may be compared with a bird in flight; aggressiveness is represented by one wing, and religious retreat by the other. During flight, the two wings must balance each other's movements, and they must compensate for each other's adjustments during gliding.

The fact that most so-conceived greater-than-human configurations of reality have traditionally been encountered as personal deities, happens to be a quite rational happenstance. A *Homo sapiens,* who defines his own existence in terms of intelligent personhood, cannot forever avoid to face the puzzle of its own vulnerability along the biological food chain. Existential threats encroach on intelligent minds, as much as, once upon a time, have impinged on ancient hunters the claws and teeth of greater-than-human predators. *Homines sapientes* are challenged to recognize personality status in any "thing" that reveals itself as being a little greater, coming from the outside or from beyond. Upon the Teeter-Totter of life, denying one's finitude, caught up in the existing threefold proportionality, or disallowing the common-sense need to thrive near the middle of one's experiential spectrum, somewhere between the extreme points of "eating" and of being "done in," would be tantamount to insisting on lopsided divine status for oneself.

While it endures passively or sometimes falls asleep, a reflective human mind cannot escape this query: if the ontological stratum that defines the human ego, that has given birth to it as a self-reflective entity, is not somehow personal—if the "ground of my being" is not personal—then what is "I"? Then, what is a person? And then, what is consciousness? What is the value of human efforts? What are human rights or how low is human dignity?

In my younger years I built a sailboat. During a stormy episode, while crossing a lake in Kansas, I noticed myself talking to my own handiwork as if it were a person. While rationally and scientifically manipulating sails and rudder, I was subconsciously repeating what all our ancestors might have done in similar situations. I uttered pious words of encouragement to the only tangible greater entity present that was able to keep me above water—safely and in accordance with presently known laws of physics. My threshold of Fascination had moved, even if only temporarily. Once again in the course of human evolution, a new greater-than-human manifestation of reality—the able agency of a personal saving reality—has begun intruding on a vulnerable mortal. And so, while I attribute the religious discovery of personal attributes among so-encountered greater-than-human configurations of reality to active human intelligence, I also must insist on the more general truth, that certain styles of human reasoning necessarily do transcend and reach beyond the narrow goals of utilitarian analysis.

To confront less-than-human things analytically, and to manipulate them scientifically, may be deemed a reasonable undertaking, provided the things to be controlled are indeed less than human. Our short-term survival depends on the success of these "rational" estimates. However, seeing oneself confronted by greater-than-human reality, and responding with Fascination, Awe, Fear, Tranquility, or Surrender, may be equally realistic. Running from a dangerous predator, from a fire-storm or tsunami with fear may be the most rational thing a person can do. Human rationality cannot be established by either the presence or the absence of analytic hunger, greed or cunning; nor can it be judged only by the presence or absence of poetry or mystic bliss that might linger. The acid test for human intelligence, in the end, will always be the achievement of a realistic balance within a person's three-fold ontology—among so-encountered equal, lesser, and greater configurations of reality.

In relation to this ontology, the mind of every *Homo sapiens* must continuously renegotiate its existential balance for survival. A narrow analytic or scientific application of human reason, that ignores equals or greater realities, is destined to collapse into foolish despair or self-destruction as soon as a next larger context looms or overwhelms.

Behavior-ology of Religion

Some decades ago, the section that follows here would have been labeled "Psychology of Religion." I will refrain from doing so here because psychology as study of the soul has quietly evaporated from the academic landscape. With the increasing uncertainty about whether, objectively speaking, there is such a thing as a soul *(psyche)* to be studied, the discipline has for all practical purposes been turned into Behavior-ology. The fate of this intellectual endeavor furnishes us with excellent introductory considerations.

The evaporation of the central concept of a subject matter, in a recognized science, follows naturally the internal logic of human finitude. Scientific "psychology," having been increasingly modified by its own imitation of experimental methodologies of the Nature sciences, has gradually noticed that its psyche, or soul, which initially had been its central subject matter, has forever remained beyond arm's length and out of reach—and this discovery persisted until the core concept of the "psyche" itself had to be abandoned as an unverifiable hypothesis. Two and a half millennia ago, the Buddha came to a similar conclusion by way of reasoning introspectively, along a religious track.

Within the context of human evolution, analysis represents the mental equivalent, or an extension, of ordinary cutting skills that already our most distant hunter ancestors had acquired. The subject matter of soul, as life principle, appeared alive and real while humankind, as scientific hunters, kept chasing it as the life-emanating entity of an animal body. But it appeared inert, just moments after the human knives of analysis, or the acids of digestion, had accomplished what was expected of them. When formerly a deer had been tracked and felled by archaic Navajo hunters, the visible soul form of Deer-ness, butchered and consumed, was seen trimmed down to bare bones, literally. Ancient hunters suspected bones to be the substantial core/ soul of animals. The soul-power of observable self-mobility was no more. In a similar manner, psychologists scored their analysis of the of the personality of other human beings like a hunter's victory. The price they paid for this triumph is the fact that psychological therapy henceforth no longer can be used to heal "persons," but instead, to readjust or to repair "response mechanisms." Modern theory about the wellbeing of human persons now presupposes that a client-person is a machine that "lives in danger of breaking apart."

The teeter-totter scale can help us conceptualize why the scientific method, as such, is not very useful for understanding equal and greater-than-human configurations of reality. The psyche or "life principle," to be studied and treated as an object of science, needed first to be postulated as an "object,"—to prevent the "souls" or "minds" of the analyzers from confusing themselves with their own handfuls of declared experiment-able subject matter. Analyzers cannot objectify their own minds without risking confusion and self-mutilation by their own methods of treatment. Fragmented patient data needs to be hermetically sealed in bags of scientific hypotheses. A human observer-soul finds itself to be an out-of-bounds agent that professionally sees itself as a technician. To continue working scientifically, as behaviorists, we are restricted to interpret and to contemplate superficial activities and behavior—thus data in past tense, which after analysis and with luck, end up on our work benches still with some of their aspects intelligibly labeled.

During sessions of being observed, the psyche itself vanishes from view.[2] This happens precisely at moments when an observer's analytic mind assumes itself to be a greater than ordinary likeness of human souls. As a result of this close encounter with greater-than-human reality, the observer's psyche melts from view. This outcome is unavoidable. The observer's mind, though it may imagine

---

[2] My allusion to this linguistic flaw, in the history of "psychology," need not be taken as a criticism for the discipline as such. If the concept "Nature," which is utilized to furnish basic meaning for "natural sciences (*Naturwissenschaften*)," were not kept intentionally general and vague, the category of "Nature-Science" would become equally problematic, as already has become the subject matter of psychology. There exists no entity named "Nature" that could be placed on a workbench for observation and scientific testing. This happens to be an elementary deficiency of which nature-scientists have been accusing theologians for centuries. Some oversized word symbols, like God, Nature, or Psyche, cannot be manipulated to fit decently into crossword puzzles concocted by mortal *Homo ludens*.

being capable of omniscience, nevertheless stays constricted and contained within a human body, posing as a riddle, similar to the ones that await to be analyzed. No objective perspective regarding its integration or identity seems possible. Externally, we see a bag of skin that is capable of movement and somehow also capable of exuding patterns of symbolic communication. After having cultivated hunting and butchering skills, the descendants of ancient hunters—modern analysts—no longer can feel the vitality that used to surge in the arteries of a hunters' victim—or later in the bodies of patients or "subjects."

Therefore, while facing our existential and epistemological predicament openly, there remains no strong reason why a historian of religions should not also say something that can be sorted out under the empiric heading of behavior-logic. To explain empirical data, or to estimate intensities of religious experiences and responses, we have designed a teeter-totter scale. It serves as a bridge between varieties of religious experience and scientific justified behavior. Perhaps a researcher in the field who visits people in a foreign culture will be the first to scale the beam of their teeter-totter bridge. Until a religious studies field researcher learns the local language, or while interpreters and recording devices do their tasks, the researcher may utilize time productively by "reading" the more basic language of gestures and bodily demeanor. Interpreters and linguists may argue about the meaning of words, symbols, metaphors, and syntax. Here, as elsewhere in human life, actions speak louder than words. Intelligent creatures who can communicate by way of language are, by that very ability, empowered to adjust and to compose fiction and lies as frequently as they wish. In order to recognize spoken truths, and to distinguish them from convenient rationalizations or teasers, unspoken behavior, also, must be understood by observation and by limited participation.

The first level of encounter with human behavior usually is visual. At the aggressive side of our scale, eyes focus on some smaller or conquerable reality. When eyes focus to achieve a better resolution, they must sacrifice scope. Eyelids are frozen in a half-open position to avoid blinking and missing opportune moments of the subject's vulnerability. At the point of Familiarity, communication from one pair of eyes to another is permitted to lapse. At the point of Fascination, eyes begin to open wider. This happens to be the point at which people fall in love with someone or something—and people who are in love, tend to open their eyes and souls to the point where they become vulnerable. At the point of Awe, the religious midpoint, eyes tend to become transfixed in anticipation of eventual union or Surrender. At a point still closer to Surrender, eyelids no longer may find it necessary to close defensively. They may flicker. Unmanageable vision of "all light" may alternate with seeing "no light." This may mean blindness. A contrast can be found among history of religions data by considering Saint Paul's surrender and blindness that was caused by a vision of light on his way to Damascus. By contrast, the beatific vision of Saint John of the Cross was experienced as "dark night of the soul."

Generally, a mouth can communicate attitudes in situations where eye contact no longer is essential. Teeth tend to clench as they engage at the Aggression-side on the scale. The most basic form of conquest and control among all living creatures is killing and eating. Even if the physical activity is sublimated into mental digestion, the clenching of teeth anticipates victory through biting. Beyond the point of Familiarity, along the dimension of Retreat, lips dare to kiss. In a state of Fascination, wherein kisses become more intimate, they entail a measure of surrender. Lips meet other lips, teeth approach other teeth, and one tongue may play with another while engaging in all the aforementioned.

The encounter is fascinating and thrilling. Why? Because the most dangerous equipment on a human body, its teeth, are thereby held in check by trust, by affection, and by the implied possibility of blissful and safe surrender—on its way to pleasant rest—stopping short of actually getting eaten. In a state of Awe, the mouth tends to forget to close occasionally. Along its path to atonement, a mouth that had been committing the "original sin" of aggressive eating—may attempt to enlist the grace of a deity. This may be accomplished by submitting a share-offering, or by way of speaking a prayer, petitioning a deity's participation, blessing, or permission.

Permission to kill and to eat may be symbolized by rites of sacramental eating—by the deity sharing its own substance voluntarily. Or eating may be legitimized by conforming to special dietary restrictions or by observing prescribed periods of fasting. In some American Indian ceremonies, such as Navajo and Hopi Indian, I have observed vomiting (i.e. backward eating) practiced as an activity that would symbolize Retreat behavior.

Voice is projected forth by the mouth. Near the point of Control, audible growls tend to imitate the snarls of aggressive predators. Intense sounds rise to sustained pitches. In a more socialized form, growls are audible as threats or forceful commands. Around the midpoint of Familiarity, egalitarian conversation bent on sharing information becomes the norm. Spoken language, from left to right along the scale, tends to transform prose into poetry. At some point near the dimension of Retreat, structured poetry gives way to less structured song—with pitch added as substitutional discipline. At this point, there still remain degrees of structure, of rhythm and pitch (modified styles of control). But then, somewhere between Awe and Surrender, heightened feelings of exultation may collapse the speech of finite humankind into nearly unstructured glossolalia.

All the while, audible voice may also be negated by silent prayer, or by a vow to practice virtual silence—in anticipation of eternal silence. Stillness also may mean surrender to the only power that, in holy moments of surrender, appears to own all speech. Blissful surrenders sometimes emit guttural groans that drop and fade into silence. It is the opposite of a predator's aggressive snarl, at the opposite end of the experiential scale.

In a less spectacular manner, laughter or a smile may signify a measure of retreat behavior—either real or feigned Retreat. The "smile" or grin of an ape places that animal at a point near Fear and Trembling. By contrast, human smiles and laughter are intellectually more complex and are able to communicate attitudes and alternate meanings over a wider range. All the while, analytically active eyes and mouths, which otherwise could be aggressive and tense, appear relaxed when laughter or smiles are added. Eyes and mouth are surrounded by an array of relaxed muscles that appear silly and harmless. However, a human laugh or smile of Aggression, along the scale's dimension, may be contrived and applied deceitfully. Around the middle of the scale, an apologetic smile, alternating with progressive/aggressive reasoning, may be a teacher's best tool for luring students into the comfort zone of Familiarity, to share knowledge and induce learning.

Prominent among bodily members, human hands also prove suitable for communication. When, in the flow of evolution, hominid hands got freed from serving the function of locomotion, they could be used more readily to feed the mouth. The evolution of human hands, as the evolution of the human brain, was challenged by hunger and by the inadequacy of human teeth—all the while, competing with and trying to imitate the more effective natural predators. Humanoid hands have developed a complex industry of substitutionary weapons, "false teeth" or "brain-tipped teeth," for self-enhancement. In the flow of this process, a variety of aggressive manual skills have rendered the repertoire of hand gestures more complex. Nevertheless, basic Aggression still is expressed by way of clasping tightly or by holding. At the point of moderation and Familiarity, when two people meet, they frequently extend right hands for a mutual handshake—to express and to balance their commitment to coexistence. They surrender to each other their fighting arms and they agree on covenants of the "live and let live" variety.

Religiously, hands are folded in prayer as if fettered and bound. A comparison to man's closest friend, the dog, is enlightening. The dog extends and uses its tail as a rudder when it pursues a potential victim. Therefore, when assuming an opposite "religious" posture, to signal Retreat, this same animal draws its proud tail between its hind legs. During the assertive pursuit of their goals, human runners utilize their hands and arms as side rudders. Therefore, in the religious mode their hands may be folded to express prayerful retreat. To express the religious opposite of grasping, hands may be displayed open and empty, to implore—a begging gesture that also chimpanzees use. Hands may be uplifted in praise, flattery, or capitulation. In Eastern religions, the hand gesture of a yoga practitioner, where thumb and middle finger touch gingerly, has traditionally signified an attitude of Retreat. It negates what anthropologists meanwhile have begun to celebrate as "the opposable thumb" or as "precision grip" which, supposedly in evolution, has driven the development of humanoid aggression.

Not only limbs but also the posture of an entire human body communicates religious as well as defiant and less religious attitudes. It appears that the human rational animal, when it switches to acting religiously, retreats not only spatially but also in the dimension of time. It revisits the past as, occasionally, it also bolts ahead to embellish the future freshly and imaginatively. With added mental ability, our species has found the road of nostalgia that leads back to a simpler past. In fact, with our mental ability to effect nostalgic revisions, we can travel back farther in time than ordinary mental recollection can reach. We respond to primitive more ancient norms of behavior somewhat subconsciously. This fact becomes apparent as soon as we dare to compare human behavior with that of animals whom we allow into our proximity. While normally a dog exists and functions well at the level of healthy quadrupeds, during an act of religious penitence, nevertheless, this same dog may cower to an earlier reptilian posture. It may approach its master guiltily, crouching and dragging its belly.

In similar proportion, humans, as *Homo erectuses*, retreat religiously from their aggressive upright bipedal posture toward the more primitive posture of their ancestral quadrupeds. They kneel and bow. Certain practitioners of Islam and Tibetan Buddhism prostrate themselves to retreat to de facto prone reptilian positions. And most of us, as we go to sleep, cherish the habit of surrendering unto our sides or backs—even as far as curling into a fetal position.

Physical postures are not the only ways of expressing attitudes of religious retreat. Mental attitudes, as well, range across the scale of the experiential Teeter-Totter—all the way from aggressive conquest or analysis to self-effacing retreat and mystic surrender.

This is what the miracle of human reason has come to. It is capable of mentally imaging the entire experiential teeter-totter up close, at the left and toward the point of Hypothetical Rearrangement. On the other side, where the intellectual posture of mystics becomes passive, even their limited analytic alertness is getting dimmed. About midway between analytic conquest and surrender, rational minds occupy themselves with performing random acts of synthesis. The ultimate degree to which philosophical synthesis can be pursued is achieved by mystics. The "All" of reality will not reveal itself to greedy minds that habitually are filtering out phenomena of greater than human reality. Nevertheless, even during philosophical discourse, self-esteem still rises and ebbs along the same teeter-totter scale. People who engage in variant styles of philosophical temperament, in actual debate, display gestures that resonate with either aggression or with apologetic flight behavior—of which both were anciently enacted already in animal strata, along the trails of evolution.

Theological reasoning yields a similar pattern. Back in time along the evolutionary track, at the left on the experiential scale and at an early level of animal existence, acts of killing and eating constituted the "original sin" or existential crisis, as well as imbalances among hunters.

At the opposite extreme from acts of killing and eating lies the passive experiential possibility of being killed and eaten. These original natural opposites are far more intense than the religiously modified, or compromised degrees of sacramental eating or of temporary fasting. Sublimated by broader theological reasoning, this basic datum of life, of being killed, eaten, and absorbed, translates into the mystic formula that the Apostle Paul adopted from the philo-sopher Aratus: "In him [God] we live and move and have our being." Rational mysticism, prefigured physically at the animal level —raw and "red in tooth and claw"—does indeed allow "surrender" to mean being eaten or absorbed by greater-than-human reality.

In the final sense, two directional perspectives are possible in which life-processes, and the food chain can be viewed from opposite sides. There is the perspective of predators and the perspective of prey. Rationalized aggression derives directly from aggressive ancestral hunters who lived and roamed amongst their totemic predators. At the same time, many of our symbols of religious retreat derive from fearful encounters with totemic animal masters, possibly even predators who "owned" or represented subjected animal species. Predators, in fact, have acted as the masters of those who have succumbed and become victims, of animals and of humans alike.

Culture versus Religion

Explanations in this section are added to facilitate discourse between the history of religions and anthropology. Readers who are not immediately involved in evolutionary questions are free to skip this section and return to it later.

Religious retreats are behavior types of individuals as well as of groups. Anthropology and sociology, as well as questions of societal ranking, therefore become relevant for this study. If I coerce someone to retreat as I do, I do not act religiously toward that person, but rather aggressively. However, if that person retreats by way of imitating my retreat behavior, both of us act religiously. Managed or organized retreat behavior can, therefore, never be com-pletely religious for those who undertake the organizing—and it need not be. Humanistic concerns naturally blend into religion.

A similar ambiguity exists along the expanding culture and aggressive side of the scale. For example, a soldier who obeys a commanding officer's order to attack an enemy position, acts aggressively toward the enemy; he acts religiously toward his commander and the entire superior chain of command. Each superior in that chain acts religiously toward his next superior and acts aggressively toward subordinates—unless he disobeys an order and suffers consequences. In the case of such resistance, the sufferings of punishment absorb into themselves the religious behavior that would have accumulated down the line to the soldier and the enemy. Meanwhile, any type of organized and aggressive or defensive movement, whether individual or communal, can never be fully devout or be religiously justified in an absolute sense.

As I have alluded herein frequently to latter-day cultural struggles, to reach for another analogy farther back in time, such were presaged in the simple quests for food among primitive hunters. Aggressive scavenging, hunting, killing, and eating are followed steadily during the basic life process. Religious retreat behavior corresponds to inactivity that sometimes is associated with remorse and fasting, or with other restrictions imposed during an ordeal—or simply with a feeling of satisfied fullness while food is being digested. Such limitations were explained by primitive hunters most often religiously, as having been imposed on them by greater-than-human personages or circumstances. In modern atheistic speech, the effect that greater-than-human obstacles have uploaded unto human souls continues to register as conscience; that is, as "con-science" in the negative sense of being contra, "con-" to aggressive "science." Inasmuch as religious retreats generally do imply a show of weakness, the forced imposition of religious behavior, on groups of people, will inflict unbalanced embarrassment or even shame. Aggressive individuals tend to disparage pious people for a variety of sublime intellectual expectations. Among these reasons crawl feelings of embarrassment for having enabled the exploitation of other beings. And thereupon, if bullied arbitrarily and continually, even the most pious person may generate resentments that seek to justify either a defensive or a fresh aggressive round of behavior.

If left to themselves in peace, people ordinarily engage in religious retreat behavior together. They think religious thoughts naturally and voluntarily. Within communal bounds of safety, they may organize to withdraw and retreat in unison for mutual comfort and assurance—which is, for encouragement and trust toward each other as individuals. They share their retreat behavior. They trust those whom they find to be on matching paths of retreat. In shared states of weakness lie comfort and trust—rests also the strength for a joint resurgence, as well as for joint aggression and abuse. Religious folk tend to acknowledge and to submit to benevolent greater-than-human realities together—submit to divinities who endorse, sustain, and tolerate their survival as devotees.

All individuals survive by balancing their aggressive selves, embedded in modes of cultural aggression that are religiously and collectively justified, as well as scientifically rationalized. Religiously they are justified by way of retreating. Every social group, every culture or civilization, survives by trying to maintain some state of balance. They will endure as long as they can, by cultivating the focus that helps stabilize overall structure. It all happens along points on the teeter-totter scale, the scale of rationalized methods and rituals—of predatory aggression, nurture, mystic acceptance and opening up to the least embarrassing available modes of surrender.

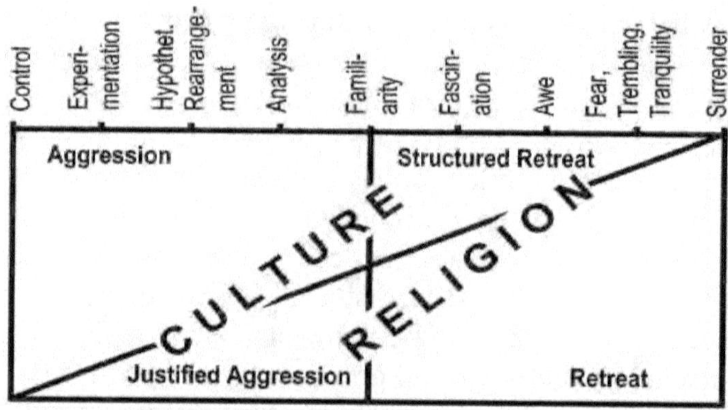

Figure 2. Religious Experiences and Responses in relation to aggressive "culture-building" and "organized religion."

Collective balancing on the way to either extreme, of aggression as well as retreat, will sooner or later evoke reactionary movements or counter-adjustments in opposite directions, which then will tend to overshoot again their points of balance. Aggressive military campaigns and penitential religious pilgrimages alternate in the ebb and flow of tribes and nations. The necessity of achieving rational balances determines the status and the stability of all strata of society, even in situations where at one or the other behavioral extreme, at points of either Control or Surrender, an elite stretches its theatrical high wires to perform upon.

Aggressive heroes provoke religiously regressive pious folk who pose as a challenge to haughty scoffers—while scoffers provoke humble folk into becoming first defensively and then piously proud. Their offspring in turn, raised piously, grow up and mature to be piously aggressive and eventually aggressively proud. No generation of Homines sapientes knows in advance the type of ontology that their offspring generation requires to attain their existential balance that will be necessary to assure survival into the future.

Religious soteriology, initially, is predicament-specific. Religious gospel messages are found to have gotten evoked by specific socio-cultural problems and imbalances. Generally speaking, they come into being to alleviate prevailing modes of violence. They exist to balance the effects of chronic hyper-domestication, aggression, and collective "original sins."

Aggressive hyper-domesticators oppress sensitive people to a point at which they will identify with doves and lambs. Stubborn martyrs will suffer in hope of shaming their tormentors into repentance. Kings on horseback have, at some point in the history of Near Eastern civilization, evoked a political climate of contempt that a poor rabbi, riding on a borrowed donkey, would be hailed as supreme King of Kings Eternal.

Up to this point, I have delineated culture and religion from a behavioristic perspective, as opposites in movement from one extreme toward another. To understand the origin of a religion historically, one must examine the socio-political dynamics from and against which religion arose. Our approach posits Retreat behavior categorically in contrast to Aggression. The primary thrust that builds and supports culture requires the imposition of organized structure—entails assertiveness, the extreme modes of which can easily and inhumanely deteriorate into violence, "red in tooth and claw."

Religious behavior is manifest by its essential readiness for Retreat within the larger organizational enterprise. At its most extreme, religious Retreat accepts the total surrender of the human ego. In a person's struggle for survival within organized hyper-domestication, and as a matter of course, ego-postures must often be compromised. Analysis, and then Hypothetical Rearrangement, are the products of Culture and Aggression. They are developed to enable communicational and organizational leverage.

While Structured Retreat behavior tends to become "organized," organization itself implies that it will be "compromised." By way of excessive compromise it may even blend and slide into the general realm of Aggression, and so we can also posit the subcategory of pretentious Justified Aggression. Yet, aggressive behavior, for the sake of cultural balance and survival, still must derive its justification from some type of ontology in the field of Structured Retreat at the opposite side of the scale. Inversely, Structured Retreat, for the sake of communication and organization, is obliged to draw its cultural skills and tools from aggressive behavior in the realm of cultural assertion. The category of Justified Aggression easily gets compromised by allowing it to degenerate into unchecked and pre-emptive Aggression. These possibilities have been diagrammed in Figure 2.

By Justified Aggression—that is, by organizational and political compromise, religions will die. By enabling and rationalizing Structured Retreat, specific cultures can to some degree be tweaked to become better mannered. Thus, for the purpose of engaging in a constructive dialogue between the fields of anthropology and the history of religions, the concepts of Culture and of Religion may be distinguished as follows:

Culture participates foremost in the dimension of aggression-enabled organization. It is legitimated by the method of cultivating select religious beliefs that justify the chosen circumscribed measure of aggression. A culture deduces its ontological validation for Justified Aggression from the greater-than-human realities that are acknowledged within the full dimension of Structured Retreat.

Religion is complementary to Culture, and basically it remains anchored in the thought-dimension of full Retreat. But it is conceptualized and communicated with categories from its intermediary subregion of Structured Retreat. All these categories are supported, organized and institutionalized as part of Culture, more or less aggressively empowered by the religious and cultural dimension that we have labeled Justified Aggression.

An emphasis on Justified Aggression, which ignores its roots in Retreat ontology, ceases to be religiously balanced—whereas Pure Retreat behavior, by itself, contributes very little to the body of Culture. Only structure that organizes can add fiber and build body for visible change. Organized religion, at its best, contributes balance to Culture by stabilizing and limiting aggression as well as retreat behavior. All the while, the heart and soul of a religion lies in the core dimension that we categorize as "Pure Retreat." A religious organization can easily corrupt and spoil its purity by constantly operating in the mode of alleged "justifiable" Aggression. A religious organization can decay to the level of becoming a meager segment of secular Culture. The offspring of religious people, as of all humankind, are born with the same ability to grow teeth and nails. Religious retreat behavior and culturally aggressive behavior are opposites. To some extent they are expressed by all living beings, all the time.

Among higher and rational animals there is co-present and grows, as a result of rational engagement, an increased ability of self-reflection on one's own dependence, retreat, and "con-science." This ability is nourished by the general disposition of having second thoughts —about one's own socio-cultural standing and analytic assertiveness.

Aggression and advance at one side, and withdrawal on the other, do interplay in human society as checks and balances, as naturally as do the alternatives of inhaling and exhaling. After every intake of breath follows an exhalation, with nearly equal volumes of exhaust. The same functionality of life-enabling intellect (spirit) is present for the opposing behavioral foci. Culture and religion are contrary interdependent modes that together pulsate human life. Expressed after the fashion of *Ecclesiastes* 3, there is, for all living beings, a time to grasp and a time to let go. Religious traditions cannot render the lives of mortals completely perfect. At best, they can help moderate and balance the lives of otherwise overly aggressive individuals. Religions can help organized societies survive collectively into the future—longer probably than these would survive without.

Near the midpoint of the existential teeter-totter scale, all individuals may together contribute checks and balances to an equilibrium that favors survival, supported by rituals which imply, rationalize, and stabilize a habit of following the Golden Rule. There, along the teeter-totter beam, near the egalitarian point of balance, between culture-shaping bouts of aggression and commonsense religious retreats, potential equals share, compete, coexist, inspire, mate, multiply, enjoy, and endure one another. They live. They argue and concede. They read and write, and as neighbors they learn to tolerate and endure one another. They write books to share.

Evolutionary Context —a Preview for General Orientation

Gatherers and hunters began to domesticate plants and animals in larger numbers, perhaps som twelve millennia ago. Progressive men did hyper-domesticate; they controlled and began to own fellow humankind as well. Rulers who enslaved humankind acted as Sons of Gods. In ancient Egypt they descended, i.e. emanated from, were procreated by, or were initiated into the "totemic cliques" of mighty raptor and other predator deities.

Sons of God were would-be human immortals whose deaths were deemed fortuitous. When death nevertheless occurred, then, in order to hold on to authority over a group, they needed to resurrect into the bodies of their successors—preferably the bodies of their own offspring. Ceremonial mystery-plays maintained the status of deified rulers and their dynasties. The pharaohs of ancient Egypt ruled as Sons of God. Later conquerors of Egypt, such as Darius the First, Alexander, and Augustus Octavius, they all learned in Egypt how to rule as Sons of God.

Inspired by Augustus, the Caesars of Rome sought post-mortem deification (apotheosis) and imperial Son of God status. They ruled their empires assuming to be de facto Sons of God. De facto "resurrection" was what imperial Sons of God hoped to achieve. Therewith they empowered, deified and stabilized their dynasties for future generations. But it could not last.

Jesus of Nazareth, a commoner Jew who preached the Empire of Heaven, was executed by crucifixion under Tiberius, a Roman emperor who ruled as de facto imperial Son of the God. Jesus was crucified for having acquired the reputation of being the Messiah, a de facto Son of God. The evolving faith surrounding the Resurrection of Jesus presumed a higher divine status than what any deified Roman emperor could claim for himself.

Therefore, the political question still is pending today: Can the revolutionary resurrection story of Jesus of Nazareth, a commoner, be deemed less, or more, rational than the imperial deification rites or the claims of hyper-domesticators during the preceding three thousand years BCE? Regardless of our answer, the Christian story about a commoner's resurrection has changed the course of history. It has changed entitlements to equal status among commoners, as children of God and as brothers and sisters of Jesus Christ. It continues to affect human history today. Among the secularized children of Mother Nature, claims to "equality" persist.

When Constantine won the Western half of the Empire, against Maxentius, and the Eastern half against Licinius, the traditional gods of Rome were enlisted by his competitors. But with his Christ-Emblem ☧ mounted on his labarum, Constantine did win his battles against them. He thereby gave credit for his victories to the God of Christianity--to Jesus Christ, as member of the almighty Trinity. The "Only begotten Son of God" out-ranked the imperial "made" Sons of God. The Emperor Constantine also held the office of Pontifex Maximus--of High Priest or Supreme Pope--as such he presided over all religions that were tolerated in Rome. The Emperor Constantine favored Christianity; but understandably, as the "pagan" Pontifex Maximus of all Roman religions, he postponed Christian baptism until his deathbed.

2

Religion and Culture in Evolution

The process of "evolution," as it has been refined in anthropological theories during past decades, no longer means what it meant in the Nineteenth Century—progress from lower to higher levels of existence. Modern anthropological evolutionists may, to the extent that archaeological data support such inferences, nevertheless recognize a gradual increase in the complexity of cultures over the long haul. The technological "primitiveness" or lack of complexity, among earlier cultures, is not an indication of the role or the quality of coexistent "primitive" religion. More is not necessarily better. However, cultural complexity implies commensurate styles of aggression or corresponding cultural "sins." These, in turn, require specific styles of "religious" retreat behavior for balance and justification.

ca. 300 years ago: democratic revolts

ca. 3,000 years: religions of universal salvation

ca. 5,000 years ago: hyper-domestication

ca. 12,000 years ago: domestication

ca. 3,000,000 years ago: gathering, scavenging, hunting

Figure 3. Eras and Strata in the Evolution of Cultures and Religions

Inasmuch as in the previous section we have outlined the reciprocal relationship between culture and religion, there no longer exists in the history of religions field a need for holding evolutionary thinking hostage to the old ghosts of our progress-oriented forebears. Religion, defined as retreat behavior, never can mean "progress."

Thus, religions may entail not only retreat behavior in space, but also may nurture thoughts of retreat nostalgia and rites of penitent remembering along the larger dimension of time.

There is not a single religious founder, documented in the annals of our discipline, who has not in some way returned his or her followers to an earlier or simpler relationship with greater-than-human reality. These founders have lured whole cultures and nations unto nostalgic paths that lead back to what is remembered as having been simpler and in the longer run, as having been still more rational under better balanced circumstances.

Another common misconception about "evolution" must also be put to rest. The evolutionary eras, suggested in Figure 3, are not successive portions of time that followed each other progressively; rather, they are vertically accumulated strata. All culture strata may be visualized as additional layers of data that, somehow together, have been propagated into the present.

For example, hunter-gatherer cultures and their corresponding religions are still with us and in some remote corners of the world are still ethnologically alive and exposed to sunlight. This author himself has lived and participated at all the evolutionary culture strata indicated in the diagram. Of course, people who pursue different livelihoods, and those engaged alongside, commit different "sins" of culture-defined over-assertion.

While participating in different cultural contexts, this author himself became existentially involved in the assertiveness of other peoples. He has acquired, and has become entangled in, the collective guilt of culture-specific sins. He also has participated in some of their religious "retreats" — in their pilgrimages and rituals that sought atonement for the same. Some other people differ from him only because during their collective struggles for survival they have become stranded in other specialized culture contexts — which means they became entangled in cultural quests for survival along different paths of religious justification. They therefore seek their balance in "faiths" concerning greater-than-human realities that seem different. The general evolutionary eras, postulated in this essay can be integrated into most current anthropological theories pertaining to the process of evolution. Inasmuch as cultures move forward by leaps that periodically do sloughen into recession, the lengths of their evolutionary episodes differ accordingly.

Gathering, Scavenging, Hunting

The span of time in humanoid evolution that is alluded to here, with its activities of gathering, scavenging, and hunting may be estimated in excess of three million years—as having begun at least with the manufacture of stone weapons and the use of fire. In isolated regions on our globe, remnants of this Stone Age hunter stratum survive today. Subsistence within earliest culture strata depended on abilities to forage and to kill animals. Gatherers, scavengers, and hunters have principally interfered at the end of the life cycles of their victims. They exploited natural deaths, learned to inflict deaths, and assumed full control over the bodies of their victims. They butchered, prepared and consumed them, accordingly.

An increase in intelligence, driven by desire for better weapons, has increased the human mental ability to the point of also recognizing societal guilt as well as fresh paths of justification. Hunting is trickery par excellence. Hunter gods frequently were seen as greater-than-human "hunters" who appeared in animal form as predators. To these superiors, some hunters paid share offerings from among the carcasses of the victims they killed. They atoned for violent aggression and for sins of unfair competition. Primitive hunters performed "religious retreat" or "back-off" rituals. Ceremonially they rebuilt damaged relationships with their victims whom they recognized as fellow persons and, occasionally, as gods. By double refraction even some victimized species—such as Deer or Lambs—became totemic sponsors of guilt-ridden human hunters or herders.

Domestication

Domesticators claimed ownership of seeds, plants and livestock. They paid back their gods with sacrifices in kind—often whole animals or sheaves. Domesticators are known for having taken control over entire life cycles of plants and animals, from conception to consumption. They no longer interfered merely to inflict death on their victims as hunters did. Domesticators claimed ownership of the land and the dwellings that they occupied, whereas newly discovered creator gods vouched for these possessions and underwrote human entitlements. Herders continued the nomadism of their hunter ancestors for a time, whereas domesticators who practiced planting needed to settle, dig more permanent caves or build huts. And as they became sedentary they became targets for hunter bands turned warriors.

In all likelihood, in tropical areas the earliest pursuit of horticulture was dominated by women, whereas men continued to specialize in hunting. Success in horticulture, in some areas helped produce an increase in population which, in turn, resulted in an increase of eligible hunters. This increase left fewer animals for the men to hunt. It has saddled huntsmen with the burden of having failed as providers.

Secret warrior societies, cults of headhunting and cannibalism were some of the religious and cultural adaptations with which the egos of decadent hunters became entangled. Subsequent aristocratic warrior societies and priesthoods, together, have derived much of their ethos from the crises of adjustment that separated and united men during their transition from hunting to domestication.

On pasture lands, where hunters took to shadowing remnant herds and where they claimed these herds, men remained primary providers. By contrast, women in semi-arid regions of northern Africa, in the Near East or Central Asia, reached higher status with greater difficulty. In comparison, cultures that practiced a mixture of gardening, animal husbandry, and simple mechanized cultivation with draft animals, were able to distribute labor, authority and gender roles a little more evenly.

Grand-, Over- and Hyper-domestication

The grand-, over-, or hyper-domestication phase is important for understanding all of human evolution and recent history.[3] All phases represent simple logical outcomes of exaggerating the ordinary practice of domesticating plants and animals. Hyper-domestication began where ambitious domesticators—men with herder skills and greater goals—pushed beyond the limits of merely controlling the life cycles of plants and animals.

They also proceeded to control human groups as their herds. They organized them under gods who then, figuratively, presided over herded human subjects as well. Totemic hunter gods and predators formerly presided over herds of wild animals. Domesticators usurped the function of divine animal masters as new owners and herders. Both animals and humankind were acquired from the gods. Hyper-domesticators paid for each species with share-offerings of the same.

---

[3] Designations of Civilization, Grand-domestication, Over-domestication or Hyper-domestication, for this writer, do cover connotations that range from appreciation to repugnance.

The most conspicuous methods for over-domesticating humankind were militarism, slavery, human sacrifice, castration, bureaucracy, including the over-regimentation of religion and human labor.[4] Methods for domesticating the gods of subjugated peoples required building stately "barns" (temples)—setting up the gods as lords in proxy, as statuary presences at their tables (altars). Positioned mysteriously in sanctuaries, behind curtains, some were set up permanently invisible.

Where deities came to feed at their tables, groups of people could be scheduled according to sacred calendars and festivals. The people's hours of paying homage could be made to coincide with the feeding hours of the gods. All this could be managed by priests and high-priests—chief butchers—for their warrior-bosses who rose to be kings. Many hyper-domestication schemes began religiously and innocently enough, with the full collaboration of subjected peoples.

Defensive efforts against other hyper-domesticator hordes required strict military organization under some kind of Chief of chiefs who, in turn, derived his authority from the next superior God of gods. Thus, by their transcendent placement, great divine beings functioned as administrators and "saviors" of warrior peoples that gathered, allowing themselves to be organized to increase safety and power for defense and proactive aggression. In a human world order, defined by competition among hyper-domesticators, it was easy for sedentary people to be rendered vulnerable and be subjected.

---

[4]One of the reviewers at Amazon.de, of my book *Jägertempel am Göbekli Tepe* (2015), well-intentioned, has attempted to improve on my term *Über-domestizierung* by proposing a German translation of his own: *Verhausschweinung*. As a farmer's son, I am keenly aware of other connotations and that, as a species, pigs were the most severely victimized among our farm animals. I certainly would not wish to impinge on their remaining dignity with this questionable hyperbole. Besides, it was not the farmers, it was the nobility and royalty—"*die besseren Leute*"—who inflicted "*Verhausschweinung*" on humankind. Yes, farmers domesticated pigs. And in return, to pay for their successes in domestication, they were conscripted or "installed" as grunts, or were "*inhaftiert im Burgverlies*" by royal officials—who often themselves were treated like pigs. Culture-specific language has a way of adding lopsided connotations and can be applied from the points of view of oppressors as well as of victims. Grand-, over-, and hyper-domestication refer to various intensities of the same human activity. These three attributions vary by connotations only, not in kind—but rather in relation to their degrees of cruelty toward fellow humankind.

Under conflicting conditions, people could survive only if they allied themselves with strong hyper-domesticators, who themselves claimed to huddle under still more powerful divine sponsors, for empowerment and justification.

Whereas warrior, headhunter, or cannibal societies may be considered primitive, early forms of over-domestication, the practice of human sacrifice in any form, represents a more extreme degradation of hunting and butchering, arranged by obsolescent and decadent hunters for purposes of blending their killer activities with the domesticators' logic of owning living subjects. By sacrificing a specimen from his human herd, a grand-domesticator paid his "share" to own and to claim the remainder of the herd as his property. He legitimized his ownership by solemnly "purchasing" livestock and other property directly from the divine creator. Human share sacrifices to the gods, legitimated (or at least demonstrated) the grand-domesticator's claim to absolute power over his human subjects. The more they killed in war the more they "sacrificed" and deemed to pay to the gods, ...the more "human breeding stock" they acquired to enlarge their "herds."

Egypt, the mother of Western Civilization was a grand-domestication system par excellence. The Hebrew Exodus tradition has defined itself as a reaction against slavery in Egypt, later—by way of arguing from presuppositions advanced on behalf of the Davidic monarchic reform. Greek philosophers, too, reacted to the problems of grand-domestication, and for their argumentation they drew old ontology from Egypt. Then, from the heartland of its own Near Eastern origin, Christianity inherited the Hebrew reaction against Egyptian grand-domestication. But alongside the prophetic sentiment, for balance, it learned from ancient Greek philosophy some metaphors that also were anchored in Egyptian ontology and theology.

Hebrew monotheism, under King David, appears to have reacted somewhat against hyper-domestication culture, whereas David's successor, King Solomon relapsed by moving his entire reign toward institutionalizing the glories of hyper-domestication. In the larger perspective of evolution, our history of religions approach need not follow slavishly the valuations of regular field historians who, since times immemorial have been singing praises, and speaking flattery, on behalf of tyrants and their empires—extolling glories on the hyper-domestication schemes of their respective employers and paymasters.

Kept on the payrolls of hyper-domesticators, scribes have repaid their masters with valorizing and glorifying grandiose aggressive schemes as "civilization." Let the historians of hyper-domestication glorify the battlefronts and victories of empires; it remains the task of historians of religions to detect and to understand institutional deficiencies and to identify past types of religious Retreat solutions. Historians of religions are interested in the evolution of common-sense compromises, in escape and retreat behavior, thus, in movements which have attempted to reduce aggression and violence and have striven to lessen selfish human hoarding of resources and power.

Universal Salvation Religions

Universal salvation religions are torchlights, of peoples who lived in gloom and toiled in the shadows of hyper-domesticated "civilization." They are popular patterns of religious flight responses that, when possible, attempted to establish universal dignity for all people, regardless of imperial boundaries, wealth, inheritance, or aristocratic privilege. Theologically they would deny, and at times would even dare to mock, the claims to grand-domesticator status of their superiors. Symbolically and by religious faith, they dared to insist on being fellow equals. Their own faith provided competitive assurances against organized aristocratic religion. They derived their dignity from the highest imaginable creative authorities, from gods. They struggled to find theologies that would match or surpass the beliefs of those who subjugated them. Universal salvation religions are movements that spread on behalf of the masses of people. They are faith systems that succeeded, in some form, emancipating peoples from the fetters imposed by hyper-domestication ideology. They are low-key revolutionary solutions that, where people break free from their constraints, may grow into international movements for greater freedom—for a time.

Approximately during the thirteenth century BCE, the biblical literary Moses figure is said to have led a group of Hebrew slaves to freedom under the auspices of their God, Yahweh, whom they accepted as being superior to the God of gods of the Egyptian empire who was referred to as Amun. The formalized religion of ancient fugitives, in reaction to slavery in Egypt, survived partially in Judaism and Samaritan-ism. Strong trends of its theological impulse continued later in Christianity—and still later in aspects of the Islamic prayer ritual. The number of Israelites who could have escaped from slavery in Egypt, and the story of their escape, has meanwhile gotten reclassified and revised as historicized myth or legend. The Hebrew narrative of the Exodus, from the start and again today, appears to have gotten politicized for goals of self-legitimation. The story of the Exodus appears to have been intended first to establish an advantageous covenant among the earliest (ostensibly united) Israelite peoples and their God. Its political purpose initially was to bind together Israelite and Judaic tribes into a confederacy that King David had been trying to mold into a kingdom. The preponderance of present archaeological evidence, however, suggests that the foundation stories of David's monarchy were told later to establish hyper-domestication rights for royal heirs of his dynasty.

Around the middle of the First Millennium BCE, the man remembered as Zoroaster, 628-551(?), effected a religious-political reform on a herder priesthood that derived power from animal sacrifices. With the help of King Vishtaspa, a benign grand-domesticator, he introduced worship of a supreme deity, Ahura Mazda.

During the Fifth Century BCE in India, Gautama, the founder of Buddhism, disallowed the authority of the traditional Aryan priesthood, which was similar to the old Iranian priesthood. The authority of these herder priests swelled by the performance of spectacular sacrificial festivities that procured blessings and authority from the gods. Along with the Aryan organized tradition, Gautama rejected the religious endorsement of his own inheritance of royal prosperity and wealth. He dropped out from his aristocratic class and became a mendicant hippie-monk who, like many contemporaries, sought an escape route from *samsara* and the effects of *karma*.[5] He found a somewhat moderate path to happiness and nirvana.

Soon thereafter, in China, the sage Lao Tzu recorded his philosophy in a little book that gave prominence to the need of living in harmony with the universal *Dao* (the Way). He gave his readers the mental tools with which, over time they could ignore mongering warlords and ambitious hyper-domesticators. Some Daoist faithful, such as those at the White Cloud Temple in Beijing and in the education of peasant shamans in China's western provinces, still revere this ancient hippie-philosopher as Lord Most High.

---

[5] Samsara, in Hinduism, is the process of transmigration and reincarnation of souls. Karma is the cosmic law which in the physical world determines the level at which souls become reincarnated.

Also, in China, at about the same time as Lao Tzu, the sage Kung Fu Tzu (Confucius) taught a doctrine of universal ethics to establish a more decent government. This doctrine imposed the Reign of Heaven and the formal veneration of ancestors to guide social relations. His ethics eventually put ambitious hyper-domesticators on the defensive. Under the tutelage of Heaven, and in the tailwind of "wise rulers of long ago," he prescribed a gentlemen's code of behavior. When his behavioral and ethical recommendations gradually took hold, and when, finally, they were endorsed by some farsighted grand-domesticators, they helped stabilize China for two thousand years.

The several "good" heavenly emperors of Chinese Daoism—who lately have risen again in popularity—constitute a multiplicity of religious hopes, similar to the "kingdom of heaven" anticipation that Jesus imparted to Christendom. Chinese Daoist priests balanced their traditional problem—of having earthly grand-domesticators rule the Middle Kingdom (China) selfishly—by accepting each as a legitimate Son of Heaven.[6] They balanced successive emperors who ruled on earth with counterweights of several "good" Heavenly Emperors who then commanded some eighty-seven good heavenly generals. In historical evolution, this multiplicity of potential heavenly savior-generals may reflect a prior awareness of hosts of Buddhist bodhisattvas, living in the heavenly canopy above the human realm.[7]

The issues that Daoists encountered with hyper-domestication systems resulted, to some extent, from the generous endorsement that early Confucians provided for the office of the imperial Son of Heaven. The celestial realm of Daoism is still conceptualized as being managed and balanced by several heavenly emperors, as a somewhat benign imperial bureaucracy. In any case, the sage Confucius need not be held responsible for all exaggerations that in context with the later

---

6 This may suggest that, for similar reasons, such status may have gotten ascribed in Western Civilization, to Jesus Christ, the Anointed (Messiah), as Son of the un-nameable God (Yahweh).

7 I visited the assembly of statues of these "Celestials" at the White Cloud Temple in Beijing, but I did not take the time to verify the count of eighty-seven statues of these generals. See also Karl W. Luckert and Zuotang Zhang, *Yin Yang Shamans of Ningxia*, China, 2002-2004, a Youtube video.

imperial history of China have become attributed to him. He lived and taught during times of unrest, when it seemed that the emperor had lost his heavenly mandate. Confucius hoped and labored for balance and moderation among the ruling elite. In his own days, he was convinced that the imperial office was necessary to restore and to maintain a semblance of order.

During the first century, in Palestine, a man named Jesus was recognized by people as a "Son of God"—a title that for three thousand years in the Near East has meant "heir of a divine emperor." He quite obstinately lived the role of a poor people's Son of God, and masses of people continued to follow him even after he had been publicly shamed and crucified. The people celebrated his resurrection from death as their salvation. In the religious movement that ensued, people became brothers and sisters of this Son of God, destined to enter the Empire of Heaven with him. Kings and local terrestrial emperors began to lose followers to this universal "King of Heaven." The promotion of Christ's followers to the status of being their Savior's brothers and sisters—thus, God's adopted children—raised them all to a level of equality with their high priests and kings. As the centuries passed, generations of secularized Christians began to trade their religiously inherited "saved-for-deification" status for "natural" equality and "secular" democracy.

During the seventh century, in Arabia, Muhammad the "Messenger" organized a semi-nomadic people who had been dwarfed in the shadows of two over-domesticated universalisms: Zoroastrian Persia to the northeast, and Christian Byzantium in the northwest. At a time of competitive warfare with these powers, his universalism of calling all people as fellow equals, to submit to Allah, quickly arrived at a synthesis and brought the religion of Islam to assimilate the political mindset of grand-domestication. Whereas it took the Christian universal salvation religion three centuries to re-accommodate grand-domestication, under the Emperor Constantine, such accommodation happened in Islam during the lifetime of its founder, Muhammad.

Democratic Revolts

Revolutions in recent centuries, which in Europe, Asia, and the Americas deposed hereditary kings and instituted democratic and socialist forms of government, drew their sanctions from a long history of ideological wresting and conditioning. For about two thousand years, Christians in Western Civilization have been accustomed to think of themselves as brothers and sisters of Jesus Christ—who, as a lowly type of Son of God also was hailed as "King of kings" (thus, by the title of a contrary divine emperor). All along, the Christians have preserved a spark of that ancient hope of living with their Savior in his heavenly Kingdom.

Nevertheless, secularized descendants of peoples whose forebears knew themselves saved by Christendom's universalism, became disillusioned with the over-domesticated state of religious organizations. They presently still labor to abandon five millennia of old political patterns of organized reasoning. Secularized humankind continues to cling to much of the reactionary Christian ethics of universal salvation, though. They continue to dream of universal salvation without also having to carry the burden of politically compromised ancient theology and hyper-domestication.

It is widely asserted by students of intellectual history, that Western democracies were the true offspring of Hellenic and of Western European Enlightenment philosophy. This view appears to be only half true. Indeed, the Renaissance and Reformation loosened the grip of the Christian mandated state, and secularized Enlightenment mythology took root in the "Social Contract" philosophies of Locke and Rousseau. Social Contract theory has summarized and justified democratic and egalitarian goals; it could nicely be combined with the newer faith in Nature—without having recourse to the ancient God of the Egyptian-Hebrew-Christian inheritance. Ancient biblical "covenants" with God were replaced with social "contracts" by groups of people who ceased hoping for Paradise but still thought of themselves as being "exceptional" while anticipating Utopia.

"Social Contract" theory was modern parabolic mythology. It was religious assurance, projected back into the greater mythic beginnings of human evolution. Nevertheless, there exist no anthropological or archaeological data that a primeval social contract was ever agreed to in an ancient assembly. Rather, the legend of the "Social Contract" did ring true during democratic revolutions—truer than did the earlier theologically legitimized mandates that continued to be promulgated by monarchs. The new mythology was told to rationalize fresh waves of nation-building under diminishing theological justifications, but with an increase in nationalistic and democratic confidence. The Social Contract was cherished in England to legitimize and to valorize the *Magna Carta.*

In a similar fashion, Marxist ideology reached back to mythical beginnings to establish norms for human sociology with faith in a classless society. This strata-less social order was imagined as a type of Utopia to which some early democracies and communes hoped to return their people. Both streams of revolutionary fervor, Western democratic branches that reached America, and the Communistic wave that rolled eastward, attempted to derive authority from preexistent and greater-than-human conditions, quasi-religiously. Both streams started flowing as universalistic yearnings for salvation, against enslavements of hyper-domestication and "civilization."

The Christian Kingdom of Heaven may all along have been a "pie in the sky" notion, as Marxist ideologists have teased, but Christian hope, surely, also was the power that depreciated the status of hereditary despots and kings to a point where their subjects—the parent generations of later revolutionaries—could begin to think about deposing and reducing them to the status of equals.

Karl Marx came out of Judaism, and Friedrich Engels came from the conservative Christian *Alt-Pietismus*. Their Communism need not surprise us—not in light of the fact that primitive Christianity began as a communistic Jewish social movement. The "commune" idea is a historical datum in the early records of Christendom. Kibbutzes still exist here and there in the modern state of Israel. But both Marx and Engels became dissatisfied with organized religion during the hypergrowth of the Industrial Revolution. Both remained nevertheless blessed with the scriptural prophetic insight that a Judeo-Christian God, who during the Industrial Revolution was utilized to justify the exploitation of workers, could not be real. Marx and Engels chose for their Communist ideology the reactionary ontology of atheism. As prophetic revolutionaries, in their time, they may have had no choice. When theologies or ideologies can no longer be repaired, when their mythic languages can no longer be understood in historical context, they need to be restudied.

Following the reactionary trail established by Marx and Engels, we note that Communist liberation armies of Russia, China, and elsewhere spread the Judeo-Christian ethos, minus its God-story. Questions of social justice and ethics are like eggs from which mutations of theological doctrine are hatched. Secular armies have unknowingly spread their ethics-embryos—like a heron's legs that carry the eggs of fishes from one pond to another. As the Christian religion acquires new followers in lands where Communist systems are being reformed, this happenstance does not result merely from the lure of capitalism that emanates from compromised Christianlands. Latter-day followers of Communism have for decades been imbued with a radical portion of the Judeo-Christian ethos, minus its theology. Some of them are simply trying now to discover their own implicit theological and ontological roots, which had been buried among loads of materialistic and atheistic dogma.

Revisiting Near Eastern Religions

Within the history of religions field, perhaps no other geographical region of the world has been studied and re-examined as much as the ancient Near East. Why, then, is another book and a fresh look necessary? What can the general history of religions contribute to a field of study that has been examined by thousands of specialists? Obviously, one more edition cannot hope to provide much more detail in proportion to what is already available. But it can offer a wider view, with glimpses of interrelatedness among a variety of Western cultures and religions—of four distinct academic fields: ancient Egyptian religion and civilization, Hebrew tradition, Greek philosophy, and early Christianity itself.

Individual religious traditions generally are studied by specialists who begin at moments of inception, with the biographies of their founders. The histories of selected religions are then traced forward through time as far as records will carry. For a broader scope, historians occasionally will look sideways to parallel traditions that thrived nearby, or they will apply a variety of perspectives borrowed from ancillary academic disciplines. But rarely do they position themselves at the beginning of their favorite tradition to appreciate the full evolutionary process surge toward them—and then watch the political flow of this process as it saddles religious founders with the obligation of having to act as reactionaries and contraries. None of the great religious founders have set out to establish exactly the organization that later became associated with their names.

Ancient Egyptian civilization—a strong system of hyper-domestication—and the concomitant theology of the pharaonic burial cult, have provided Hebrew tradition with ontological ignition points for future systematic protest and development.

For instance, Egyptian royal soteriology offered to pharisaic Jewish minds an opportunity to contemplate concepts that helped rationalize the possibility of "resurrection for dead Osiris-es." Hebrew and Egyptian theological notions together contributed logical structure to what was to become trinitarian Christian theology—altogether rendered credible by so-called Neo-Platonism. Christianity and Judaism, in competition, also passed on some early thoughts to Arabic Islam.

The Judaism that co-existed with early Christianity was not the new religion's father. From the point in time at which Christians became visible, both religions were competing rather like siblings.[8] Judaism, the older sibling, was nurtured by the memory of an Escape from Egypt as well as by love for an early monarchic temple cult, whereas Christianity broke away from both—from the temple when it was destroyed in 70 CE, and from the tribal consciousness of Israel and Judah. During the period of their Babylonian Exile, Judaism was reorganized around synagogues.

Later, alongside Christianity, Judaism found its new path with somewhat less tribal identification and without refocusing on a temple.[9] Christian churches, thinking of themselves as a new type of Israel, managed to withdraw from older tribal traditions more thoroughly. They spread into the larger Roman Empire to mingle and to fuse. Recognizing this historical development head-on may, gradually, help our secular society understand better what it may be that periodically confounds regional populations with "anti-Semitism."

Our statement is meant to be neither a personal evaluation nor a criticism. We merely try to identify historical events and differences. Whenever Christian missionaries insist on converting the Jewish eth-

---

[8]Regardless of how seriously one evaluates the Jewish Jamnia Council (90 CE), as a fork in the early Christian path away from Judaism, there remains the Egyptian dimension of early Christian history. It might be better to restrict the popular category of a "Judeo-Christian Tradition" to its latter-day ecumenical meaning, for managing life in America—rather than to force it retroactively into the Near Eastern history of religions. The theological breach between Judaism and Christianity, in competition with the Roman emperor cult, called for an entirely new revolutionary God-story.

[9]Their ancient temple was built twice (Solomon—952 BCE, Zerubbabel—516 BCE; was expanded by Herod the Great (starting 20 BCE). It was destroyed twice (Nebuchadnezzar—586 BCE; Titus—70 CE). During the First Millennium BCE, the temple cult gradually became obsolete. Muslims claimed the Temple Mount in 638 CE, and Christian Crusaders took control from 1099 to 1187 CE.

are spawned when Jewish scholars explain away the divine mission or nature of Jesus of Nazareth, i.e. the Christians' Son of God, by trying to recapture and reduce him to the level of a marginal rabbi who, as an offspring of Abraham or an heir of David, should forever be held indebted or be Jewish cultural property.

None of these presuppositions will sit well in the longer run. Both will produce cancerous conflicts even among secularized Jews or Christians who no longer do take the stories of their inherited or divinely granted status seriously. Extinct volcanoes can erupt again, and some well-nigh dead religions can be resurrected as banners to rally troops for tribal or nationalistic battles. Outsiders who capture the battle flags of insiders are demonstrating to those who lose the symbol of their identity, that their ambiguous tradition belongs where it was meant to be—onto the ash heap of history. Of course, all sentiments generated by a loss of identity, at any level of sophistication, tend to mutate to irrational exaggerations born of competition, of hostile action, reaction and emotion.

As far as Christianity and Judaism are concerned, they both had the fiery ancient Hebrew religion as their father. Our essay does not detract anything from that well-documented paternal heritage and history, nor will we depreciate the broader Semitic context of Judaism within the Greater Near East. But with that same historical objectivity we acknowledge also the ancient Egyptian imperial religiosity that served as Christendom's quietly aging mother—even more so than she gave shape to the escape-minded and Exodus-oriented reactions of Judaism and the latter's theology.

Christianity began with two Jewish founders, John the Baptizer and Jesus of Nazareth, and with approximately a dozen Jewish followers whom these men inspired. The Apostle Paul, another Jewish rabbi, may be rated as Christianity's third founder. Then, the oldest written texts of Christendom were spawned within the Hebrew-Aramaic linguistic context. Christians adopted much of the canon of Hebrew scripture as their "Old Testament"—as a record from which an older notion of a theocracy of ancient Israel could be resurrected by prophets, into a revised Kingdom of Heaven or a Kingdom of God anticipation.

The First Millennium BCE saw the evolution of a special Covenant (Deal), as title to land and a basis for the tribal monarchy, deeded to a chosen people. Even though Christian leaders went international and almost completely ignored the tribal basis of the old covenant stories, narratives pertaining to the legitimation of ancient Israel were cherished by Christians as their first installment to the Kingdom of Heaven proclamation of Jesus. In spite of Christianity's multinationalism, the sublimation of Israel as an older "Deal" or special "Covenant Nation" has become an article of faith for groups of Christians who blessed themselves with the notion of becoming themselves tribal again. But by and large, Christians who try to convert Jews, and Jews who re-historicize Rabbi Jesus for Christians rarely make things nicer at their places in the world.

Jesus, as a Son of Man and a Son of God, was accepted by Christians as a messiah (an Anointed One) to sit enthroned next to God the Father. The Christian proclamation therewith proceeded to remove the ritual boundary wall that stood between Judaic Christians and the Gentile Roman empire. It opened doors to the wider world. The corpus of Hebrew scripture, dubbed "Old Testament," continued to serve Christianity as prehistoric and anticipatory introduction to its faith. Occasionally, it also became the unlucky foil of their gospel.

The importance of traditional Hebrew scripture was diminished by Christians in contrast with their New Testament. First-Century Christians began to write their New Testament in Greek which, since the time of Alexander the Great, had become the literary medium for what eventually became the Eastern Roman Empire. With several older languages having contributed a polyphony of meanings, Greek challenges alone could not account for the entire Christian re-orientation.

From a Jewish perspective, the Christian New Testament represents a sectarian fringe from along the periphery of first-century Judaism. In the larger historical context, however, the theological emphasis of the New Testament also signifies a wide breach in the dike of Judaism. This rupture enabled a rivulet of Hebrew religious thought to flow outward into the larger estuary that was the Roman Empire. It broadened and diffused to become orthodox Christendom. The flow carried a distinct theology and soteriology—a combination of Babylonian Christology (i.e. Cyrus-inspired Messianism) and Egyptianized Graeco-Roman Numenology and Mariology. The distinct Christian strain of Trinitarianism surged. It brought the time-tested ancient Egyptian process theology to the surface and therewith Christendom, for a while, has united Western Civilization as Christendom.

With historical hindsight, the controversies during the early Christian centuries, pertaining to the natures of Jesus Christ, to Mary and the Holy Spirit, can best be understood as mental birth pangs that accompanied the emergence and organization of Christendom. The new religion introduced a fresh profile for understanding God as a loving almighty Being, and of Man as a defective but improvable image, or as a child of God. These pangs, while almost forgotten by the offspring, were, nevertheless, real labor pains on the part of Christendom's mother—the expiring religion of ancient Egypt. This Mother religion died in the centuries during which her vigorous offspring emerged and began prospering in the Mediterranean world.

The Mother's labor pains were also her death pangs. For almost two millennia, the Daughter religion, Christianity, remained relatively well informed about her ancient Hebrew paternal origins, being reminded of it constantly by narratives stored in its Old Testament. Despite the close resemblance of Christendom's orthodox legacy to Ancient Egypt's theological and soteriological orientation—and aside from the pharaonic double crowns that the Christian bishops kept wearing at festive occasions—Christianity has remembered not many specifics about the deceased Mother religion. Pyramid- and Coffin-texts survived unreadable, in hidden oblivion.

Beginner Questions

Fresh and rational perspectives beg new questions. When new questions are focused on a revised historical grid, some better answers snap into focus. To assist readers of this volume at the start of their refocusing, a few starter questions shall be introduced here. No attempt will be made to answer these systematically. The remainder of the book will trickle forth the answers.

How did the Christian gospel, of God "begetting" a Son, ever make sense to Jewish minds who all along had been living under the influence of a monotheistic interpretation of Yahweh theology? Is it really conceivable that the apostles of Jesus Christ, as Jews, were favorably impressed by Greek mythological models—as, for instance, by the lewd affairs attributed to Father Zeus, which resulted in a variety of interspecies begettings? Or must one look for meaningful antecedents elsewhere in the history of the Near East?

How was the "logos" concept, the creative Word of God, initially understood? Was it derived from the commands that God has spoken according to the creation account in *Genesis*? Or did it spring from the orthodox tradition of Egyptian monotheism, monism, and known strata of emanation? Religions contain mythologies, rituals, liturgies, theologies, and more. They may, nevertheless, also be meaningfully contemplated as large linguistic and symbolic compilations of knowledge which, in the embrace of time have been rolled into the processes of life and evolution. Humankind were being carried along. As scientific languages, specialized on contents of reality, so also the languages of various religions sought to achieve clarity among human relationships toward greater-than-human circumstances and conditions. Rationalized religious faiths are the primary bulwarks of defense against greater realities that threaten to overwhelm.

How has Christianity gotten its Trinitarian theology? Were Indo-European tripartite models really the basis, as many scholars have suspected? Or should one rather look to the first Trinity of the Ninefoldness (Ennead) at Heliopolis? Was the early Christian debate concerning the "Holy Spirit proceeding from the Father and/or the Son" provoked by Egyptian or by Greek theology and logic? Or by both?

Upon what basis of Jewish logic could the Pharisaic faith in the resurrection of the dead have evolved? It seems obvious that it could not have sprung from Greek philosophical reasoning, according to which only "souls" survive human death. Was it derived from Iranian Mazdaism, as some scholars think? Or is it more likely that ancient Egyptian funerary orientation provided the initial direction?

Why, in the early history of Christendom, was the "Kingdom of Heaven" message converted so quickly into a personalized "death and resurrection" eschatology? Could that personal dimension have stemmed from popular funerary practices, earlier during Egypt's New Kingdom era? Could wider strata of people, in Egypt, have usurped funerary practices to acquire eschatological privileges formerly held exclusively by the royalty?

Concerning the Kingdom of Heaven, proclaimed by John the Baptizer and by Jesus of Nazareth, as antithesis to hyper-domestication kingdoms in the mundane realm—could their message have solely been based on visions anticipated by Hebrew prophets? Could Hebrew "kingdom criticism" have gotten evoked also by Egyptian and Babylonian imperialism?

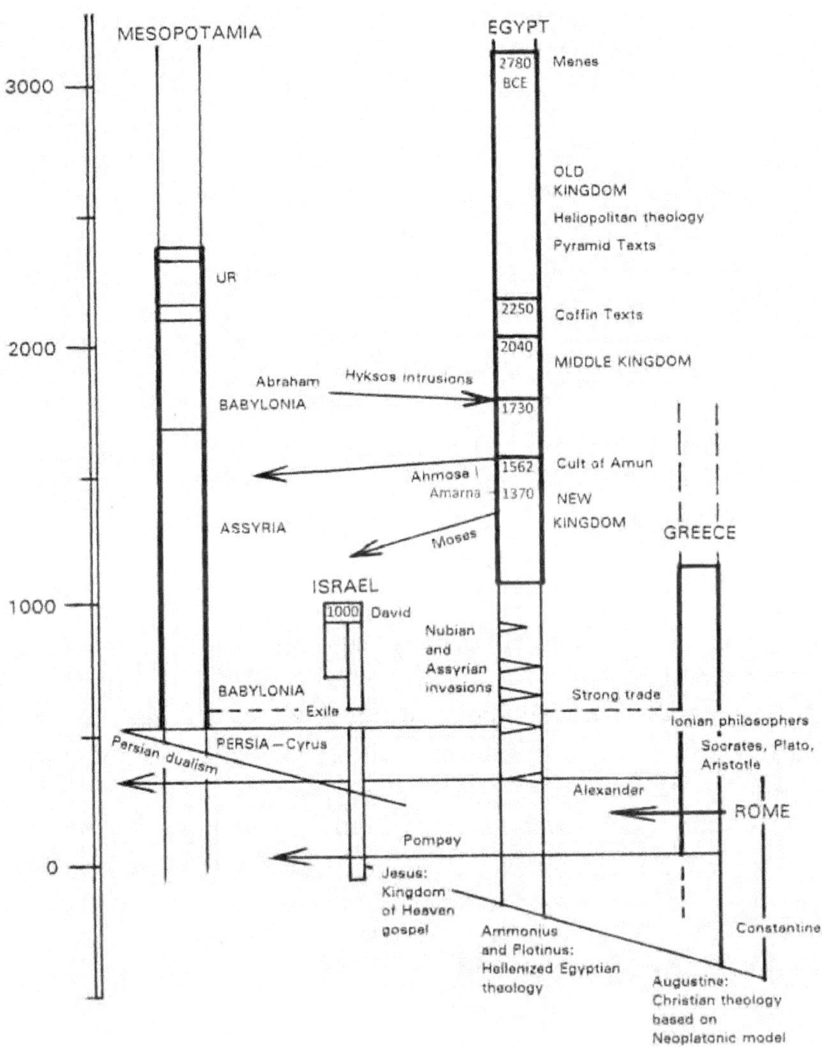

Figure 4. Schematic drawing, depicting the ancestry and birth of Christendom among Near Eastern Civilizations: Hebrew religion was its father; Egypt was its mother; Mesopotamia stood as God-parent; Hellenism served as midwife.

How Judaic or how non-Judaic was the pantheistic theological accommodation with which, according to *Acts* 17:28, the Apostle Paul addressed his Athenian audience? The "in Him we live and move and have our being" generally is credited to Epimenides of Crete; and the "for we are indeed His offspring," suggests the earlier

Phaenomena, by Aratus. Both quotations appear to harmonize better with ancient Egyptian theological common sense than with Jewish or Greek traditions. If we define religion as a human response to so-conceived greater-than-human configurations of reality, then what or who is God? Is Saint Anselm's answer to this question good enough? He referred to God as being "That-than-which-nothing-greater [or better] can be conceived." I will not accompany Anselm on his next step of trying to construct a full ontological argument for the existence of God; rather, I go with him as far as the human limitation takes him. Of Anselm's "that than which nothing greater can be conceived," I accept the happenstance that God may be talked about allegorically, and also the fact that a human mind is limited when it comes to comprehending the entire scale of greatness. Then, aware of those limitations I can also accept the statements of Saint Paul and Epidemides of Crete as being somehow factual:

It was our mother who first was assigned playing the role of God toward us. In her we lived, literally, and moved and had our being for a while. Thereby God became for us the greater-than-human Mother—including the "Mother Plus" dimension of the world in which she herself moved about and into which she delivered us to continue our process of learning. Of course, this type of infant-religion remains valid only until the child and learner recognizes the face of a Daddy peering over the mother's shoulder. From that point on the Greater-than-human showed itself jointly as Mom and Dad. Nevertheless, their joint status could evolve only as far as human fathers and mothers can emulate God by pointing beyond themselves. And being unsure of themselves, this they often do.

But then, any greater-than-ordinary status we perceive, while we ourselves are growing or getting greater, must eventually be either updated or abandoned. As the next generation steps into their own pitfalls of love, life, and dangers toward survival—they can play their God-impersonation roles only for a while, until the offspring either escapes or the parents surrender the mammalian authority that was vested in them. Being active as fathers or mothers, in most instances, ends when children themselves become fathers and mothers. Play-acting divine parental roles toward weaker offspring remain an inflationary possibility only until general parental authority diminishes.

The situation in the wider flow of history and evolution is similar. Microcosm imitates macrocosm. Our Stone-age hunter ancestors discovered the That-than-which-nothing-greater-exists as some greater-than-human killer, as hunter, archer, wielder of clubs and spears, or as a spider-like trapper—a predator or raptor, a cannibal, giant, or dragon. Temporarily, all these were primitive types of greater-than-human realities for primitive human hunter folk. Of course, the existential distinction between good divine models, and bad models, has always been present. And there will always be born generations of *homines sapientes* who favor and elevate bad greater-than-human models to justify their own malevolence.

During the era of domestication, greater-than-human reality was needed to educate and to justify gardeners and herders—to help identify good gardening as opposed to bad gardening and good shepherding as opposed to bad shepherding. When domesticators became hyper-domesticators—such as kings, emperors, and owners of humankind—the ordinary greater-than-human dimension was getting usurped by them. During the episodes in human history that they dominated, they attempted to play roles of God—of That than which nothing greater can be conceived.

Part One:

Egyptian Gloom and Light

3

The Gloom of Civilization

The gloom of civilization is man-made. Since I first published *Egyptian Light and Hebrew Fire,* in 1991, fresh archaeological data from the Göbekli Tepe excavations, in eastern Anatolia, have helped illuminate some of the prehistoric horizons of religion and of civilization in the early Near East. They shed light on some additional six millennia of Neolithic progress and changes—including possibilities of gloom—which together have led to what came to be called "civilization." The ancient shadows of hunter and gatherer culture, from which humankind emerged to create a general culture of domestication and warrior states, which gave us cities and empires, have now come clearer into focus. Efficient Neolithic hunters at Göbekli Tepe, during their period of transition to domestication, multiplied and depleted the fauna. Temple cults answered the need to emphasize the propagation and domestication of life. Some of the descendants of transitional hunter-gatherers became domesticators, while others began to roam as hordes of warriors to prey on the settlements of domesticators. Hunters, as warriors, became raiders of settlers who retreated into enclosures behind protective walls—behind walls that originally were intended to hold and to shelter domesticated animals.

A little over five thousand years ago, the Egyptian empire was unified by Menes (Narmer). He was a passionate hunter who killed wild bulls for pleasure and who, from similar passions and motivations, killed people to build an empire—perhaps also to the end that we later generations would continue to admire and celebrate him. The Narmer Palette (Figure 5, below) shows him doing what he knew how to do best. His three victims probably were hyper-domesticators like he himself, who may have cherished ambitions that resembled his. But apparently, they were a little slower, less brutally efficient, and therefore less effective in conquest. Human burial sacrifices, associated with the royal tombs of the First Dynasty, show the extent to which the earliest totemic Falcon-kings of Egypt, as divine

Horus manifestations, advanced their agendas of over-hunting and over-domestication. Human domestics fell to the level of being hunted as prey. They were rounded up as prisoners and slaves.

It should be noted that the present chapter follows roughly the same outline as Chapter 17, in *Stone Age Religion at Göbekli Tepe* (2013). Studies undertaken for that publication have significantly altered this author's long-held views regarding ancient Egypt—that is, the views that he published in 1991 at the younger age of fifty-seven. Two decades later, the time has come to begin explaining some changes that have taken place in my understanding of Stone Age hunter ontology. Readers, to whom our present overview appears risky, may wish to read *Stone Age Religion at Göbekli Tepe* (2013) first, and thereby contemplate the larger scope of discoveries that have necessitated this 2021 re-visitation of *Egyptian Light and Hebrew Fire.*

From Göbekli Tepe's "T-Pillars" to Egyptian Obelisks

There existed on this planet another famous symbolic world-view, one that needed to be brought into focus from a headstand perspective. In the year 2011, at Göbekli Tepe, I began explaining the "T-pillars" to Klaus Schmidt and myself as representing stone phalluses, inserted into the "Abdomen Hill" of Mother Earth. There appeared to me simultaneously the challenge of comparing, and of contrasting these T-pillars with the presence and significance of ancient Egyptian obelisks, including the shapes of pyramids. Also, there needed to be considered the Heliopolitan theogony (story pertaining to gods) or mythology (stories about greater-than-human realities) pertaining to the rising Primeval Hill, named "Atum." Far to the south of the ancient Göbekli Tepe menhirs, along the Nile River, we once again needed to relearn, how to view the world by a vertical reversal. Seven thousand years after Göbekli Tepe, Egyptian symbolism must be understood in context with later megalithic innovations—let us say, in relation to mythology that explains the primeval Egyptian deity Atum. We must learn to see these subject matters in the context of Neolithic Near Eastern world views.

Why is this effort significant? Because for the ancient Egyptians, the Earth was Father Geb, and the Sky was Mother Nut. She was born of Tefnut, who had been the unseen Hand of Atum—of Atum the All-God—who in turn gave birth to Nut and Isis. Yet, in order to begin to understand the basics of this cosmography in Heliopolitan theology, we must first abandon fantasies about builders who might have come from outer space into ancient Egypt as foreign guest laborers. We must begin afresh a sober historical review and study the self-produced and well preserved Pyramid- and Coffin-Texts, which explain early death and underworld concepts of royalty and nobility.

The exact beginnings and the history of certain ancient Egyptian obelisks have become somewhat unclear, because many of them have as souvenirs gotten dragged to foreign places by foreign conquerors. The oldest hieroglyphic depiction of an obelisk may be found in a pictogram of *Pyramid Text*, Number 1652. There the primordial mountain, Atum, is shown as a slender obelisk-like shaft, the tip of which still appears somewhat rounded. It is not yet abstracted and angled. This rounded "pyramidion" tip is pointing skyward. It may well be that the geometry of obelisks and pyramids evolved together. Their symbolic meanings appear to have been interchangeable. The god Atum, rising from Nun as from the primordial sea of Chaos, was functionally identical with all pyramid shapes. He was the creative primordial hill, the royal pyramid, as well as the reduced pyramidion tip that topped the obelisks.[10]

Sneferu and Kufu: The proof of our hypothesis is architecturally traceable in the monuments of no lesser individual than the pioneer architect and builder of the first standard Egyptian pyramid, the Pharaoh Sneferu (ca. 2613-2589 BCE). He was the father of Kufu, of the pharaoh who later built for himself the Great Pyramid. Sneferu left to posterity three vastly different prototypes of pyramids, for us to wonder about and to scrutinize. He thereby has enabled us to track the development of his architectural fantasies and designs.

The first burial edifice that he built for himself was the Pyramid at Meidum. There he tried to build something in seven stages, too steep and too high. Much of the top section collapsed. Nevertheless, judging by the contours that still stand today, his upper stage seems to have been intended to receive the shape of a drastically shortened obelisk, probably with the typical pyramidion tip.

---

10 Hans Bonnet, *Reallexikon der Aegyptischen Religionsgeschichte* (Berlin: Walter de Gruyter, 1952), 539-542.

Fortunately, we know what was on the builder's mind, because the next mausoleum that he built for himself—now called the Bent Pyramid—took the compacted and stubby form of a dwarfed obelisk. It had been kept low because of its massive weight and width. We know, therefore, that the Pharaoh Sneferu very much wanted to be buried inside a gigantic obelisk—inside the Godhead Atum himself. But contemplating the Bent Pyramid, Sneferu apparently was not satisfied. Its shape was far less elegant or erect than the first shaft-shape that he had envisioned for Meidum. Additionally, some instability can be detected along the early construction stages of the Bent Pyramid; he possibly feared another disastrous collapse. He built for himself a third structure, the so-called Red Pyramid, for which he imagined the obelisk shaft to be completely out of sight, hidden in the ground. This time around, Sneferu limited himself to building only an enlarged version of the pyramidion tip. The Red Pyramid stood solid, and it held. It became the standard design for subsequent Egyptian pyramids. Sneferu's son, Kufu, learned his lessons from his father's experimental failures, and he proceeded to build for himself the largest "Head of Atum" of all times.

In plain language, this means that those ancient pharaohs erected their burial edifices so that at death they could return to the Godhead—to the very phallus-head of Atum—so as to issue from there again as rising Sun-god Ra, and then, as Horus-Falcon, to impregnate the divine Tefnut/Nut/Isis femininity—thereafter to be reborn from, and onto, Isis who was present as Egypt's female divine Throne at the rite of coronation.

Göbekli Tepe "Pillars" in Contrast

At Göbekli Tepe, the "Earth Beneath" was the Mother, and this arrangement left the "Sky on High" completely free to be Father. It is quite obvious, now, why in Egypt the phallic Atum was rising as a hill and why Egyptian obelisks and pyramid tips point upward. They all targeted a female Sky. The goddess Nut was their goal.[11] If many thousands of years earlier one would have set a Göbekli Tepe "*T-Pfeiler*" bottom-up, one would have anticipated the function and the direction of subsequent Egyptian obelisks, adjusted for royal access

11 Karl W. Luckert, www.historyofreligions.com, a downloadable video script titled "Out of Egypt an Other Son." And please view the corresponding video by that same title, on You Tube.

to the upper-world of Egyptian divine femininity, to the end that newly deified pharaohs could be begotten on high and also be born from on high.

The ancient Egyptian Falcon-Pharaohs loved to arrive for their incarnations and re-enthronements "trailing clouds of glory" (as William Wordsworth rhapsodized)—born from on high. It is possible that typical Egyptian royals have insisted, subconsciously, on an antithesis to the Earth cult that, five to seven millennia earlier has spiked the Earth Mother with T-shaped phallic menhirs, at Göbekli Tepe.

I am still inclined to suspect that the hands and the stoles depicted on a few of the menhirs at Göbekli Tepe were part of the ceremonial paraphernalia—that they also had functional relevance for the central cult mystery of this place. And they were arrayed to be intentionally riddle-some and functional. Look more closely! None of these "pillar heads" at Göbekli Tepe has a face—not even a nose. The heads are either shown empty or are loaded with more of the same totemic animal presences as are visible along the shafts. Whether these animals were sculpted onto the surmised heads, or only along the shafts, they all were made to protrude from the rock surface as true bas-reliefs. Positive reliefs on stone were far more difficult to sculpt than simple negative engravings. This suggests that, as protrusions these figures were part of the positive "naturalistic" essence of the menhir. Like protruding arteries or veins, these bas-reliefs reveal the primary characteristic of their substratum.

At Göbekli Tepe all the explicitly positioned animals, in bas-relief, seem to be of the male gender—and they are prominently depicted as such. This feature must have been important to the sculptors and quarrymen. And one should not fail to notice that many of the male totemic animals are shown assuming some kind of ready-to-mount posture. This posture is depicted also at some of the more roundish sculpted totem pole remainders (see Schmidt, pp. 100, 110, 159). Those bird totems are holding onto heads or whatever else they may have been impregnating within this mythical world of the hunters' pre-human flux. Even the crouching canine or boar, and other high-relief animals at Göbekli Tepe, are raised in a manner that suggests a readiness for sexual mounting. With all that male excitement, a female entity cannot be far away. The ornamentation opens up the possibility that the faceless and cubic tops of the T-shaped menhirs have, all along, not been abstractly squared heads but squared testicles instead—that is, squared just enough to keep the uninitiated out of the loop. With all these imitation menhirs, the Göbekli Tepe Mountain-Woman became pregnant and her abdomen expanded.

While intentional abstraction might initially seem to be an attractive academic designation for the squared shapes of Göbekli Tepe menhirs, we must not overrate it. Abstraction may have happened here somewhat unintentionally. The thicknesses and sizes of the menhirs seem to vary in proportion to the available dimensions of lenticular limestone slabs that the quarrymen were able to loosen. This means that a quarryman, as a potential sculptor, would at the outset have admired his block as a nice, coherent stone surface. Rather than smashing it to rubble, in hope of freeing up flint nodules, he drew an outline of the most important thing that came to his mind. It is even possible that a portion of its first outline was cracked naturally, and that this omen could have given him the outline of what actually was hidden in the slab of limestone. The resulting contour resembled a T-shaped phallus, and the men kept chiseling to improve on its natural geometry. The better they could square those blocks of limestone, the more their masculine skills and powers over the Earth-Mother's ovaries would be demonstrated.

The human mind has always dangled along the boundary line between science and magic. From the smooth surface and the improvised outline may finally have resulted a technique of squaring for what, twelve thousand years later, can now be explained as artistic abstraction. It seems quite possible, though, that the word here should rather be "simplification" or "rectification." Or possibly, it was understood as a "dare" or a "challenge" by which an archaic sculptor could show himself to be a hero who, within the cult, mastered the art of dealing with the very "bone-substance" of the maternal Earth-deity.

Into the pre-literate cradle of Near Eastern civilization, beginning some nine thousand years ago with *Çatalhöyük* and continued more massively before five thousand years ago in Mesopotamia and Egypt. There texts were getting written. Stories were composed about how all those good things of civilization had come to be. For instance, still in biblical scripture we are given hints about mighty heroes, sons of gods, who lived in prehistoric times. This divine offspring belonged to the human species, as they took for their wives the daughters of humankind (cf. *Genesis* 6:4.) We are given a few names of heroic hunters who transformed themselves into men of of war, into kings or builders of cities. Kings also gathered entourages from among progressive scribes, who themselves were anxious to compete with earlier more old-fashioned skilled elites, such as the still illiterate stonemasons and limestone sculptors at the ancient Göbekli Tepe temple site. We might safely assume that they competed also with other types of public and priestly actors.

While orators recited epics and told legends to educate or to entertain, aspiring scribes recorded similar stories simply to practice writing. On fragments of their writ we find the names of ancient kings and hunters like Gilgamesh and Enkidu, Nimrod, Sargon, Esau, Menes, and the like. The actual historical content in these fragments is generally meager. Some may refer to early mighty men, while others may prove only that there must have been a time when a scribe knew that some men of old built cities and that these men coexisted in the proximity of hunters and wild men and, also, that mighty men and hunters sometimes became the conquerors and controllers of cities. The general drift, along which obsolescent hunters became heroes, also explains how heroes became gods and then founders of theocratic city-states. These are the themes that our present chapter is trying to illuminate, obliquely.

Legends occasionally reveal the courage of ancient scribes to think afresh about their history. But by themselves, most of their literary productions contain also the dubious data of raw contemporary politics. Fortunately, in some situations, archaeology has brought to light material vestiges that allow fresh interpretations of bygone conditions. In our days, when the skin-wrapped bones or mummies of divine kings are gathered into museums, to be displayed, surely some polished layers are getting scoured away from the halos of those ancient and venerable deified tyrants. While according to nostalgic dreams, some of the earliest cities in the Near East were built by hunters, suspicions are justified that the first settlements were far more often destroyed by hordes of hunters who acquired warrior status, rather than having been built by them.

Obsolescent bands of hunters did not easily convert to being peaceable domesticators. Based on their prior livelihood and training as hunters, it was easier for them to become bandits and warriors—i.e. hunters of humankind. Some early cities were repeatedly destroyed or held in submission and then rebuilt at the command of such conquerors who, quite likely, were interested in acquiring fortified walls for their own protection. They transformed domesticators and denizens into hunted prey, to enslave and exploit them as future resources. Warlords found protective walls useful for spending their nights, and within these walls, they employed writers who knew how to inscribe housekeeping ledgers and compose supportive propaganda in the form of legends and myths. Legends that boast of how early conquerors have built cities are lacking in precision. Very likely, such stories never were meant to be true records of history, but handles on power to shape history. They served as aristocratic propaganda, mandates, and as entitlements to real estate. Their practical motifs helped, rather than hindered these stories in becoming holy writ or divine law. In any case, the stories supported the titles and the hype of hyper-domesticators.

Orthodox and roaming hunters, when hungry, turned into robbers, warriors, and conquerors, and then became creative planners of still larger hyper-domestication schemes. They made policy and virtue of rounding up and of holding captured domestic animals, and of commandeering human domesticators. They invented and improved weapons to enlarge upon the ambitions of their ancestors who, millennia earlier, had mastered the art of manufacturing artificial "teeth and claws," of flint.

While early hunters quite likely were not the actual hands-on builders of ancient cities, they might nevertheless have been history's "sheep dogs" who rounded up human gatherers, planters, and herders into corrals, together with their animals and possessions, for tighter control. They held them available as resources to be used and exploited as needs and opportunities arose. After the first rounds of city conquests, destruction and supervised rebuilding had taken place, as competition among marauding armies became more fierce, the wiser among warlords decided to become sedentary protectors of the settlements they had taken. If they robbed and destroyed the places completely, and if after each occurrence they retreated to the hills, there would be nothing to return to and "harvest"a year later. If a chief of bandits did not watch his booty, another hungrier horde would be waiting in the hills to replace him. It was more profitable to colonize a settlement like a living bee hive, to confiscate a share of its produce regularly in a somewhat disciplined manner, and in return provide protection for the colony's laboring inhabitants, who thereby have become de facto slaves.

Hunting humankind was the warriors' way of practicing hyper-domestication. Under the conditions that they imposed, the status of sedentary subjects was reduced to the level of domestics and slaves. They were owned as, all along, animals have been held by domesticators—as livestock. Systematic fleecing of a city's denizens became established as an honorable and noble profession.

This was the beginning of individual city-kingdoms. The subsequent annexation of neighboring city-kingdoms was the beginning of empires. In common history books, such schemes of hyper-domestication are referenced as "civilization." Indeed, by administering the better policies of a wise ruler who employed decent officials, hyper-domestication systems for larger populations could, occasionally, look somewhat normal or even humane—until misfortune befell the pretender's dynasty, or a foolish princeling inherited power.

To postulate such arrangements and conditions in the longer flow of human evolution, it would, understandably, have taken thousands of years of incremental insights and adjustments before a group of rebels could have gotten the idea that initially all humankind might have been intended to be equal.

Occasionally a stark contrast is needed for humankind to notice the commonplace and the obvious. Several years ago it was an eye-opener for this writer when, at last, I looked at the earliest known organized stratum of Chinese civilization. Among the earliest scratches of Chinese writing, engraved on shoulder blades of oxen and on tortoise shells—collectively known as Oracle Bones—one can discern the testimonials of marauding hordes, of ex-hunters arriving as warriors along the Yellow River. They claimed domesticator- settlements among their captured properties. The Shang aristocracy was such a horde, fully engaged in establishing their own kind, and puffing themselves up as hyper-domesticators.[12] For extra leverage they invented the art of writing. Divination was supervised and manipulated to justify royal authority. Some three thousand years and a few centuries ago, a bureaucracy of about two hundred scribes and diviners was managed by an ambitious Shang ruler who had veto power over everything that was written—and over anything that the gods or the ancestors communicated in rituals of cracking Oracle Bones while red-hot metal rods were applied.

---

12 For more detailed documentation of these matters, see Karl W. Luckert, Stone Age Religion at Göbekli Tepe..., Chapter 19 (Portland: Triplehood, 2013).

As a surprise to me, the first historical strata of Chinese civilization closely resembled those which I had been exploring in ancient Middle American ceremonial domains, some decades earlier.[13]

Primitive hunters, there, were perfectly capable of building something that looked like a jade, serpentine, flint, obsidian, basalt and limestone-laid civilization. The highest "spiritual" level to which some of those ex-hunter warriors, butchers or priests, were able to sublimate their skills was to cleave rock boulders instead of merely smashing skulls, or to enable sacrosanct butchers to cut open rib cages and sacrifice human hearts to a celestial Serpent.

Hunters were our first deified rulers. The Mesopotamian Gilgamesh, a hyper-domestication prince, quested and sought a level of divine status that had been attributed to totem-devotees of old. His story provides insights into how the early aristocrats wanted to be seen by those whom their stories were meant to impress. Whereas Prince Gilgamesh achieved for himself something like a low-level divine status, his more archaic huntsman partner, Enkidu, acted the role of a leftover hunter-buffoon, as a foil for comparison and contrast. Prince Gilgamesh's quest illustrates the efforts of ancient Mesopotamian nobility to achieve divine status. Hyper-domesticators sought to adorn and to justify themselves with a literary veneer of fake piety. In comparison, the earliest Egyptian pharaohs, as devotees of a genuine Falcon totem, a natural raptor, were less humble and more forthright about their divine status.

Egyptian rulers aspired to high divine status early on, and for those ambitions they still are admired today. But let us look at their careers historically, in sequence and in the dialectic of their evolution as hunter-, robber-, and warrior-upgrades—rather than merely enacting the role of a lofty Falcon totem named Hor, or "Horus" in Latin, the ruling god-kings of Egypt can be tracked throughout their history as passionate earthbound hunters who upgraded themselves enough to pose as legitimate divine hunters of men. They gave depth to their hunter egos and passions with violent accomplishments as something that could be evaluated as Ancient Egyptian Civilization.

---

[13]See Karl W. Luckert. *Olmec Religion, a Key to Middle America and Beyond,* Number 137, Civilization of the American Indian Series (Norman: University of Oklahoma Press, 1976).

Menes (Aha), ca. 3100-3038 BCE

Figure 5.
The Narmer Palette
Courtesy: Trusties of the British Museum

Menes was the founder of the Egyptian empire, of the first installment of what came to be known as Western Civilization. He set Egypt's direction. He combined two kingdoms that became known as Upper and Lower Egypt. The names by which he has been identified in history are Menes, Narmer, and finally Hor Aha.

The last of these names was ascribed to the occupant of the first royal tomb of the First Dynasty. Under the name of Menes, this pharaoh earned the reputation of a heroic hunter. To pharaohs who thought of themselves still as superior hunters, the most meaningful manifestation of their authority to govern was their ability to kill. Among all the skills of which archaic hunters were proudest, their talent to kill ranked as their *summum bonum*.

There is a story about Menes having been attacked by his own hunting dogs. He rescued himself by riding across Lake Moeris on the back of a crocodile. This feat of daring, to mount a most dangerous reptile, signifies mastery over and above ordinary hunting skills. The people saw in this king a hunter who belonged to the superhuman order. Their master was a tamer of crocodiles who, surely, also made people toe the line.

The tale was told by a priest whose god was Sobek, the divine Master of Crocodiles.[14] By incidental circumstances, Menes was implicitly given credit for founding the city of Shedyet (Crocodilopolis). A priest at the primary sanctuary, at this place, had a vested interest in suggesting that his temple, as well as the city, were as ancient as Menes, the divine founder-pharaoh of Egypt. While tillers of the soil domesticated cattle, the aristocratic priests of Sobek managed crocodiles at their temple.

Apparently not all of Menes' extraordinary hunting feats were remembered in the form of fantastic legends or hype. The story of his death sounds more realistic. Having been a hunter all his life, and after having reigned over Egypt for sixty-two years, Menes was out hunting by the River Nile and was killed by a hippopotamus. Grave goods in the tomb of Aha, the First Dynasty's first Osiris, included over four hundred sculpted bull heads affixed with natural sets of wild bull horns. It is conceivable that this pharaoh accumulated the horns himself as trophies over the course of his reign. Buried with Aha were dogs, young lions, male servants, women, and dwarfs.

According to the earliest clues, in the Pyramid Texts, any ancient Egyptian pharaoh became the god Osiris when he died. By way of continuing his divine mystery drama, according to later reckoning at Heliopolis, this Osiris rose in the form of his successor as a totemic Horus Falcon—so as to appear at the proper time, completely transfigured for coronation, to sit on the throne of Egypt again in his full human shape and glory. In this manner, every ancient pharaoh was his own predecessor as a ruling Falcon. He was transformed into an anthropomorphic Osiris mummy when he died. Eventually he became his own successor, as the next Horus manifestation. Thus, with each generation of rulers, since Stone Age hunting days, this ancient totemic raptor deity transformed himself for re-enthronement, as Falcon deity and king.

Still quite in harmony with the transformational prehuman flux mythology of archaic hunters, a dying pharaoh went to his tomb transformed into Osiris. He rose to rule over Egypt as a single deity,

---

[14] Diodorus Siculus, in *Bibliotheca Historica*. See Joseph, Frank, *The Destruction of Atlantis* (Rochester, VT: Bear and Company, 2004), 99. Citation in Wikipedia.

comprising each pharaoh in the lineage—past, present, and future. At some point between his funeral as Osiris and his reappearance as Horus he was transformed by resurrection.[15]

The Egyptian mystery of royal death and resurrection was not restricted by visible material bodies. It was not the case that each body would house a divine spirit. Rather, the sequence of divine kings in Egypt comprised a single personal-divine essence. Each king appeared in dual manifestations of life—as the flashy *ka* and as the shadowy *ba*. *Ka* was the bright spirit-soul which after death returned to Atum, the Godhead, whereas *ba* was the shadow-soul that lingered with the body, with the mummy that was Osiris. During their reigns, ruling pharaohs would portray themselves as a Falcon-deity who continued to be divine, impossible to kill, and everlasting. The God-king existed by the inherent logic of totemism, by transformation and resurrection, which was derived from the prehuman flux of hunter ontology. The notion of prehuman transformability and resurrection enabled the Egyptian System of hyper-domestication to remain logically coherent for approximately three thousand years. This Egyptian political ideology was similar to ideologies that later were embraced, in part, by King Solomon or by King Hezekiah of Jerusalem, by Darius the First of Persia, Alexander the Great of Macedonia, by Caesar Augustus of Rome and some of his successors. These rulers all knew themselves to be Sons of God, essentially and forever.

The theocratic-imperial tradition eventually evoked competition on the part of lower ranking populations. Patricians during Egypt's New Kingdom Period availed themselves of ancient copies, fragments and elaborations on copies, of the imperial soteriology (doctrine of salvation). They had themselves buried with funerary texts written on papyrus scrolls. Today these are known as a collection of the *Egyptian Book of the Dead*. During the first century CE, Egyptian commoner converts to Christianity were upstaging this earlier Egyptian trickle-

---

[15] "Prehuman flux" in hunter mythology is a term first coined in Karl W. Luckert, *The Navajo Hunter Tradition* (Tucson: University of Arizona Press, 1975), 133ff. It refers to mythical conditions, thus, to a time when gods, humans, animals, plants, and other natural phenomena were still one kind of "people." These primeval people exchanged their skins and appearances after a manner in which humanoids change masks and clothes. Participating thus in the lifestyles of all kinds of imaginable, more-or-less divine species, they lived together in harmony and still spoke a common language. Aside from *The Navajo Hunter Tradition*, 1975, see also Karl W. Luckert, *Stone Age Religion at Göbekli Tepe*, Portland, 2013, Chapters 14, 15, and elsewhere.

down soteriology by way of preferring a crucified foreign victim over those deified imperial champions of hyper-domestication—reasoning along the same ontological stepping stones. But their Son of God was a commoner about whom they insisted that he was born of, and resurrected by, God-Father. The Gospel of Jesus of Nazareth proclaimed the Kingdom of Heaven, or Empire of God, as a radical religious alternative. The divinely begotten status of earlier Roman emperors was implicitly canceled by the Nicene Creed, which clever Christian theologians (Athanasius foremost) got endorsed under the Emperor Constantine's own supervision. Jesus Christ was thereby established as "the only-begotten Son of God." The divine title of Roman emperors was on that account officially abolished under Emperor Flavius Theodosius Augustus, who ruled from 379 to 395 CE. He ceded the title "Son of God" to Jesus the Christ (the Anointed), who as a shamed Jewish victim had been crucified under Tiberius Caesar Divi Augusti Filius Augustus—thus under an earlier imperial Roman Son of God.

First Dynasty Human Sacrifices

The ancient Egyptian style of hyper-domestication is documented archaeologically by human sacrifices that were found at all the imperial tomb sites of the First Dynasty. According to the archaeological record, the royal tombs of the First Dynasty (ca. 3000–2800 BC) have yielded a total of 860 so-called "subsidiary burials."[16]

In light of the fact that these graves have been looted and disturbed, one cannot be sure that all subsidiary burials were sacrifices. However, it seems that a large portion of these tombs, if not all, may have held retainers who were given no other choice but to die at divine-royal funerals. The heirs and successors of deceased pharaohs, or their handlers, probably thought that Egypt would be a better place, or at least be easier to govern, when some of these people were promoted into the underworld.

Even though these Egyptian numbers look smaller than those of the Middle American sacrificial cults, where totals ran into many thousands, or better than Shang and Chin Chinese numbers, where totals may turn out to be tens of thousands, the notion, that human beings were captured, kept and wasted as inferior properties, is evident. Peoples captured by hyper-domesticators were thought of as prey, property, or trophies.

---

16 Caroline Seawright, "Human Sacrifice in Ancient Egypt," http://tour-Egypt.net/feature stories/humansac.htm.

If we took a divine scion from totemic hunter stock, grafted it onto the throne of Egypt and let it be born of (or hatched by) Isis, then the deity that grew from her nest would grow up to be a Horus, a raptor, a divine killer.

Some historians interpreted the number of subsidiary burials and sacrifices in Egypt to reflect the greatness of the kings for whom they were sacrificed. Indeed, there had to be a corresponding degree of stability, of fatalism sustained by fear, when significant numbers of the former king's retinue could be sacrificed for him without serious repercussions. But in this writer's opinion, all these numbers reflect an offset sequence. Djer apparently sacrificed thirty-three retainers of Aha to ensure his secure takeover from his predecessor. Djet thought he needed to eliminate 318 to secure his position, and his widow Merytnit and her military backers together resolved that they needed to rid themselves of 174. The system, then, seemed to have held itself afloat with a transitional queen-widow on the throne. When her son Den was old enough to rule, the system had been cleansed, by and large, and the trustees were already committed to support him. He and his closest retainers felt they needed to get rid of only 41 expandable characters. Den himself probably had little say in these matters. But overall I suspect, that the weaker the political position of an heir was, the greater a compensation payment, a sacrifice, was required. The next leader might win status for himself, as well as empowerment for his allied ceremonial executioners who were positioned to serve as his ministerial thugs.

The first king of the Second Dynasty, Hotepsekhemwy, sacrificed a token of 26 victims to his predecessor at Abydos in order to inherit the First Dynasty's mandate. Then he left Abydos and moved downstream to Sakkara. For all we know at this point, his successors there abolished burial sacrifices and substituted carved figurines.

Most commentators on First Dynasty human sacrifices tend to accept the original cult story at face value, that it ensured proper afterworld arrangements for the deceased king. But to this writer's mind, such apologetics for human burial sacrifices are not very convincing. The additional rationalization, that in First Dynasty days a distinction was made between slaves and devout free servants—suggesting that servants might have been willing victims—also appears doubtful. Still, quite in harmony with transformational prehuman flux hunter mythology, a dead pharaoh, at his funeral went to his royal tomb transformed. Whereas dying kings may have given hints on who should die and who should live, the primary decisions of who should die and who should live were probably made by successors—by royal heirs and their conspiring thugs.

The system was implicitly structured to create its own victims. If you were a servant and wanted to be kept alive by the next Horus, you might ingratiate yourself to the prince as best as you could. But everyone would notice what you are doing. If in the last moment an inner circle of priests and regents enthroned a successor whom you did not expect, then you had been betting on the wrong prince to be Horus. You could be under suspicion because you have demonstrated uneven loyalties, or you could be distrusted because you have shown yourself as being too wise and too efficient in performing imperial chores. From a royal successor's point of view, the safest solution was to "promote" ambivalent servants to serve the Osiris in the underworld. You likely would then have been sent on another tour of duty with the old king.

But certainly, it is a reprieve to see that Egyptian pharaohs, in their hyper-domestication initiative, were not the worst exploiters of humankind our planet so far has seen. Nevertheless, deified masters expected their servants, and even some of their high-level ministers, to accompany them into their afterworld.

If this is what the pharaohs expected of those who helped them build up their inheritances, then what could one expect from their behavior toward common people whom they never needed to face? Their system implied that the sovereign owned subject peoples as property. The expertise of hunter-born totemic emperors—of men skilled in the art of killing—has exaggerated domestication skills to the point where they ripened into hyper-domestication schemes. Perhaps it was the moderating influence of smaller nomadic herder clans surrounding ancient Egypt, that contributed certain religious compromises which, following the First Dynasty, helped devalue subsidiary burials. There may have been only a trickle of reform-minded people preceding the Hyksos invasion, over the course of nearly a millennium.[17]

---

[17] The Hyksos, known as foreign "Shepherd Kings" or "Princes of the Desert,"had their capital at Avaris, in the northeastern part of the Delta. Their occupation lasted from about 1783 to 1550 BCE, through the Second Intermediate.

It can be assumed that in surrounding realms, freedom-loving herders roamed and tried to resist when hyper-domesticators garnered too many possessions for themselves. Lesser royal upstarts, and to some extent the imperial pharaohs themselves, appear to have added some herder ethos to their hunter instincts. Pharaohs were depicted carrying symbolic whip insignia, as drivers of animal carts or as supervisors of slaves did. Additionally, already during the First Dynasty, some pharaohs were shown carrying the symbolic crooks that shepherds utilized to hook animals by their hind legs to manage them. Obviously, domestication symbols by themselves could not humanize the imperial system. It was the destiny of herd animals to be slaughtered, as surely as wild animals formerly were killed and butchered by orthodox hunters. So it could have been the cultural exchanges between Egyptian hyper-domesticators and marginal Near Eastern herder traditions that eventually, and to varying degrees, made a "good shepherd" ethos necessary and possible. This ethos became imprinted on Judaism, Christianity, and Islam. The "good shepherd ideal" presented itself as a foil to hunters turned warriors, or to shepherd-rulers who evolved into bandits and who were known to lurk in the dark. But this meager herder-humanism failed to save all human victims from Egyptian slavery or from death.

The fate of being owned also befell those captured as prisoners of war, as victims in conflicts that they did not instigate. It also caught up with groups that were enslaved by divinely mandated rulers. Hunter totems, like those which at Göbekli Tepe were flattened down to limestone bas-reliefs, were still roaming freely at the beginnings of sedentary civilization in Egypt. The birthplace of Western hyper-domestication was ruled by totemic Horus falcons. These insignia survive in Western lands still today, where eagles serve as totemic emblems on flags and on monetary notes.

Here in the United States, we honor our Egyptian roots with our bald-headed native American fish-eagle, with a gigantic obelisk that memorializes our first president, and with the image of a pyramid printed on our one-dollar notes, which, to boast authenticity also do sport the eye of Horus. Our gigantic obelisk in Washington, DC, has been built, thoroughly hollowed out—democratized for our citizens' pleasure, to enter there as tourists, with strong chances of entering and coming back out alive.

Ancient Egyptian Ontology--Preview

Gods are emanations of All-Being who, as deities, frequently still choose to appear in prehuman flux combinations. This theoretical untidiness is not the result of faulty logic. Misunderstandings of this logic derive from the fact that Western scholars hitherto have read Egyptian theological statements as if they pertained to a multitude of stubbornly individualistic divine personages. Theological statements have been interpreted in accordance with what Westerners, after accepting monotheism, conjectured polytheism to be. They saw an incoherent collage of idols that conflicted with the arithmetic of Hebrew monotheism... or that corresponded to what Greek philosophical atheism had already dismissed.

All the while, the ancient Egyptian blending of divine natures and functions could have been understood rather easily by remembering the simple fact, that learned ancient Egyptians persistently believed that one indescribable and all-inclusive Deity has been staging the entire polytheistic show. Not less than nine divine personages were named, combined, and fused at Heliopolis into a single Ennead--a Ninefoldness--a Trinity Squared!

4

Sun-Theology at Heliopolis

The ancient Egyptian cult center Junu, named "On" in the Hebrew Bible, was renamed Heliopolis by the Greeks in recognition of the happenstance that the Sun-god Ra ("Helios" in Greek) presided there. Junu is mentioned in the Pyramid Texts as the "House of Ra." Nevertheless, Heliopolitan Ra theology had another and more mysterious dimension. It was Atum.[18]

Many basic Egyptian notions of thinking about gods, animals and humankind together, definitely date back to an ancient hunter-gatherer stratum of prehuman flux mythology. However, the basic Heliopolitan theological notions belong later in the evolutionary sequence of Egyptian culture and religion. They correspond to efforts of balancing domestication and grand-domestication. The basic Heliopolitan theological notions could have been formulated by the founder of the First Dynasty (ca. 3100 BCE). Overall, the theology of Junu was well suited for the justification of imperial grand-domestication by which the Lower and Upper Egyptian dominions were united and a variety of regional cults were accommodated.

As a system of thought, the theology of Heliopolis was recorded during the Fifth and Sixth Dynasties (2494–2181 BCE) on interior walls of seven large pyramids. This theology has thereby survived in

---

[18]Inasmuch as the cult at Heliopolis remains archaeologically obscure, its linkage with Pyramid Texts also remains somewhat hypothetical. The discussion of ancient Egyptian religion in this book is indebted to the works of a large number of Egyptologists, especially to Bonnet, *Reallexikon der Ägyptischen Religionsgeschichte* (Berlin, 1952); R.T. Rundle Clark, *Myth and Symbol in Ancient Egypt* (London, 1959); Adolf Erman, *Die Religion der Ägypter* (Berlin and Leipzig, 1934); Henry Frankfort, *Ancient Egyptian Religion* (New York, 1948); J.H. Breasted, *Development of Religion and Thought in Ancient Egypt* (New York, 1912); Siegfried Morenz, *Ägyptische Religion* (Stuttgart, 1960); and Eric Hornung, *Geist der Pharaonenzeit* (Zürich, 1989).

the masonry afterworlds of deified pharaohs. Together these inscriptions have been published as the *Pyramid Texts.*

Pyramid inscriptions reflect a time when Heliopolis was the major cult center of the united Upper and Lower Kingdom. Atum was the name, given to the God of gods who was the source and the essence of all Egyptian god-manifestations, and of everything else. In the dynamic self-manifestation of Atum through lesser divinities in this world, even the ancestry of the human progeny could be included as pharaohs —as representations of the Godhead—this is what the politicized Egyptian high theology was about.

The Helipolitan version is the clearest formulation of any Old Kingdom theology; though, by present standards it can scarcely be called systematic. In the form of funerary texts it became the dominant orthodox strain of thought by which most derivative Egyptian religious notions and rites of power were oriented.

Later theological formulations in Egyptian religion showed a need to embrace antecedents, to absorb them as much as possible. This endless incorporation of inherited theological formulas has, to this day, held our understanding of Egyptian royal religion in suspense.

Western minds accustomed to disjunctive logic may, in reference to ancient Egyptian religion, recognize only irrational conglomerations of obsolescent god-stories and burial rites. Characterizations ascribed to one Egyptian deity could be applied to others as well. In the Egyptian system, gods are emanations of All-Being who, frequently, chose to appear in combination with others. This theoretical untidiness is not the result of faulty logic. Misunderstandings of this sort derive from the fact that Western scholars hitherto have read Egyptian theological statements as if they pertained to a multitude of stubbornly individualistic gods. Theological statements have been interpreted in accordance with what Westerners understood polytheism to be. They saw an incoherent collage of idols that conflicted with Hebrew theism and arithmetic—even with what Greek philosophical atheism has rejected. All the while, the ancient Egyptian blending of divine natures and functions, could have been understood rather easily by the simple fact, that learned ancient Egyptians persistently believed, that only one indescribable and all-inclusive Deity has been staging the entire polytheistic show. No less than nine divine personages were named, combined, and fused at Heliopolis into a single Ennead—a Ninefoldness. A Trinity Squared.

On what grounds could a Christian theologian, later, classify his faith in a Trinity as de facto monotheism and keep insisting that the Heliopolitan Ennead (Trinity Squared) belonged to polytheism? The monotheism of the pharaohs had no difficulty sponsoring, embracing and absorbing lesser provincial deities throughout Egypt, as offspring or as manifestations of the divine Ennead. Also, lesser cults were sponsored by human imperial Horus descendants of that same ninefold divinity. Primitive "archaic" shamans, whom this author has visited, had no difficulty thinking of their multiple gods as being One. Theology need not be hijacked into mathematics.

Priesthood, Royalty, and Aristocracy

The oldest substantial amounts of Egyptian textual materials containing religious information, are inscriptions on walls of royal pyramid chambers (2494–2181 BCE) of the Old Kingdom, continued in patrician coffins that reach into the First Intermediary (starting 2250 BCE). As mentioned above, these are named accordingly Pyramid Texts and Coffin Texts. By the time these texts were drawn, and later written onto papyrus, the Egyptian subject matter of religious ontologies and eschatologies had been many centuries in the making. They had plenty of time to become complex. The *Book of the Dead,* copied and rewritten by craftsmen who knew little theology, suffered artistic modifications that helped amplify the process toward complexity and obfuscation.

The academicians' grasp of ancient Egyptian religion is patchy at best, but for our present task, abstinence and willful insistence on faddish impossibilities would yield worse results than imperfect hypothetical grasping. In ancient Egypt, as was the case anywhere among the world's civilizations, the scribes invented writing and they understood what they wrote. Thus, the first stratum of religious texts belonged to an elite—to royalty, to their aristocratic and priestly propagandists and an entourage of retainers.

The religion of the common people in ancient Egyptian civilization, generally, has not fared very well in historical reconstructions. Most of what has been said so far about the lives of the common people is necessarily based on information inferred from statements made at the apex of the imperial hierarchy. Imitative commoner religion was derived largely from the funerary cults by which royalty and aristocracy memorialized and established themselves for the future.

Commoners had no alternative but to find their salvation by competing for spill-over and trickle-down advantages from their superiors.

Only at the apex of the hierarchy were the tenets of ancient Egyptian religion recorded in writing, and memorialized on monuments, massive enough for survival. The lacuna in our knowledge of commoner religion becomes especially glaring as we enter the first millennium BCE. When during that millennium foreign armies periodically clipped the Egyptian apex, official records concerning the mysteries of their gods, concerning life after death, necessarily slowed to a trickle. Later, as Greek writing became more widely used in the larger Hellenistic ferment, some ancient Egyptian notions spread forth into Mediterranean daylight.

Imperialistic nations that owned the libraries during the centuries of Egypt's decline, that also produced books of which lucky samples have survived, were not especially interested in what appeared to be the superstitions of Egyptian natives and commoners.

Genealogical Fallacy versus Emanation

The political dimension of the Heliopolitan theological system has been the subject matter of frequent academic discussions of which not all need to be belabored here in their entirety. A single such interpretation suffices to make our point. Rudolf Anthes has concluded that the theologians at Heliopolis postulated a genealogy of five generations of gods, and that they did so to establish the divine and primeval character of the ruling king. Accordingly, the lineage of Horus, the god with whom ruling kings of Egypt were identified, "encompasses cultivated land and desert, heaven and earth and whatever lies between these, as well as the ocean from which Atum arose." The Heliopolitan theogony, therefore, may be understood as a "systematic demonstration that all the world was identified with, or belonged to, the realm of Horus."[19]

As reasonable as such an explanation of political divine claims may appear by standards of political theory, by Greek mythic genealogies or aristocratic histories, it also is a fact that Heliopolitan priests have included in the realm of Horus all conceivable aspects of their cosmos.

[19] Rudolf Anthes, "Mythology in Ancient Egypt," in *Mythologies of the Ancient World.* S. M. Kramer ed. (Garden City, N.Y., 1961), 42.

They pursued their habit of inclusion far in excess of what an Egyptian king could ever hope to govern. This happenstance invites us to examine the larger cosmic dimension, specifically in relation to a pharaoh's need for religious justification and overlapping theological and political relevance.

It appears that our Western preoccupation with the metaphor of a divine genealogy, after the manner in which kings used to keep track of their authoritarian ancestors, has thus far unduly hindered our understanding of the larger Egyptian divine/political order. A discussion of the Heliopolitan God-story ought never lose sight of the fact that the supreme Egyptian deity has emanated the gods as well as humankind—although the All-god may have altered his/her own manifestation over time, or even preferred invisibility. During all his phases of transformation, the deity has never ceased to exist. As soon as this simple concept is recognized, the Heliopolitan sequential genealogy which Anthes has postulated evaporates from its own outline. The supposed generations of gods are discovered as episodes in an ongoing process that generates a multitude of *ba* mutations, which all are expressions of one timeless eternally living God-essence or *ka*.

As mentioned previously, the Egyptians called the invisible life force, the spark of life that energetically manifests itself from within, the *ka*. They named outward visible manifestations the *ba*. In human awareness and in epistemology, a *ba* unit registers as phenomenon or as a phenotype mutation of the life force. Both *ka* and *ba* are what we might call "soul." A *ba*, appearing along the outer reaches of a *ka* emanation, is a visible, shadow-tainted, and estranged unit of *ka*, whereas the *ka* unit, as such, may be understood as a pure aspect and eternal participant in the original plethora of divine essence. Thus, the *ka* represents divine essence and as such, it exists in and emanates from the divine Source-Being. True to the ancient prehuman flux mythology of hunters and gatherers, the gods of Egypt continued to appear in any garb or *ba* they desired—of any animal, fish, bird, plant, or other natural phenomenon—as well as in the human figure of a ruling pharaoh.

God and gods also could appear in prehuman flux twilight, in half-dress as half-animals or half-humans. In contrast to the gods, humans were enabled to transform their *ba* substantially only by dying. Accordingly, Egyptian ghosts, who alongside the gods got caught up in the condition of prehuman flux, lingered in Egyptian memory throughout the ancient period. They were known to appear in the shape of animals or half-animals, in accordance with the still older ancient mysticism that is typical of the ancient hunter-gatherer world-view and religiosity.

The entire plethora of Atum's generative emission or flux means that, within the larger Egyptian cosmic schema, we are not looking at five generations of divine personages. Nor are we faced with an assembled pantheon of separate individual deities. Instead, we behold with our very human eyes the manifestations of a single Godhead along his more or less visible periphery—a horizon that, as far as can be perceived from our low-level perspective, displays an ever evolving panorama of visible light and shadows. But all the while, the one God, within Him- and Herself, remains eternally the same living source of All-Being.

Heliopolitan theology, ancient Egyptian orthodoxy, is best approached from its two oldest strata of extant data, namely, from the funerary literature that has survived as Pyramid and Coffin inscriptions. Excerpts and phrases from funerary liturgies, comprising spells for good fortune in the hereafter, were inscribed on royal pyramid chamber walls and in coffins of royals and patricians. The oldest of these texts, in the pyramids, were intended to establish a hallowed intellectual context for the return of a deceased pharaoh to his next state of fulfilled godhood. Thus, by and large, the Pyramid Texts delineate the royal soteriology of returning from an estranged human condition to a more unified and divine mode of existence.

The road thither corresponds exactly to the road that has led a human *ka* portion or life-spark hither.[20] This is to say that in accordance with Heliopolitan theology, soteriology traces the story of the cosmos in reverse. Inasmuch as the greater-than-human cosmos in ancient Egypt was deemed personal and divine, cosmogony

---

[20] Our procedure of rendering *ka* as "life-spark" or "life-soul" may seem unduly redundant. The word "soul" by itself would signify as much. But in Egypt, we also have the *ba* to compare, a concept of soul that may be defined as "apparition-soul," as "visible soul," or as a kind of "shadow-tainted soul."

equaled theogony (Story of God) and their soteriology was therefore a theistic theory of salvation that sustained faith in overcoming misfortune and death.

The entire Heliopolitan theological system can be visualized as a flow of creative vitality, emanating—that is, radiating outward from the Godhead, thinning out as it flows farther from its source. Along its outer periphery, this plethora of divine emanation diffuses into what begins to appear as the light and shadow realm of our material world. So it becomes visible. Farther out, beyond the periphery of visible matter, lies the realm of Non-being which in Egyptian mythology was conceptualized as Nun, watery chaos and utter darkness. Thus, the boundary realm between divinely generated Being and Non-being is what contains our apparently concrete experiences of world, of life and death. Were it not for the fact that dichotomies of ideas and things, of mind and matter, are not really distinguishable in an ontology of emanation, this could be called a Concrete Philosophical Idealism.

Along its outer periphery, the plethora of divine existence, of generation, of emanation, of being and life—namely, the divine stream of *ka* radiation—becomes visible as a multitude of *ba* apparitions. Along its outer periphery, Being encounters Non-being. It is stunned by Non-being and, as a result, it curls back and inward on itself. Individualized and estranged *ka* units; that is, *ka* spark surfaces, become visible as *ba* materializations—impacted by Non-being. They may along the periphery of divine emanation swirl or curl for a time as ghostly apparitions, estranged, bewildered, lost—as a waterfall churns where it hits the ground. But all these *ka* souls may—according to their nature—also get meaningfully re-oriented to travel home again toward the source of their being, which is the Godhead.

While the sole and hidden deity has been generating and giving birth to its self-emanations, in external visibility as if it were an ongoing process of exhaling, this same sole divine Source also has been inhaling its own life essence—attracting its own periphery by its own magnetism. Along the outer edge of human ontology and epistemology, these essences, perceived as finite manifestations, have been stunned by the kiss of death—by Non-being and by Darkness. They turn back and are thereby "resurrected" with the assistance of priestly funerary rites. Divine generation from the Godhead, and the nostalgic return of estranged souls to their Source, happens along a busy two-way road or flow.

The creative process of descending outward emanation ends in the cul-de-sac of life made manifest, as if getting caught up at the curve of a U-turn. The entire path of creation leads hither, from God to humankind, pushing toward finitude. The path of resurrection and salvation leads home toward the heart of God.

Emanation Through Five Hypostases

The First Hypostasis (Level 1)

At the starting point of generational flow, directionally in Heliopolitan manner, minds may visualize the source of All-Being as manifesting itself concretely, in the form of a phallic primeval hill, of Atum on the rise. His creative emission or emanation may be visualized, more aptly perhaps, as Ra, the rising, radiating, and life-evoking Phoenix or Sun deity. For a still clearer ancient perception, one may visualize our world from the vantage point of the Sun-god, or even from the vantage points of descending sun rays. At the turbulent terminals of their path of emanation, at their points of impact onto Non-being, these sun rays evoke for us here on earth certain sensations that cause the phenomenal or material world appear around us, substantial and in color—that even cause us to appear to ourselves.

The notion of Atum rising as a hill, from the chaotic waters of Nun, was sublimated to account for the facts of theriomorphic as well as anthropomorphic generation and procreation in this world. The rising hill of Atum was a rising phallus. As such, it was replicated on consequent masculine hypostases like Shu, Geb, and Osiris. Atum's fondling hand became the prolific vagina of Tefnut, Nut and Isis, without ever ceasing to be Atum's own hand. All these generative divine "organs" in successive hypostases, male as well as female, could be contemplated in singular androgynous as well as plural forms. The Heliopolitan Ennead in its entirety was Nine as well as One—thus a Ninefoldness. It also manifested itself in any number between one and nine, or futuristically multiplied beyond these numbers. In the beginning, Atum arose from Nun the chaotic primeval waters (Figure 6). Nun is the inconceivable and chaotic nothing, a moist void that can be said to be only potentially there.

By contrast, Ra emerged as phoenix or sunburst above Atum. Together they comprise Atum-Ra, the total Godhead of Heliopolitan theology. Atum arose as a primeval Hill amidst Nun; he was the first solid someone or somebody.[21] Not unexpectedly, this rising Hill was visualized by male priestly storytellers principally as being a masculine generative divine force. And again, not unexpectedly, it turned out that Atum's sanctuary, at Junu, had been built exactly upon this primeval cosmic height.

Figure 6. In the beginning, within chaotic Nun, Atum arose as primeval hill. Author drawing.

Many writers have alerted to the fact that, following the recession of flood-waters from the Nile valley bottom-land, which was an annual event before the Aswan Dam was built, the re-emergence of hillocks and land was regularly displayed for Egyptian cultivators.

Although the exact experiential moment when Atum became identified with the Sun-god Ra can no longer be determined, it already was standard practice in the Old Kingdom to refer to these polar manifestations together as a single Atum-Ra. Cosmologically, one can visualize the two together as Sun rising above the primeval Hill. In time, the hidden Atum was contrasted with

---

[21] Cf. especially *Pyramid Text* 1652, below in Chapter 5.

the radiant Ra of daytime. That is to say, Atum in his original hidden form corresponded to the very Sun-god himself as he set in the west to hide again in darkness.

Politically, the upward and sun-ward orientation of Egyptian kings, as Horus-Falcon deities soaring toward the Sun, provided an easy directional association of royalty with the rising Ra (see Figure 11, Levels 4, 5). By logical extension, this orientation accomplished a fusion of the rising Hill with the ensuing Ennead. Being Horus-Ra, and being supported by the solid masculine Hill-power of Atum, the Egyptian god-king hoped to survive death, to rise and to rule another generation of people, in solar glory, splendor and authority.

The Second Hypostasis (Level 2)

Heliopolitan mythology and theory of evolution begins with the conceptualization of a divine generative process, which developed from there towards a sexual process of generation. Shu and Tefnut, male and female together, are the second hypostasis "generation" in the emanation and manifestation of Atum's pleasure. Shu and Tefnut sometimes are mentioned together as Ruti, a pair of divinities who become visible in the *ba* apparitions of a male and a female lion. Thus, at its second hypostasis, Heliopolitan theology is basically monotheistic. Focusing on two aspects will render it di-theistic. Contemplated by an analytic human mind, any single "One" will, sooner or later reveal its two, three, and more sides or aspects.

Whereas the Ruti dualism represents a convenient accommodation to the local cult of Leontopolis, Shu and Tefnut in their indigenous Heliopolitan context were still thought of as forming a trinity with Atum, from whom they proceeded. Within this trinitarian frame of reference, Shu personifies the masculine phallus-semen-life-breath extension of Atum, while Tefnut personifies the female hand-womb-mouth or order-and-containment dimension.[22] Both dimensions together continue the creative activity of Atum's "spitting," which originally has generated them. In this manner, in turn, they generated a next hypostasis, one that would exhibit slightly more visible detail, or more easily imagined contours.

---

[22] See *Pyramid Text* 447, below.

Atum, in the form of Hill, created Shu and Tefnut, the brother-and-sister twins. In terms of cosmographic visualization, Shu pushed forth from the solid Hill as the force of life—a soul-charged divine breath of air. Around Shu, and towards the limits of Shu, there arched a kind of feminine order, an enclosure or firmament. In the Hebrew creation story, this firmament was established by God for the orderly purpose of separating the waters above from waters below (compare *Genesis* 1:6–7). Theologians at Heliopolis knew this firmament, or this contained order, as Lady Tefnut or Lady Mahet. It was she who enclosed and held back the enveloping domain of chaotic Nun.

This entire trinitarian parent portion of the Ennead—the All-God Atum together with Shu and Tefnut—was with the demise of the Egyptian archaic period transposed by Plotinus into Greek-resembling philosophy: into One Father-Atum, Mind-Mahet, and Soul-Shu. In Alexandria, around the time of Plotinus, the Egyptian theology was also transposed by Christian theologians into Father (Atum), Son (Shu), and Holy Spirit (Mahet).

Modern connoisseurs of origin stories may be baffled by the very basic anthropomorphic demeanor of Egypt's high god, Atum. Egyptian theologians were no Indo-European dualists; their material world was not hopelessly severed from a qualitatively distinct and superior spiritual realm. They were not even dualists who easily could have converted to making Zoroastrian or Manichaean sharp distinctions between the personified Good and Evil.

These ancient Egyptians felt only slightly uneasy about promulgating a masturbation metaphor in their high theology. Their uneasiness stemmed not from a realization that sexual prowess was unbecoming of a God-of-gods. On the contrary! It rather derived from an awareness that the God's sexuality could, effectively, be activated somehow at a low human level—at a scale far too low to be kept lastingly in reverential focus. They therefore broadened their sexual metaphor of divine emission, in light of a somewhat larger analogous process. "Spitting" and "expectoration" were synonyms that were scarcely more endearing to the dualistic sensibilities of subsequent Indo-European theologians and philosophers.

The Third Hypostasis (Level 3)

At this level, Geb and Nut are the manifest divinity. Together, they represent a hypostasis in which anthropomorphic conceptualization and cosmological visualization come together. The introductory illustrations (Figures 6, 7), which depict the early hypostases of the Egyptian God-story, we have envisioned and illustrated on the basis of extant literary descriptions. We have dared to draw them with our own hands. In stark contrast, ancient Egyptian artists were far more explicit when they illustrated this same hypostasis. They were in the habit of showing the contours of Geb and Nut in various degrees of anthropomorphism and sexual explicitness (see Figure 8).

Figure 7. Atum spat forth Shu and Tefnut, Life and Order, to expand himself and to prepare the realm for life and offspring. Their nearly invisible union defies illustration and has generated Geb and Nut. Author drawing.

Although Geb served a familiar role as Father Earth, and Nut did the same as Mother Sky, they nevertheless constitute an anomaly among the mythologies of humankind. In most other cosmogonies, the Sky is Father and the ever-bearing Earth is recognized as Mother. But Egyptian royalty identified unambiguously with the life-evoking splendor of the Sun. Kings preferred to be born from on high, "trailing clouds of glory," as William Wordsworth would have said.

The geo-focal myth that describes the emergence of Atum as a rising hill, or a rising phallus, gave direction to the generative nature of all subsequent hypostases. It established the primacy of the masculine dimension of Atum-Ra as Godhead in the personas of Shu, Geb, and Osiris. It kept Egyptian royal masculinity anchored solidly on Planet

Earth and it bestowed on pharaohs the authority to administer and rule the "heritage of Geb," that is, the visible earth. The pharaoh, as a divine raptor and Horus-Falcon, having been born from on high, was thereby empowered to rule all that lived or grew on earth. By extension, he ruled everything that was mummified and buried in it.

Figure 8. Geb, as Father Earth, represented in person and by his emblem, the Great Cackler, on the left. He rises to meet Mother Sky, Nut, who arches above him. Their Father Shu, on the right, proceeds to separate them. They illustrate the Egyptian cosmos theology in the anthropomorphic mode. Twenty-first Dynasty, Papyrus of Tameniu, British Museum. Author-drawn after Ions.

Onward from Level 2, the texts read as though the deity Atum is emanating almost as if by perpetual sexual union between its Shu and its Tefnut aspects.[23] Cosmo-graphically speaking, from the perspective of an earthling who exists at Levels 4 and 5, but who is still able to notice Level 3, it would also have been difficult to perceive how far the body of Geb, the male, reached and where the body of Nut, the Female, began. Some descriptions given in the Pyramid and Coffin Texts are, nevertheless, very "explicit Theography"—and per-chance they can be explained more precisely as porno-graphic Theography.

---

[23] Cf. especially *Coffin Texts*, Spell 80, below.

That such an intimate allegory would lead to pregnancy and offspring, as the next hypostasis showed, should not surprise anyone. After all, this story has been composed for the benefit of mammalian human minds. All the while, no negative valuations have been intended by our depictions. The visible world, which was the subject of graphic, sculpted, and scribal storytelling, was never more and never less than low-intensity divine reality. Our low-intensity materialized reality can, indeed, still be visualized by human eyes as being generated by *ka* energy—as emerging from shadowy contrasts, within the realm that in its totality, ontologically speaking, amounts to less. *Ka* energy, at the human level, gets entangled with, but remains distinct from, chaotic or shadowy Nun (Chaos and Non-being) and thereby appears as *ba*.[24]

Atum, that is Shu and Tefnut together, procreated Geb and Nut. His two offspring are more or less the visible Father Earth and Mother Sky pair. Cosmographically, it may be observed that the creative emissions of Atum, by which Shu and Tefnut came to occupy the combined realm of life and order, have with the appearance of Geb and Nut only come into sharper focus. Father Geb can be felt, seen, and understood much more easily than his largely invisible Father Shu. Geb's concrete outlines can clearly be discerned and can even be modified by human hands and skill. Mother Nut can be visualized as well in the azure sky. However, everyone will admit that seeing her, while she tries to conceal her nudity, requires a robust dose of masculine imagination—which, we may safely assume, has presented no real obstacle to Egyptian priests.[25]

---

[24]Some among our Western readers, in the tradition of highly dualistic Puritanism, may have felt disgust on account of the pornographic theophany depicted in Figures 7 and 8. Their response, of course, is no solution to the ancient problem. It is merely a symptom of the ten-millennia conflict among hunter, herder, and planter cultures and their concomitant religious rationalizations.

[25]I readily admit that prior to 1987, this visualization of Sky, as Lady Nut, presented to me some difficulties—until, somewhere in Xinjiang, while describing a waterfall, a Kazakh elder explained that the falling curtain of water was a nude maiden. When the girl discovered that she was being observed by men like us, she started diving into the creek below. Because she is still diving there, in the shape of a waterfall, it has become easier to envision Mother Sky arching along the Egyptian azure. .

A patient reader who follows this line of inquiry to its completion will discover that many obscenities in Near Eastern and Western civilization, including wars brought to a boil in the name of religion, have been aggravated by the inherited tension between Near Eastern civilization and its outreaches farther West. They have been aggravated ideologically by the inherited conflict between Egyptian monism and northern or Indo-European dualism. Our monastic Puritan scruples have gotten cultivated while the people were getting squeezed between those two very different ancient world-views.

The Godhead, Atum, displays his otherwise hidden nature by way of revealing his invisibility through the likewise mostly invisible personae of Shu and Tefnut. Of course, further down and outward along the flow of divine emanation, as that flow exposes itself in the *ba* modes of Geb and Nut, the Godhead's *ka* essence appears to get fragmented and thinned out. All light-and-shadow apparitions happen for the benefit of human eyes to accommodate the human ability to perceive, and to learn about lesser things as well. However, the whereabouts of the dark outermost boundary of All-Being remains invisible to us. Black holes and Nun-tainted nothingness may remain questionable forever.

The Fourth Hypostasis (Level 4)

With Mother Sky and Father Earth having come into better focus, the Egyptian world was ready for still smaller specific divine births. From Geb and Nut were born two brother and sister pairs of twin gods: Osiris with Isis, and Nephthys with Seth (see Figure 9, page 88). These pairs of twins were envisioned anthropomorphically, or were sometimes seen as existing in a twilight condition of prehuman flux. As gods at Level 4, they appeared and operated on a smaller and more visible scale than did their greater parent, or parents. At this level of specificity, the Egyptian Godhead renewed and sponsored divine-human sovereignty over the world of Egyptian planters and domesticators in the realm that was to be the All-God's remotest visible level of emanation.

Gods of the Fourth Hypostasis function primarily along the outer edge, along the turnaround curve or perimeter of divine emanation. Nephthys, as goddess of the home fire, was credited with having suckled and nurtured young Horus kings. Seth, as god of desert heat and enemy lands, has been saddled with the blame of stopping pharaohs in their tracks, with changing them into corpses, with causing them to die. Because he was the one who stopped living Horus Falcons, he also was the one who transformed them into Osiris shapes. Inasmuch as this final wrought transformation left them as bona fide members of the Ennead, one can assume that somehow Atum's phallus also was on Seth. However, the sexual distinguishing mark of Seth is a hunter's or warrior's phallic aberration: a deadly dagger, made to stab and to kill. By contrast, Osiris is the creative phallus-bearer of his generation of gods within the Ennead. He procreated all subsequent Horus kings of Egypt, while Isis, as divine mother, gave birth to and nurtured all his offspring.

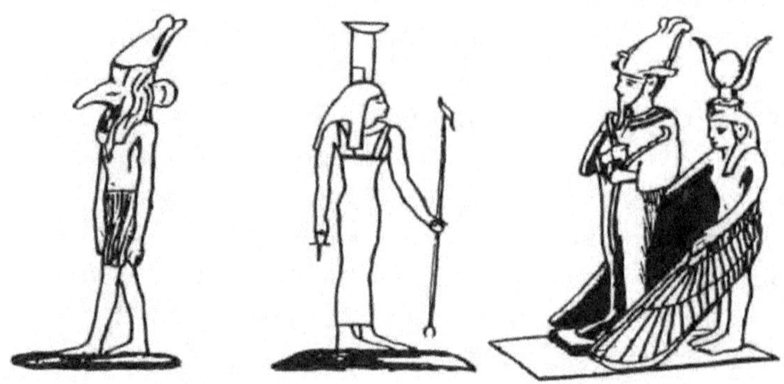

Figure 9. Seth and Nephthys, Osiris and Isis. These children of Geb and Nut occupy the lowest rank in the Heliopolitan Ennead, at Level 4; they exist low enough to participate intimately also at Level 5, in the human experience of life and and death. Drawn after Bonnet and Erman (1934).

The Turnaround Realm (Level 5)

The gods mentioned together with the outermost generation of the Ennead, and in association with the Turnaround Realm, played major roles in Egyptian funerary proceedings, at least insofar as these proceedings happened in light of Heliopolitan theology. Foremost among these lesser gods may be mentioned Horus, Thoth, and Anubis (Figure 10). As noted earlier, Horus represented any duly installed Egyptian king—a divine Falcon-King. The ibis-headed Thoth was scribe and keeper of the divine words; he later served in Memphite theology, appropriately, as tongue of the All-God, Ptah. Thoth and the jackal-headed Anubis belonged to some kind of lower or lesser "Ennead" (Figure 10). At the same time, Horus, in the Turn-around Realm (Figure 11), became associated more personally and intimately with the "great" Ennead. As the son of Isis and Osiris, he seems to have functioned almost as the

Ennead's transitional tenth member. Of course, at that level in the process he also was the Enneadic Shu-Geb-Osiris.

From the Heliopolitan perspective, these lesser gods were created like everything else in the cosmos, by that same emanation that also generated the primary hypostases of the Ennead. All creatures, all that live, move and are, have their being from within this process of emanation.

The cosmos was generated by Atum alone, first; and from that point of generation continued onward, simultaneously, by the trinity of Atum, Shu, and Tefnut. By the same breath of Shu and the receptive presence of Tefnut the visible cosmos was procreated—by Atum himself, and by this Trinity, simultaneously—for the All-God to become increasingly more apparent to humankind as Geb and Nut (see the schematic drawing, Figure 12).

Figure 10: Left to right: Horus, Thoth, Anubis. Drawn after Erman (1934).

Various Egyptian local traditions cultivated additional divine manifestations and saviors to be reckoned with. The wise theologians at Junu knew how to accommodate them all into their system. Some of these divinities found new roles to play along the lower end of an already variegated Enneadic emanation. There, they found new ways to surf, as it were, on the coastal waves that surged along the outer perimeter of Atum's emanation. They helped reverse the fates of *ka* sparks; they re-oriented the movement of life-souls who had become estranged from their source and had gotten caught up in the shadow play and confusion that prevails naturally in the vicinity of moribund bodies.

Some lower gods were called on to serve as ceremonial assistants, guides, and conveyors of life-souls during funerary proceedings. Anubis was undertaker, and Thoth officiated as priestly scribe. In performing their tasks, these gods interacted with some of the lower divinities of the greater Ennead. Nephthys and Isis frequently provided Turnaround assistance. Reliance on Horus became more widespread in Egyptian soteriology when, during the Intermediary Period (2181–2040 BCE) patricians, too, began to avail themselves of the royal Heliopolitan means of salvation. In *Coffin Texts,* the god Horus is recognized as a living savior with whom a homeward-bound soul, on its way back to the Godhead, could hitch a ride for easier travel. For some returning souls, the Horus-person himself has become the mediator for mystic re-identification with divinity.

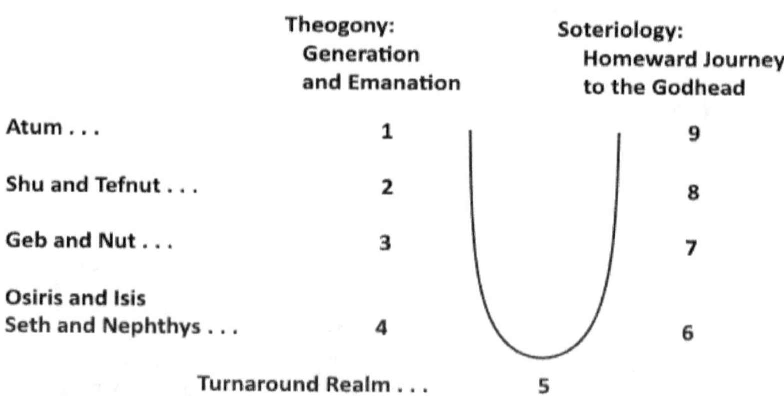

Figure 11: Directionality and levels in Heliopolitan Theogony and Funerary Soteriology.

The ability of Horus, to function as the divine Falcon-King of United Egypt, a Son of God and savior of humankind, is underwritten by Heliopolitan imperial mythology, namely, by his status as Son of Osiris and Isis. For the purpose of enthronement rites, Isis as Mother embodied the Egyptian throne. Every divinely installed Egyptian king was ceremonially reborn—upon her and from her, as the Throne. Then, when a ruling God-king came to the end of his career, he was transformed. First, his human appearance, his *ba,* was transformed by Seth into an Osiris kind of *ba,* a corpse apparition. His *ka* was thereby liberated from its own shadow. The *ka* got resurrected to return to the Godhead and to remain on call, to be "reborn."

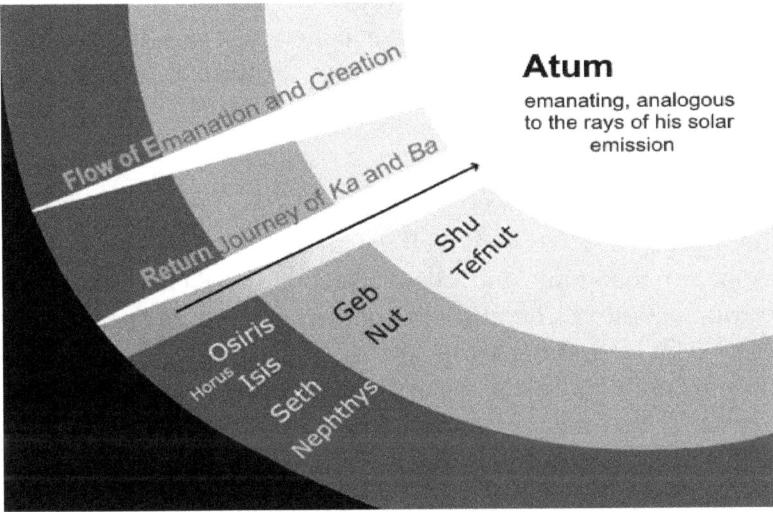

Figure 12: Atum emanating, analogous to the rays of his solar emissions.

When a deceased pharaoh was put into his coffin, he represented the masculine and potentially creative Atum-Shu-Geb-Osiris "phallus" dimension. At the same time, Isis—and we may refer to her as representing the feminine Atum-Tefnut-Nut-Isis "hand and womb" dimension—hovered over the entombed royal body of Osiris, waiting to be impregnated by him again.

Depicted at the inside of many ancient Egyptian coffin lids was an image of Isis. This practice obviously alluded to the Osiris-Isis myth as it pertained to Osiris's sexual resuscitation—conception by Isis, and the expected rebirth of Horus. As will be shown later in Coffin Text Spell 84, the soul of a deceased person may be expected to issue forth from Isis anew, as a son of her, named Horus, and from there to journey homeward. As a result, in her next form as throne, she gave birth to the new Horus. That these combined wedding, burial, rebirth, and enthronement rituals constituted Atum's selfsame emanation becomes evident when one contemplates the Heliopolitan system in its entirety.

Repeatable cycles, of God begetting a Son to rule the human realm of Egypt, and then retrieving this Son again unto himself, are what throughout the millennia of known history gave to the Egyptian hyper-domestication system a measure of stability. An offshoot version of this Egyptian rotational stability, enveloped by a new form of Heliopolitan trinitarian theology, has later taken shape in Western history. It gave coherence to Christendom and its regions in the Christianized Roman Empire throughout almost two millennia more—at least to the days of Saint Augustine and then as far as Martin Luther.

The Homeward Journey

In the Pyramid Texts, as well as in the Coffin Texts, the total Heliopolitan theogony and cosmogony is implicitly referred to as background context. The primary concern of all these ancient Egyptian funerary texts was, necessarily, the immediate homeward journey of *ka* souls to the Godhead, plus, taking proper care of the dawdling *ba* aspects. It becomes therefore necessary to approach the process of generation/emanation, and even the Turnaround Realm as derivatives of the larger Heliopolitan theology.

Levels 6 through 9 can be understood by turning directly to the textual data. Excerpts from Pyramid and Coffin Texts, presented next, will provide samples directly from Egyptian soteriology. Materials as foreign to modern minds as funerary utterances of several millennia ago are easiest to understand when they are allowed to disclose their own former contextual function. At the Turnaround Point, where life encountered death and where light and shadows were severed to highlight the ultimate boundary, the reasoning of ancient Egyptians took on exceptional clarity. The ancient Egyptian funerary literature is, therefore, an excellent place to begin to contemplate general ontological axioms, as well as political and religious policies and issues of human co-existence.

Commentaries in the next two chapters will be kept to a minimum. They can be simplified further with the help of reference numbers introduced by Figure 11. These numbers will help us see the hypostases of creation (Levels 1 through 4) as way-stations past which, after death, a liberated soul journeys homeward to the God-head (Levels 6 through 9).

All the while, it is helpful to keep in mind that reference numbers for hypostases, along the generative flow of the divine *ka* force, correspond to another set of numbers that we assigned along the homeward path in an inverse manner. In Figure 11, Number 1 corresponds to 9, while 2 goes with 8; 3 goes with 7, and 4 is the same level as 6. The number 5 represents the Turnaround Realm, within which the material world, life and death, are experienced physically and to some extent visibly. The use of these ancillary code numbers, in Figure 11, makes our exposition of *Pyramid Texts* and of *Coffin Texts* considerably easier.

The moment has now arrived to comprehend the larger outline of ancient Egyptian ontology, to contemplate the larger view of Heliopolitan theology. The Sun deity, Ra, is the life essence of Atum that was ejaculated at the first moment of creation. Ever since this creative event happened it has been repeated daily when Atum-Ra rose in from the nightly gloom of chaotic Nun, the east. This cosmic event has been expanded along the eastern horizon of Geb (along the land *E-Geb-t*) into the domain of Nut. Before moving on into the next Chapter, a curious reader might benefit from reviewing briefly the essentials illustrated in Figures 6 through 12.

Preview--The Heliopolitan Theological System

can be visualized as a flow of creative vitality, emanating--that is, radiating outward from the Godhead, thinning out as it flows farther from its source. Along its outer periphery, this plethora of divine emanation diffuses into what begins to appear as the light and shadow realm of our material world. So it becomes visible. Farther out, beyond the periphery of visible matter, lies the realm of Non-being that in Egyptian mythology was conceptualized as Nun, watery Chaos and utter Darkness. Thus the boundary realm, between divinely generated Being and non-generated Non-being contains our apparent concrete experiences of world, of life and death. Were it not for the fact that apparent dichotomies of ideas, and distinctions of mind and matter, were of minor significance in an ontology of emanation, the entire theological system could be called a Concrete Philosophical Idealism.

5

Sun-Theology in the Pyramid Texts

This chapter focuses on a small selection of Pyramid Text samples that may be helpful in sketching the total of Heliopolitan theology somewhat coherently. Critics of our present perspective on ancient Egyptian religion, who hitherto have prejudged Egyptian "polytheism" for contrast vis-à-vis presumed exceptional ancient Hebrew "monotheism," very likely will insist on the individuality of each and every Egyptian divinity. While allowing such habits to rest, this author is saddled with the historical obligation to visualize the beliefs of ancient peoples in light of what they themselves most likely would have believed and how, in their finitude, they have responded to greater-than-human reality—how they themselves attempted to improve their temporal fortunes in light of their own glimpses of eternity. Hebrew religion, Greek philosophy, Christendom and Islam are late-comers. During their histories, core concepts of earlier Egyptian thought have continued to leak to the surface. This means that problems of civilization, as well as religious responses to these problems, have been surfacing together.

We need not abandon logic if we try to understand human existence the ancient Egyptian way. From the perspective of divinely radiated life-energy, from within emanations of divine purpose, Egyptian sun rays have engendered what nowadays we understand to be protoplasm and genes. The ancient stream of a Godhead's conscious emanation probably will outlive our momentary spans of memory, our traumas and multiple personalities. Time itself will arbitrate between our moribund disjunctive reasoning and the more holistic reasoning that ancient priests, at Heliopolis, have cultivated to rationalize their world and their existence.

Pyramid Texts 1248-49

Liturgical utterances that we consider, affirm at the outset the self-creation of Atum and suggest a perspective in which the Godhead might fittingly have issued his first dual hypostasis, Shu and Tefnut. The necessity of having postulated a creation of male and female genders, early on, seems reasonable. Concerning Levels 1 and 2, we are given an anthropomorphic analogy in the form of theogony (God-story). Ancient teachers regarded the human experience as a worthy basis on which to construct their emanation ontology, mythology and theology with analogies from human life.[26] **The author assumes that serious students will want to scrutinize the summations for themselves, in direct comparison with the published materials.**

Atum is he who [gave pleasure to himself] in On [Junu]. He took his phallus in his grasp that he might create orgasm by means of it, and so were born the twins Shu and Tefnut. May they put the King N. between them.[27]

Rather than merely acknowledging the unique situation of an individual deity, as having created things in a peculiar manner, Kurt Sethe's translation implies the primeval moment of the phallus-in-hand scenario, explaining best the entire creative process:

Atum ist der [von selbst] entstand, der mit sich onanierte in Heliopolis. Dem sein Phallus in seine Faust gelegt wurde, damit er sich geschlechtlich vergnüge mit ihm, und geboren wurden zwei Kinder verschiedenen Geschlechtes, Shu und Tefnut. [Diese] setzen sich nun den N. zwischen sich.[28]

---

[26] For hypostasis level designations see Figures 11 and 12, above.

[27] All English translations of Pyramid Texts quoted in this section, except the German version just quoted, are kept in line with R. O. Faulkner's translation, *The Ancient Egyptian Pyramid Texts* (Oxford, 1969) portions, reprinted in *Egyptian Light and Hebrew Fire.* Permission of Oxford University Press. While Faulkner's translation "Atum ... who masturbated in On" may be considered literally correct, his rendition appears nevertheless somewhat banal—at least in as far as the original statement surely has originated in a liturgical setting. Our modified rendition of "Atum... who gave pleasure to himself" seems sufficiently precise and more appropriate for the decorum of its ritual context. In addition, Faulkner's renditions of "Tefenet" have been adjusted to the now more common orthography as "Tefnut."

[28] Kurt Sethe, *Übersetzung und Kommentar zu den Ägyptischen Pyramidentexten,* Band 5 (Hamburg: J.J. Augustin 1962), 147.

This soteriological utterance, which returns a king, N., to the moment of all creation, delivers him as an Osiris offspring back directly into the creative embrace of the Godhead. It happens at Levels 8 and 9, which, of course, also corresponds to Levels 2 and 1 along the path of emanation. More precisely, the deceased king is placed smack between Shu and Tefnut. He has returned to the primeval moment and condition in which all subsequent gods and *ka* souls had prior existence. Atum's emanation as Shu and Tefnut constitutes a Trinity. One must keep in mind that both aspects of the deceased, his Shu as well as his Tefnut relatedness, continue subsequently to be engaged in creative sexual union, so that between these two there is no empty space for a separate royal personage to coexist. The king is therefore thought of as being "set among the gods," after the manner in which all gods and hypostases still existed at that primeval moment. Being an Osiris spark of *ka,* the deceased king still is contained in the All-God and participates anew at the starting point of the divine creative emission and emanation. He is intimately located where Shu and Tefnut are joined—intimately, as one who at an earlier moment has suffered separation, having been emitted to be born and to die. In the final analysis, the king, "set among the gods," is back in God. He returned to the source of his initial procreation at Level 1 and 9.

Pyramid Texts 1652-55

The royal pyramid, dedicated by the words that follow next, has been built into the realm of ontological Turnaround, at Level 5. All the while, the theogony is invoked along its entire dimension. The entire creative Ennead is mentioned in its full spatial presence (Levels 1-4). This is done to establish a mystic primeval union of the king's pyramid with the original Atum as the primeval pyramid-mountain. By dying, the ruler achieved a mystic union of sorts with the edifice that he had built. The king is placed to rest within his own mighty architectural "erection" as an Osiris corpse. It is Atum's own embrace, at a deceased king's funeral, that bridges and reduces the distance of Levels 5 through 9:

O Atum-Khoprer, you became high on the height, you rose up as the *bnbn*-stone in the Mansion of the Phoenix in On, you spat out Shu, you expectorated Tefnut, and you set your arms about them as the arms of a *ka* symbol, that your essence might be in them. O Atum, set your arms about the King, about this construction, and about this pyramid as the arms of a *ka* symbol, that the King's essence may be in it, enduring forever. O Atum, set your protection over this King, over this pyramid of his, and over this construction of the King, prevent anything from happening evilly against it forever, just as your protection was set over Shu and Tefnut. O you Great Ennead which is in On: Atum, Shu, Tefnut, Geb, Nut, Osiris, Isis, Seth, Nephthys. O you children of Atum extend his goodwill to his child in your name of Nine Bows....

Pyramid Texts 167-78

Defeated by Seth at Level 5, the Egyptian Horus-King was transformed into the condition of Osiris who appears at Level 4 and 6. It is noteworthy, regarding the liturgical utterances that follow, that its writers have not found it necessary to acknowledge the god Osiris apart from his presence as the mummified body of the king. Had they wanted to do so, Osiris would have been invoked between the lines that address Nut and Isis. This means that the presence of a dead king, at his funerary ritual, was deemed sufficient recognition of the presence of the god Osiris. It also suggests that during his funeral, the deceased king was considered to have been firmly merged with Osiris, as a divine member of the greater Ennead. The presence of a lesser Ennead, for contrast, adds variables for interpretation.[29]

> O Atum, this one here is your son Osiris whom you have caused to be restored that he may live.
> O Shu, this one here is your son Osiris . . .
> O Tefnut, this one here is your son Osiris . . .
> O Geb, this one here is your son Osiris . . .
> O Nut, this one here is your son Osiris . . .
> O Isis, this one here is your brother Osiris . . .
> O Seth, this one here is your brother Osiris . . .
> O Nephthys, this one here is your brother Osiris . . .

---

[29] Sethe (1962, Vol. 1, p. 87) explains the Lesser Ennead as having been postulated in contrast to the honorific appellation "Great Ennead," which was misunderstood in a numerical sense. This may be so. But I suspect that in this prayer sequence the addition of Thoth and Horus adds up to an extended Ennead. The Lesser Ennead, therefore, could refer to the inclusion of lesser gods—that is, to the extension or temporary "peripheral thinning" of the Great Ennead in the minds of human kings or humankind in general. In the shadow realm of mortality, this would refer to the immediate context and conditions that prevail during the funeral proceedings.

O Thoth, this one here is your brother Osiris . . .
O Horus, this one here is your father Osiris . . .
O Great Ennead, this one here is Osiris . . .
O Lesser Ennead, this one here is Osiris. . . .

Pyramid Texts 1660-62

Inasmuch as the temple compound at Junu contained two sanctuaries, one for Atum and another for Ra-Herachte, the duality of the Godhead as rising Ra and setting Atum seems to have been an early aspect of the Heliopolitan cult. Therefore, even at its cultic core, the theological Oneness of the Godhead contained this practical directional East-West duality. The exact process of reasoning along a historical path on which the one dual God, Atum-Ra, was first perceived as a Shu and Tefnut duality is perhaps no longer traceable. In the text quoted next, it appears as though initially at Heliopolis, Shu and Tefnut had distinct cultic realms assigned to them as well. It is significant that in the case of Shu and Tefnut, the theologians at Junu adhered to their Two-as-One formula as they had been doing all along while contemplating Atum-Ra. They continued doing so with regard to the subsequent divine generation of Geb and Nut.

O you Great Ennead which is in On (Junu, Heliopolis), make the King's [name] endure, make this pyramid for this King and this construction of his endure forever, just as the name of Atum who presides over the Great Ennead endures. As the name of Shu, Lord of Upper Mnst in On, endures, so may the king's name endure, and so may this pyramid of his and this construction of his endure likewise, forever—as the name of Tefnut, Mistress of Lower Mnst in On, endures.

Pyramid Texts 447-49

The soteriology expressed in the next selection focuses on Levels 8 and 9, thus on Ruti and Atum. Shu and Tefnut as lion pair [Ruti] are implored to grant to the deceased king safe passage past their own divine presences along the horizon. It indicates that the deceased is now on his way home to the First and Eternal One, Atum.

You have your offering-bread, O Atum and Ruti, who yourself created your Godheads and your persons. O Shu and Tefnut who made the gods, who begot the gods and established the gods: Tell your father that the King has propitiated you with your dues. You shall not hinder the King when he crosses to him at the horizon, for the King knows him and knows his name: "Eternal" is his name. "The Eternal Lord of the Year" is his name.

In support of Level 8 and 9 soteriology, this passage also refers to Levels 1–2 along the generative outward track of the theogony. Atum is acknowledged as the original Godhead who created his own masks and personae, the duality as well as plurality of the gods. Shu and Tefnut are credited with subsequently having begotten other gods. And, as everywhere in the Heliopolitan system, so also in this passage, soteriology is based on the trinitarian theogony—on the theology that combines Atum, Shu, and Tefnut into a single process of emanation.

Pyramid Texts 552-53

The deceased king's identification with Shu and Tefnut, at Level 8, explains his new mode of existence. His hunger and thirst are satisfied after the manner in which gods satisfy theirs. The "morning bread that comes in due season" provides a cosmological hint: Shu as air—and Tefnut as sunlight that envelops order, perhaps—appear to be nourished when together they consume the morning dew: I will not be thirsty by reason of Shu, I will not be hungry by reason ofTefnut.... My hunger is from the hand of Shu, my thirst is from the hand of Tefnut. I live on that whereon Shu lives, I eat of that whereof Tefnut eats. [Thus, in actuality, I am Shu and Tefnut].

Pyramid Texts 1817-18

Although the syntax of the next text is somewhat problematic, it nevertheless is clear enough to provide a hint about the interrelatedness of Shu and Atum. The phallus of Atum is also on Shu. By extension, and in light of the importance of the phallus for Osiris-Isis mythology, as for funerary and coronation mythology in general, one can surmise that therefore this same phallus also was on Geb and Osiris.

O Shu, you enclose for yourself all things within your embrace ... this Osiris the King; may you prevent him from escaping [from your embrace; i.e. the embrace] of Atum, whose phallus is on you, that you may be [... ?] his *ka*; may you protect him....

Pyramid Texts 2065-67

The various hypostases of the Godhead are in the course of a funerary washing rite visualized as a flow of pure water that originates with Atum [the Father] or with Shu and Tefnut [the Son and Daughter]. Immersed in this [combined baptismal flow of living water], the king is made divine for his return journey to the Father:

Behold this King, his feet are kissed by the pure waters which exist through Atum, which the phallus of Shu makes and which the vagina of Tefnut creates. They have come and have brought to you the pure waters with their father; they cleanse you and make you divine, O King. You shall support the sky with your hand, you shall lay down the earth with your foot.

Inasmuch as in Egyptian iconography Shu frequently is depicted as the one who lifts up Mother Sky (Nut) with his hands, the last phrase in this statement may provide a cosmogonic hint about Nut and Tefnut combined. By contrast, she seems to be the one who laid down Father Earth, with her foot—perhaps also with the rays and beams of her light, which do introduce order.[30]

Pyramid Text 1405

An invocation addressed to Tefnut provides an additional hint about her place in cosmology and theogony: The earth is raised on high under the sky, by your arms, O Tefnut, and you have taken the hands of Ra. . . .

Thus, Tefnut's function is complementary to that of her brother Shu. As masculine manifestation of the divine life force, Shu supports the arching sky goddess Nut, for the benefit of Geb. Tefnut as female life force is balancing the Heliopolitan cosmology on a next larger scale than Nut. Her presence delimits the masculinity of the Earth-god, Geb. She sustains his passion and his masculinity, and invites it to rise skyward.

---

30 The "foot" of the Mother, a sky goddess, begs a naturalistic explanation, so that somehow it fits the larger Egyptian experience of Tefnut as a cosmic being. I am reminded of Navajo Indian "roots" or "feet" of sunlight—spectacular streaks of sun rays breaking through billowy clouds, which visibly touch the earth. Tefnut's activity of "shining" seems better expressed later in some Coffin Texts, as in Spell 78.

Pyramid Text 1443

The deceased king presents himself to the Sun-god Ra in hope of being given conveyance across the sky. The Sun deity is acknowledged here as being born from Nut, on the arms of Shu and Tefnut. No contradiction between this scene and earlier selections is implied. The sky-goddess Nut manifests herself as daughter "from within" her mother Tefnut, and participates as well in the function of the "hand" of Atum. The daily birth of Ra in the east, repeats the primordial sunburst of light that issued from above Atum's phallic hill: The face of the sky is washed, the celestial expanse is bright, the god is given birth by the Sky upon the arms of Shu and Tefnut, which, of course, are also the arms of Atum.

Apparently, the deceased king, though he introduces himself later in Pyramid Text 1448 merely as a son of Geb and Osiris (Levels 3 and 4) nevertheless identifies here his own arms with the primeval arms of Shu and Tefnut (Level 2)—to obligate the Sun-god toward him as a brother, perhaps. Remember, divine personages can change shape; they can overlap and merge with others.

Pyramid Text 1066

The sequence in which the soul returns to Atum may have been determined by the theogonic sequence. The emanation called "Tefnut" emerged from Atum "behind" her brother Shu.[31] It would therefore follow that on a corresponding return journey of souls to Atum, at Levels 8 and 9, the sequence of these divinities appears reversed: I am a man of Dendera, I have come from Dendera with Shu behind me, Tefnut before me, and Wepwawet clad [?] at my right hand.

Pyramid Texts 1466-69

Egyptian priests were capable of reasoning at various ontological levels. This is demonstrated by the text given next. Indeed, everyone knew how Egyptian kings were born first of human mothers, bodily, onto this earth. And surely, many people also knew that during coronation rites, their kings were participants in

---

[31] This question of the sequence in the emergence of Shu and Tefnut is developed more seriously in the *Coffin Texts*; see especially Spell 76.

the lowest Enneadic hypostasis. Isis therefore dwelt conveniently "in the Lower Sky." All the same, the king has existed within Atum from the beginning of creation as a spark of *ka*—an Imperishable Star. Or, should we say he existed "as a gleam in the All-Father's eye"—eternally recyclable—perhaps?

The King's mother was pregnant with him, [even he] who was in the Lower Sky, the King was fashioned by his father Atum before the sky existed, before earth existed, before men existed, before the gods were born, before death existed . . . The King will not die because of any dead, for the King is an Imperishable Star, son of the Sky-goddess who dwells in the Mansion of Selket. Ra has taken this King to himself to the sky so that this King may live, just as he who enters in the west of the sky [still] lives when he rises in the eastern sky.

This text resonates in harmony with such famous post-Egyptian statements as "before Abraham was I am" (Jesus of Nazareth) or "the child is father of the man" (William Wordsworth). In any case, the deceased king returns to his point of origin. He participates in the eternity of the Sun-god Ra as well as in the larger Godhead, Atum-Ra.

Pyramid Text 841-43

The liturgical context of the next statements is not difficult to surmise. They belonged to a purification rite performed during the funerary proceedings.

O King, stand up, that you may be pure and that your *ka* may be pure, for Horus has cleansed you with cold water. Your purity is the purity of Shu; your purity is the purity of Tefnut; your purity is the purity of the four house spirits when they rejoice in Pe. Be pure! Your mother Nut, the great Protectress, purifies you, she protects you. "Take your head, gather your bones together," says Geb. "The evil which is on this King is destroyed, the evil which was on him is brought to an end," says Atum.

The exhortation to the deceased king begins here in the Turnaround Realm at Level 5. It covers the entire distance from there, back to Atum at Level 9. The purity that is achieved provides the rising and returning king with an affinity to all major hypostases or divinities along the way—to four house spirits, to Nut and Geb, and to Shu and Tefnut—guaranteed and decreed all along by the eternal Godhead himself.[32]

Pyramid Texts 2051-53

Many commentaries on Egyptian religion fail to recognize the unity of the Ennead as constituting a single Godhead. The English rendition of the next text provides an occasion to address this issue:

If the King be caused to be embalmed, the [female] Great One will fall before the King, for the King's mother is Nut, the King's (grandfather) is Shu, the King's (grandmother is Tefnut), they take the King to the sky, on the smoke of incense.

As a meticulous translator, R. O. Faulkner has added the parenthetical generational indicators (grand)father Shu and (grand)mother Tefnut. That would definitely be an improvement if, in an absolute specific sense, the goddess Nut could be identified as the King's mother. But divine relationships in ancient Egypt were never that static or specific. While the king still ruled as Horus divinity on the throne of Egypt, the proper "generation" of his mother would have been Isis; that designation would have rendered Nut to be his grand-mother, indeed, and Shu and Tefnut to be his great-grandparents. However, now that the king lies dead and is transformed and promoted into his Osirian condition, Nut indeed is his proper mother, and generationally speaking, his (grand)parents are those whom Faulkner has designated. Nevertheless, theologically speaking, no family tree with branches needs to be planted in this instance. Heliopolitan theology regards all masculine manifestations in the nine-fold Godhead as one Father. Likewise, it regards all feminine manifestations as one Mother.

It makes little sense to speak here of specific generations of gods as if their family tree had become known in linear time, as happens to be the case with mortals. Family trees with past immutable branches make sense only in the realm of mortals among whom sequences and death are significant existential boundary markers. All along in this presentation, the term "generation" must be understood in its gerundive sense—of the Godhead "generating" or "procreating" his

---

[32] The four house spirits at Pe, or Buto, may be the four "children of Horus" or "sons of Osiris." They were Amset, Hapi, Duamutef, and Kebehsenuf. Hans Bonnet, *Real-Lexikon der Ägyptischen Religionsgeschichte* (Berlin: Walter de Gruyter, 1952), 129, 315f.

very own hypostases. Enneadic theology enlarges the divine "family tree" into a single process of emanation. Divine generation that precedes human existence does not cease to be. Atum is Godhead, he lives as Shu and Tefnut, and all three continue to live manifest in Geb and Nut. The entire Godhead exists as Ennead, combined.

Thus, the deceased king in this instance is carried as *ka* or divine Osiris-soul to the sky, ritually carried on the smoke of incense, but soteriologically carried by Shu and Tefnut. These parental deities lure him past the hypostases of Geb and Nut, homeward to Atum.

Pyramid Texts 1687-95

The deceased king has traveled in the barge of the Sun-god toward the western horizon, as though he were the very son of Nut, the Sun-god Ra himself. Before he died, the king had lived in human form temporarily for the worthy purpose of ruling Egypt. When he died, he returned to the gods to continue ruling from within their midst. Boys will be boys, and kings will be kings! It stands to reason that to enable an Egyptian pharaoh to retain his identity as a ruler, the gods graciously assembled to play a game of "monarchy" with the newly arrived. A freshly deceased king, still saddled with imperial ambitions, was thereby given an opportunity to play-act his royal skills a while longer, or perhaps forever. Concurrently, of course, he also was expected to provide moral support for his own royal successor and identity on the throne of Egypt—who, on that throne, continues his very own existence upon Geb (E-Geb-t), as follows:

Go aboard this bark of Ra.... in which Ra rows to the horizon, that you may go aboard it as Ra; sit on this throne of Ra that you may give orders to the gods, because you are Ra who came forth from Nut who bears Ra daily, and you are born daily like Ra.... "Who is like him?" say the two great and mighty Enneads who preside over the Souls of On. These two great and mighty gods who preside over the Field of Rushes install you upon the throne of Horus as their firstborn; they set Shu for you on your east side and Tefnut on your west side, Nu on your south side and Nenet on your north side; they guide you to these fair and pure seats of theirs which they made for Ra when they set him on their thrones.... Do not be far removed from the gods, so that they may make for you this utterance which they made for Ra-Atum who shines every day. They will install you upon their thrones at the head of all the Ennead(s), as at the head of all the Ennead(s) , as Ra and as his representative. They will bring you into being like Ra in this his name of Khoprer; you will draw near to them like Ra in this his name of Ra; you will turn aside from their faces like Ra in this his name of Atum.

In the second portion of this important text, the individual gods gather to make enabling utterances of the kind they made when they empowered Ra-Atum, the one who shines every day and sets in the west. Of course, this is bloated poetry that reverses orthodox cosmic causality. Originally, Atum-Ra himself empowered everyone and everything else. Such ambitious texts were concocted to lend credence to state-craft and priest-craft in the lower visible regions. So, it may seem from an outsider's perspective. But what, then, is causality if all along these gods have together been a combined *ka* and *ba* manifestation of the All-God?

Be that as it may. In this case it is Ra, pushed forth by Khoprer the slow-creeping dung beetle. When he shines from on high as sun, in his manifest mode, Ra is Godhead. After he sets as sun and hides in darkness, this Godhead is named Atum. While a deceased Egyptian king travels in the company of Ra, he continues to participate in the administration of the cosmos. He went on his way to fuse his own *ka* with Atum-Ra, the Godhead.

Noteworthy in these texts is also the ease with which the plurality of the Ennead(s) is made to comprise a single Godhead. The difference between polytheism and monotheism, or pantheism for that matter, is one of perspective from afar, or of focusing up close. And this perspective or focus is, ordinarily, a function of a mortal person's degree of ego-assertion, of ego-surrender vis-à-vis God. It is a question of whether human wills can be pious enough to permit their God to show a larger single face in contrast to multiple smaller faces or, at any given moment in time, show the immensity of his or her face where shortsighted mortals fail to see any face at all. Pantheistic revelations suggest a condition of mystic surrender to a single deity, the All-God. Sincere pantheism is a mystic's fulfilled version of monotheism, where man is merged into All.

Pyramid Texts 1773-74

Here, again, the king ascends as Ra to shine back on Egypt as essence of the Sun deity. His rays descend on the land as Mahet (Order and Righteousness), that is, as the divinity that somehow happens to be co-present with natural sunlight defined by shadows. As such, Mahet is co-present with visibility and order. In this manner, deceased Egyptian kings supposedly continued to bless their land, especially at the occasion when the people celebrated New Year as the advent of another round of sunlight:

The King passes the night, having daily mounted up to Ra. The shrine is opened for him when Ra shines. The King has ascended. On a cloud, he has descended.... Mahet in the presence of Ra on that day of the Festival of the First of the Year.

Pyramid Texts 1582-83

As in the preceding text, so too in the one that follows, the king is destined to shine as Mahet, who suppresses wrongdoing. This is considered to be an extension of the royal duties he performed while ruling Egypt. His righteousness is to be radiated onto Egypt every day, along with the sunlight of Ra.

May you shine as Ra; repress wrongdoing, cause Mahet to stand behind Ra, shine every day for him who is in the horizon of the sky. Open the gates which are in the Abyss.

It seems as though Mahet is envisioned here as a form of Tefnut who, in cosmogonic sequence, emerged from Atum "after" Shu. This possibility must be considered again later, in relation to Coffin Texts, especially Spells 76 and 80--and then still later, perhaps again, in the Christian "Filioque Clause" controversy.

Pyramid Text 5

The deceased king is loved by the gods, especially by the sky goddess, Nut (Level 3). According to divine gossip, which somehow has reached the ears of knowledgeable priests in Heliopolis, Nut as sky goddess was more lovingly disposed toward this particular deceased pharaoh, perhaps more than toward her own mother Tefnut. In either case, Enneadic divine love flows (shines) outward and downstream in the direction of the king and humankind.

Recitation by Nut the great: The King is my son of my desire.... All the gods say: Your father Shu knows that you love the King more than your mother Tefnut.

Pyramid Texts 1353-54

Cosmologically speaking, the realm of Shu and Tefnut is situated in the upward direction. Hence, the soul of the deceased is "raised aloft" on the hands of these two divinities. Moving in the upward direction, the homeward bound soul arrives where Nut arches as firmament (Level 7), as celestial manifestation of Atum. We are told that previously, at Level 5, Nephthys sustained the king:

Your water jar is firm.... you are raised aloft on the hands of Shu and Tefnut in the Mansion of Her who provides, O King, because you are a spirit whom Nephthys suckled with her left breast.

Pyramid Texts 2097-99

The embalmed and wrapped corpse of the king participates in the nature of Osiris. Alluding to ancient hunter mythology, his face wears a jackal mask, and his *ka* is already wrapped in Atum's own divine flesh, which, of course, is not flesh as we know it. In this manner begins the king's homeward journey at Level 5. Inasmuch as Shu and Tefnut themselves are the primary guides, the deceased pharaoh's complete return to the Godhead is assured. The return of a king to the primordial condition happens in prehuman flux.[33]

This King comes provided as a god, his bones knit together as Osiris.... Your face is that of a jackal, your flesh is that of Atum, your soul is within you, your power is about you, Isis is before you and Nephthys is behind you, you encompass the Horite Mounds and you go round-about the Sethite Mounds, it is Shu and Tefnut who guide you when you go forth from On.

Pyramid Texts 1984-85

The deceased king's destination once again is the source of all being, Atum. As long as oneness at Level 9 is considered, Atum is the "great god." Shu and Tefnut are his designation when he is contemplated as twofold hypostasis (Level 8). Within the Trinitarian logic of Junu, to invoke the assistance of Shu and Tefnut as ferry gods, who "row," implies nothing less than that the great Trinity (Godhead) conveys the deceased king unto himself and herself... you go forth

---

33 For a discussion and samples of prehuman flux mythology, see Luckert, *The Navajo Hunter Tradition* (Tucson: University of Arizona Press, 1975), 133ff. For more examples see also Luckert, *Stone Age Religion at Göbekli Tepe* (Portland: Triplehood, 2013), 233ff.

so that you may go up to the broad hall of Atum, travel to the Field of Rushes, and traverse the places of the great god. The sky is given to you; [it is] the good great gods who row you, even Shu and Tefnut, the two great gods of On.

Pyramid Text 1739

The king's progress is assured because he is being carried homeward by Ra, or Atum-Ra. The divine-royal status of the god, as carrier of the sun, does not permit him to weaken or turn back on his path. In addition, progress on the king's journey is guaranteed because he is carried along not only by the self-conscious and dependable Sun-god, but also by the presence of the great deities Tefnut and Shu, who keep watchful eyes on the Sun-god... Tefnut seizes you, Shu grips you; the Majesty of Ra will not turn back in the horizon, for every god sees him.

Every god would notice if the Sun were to turn back. The Sun-god would thereby lose face and show himself unreliable. The bright and proud Sun-god would never risk the danger of shaming himself, or of lessening his influence and function in the larger scheme of things.

Preview--Totemic Pharaonic Horus Falcons

in human form, perched on the Throne of ancient Egypt. They ruled the birthing-nest of Western Civilization.

The totemic insignia of ascending eagles survives in Western lands where eagle images still spread fear from the flags and emblems of nations, and by illusions of real value also from monetary notes and coinage.

Here in the United States, we honor our Egyptian roots with our bald-headed American Fish-Eagle, with a gigantic obelisk that memorializes our first president, and with the image of a pyramid printed on our one-dollar notes.

To enhance their authenticity, these notes also do sport the eye of Horus (or of Atum-Ra) for good measure.

6

Sun-Theology in the Coffin Texts

The second stratum of literary sources for the theology of Heliopolis are the Coffin Texts, from the First Intermediate Period and the Middle Kingdom (2181–ca. 1773 BCE). These were written on inside surfaces of wooden coffins on behalf of patrician owners who had aristocratic status and wealth. Their material possessions afforded these mortals not only more elaborate funerals and more prestigious tombs, but also higher status in relation to the gods—professional priestly assistance with trickle-down pharaonic knowledge for a surer transition into life hereafter.

Like the Pyramid Texts after which they were modeled, Coffin Texts are spells or "strong prayers" that in the obvious presence of death affirm and insist on more life. Generally, these affirmations proceed on the assumption that the deceased person will be able to achieve an intimate mystic relationship with a great deity. The divinities on whom Middle Kingdom patricians depended were not the lowest ranking gods at Level 5 who could, just possibly, be persuaded to serve as guides to realms beyond. Rather, dying persons of rank identified themselves after the manner of superior pharaohs of the Old Kingdom. Directly they dared to address the greatest divine beings about whose presence they were informed.

Among the various theologies quoted for existential posturing, in Middle Kingdom coffin spells, the Heliopolitan theology still appears to be the most coherent system. This state of affairs attests to the fact that the priests of Junu, of the Old Kingdom, who composed spells for inscription in royal pyramids, were able to perpetuate their theological tradition even throughout the period of Egypt's first major political crisis, the Intermediary Period (2181–2025 BCE) and beyond. The Heliopolitan Ennead, the Ninefoldness, was understood by orthodox Egyptian theologians to be one All-God who, as a single divine reality and process, manifests himself in the coherent existence and sequential appearance of nine divine persons: first as Atum the Father, and then as four pairs of offspring: Shu and Tefnut, Geb and Nut, Osiris and Isis, Nephthys and Set.

Heliopolitan mythology assured that upon death, after the Osirization of a Horus-King (pharaoh), his ceremonial offspring would be born again unto the throne of Egypt as the next Horus—or Falcon-king. Such ritualizing of the political process allowed for a measure of flexibility in the choice of royal successors. It also helped rationalize the takeovers by new dynasties to be less traumatic than otherwise they could have been. Isis represented the feminine divine throne from whose lap each duly installed and recognized king was ceremonially reborn as Horus.

Nevertheless, even in the context of the highest mythology, the royal soteriology produced its own bouts of fighting between Horus and Seth. Only the intervention of another divine manifestation, Thoth, a god of scribes and wisdom, could actualize the ritualized defense of the honor of Osiris to benefit the latter's successor Horus—or could whitewash a new dynasty's violent takeover as a state of normalcy. The priest-craft of Thoth itself healed the wounds of divine combatants and thereby the new king could, henceforth be endorsed to rule Egypt as Horus, in peace.

All the while, the decisive battle of Horus, against Seth who was identified as the cause of death, was fought on behalf of mortal humankind as much as it was for the continuity of the empire—it was thereby prolonged. But this battle unto death had to be remembered by each successor-generation and be dealt with anew.

Alongside the dynamic monotheistic theology and soteriology, the divine status of an Egyptian pharaoh was anchored in the sure fact and foil of his de facto human mortality. Whereas the living pharaoh, as a divine Horus-Falcon, represented the first and highest human rank that emanated from the Ennead, a dying Horus-pharaoh returned to the Godhead along the Ennead's path of emanation, by way of being immediately transformed back into the condition of his father Osiris. The Egyptian royalty thereby oscillated between being centered in Atum at the "home" end of the flow of divine emanation, to be then resurrected and returned after death, reborn and initiated anthropomorphically—as the only-begotten Horus-Falcon divinity for the land of Geb—which is E-Geb-t (Egypt).

Dying was the birthing process in reverse. Therefore, getting oneself saved in the face of death required the homeward movement of the human *ka,* that is, swimming against the flow of birthing water and toward the original flow of the divine seminal emission. Theologically, this meant that any mortal king who wished to preserve his royal status, or any king who had just suffered the misfortune of death, was able to view himself as someone caught up in the mythic turnaround struggle that was perpetually being initiated and waged between Horus and Seth. Any mortal king, along his triumphant journey through death and his regenerative collaboration with Isis, would so participate in an Osiris moment of truth.

During the Intermediary Period, nobles of lesser rank usurped pharaonic authority. They continued doing so during the Middle Kingdom by insisting on equal burial status, commensurate with what was claimed by the ancient deified royalty. The cult that served to save dead pharaohs during the Old Kingdom (2686-2181 BCE) expanded during the Middle Kingdom to also include patricians. And then it was only a matter of time before, during the New Kingdom (1550-1069 BCE), a vogue of democratization regarding royal afterworld status was being claimed by ordinary folk. Numerous papyri of the New Kingdom period, found in the coffins of less-than-royal mummies, bear inscriptions of ancient spells that were prefigured on the earlier coffin and pyramid walls. Their existence attests to a trend of democratization—a drift toward an erosion of royal status which had been grounded existentially in afterlife dogma.

The insistence among Egyptian common folk on winning royalty-like status after death was internationalized and universalized later to spread into in the wider Graeco-Roman world under the guise of Hellenistic philosophy and various branches of "Gnosticism." It also was given a fresh form of revival by the Kingdom of Heaven movement, founded by John the Baptizer and continued by Jesus of Nazareth and Saul of Tarsus. All these trends of democratization and universalization helped undercut the divine authority that formerly had been claimed by totemic Falcon-kings and by deified emperors. In a Hebraic-Aramaic mode, Jesus of Nazareth continued to distribute divine-royal status as evenly as he could among all people and commoners who followed him as his brothers or sisters into the Kingdom of his heavenly Father—as fellow children of God.

Freedom from oppressive hyper-domestication systems—and this, modern Western reformers should understand—was achieved by ancient Egyptian commoners in competition with royalty, first on behalf of their own ancestors. Higher status for survivors and offspring could be derived from deified ancestors, and subsequently from the ranks of privileged ancestral ghosts. In the course of later Christian history, egalitarian rights were also derived from royalty status that could be assumed by religious faith, by participation in a "Kingdom of Heaven" which implied a fairer kind of world order and that welcomed all people. Equality and freedom was obtained from the greater-than-human dimension during secular modern democratic revolutions. Status could be obtained on afterlife credit, as well, by all those who were willing to die and to dedicate their dying to the cause of a more egalitarian or democratic coexistence.

Selections from among the Coffin Texts, in this section of the book, have been made on the basis of emphases and themes in Heliopolitan theology that survived into this next stratum of Egyptian literature. These selections (1) pertain to general theogony and the emergence of trinitarian theology as Atum, Shu, and Tefnut; (2) pertain to the soteriological functions of Isis and Horus, effective at Level 5; and (3) belong to the ensuing process of overt theologizing and latent philosophizing. In conjunction with our previous exposition of selected Pyramid Texts, the present selections from among the later Coffin Texts will add another level of comprehension concerning the broadening ancient Egyptian context. They will enable us to embellish our historical understanding of Hellenic philosophy, of Neo-Platonism, of the origins of Christendom, as well as of what became known as competitive trends in Gnosticism.

Theogony and Cosmogony

Some of the most informative sentences concerning Heliopolitan theogony and cosmogony in the published Coffin Texts are found among Spells 75, 76, 78 and 80. Then, Spell 80 is the most explicit and deserves to be quoted up front in larger than ordinary installments. The method to be followed for its exposition does call for a presentation of paragraph-size quotations, followed by commentary and discussion.

O you eight Chaos-gods, being truly Chaos-god of the two Chaos-gods, who encircle the sky with your arms, who gather together sky and earth for Geb, Shu fashioned you in Chaos, in the Abyss, in darkness and in gloom, and he allots you to Geb and Nut, while Shu is everlasting and Tefnut is eternity. I am the soul of Shu at the head of the celestial kine, who ascends to heaven at his desire, who descends to earth at his wish. Come joyfully at meeting the god in me, for I am Shu whom Atum fashioned, and this garment of mine is the air of life. A cry for me went forth from the mouth of Atum, the air opened up upon my ways. It is I who make the sky lighten after darkness, my pleasant [azure] color is due to the air which goes forth after me from the mouth of Atum, and the storm-cloud of the sky is my efflux; hail-storms and dusk are my sweat. (Spell 80)[34]

These opening words are put in the mouth of Atum, the "Soul of Shu." He addresses the remaining Chaos-gods as being contained in his own Ninefoldness. Inasmuch as, together with Atum, the remaining eight gods of the Ennead have also risen from chaos or Nun, the entire Heliopolitan Ennead consists of Chaos-gods. The second phrase still addresses all the remaining gods, but it acknowledges that they are one in number at Level 1, and that there are two of them at Level 2. Together, Shu and Tefnut form a triune unity with Atum, the All-Father. As such, their arms embrace sky and earth and hold them together as the next explicit parental unit in which life was to be generated and made possible. Shu, the masculine manifestation of Atum, has fashioned the other gods in Chaos, at Level 2 symbolism. He represents the creative hill or phallus of Atum that, it is said, rose from Chaos (Nun).

We also learn that the tenures of Shu and Tefnut together are everlastingness and eternity. Accordingly, in hope of its own eternity, the soul of a deceased person identifies with these divinities who, initially, contained all the primeval stirrings and all the energies of life. Mystic identification with Shu makes sense. He is air and life. To the extent that the god Shu is air, it follows that he also em-

---

[34]Unless otherwise indicated, English quotations of Coffin Texts are from R. O. Faulkner's translation, *The Ancient Egyptian Coffin Texts,* Vol. 1 (Warminster, England, 1973), by permission of Aris and Phillips Ltd. By quoting from his translation, only Faulkner's rendition of "Tefenet" has been changed to the more widely used Tefnut, and "Ma et" has been adjusted to Mahet.

bodies the very life-breath of Atum. The living breeze of Shu also brings light after darkness, at dawn, and while doing so, he radiates a pleasant color. His masculine temper occasionally erupts in hail-storms whereas morning and evening dew, it would seem, are his own gentle sweat.

The portion of Spell 80 that follows next is central to understanding the dawning of the Tefnut manifestation as Mahet. Atum has generated Shu and Tefnut, and in all likelihood, the order and containment by Mahet are here identical with that of Tefnut. For the two goddesses, Tefnut and Mahet, to achieve Atum's desired degree of separation and duality of divine names, Faulkner was obliged to disregard the predicated use of "Mahet" earlier. Compare the words: "her (Tefnut's) name is Mahet." Concerning Tefnut, he therefore translated "rightousness is her name." In our next installment from Spell 80, it will become clear that Mahet is indeed identical with Tefnut.

Also, at the beginning, Atum quite clearly decreed creative together-ness for his twin offspring, Shu and Tefnut. Shu is air, wind, breath, and life, whereas Tefnut is containment and righteous order (Mahet). But no sooner than the creative union of Life and Order has been determined by the Godhead, he continues to reflect on his intimacy with his children—as a union and expression of himself. The goal of this self-union of Atum, of the primal trinity, is the procreation of Geb and Nut—that is, Father Earth and Mother Sky.

Atum said: Tefnut is my living daughter; she is (will be) with her brother Shu. His name is Living One; her name is Mahet (Order). I live with my two children; I live with my two fledglings. For I am before them; they are behind my body to lift (me up). I live with my daughter Mahet: One (feminine) is within me; one (feminine) is behind me. I have raised up upon because of them; their two arms are behind me. It is Geb who will live, he whom I begat in my name. (Spell 80)

I have obtained a fresh translation for this passage because Faulkner's rendition assumed, wrongly I suspect, that the text refers to the manife-station of Atum as Geb. He insisted that mythologically this son would be Shu. This sort of disjunctive reasoning about ancient Egyptian theology is what has obscured for modern readers the ancient Heliopolitan riddle of life. In the larger scope of Enneadic theology, Geb was not born as an estranged or separate entity; he is never seen as being less than an emanation or manife-station of Atum and Shu. Geb is only somewhat farther out from the All-Father than his Father

Shu.[35] As Father Earth, Geb is made to appear a little more specific and concrete, that is, more visible than his immediate sire Shu, who still represents Life or the less visible breath-soul of Life. We must realize that in the Heliopolitan scheme of things, where generations of divine creative phalluses are fused as manifestations of a single primeval rising hill, a "grandson" always remains a son, and a son, in turn, continues to emit the essence of his father through his son. So, who is within? Who is behind? Who rises? Who embraces?

We are faced here with a marvelously convoluted puzzle, specifically, with the Heliopolitan riddle of cosmos and life. As one might expect, this puzzle of creation had to be stated in an inverse mode from the familiar puzzle that all along has been attributed to the Sphinx. The Sphinx is an afterworld guardian, caught up in a human and a mysterious animal existence, between the realms of the living and of those who continue to exist in a state of twilight transform-ability, beyond prehuman and postmortem flux. The Sphinx naturally belongs to the Turnaround Realm, at Level 5.

Accordingly, the riddle of the Sphinx, to King Oedipus, pertained to aging and mortality. And, true to her station in the scheme of things, this Sphinx traditionally killed her victims and therefore needed to be defeated to complete the plot of her own narrative.

But here is the much greater riddle about Atum as the source of all life and being. It pertains to the secret of the All-God's mode of creation, to his generation and his love, and to the intelligence that he inspires. How does one go about answering this riddle? What, ontologically speaking, is the creative dynamic that courses in the first Trinity of the Heliopolitan Ennead—in Atum, Shu, and

---

[35]Retranslation of this section of Spell 80, by Professor Garth Alford, is gratefully acknowledged. Translator's Note: sdr means "lift up" when used with sky determinative. May also read "(to) lift (me) up! So that I may live with my daughter Mahet." Author's Note: The two "feminine ones," who are mentioned in all the extant texts, appear nonetheless to refer only to a single "one." This text presents a case of synonymous parallelism; for example, "she is within me; [as] she is behind me." "Within me" seems to refer to Tefnut as being within Atum prior to her emergence. "Behind me" seems to refer to her two arms embracing, as lover, i.e. embracing Atum in the form of Shu. This much is suggested by what follows.

Tefnut? Can there perchance be found in the *Kama Sutra* an analogous posture or relationship? Or perchance in the *Perfumed Garden*? There is no need to make this ancient Egyptian riddle of divine life and existence any more complicated than it really is. Those who composed these Coffin Spells were human beings. There is no need to scavenge extravagances. First, the phrase "I have raised up upon because of them" surely links up, as do all risings in Atum's realm, with the original rising of Atum as primeval hill and creative phallus. However, in the present symbolic mode, the "hand" of Atum, which served to give him creative pleasure in the context of Level 1 symbolism (see *Pyramid Text* 1248) is here transferred appropriately to Level 2. The All-God's hand has become the arms and embrace between Shu and Tefnut. Shu is the life-energy that issued forth, and Tefnut is the containment, order, and firmament—hence a womb emanation of "hand," which Faulkner hesitantly has translated as "righteousness." Indeed, righteousness in the sense of orderly containment, is a delimiting factor—is what is meant when Tefnut is referred to as Mahet.

It must be obvious that this entire passage narrates a single event, the procreation and generation of Geb and Nut by Atum. For that purpose, Atum has appeared in the mode of his first Father-Son-Daughter (Atum-Shu-Tefnut) trinity. It should also be obvious that both Shu and Tefnut are manifestations of Atum at a given level of emanation. The generative Atum contains and, in turn, is embraced lovingly by both. It is equally obvious that the existential scope of Geb and Nut is made manifest, in a still more specific and more visible mode than the initial scope of Shu and Tefnut together. In turn, the offspring of Geb and Nut become manifest next and smaller on the scale; they have become manifest more clearly at the lower and more visible frequencies at Level 4.

The answer to our riddle lies at hand. Indeed, this primeval embrace of one, two, and three divine personages, with arms—and with confidence one may even add the legs—embraced the primeval Atum, who as primeval hill and phallus was contained within that selfsame embrace, namely, within a single unit of divine creative pleasure. Atum's phallus—and much of what we have discovered already in the Pyramid Texts—is present on Shu as well, for the purpose of creation.

Nu(n) said to Atum: Kiss your daughter Mahet, put her at your nose, that your heart may live, for she [they] will not be far from you; Mahet is your daughter and your son is Shu whose name lives. Eat of your daughter Mahet; it is your son Shu who will raise you up. I indeed am one who lives, son of Atum; he has fashioned me with his nose, I have gone forth from his nostrils; I have put myself on his neck and he kisses me with my sister Mahet. He rises daily when he issues from his egg which the god who went up shining [has] fashioned .... My father Atum kisses me when he goesforth from the eastern horizon, and his heart is at peace at seeing me; he proceeds in peace to the western horizon, and he finds me in his path. (Spell 80)

One Coffin Text variation of Spell 80 utilizes the plural form "they." Indicated parenthetically in the first sentence, Faulkner judged it to be an error. However, "they" may have been intended because the statement forthrightly continues to tell about Mahet and Shu. In the preceding discussion, already, we have suggested that the closeness of these two divinities has been all in relation to Atum. Moreover, we have learned from the present selection that Atum has not only kissed his daughter with his kiss of life, but he has done the same also to his son Shu. At this point in the reading there should no longer be any doubt that Mahet is indeed identical with Tefnut. Other coffin inscriptions, such as Spell 121, support this conclusion as well. The deceased, whose death has been the occasion for having inscribed in the coffin this most complete of all theogonic spells, should not be faulted for having contemplated Tefnut with an emphasis on her entire order-righteousness-wisdom-Mahet dimension. After chaotic moments of death, the ordering efforts of Mahet were expected to restore order as well as life. But whence came Atum's idea to the effect that he should kiss his daughter, or to the effect that his Shu and his Tefnut aspects should be united? This notion, we are told here, originated already while Atum was still hidden in Nun, in chaos. The original Nun somehow "knew" a thing or two about the chaotic potentiality of Atum's breath and about his potency of rising.

But then, whence did Chaos (Nun) know all these things? Perhaps it would have been wiser for our ancient author not to have attempted to explain the deepest creative mystery of Atum. At some point during ontological learning and speculation, human questions and answers will fall silent. Human minds cannot handle infinite regress. Life that is divinely given, carries within itself its own delights and sources for chaos, as well as acceptable order.

Life, or *ka* essences rising, resurrected *ka* essences soaring homeward and trailing their temporarily visible "comet tails" or *ba* appearances, this is what the Coffin Texts are all about. Atum rises daily; his emissions of *ka,* in the form of light-rays of the Sun-god Ra, demonstrate this fact. The dead look up to this divine manifestation for conveyance to travel home upon, in the direction of Atum. In contrast to his bright Ra manifestation, the hidden aspect of Atum is implied by his daily retreating into darkness and into gloom. The Ra-rays of Atum continue to give the primeval kisses that the Godhead began giving while he himself was still coiled up in gloom. These rays are intended for those among his offspring who have come forth, to live for a while in sunlight.

Our excerpts and exposition of Spell 80, which pertain to theogony and cosmogony, may be supplemented with quotations from Spells 75, 76, and 78. In various Coffin Texts, the god Shu is mentioned as though he were more important than his father Atum. This, of course, is so because Shu is the god of life and breath. During funerary proceedings, by which the effects of death are to be checked and overcome, the god of breath is in great demand. The practical funerary concern spilled over into theogony when, as an answer to the demands of mortal minds, the generative role of Atum became increasingly associated with Shu. The mythological basis for transposition, naturally, was the credo about Shu continuing Atum's emission, or his spitting.

I am the soul of Shu the self-created god, I have come into being from the flesh of the self-created god. I am the soul of Shu, the god invisible in shape.... I am merged in the god, I have become he. (Spell 75).

The unique status of Shu is based on his parthenogenetic origin. He issued directly from his Father. Atum conceived him by himself, with his own "mouth." He spat out Shu and Tefnut together to be born. Shu's primacy is getting established further by the fact that Tefnut emerged "after" him. In addition, Shu's attributes are identified as being breath of life or, more anthropomorphically, as being the breath of life that has come from Atum's throat. The eye of Atum sought out Shu and his sister Tefnut. This hint probably refers to the mythic moment when the two began mating as a pair:

I [the deceased] indeed am Shu whom Atum created, whereby Ra came into being; I was not built up in the womb, I was not knit together in the egg, I was not conceived—but Atum spat me out in the spittle of his mouth together with my sister Tefnut. She went up after me, and I was covered with the breath of the throat. The phoenix of Ra was that whereby Atum came into being in chaos, in the Abyss, in darkness and in gloom. I am Shu, father of the gods, and Atum once sent his Sole Eye seeking me and my sister Tefnut. (Spell 76)[36]

The two action metaphors of seminal emission and spitting were used separately in the Pyramid Texts (1248 and 1652). From that point on, each metaphor appears to have engendered its own train of conceptualization and of ritual responses. And so Atum's hand and phallus led the myth makers to imagine the discovery of a series of mating twins. On the other hand, Atum's spitting mouth encouraged speculation about air and breath, and eventually, this line of speculation evolved to mean the spoken divine command or logos. Spoken words are but breath made audible. This we shall find expressed clearly in Memphite theology in the next chapter. From the point of view of a dead person, Shu as god of life is understandably the most significant divine personage mentioned in funerary spells. On that account, he also is the one who is most clearly introduced. He is air, breath, and life. By contrast, the naturalistic equivalents of Tefnut are a little more difficult to make out. Spell 78 is significant because it supports what we have learned about Shu, and in addition, it gives us a fresh hint about the nature of Tefnut and her destiny to become the mother of Atum's creation. As her brother Shu does elsewhere (cf. Spell 80), so here Tefnut "shines on the gods."

---

36 Western readers who have difficulty appreciating these mystic identifications of Egyptian souls with their saving deity, and of the gods with one another, are advised to recall a saying of Jesus: "Before Abraham was, I am" (*John* 8:58), or "I and the Father are one" (*John* 10:30). These claims of Jesus, whether they were his own or whether they were later ascribed to him, sound completely reasonable in the context of ancient Egyptian ontology and discourse.

It appears that Shu's ability to shine has been a direct extension of Atum-Ra's "Phoenix in Heliopolis" (Pyramid Texts 1652). For Shu, it is the "flame of the fiery blast" and is his radiant emission, whereas the shine on the countenance of Tefnut, mentioned subsequently, appears more like an afterglow in the feminine experience of that same event.

I am this soul of Shu which is in the flame of the fiery blast which Atum kindled with his own hand. He created orgasm, and fluid (?) fell from his mouth. He spat me out as Shu together with Tefnut, who came forth after me as the great Ennead, the daughter of Atum, who shines on the gods. (Spell 78)

The priestly mind that composed this spell was well in tune with combined Shu and Tefnut mysticism, but obviously, it seems out of touch with the original metaphors that applied to Atum specifically. The priest who composed this particular spell was plagued by conscientious literalism. He no longer understood how phallus and mouth were alternate expressions for phallus and hand. His was a mind that hoped to eliminate ambiguity by way of rationalizing and harmonizing the distinct ejaculation and spitting metaphors. The result was a third metaphor, of masturbation, culminating in auto-oralism which, among us latecomers to theological analogies, may not seem to be much of a semantic improvement.

Soteriology in the Turnaround Realm

In Coffin Text Spells 131 and 335, and in other places, the god Seth is mentioned as the one who causes death. This attribution is based on the fact that, mythologically, Seth is known to have been the killer of Osiris. By extension, he also is the one who slew every moribund Egyptian pharaoh since that first creative event. And by further extension usurpation of status from the royal cult, by lower ranking folk, during the Middle Kingdom and later, Seth became the cause of death for other ranks of humankind as well. Accord-ingly, Isis the twin sister of Osiris, and even Nephthys the twin sister of Seth, became known for providing encouragement:

"Raise yourself, O my brother, so that your heart may live and that Seth may not exalt over you." (Spell 74)

The homeward-bound ancient Egyptian soul could identify with the "great soul of Osiris." This soul, as sexual opposite of Osiris, continues to enact the role of Isis, true to orthodox mythological perspective. Previously the gods commanded Osiris, to copulate with his twin sister as with his own soul [*ka* plus *ba*]. The theogonic background certifies this soteriological option:

"Go forth and copulate with your soul," say all the gods. (Spell 96)

By virtue of Osiris's participation in the primeval copulation, a momentarily deceased person for whom this spell was inscribed has likewise been remade "into his (i.e. Osiris's) living soul, according to the word of the gods."

It may be surmised that most ordinary Egyptian folk, later on, had no ambitions for being reborn as the actual Horus, as if coming forth from Isis and being destined to sit upon the throne of Egypt. They therefore also had no need to identify specifically with Osiris's emission of seed that, ceremonially, was transmitting a divine spark of life to the would-be imperial Horus successors.

Ordinary people focused their mysticism on the process of copulation itself. They interpreted the union of Osiris and Isis mystically as the God's loving embrace of their own souls, as though their souls were somehow feminine partners in this relationship.

Of course, it is also possible that Spell 96 was intended and inscribed first on behalf of a deceased woman. In that case the contrary identification with the male offspring of Isis, with Horus (as in Spell 84 and elsewhere), could be interpreted as a "masculine" variety of spells. However, it appears far more likely that the Enneadic sexual union of Isis and Osiris itself has furnished the existential model for the human soul's surrender to, and union with, the Godhead.

Reasoning in Egypt about the mystic-sexual union of Osiris and Isis, in accordance with Heliopolitan coronation theology, produced real offspring. Moribund human minds could hurry on to a quick solution and then think of themselves as liberated *ka* sparks, as having, subsequently as well as momentarily, been reborn from Isis. Joyously they could proclaim their Second Birth. "I have issued from between the thighs of Isis as Horus." (Spell 84)

Then, being sent on their way by the birth waters of Isis, the returning soul could, analogously, be seen as "going out into daylight"; it could be envisioned as swimming homeward. This swimming homeward after having been reborn cosmo-biologically, constitutes a reversal of direction from the original generative seminal emissions of Atum. In the lower Turnaround Realm, at Level 5, Seth has stopped Horus. By way of killing him, Seth has turned him around and promoted him to the condition and status of Osiris.

The role of Isis accomplishes similar turn-around results. By way of giving birth to Horus, she stopped and reversed the flow of seminal emissions that had come her way from the masculine Atum-Shu-Geb-Osiris alignment. Birth from a female is the beginning of a process of swimming back against the current of masculine emission —and in the larger context, also against the general current of Atum's generation. These mythic-biological facts brought reborn and homeward-bound Egyptian souls to a point where they could continue to swim home within, and against the current of Isis's birth waters.

> O Horus of the Netherworld, you have swum to Pe [the cult city of Horus], and the gods who were given to you by Atum have swum after you, the men who are among them have followed you, the women who are among them have turned back faint through you and through your seed, O Osiris.... (Spell 74)

Although this passage remains opaque at some points, several interesting notions can be gleaned from it. Those who swam after Horus were given and sent by Atum—and whatever Atum sends belongs, cosmo-biologically, to his emission and to the procreation of his divine offspring, so much so that at this moment in the process, the mourning women, too, can be thought of as still swooning from the seed of Atum. Of course, a Horus who enters the netherworld is no longer a Horus; he has been promoted to the full Enneadic rank of Osiris. By identifying with the virility of Osiris, as is suggested by the effect he has had on the women mentioned in Spell 74, the deceased person becomes involved, implicitly, in the general procreative activity of the Godhead. It therefore can be argued that the "swimming" metaphor of rebirth persisted as a close parallel to the initial mystic-sexual union of Osiris and Isis.

Even the best of swimmers in Egypt, along the River Nile in which crocodiles may formerly have been plentiful, was tempted to dream of a safer alternative to travel by swimming. Human salvation and the journey home to God were not immune to temptations from technology. There is an alternative to salvation by swimming. It requires rowing a boat. Accordingly, in Spell 181, Isis no longer gives birth or only stops the water-of-life current in her ordinary feminine way. Isis is mentioned as rowing a boat upstream.

Engaging Isis as a ferry lady seemed a little far fetched to another way-ward soul. His or her coffin spell preferred to seek salvation in traditional Osiris-Isis mysticism. But a mystic union with Osiris, on the part of a human soul who had learned to identify with Isis, needed to be properly augmented with cooperation from her off-spring. Salvation for souls who knew themselves as Isis, and who needed help with rowing across the waters of death and rebirth, was better left to the divine son whom the friendly goddess was able to persuade:

> "I am Isis; I have gone forth from my house and my boat is at the mooring-rope; Horus ferries me over, Horus brings me to land. (Spell 182)"

Our data are insufficient for discerning whether switching the ferry personages, Isis and Horus stood in some kind of relationship to the gender of the deceased. Perhaps this question does not really matter. Being ferried by either Isis or Horus serves as a euphemism. It is a way of claiming salvation by virtue of being "sired by Osiris" and "born of Isis" into the larger family of gods and God.

There is an inherent difficulty in the soteriology of rowing yonder. Mythologically, Horus is a king and a falcon. Egyptian kings, that is, Horus-kings existing in prehuman flux twilight, would occasion-ally avail themselves of the boats and services of oarsmen, but falcons prefer to fly and to soar. Therefore, another Coffin Spell begins to reason afresh, at the point of traditional Osiris-Isis mating mysticism:

> Isis wakes pregnant with the seed of her brother Osiris. She is uplifted, (even she) the widow, and her heart is glad with the seed of her brother Osiris. (Spell 148)

Sometime later, Isis "goes down to the Releaser who brings Horus," who apparently is delivering Isis by hastening Horus to be born.

The soul of a dying person, which is about to emerge from its bodily containment, now experiences being born of Isis, as a consequence of experiencing death as birth pangs. The proud Horus-soul promptly introduces itself as a "leader of eternity," with confident words:

"See Horus, you gods! I am Horus, the Falcon who is on the battlements of the Mansion of Him whose name is hidden... my place is far from Seth, the enemy of my father Osiris. I have used the roads of eternity to the dawn, I go up in my flight." (Spell 148)

The one "whose name is hidden," in this passage is the single Godhead of the Ennead who later in the history of Egyptian religion became known specifically as Amun, the Hidden One. The ontological mansion of this source of all being is located far from his distant Sethian hypostasis, that is, far from the lesser god of death who roams along the outermost perimeter of the Enneadic emanation.

Sooner or later, the god Seth wounded every Horus-king who ruled ancient Egypt and, invariably, transformed all of them into Osiris corpses. But then, this episode in Heliopolitan Turnaround mythology was followed by the miraculous impregnation of Isis, by Osiris or by Isis herself. Isis, in turn, has given birth to a new Horus-Falcon king. In ancient Egyptian religion, this very mythology and ritual facilitated succession on the throne of Egypt and also helped establish new dynasties. In the democratized personal soteriology, during the Middle and New Kingdoms, this same Turn-around mythology was invoked to stop and to reverse the wayward drift of the All-God's creative emanation for common folk as well. Upon having encountered Seth somewhere along the lower and outer edge of the divine Enneadic emanation, all human souls or *ka* sparks could be reborn, freed, and turned homeward. They could be liberated to swim, or to fly home against the current and the counter swirls of Enneadic generation. A number of spells inscribed in Middle Kingdom coffins insist emphatically that their inhabitants rejected the natural conditions that the gods traditionally have imposed on dead humankind. For instance, some mortals expressly put down their foot and refused to accept conditions of death, as these could have affected their appetites. They insisted on an older, more primitive version of salvation—on salvation that annuls reversals wrought by death. They refused to walk upside down or to eat excrement, even if the excrements were of the god Osiris himself!

"Eat this excrement which issued from the hinder parts of Osiris; what (else) can you live on?" say the gods to me. "What have you come to eat?" (Spell 173)

Reversal of living space and alimentary processes are commonplace in primitive notions about afterlife. Indeed, such a limited and primitive victory could seem sufficient if one's homeward journey led only to an afterworld in horizontal space. Was it really necessary for the human soul to immerse itself mystically in the entire Enneadic stream of life? Flying and soaring in the air certainly seemed preferable to the person who selected Spell 173 to be inscribed in his coffin.

He or she continued to eat the food of the living, as well as continued the habit of flying aloft—and thereby watched Egypt from on high. Impossible? Not if you are the divine Horus-Falcon yourself:

"I eat of bread and of white emmer ..."
"Be off!" say they to me. "Who pray are you?"
"I am Horus on his tall perch(?)." (Spell 173)

From Theology to Philosophy

The priestly rites and activities that dealt with human mortality, and with prospects for eternal life, inspired confidence in dealing with the gods directly. Some priests relied on methods of bureaucratic bluffing that had served them well in the environs of the Egyptian royal court. Vis-à-vis humans and gods, they learned how to function as skillful politicians, theologians, and magicians. Not many Egyptian mortals would have dared to boast in their coffins with ambitious spells such as the next one. But this particular chief magician knew all too well how Egyptian theology had been stitched together through the ages:

I am indeed the son of Her who bore Atum, I am the protection of what the Sole Lord commanded, I am he who caused the Ennead to live, I am "If-he-wishes-he-does," the father of the gods.... I have come that I may take possession of my throne and that I may receive my dignity, for to me belonged all before you came into being, you gods; go down and come upon the hinder parts, for I am a [chief] magician. (Spell 261)

These words constitute the ultimate in a mystic's daring among Egyptian Coffin Spells. This homeward-bound *ka* did not even think to bother with lesser gods like Horus, Isis, Seth, or even Osiris. He went straight home to identify with the Source of all Being: he identified with the very power that generated Atum's first appearance and emanation. This chief magician—or shall we call him a chief systematic theologian? He knew how imperial theology was reasoned and how it was amended and expanded through time. He understood the process by which greater gods do absorb smaller ones. He even understood the secret of how to transpose theology into psychology.

This magician was an If-he-wishes-he-does kind of "Father of the gods." He knew that if one wished to influence, control, or usurp a present divine power, one either had to be, or had to identify with, the next greater power on whom such a present power depended. She who bore Atum—if such an All-Mother was ever thinkable in ancient Egypt—must have been the chaotic and indefinable Nun herself. Thus, from his exalted point of self-esteem this head-strong returning soul, of a theologian, was a coequal partner of Atum. He commanded all gods to "go down and come upon the hinder parts"—to approach him on their haunches.

Fortunately for Atum's primordial status, this haughty magician or systematic theologian remained humble enough to not also claim identity with "Mother Nun" herself. Looking at the positive side, it may be said that with this man's passing, the Godhead Atum has welcomed back a confident collaborator of his, for the totality of his process of generation. In his own ancient wise Egyptian way, this chief magician either became divine himself or helped to humanize the Egyptian cosmic "All-God" with help from Helipolitan pious logic. His exaggerated mysticism may sound like blasphemy. But if that is what it was, then his spell differed from others in ancient Egypt, which also sought salvation in identification with Atum, only as a matter of degrees—of degrees pertaining to the amounts of a mortal's own ego-assertion.

Daring and selfish priests tend to become magicians. Doomed as they are to perform labors of the mind, as *Homines sapientes,* they perform, they question and try to improve inherited rituals. But then, contributions to human life made by boisterous challengers are sometimes of a negative sort. Great ideas, that can sustain human balance and survival, have most often not been hatched from conventional thought-embryos. Nearer to the heart of an orthodox ontology, still clothed in orthodox garb, great new ideas may be adopted tentatively to represent simple common-sense updates. Here happens to be such an instance:

Oh, you eight Chaos-gods whom I created from the efflux of my flesh, whose names Atum made when the Abyss was created, on that day when Atum spoke in it, with Nu(n) in chaos, in darkness and in gloom. (Spell 76)

Atum created the gods by naming them. Spoken from the point of view of the self-created first God, Atum, all the remaining eight members of the Ennead can also be designated as the eight Chaos-gods who, back in Chaos, together with Atum, began to form the Ennead. And these were created first as names. But in addition, a rational adjustment had to be made in funerary spells in light of the fact that Shu, the Son, frequently was honored as the god of life in place of Atum his All-Father.

Inasmuch as all life known to humankind could be traced back through Shu, it seems significant to learn from Spell 76 that the names of all gods—thus also human ideas about them—were thought of first by the one and only Atum, while he was still alone in Nun. The ancient Egyptian sage who composed these lines surmised that divine ideas and intelligence in the Enneadic process must have preceded the throbbing creative commotions of Shu and of those that followed. They must have preceded life and breathing. They also must have anticipated subsequent contemplative efforts among Egyptian Homines sapientes. The category of intellect has here been given precedence over empirical presences. Rational thinking demanded such a self-aware perspective for the well-being of its own process and maintenance.

In Spell 76 can be found the important seed concept that well over a millennium later, in Greece, blossomed into Platonic philosophy—into Plato's theory of preexistent and eternal "Ideas." Still later, turning homeward in the direction of ancient Egypt, a "New Platonism" was conceived. Ancient Egyptian emanation ontology blossomed anew in Alexandria, and gave birth to a genuine fruit of

Egyptian intellect, the so-called New Platonic philosophy of Ammonius Saccas and his student Plotinus. It turned out to be ancient Egyptian ontology and theology, philosophized in the idiom of Greece. It has then spread abroad as Hellenism and Christianity.

Transition to Chapter Seven

He is Amun [the Hidden One whose name is hidden], who saves whom he will, and be it from the Netherworld.... He lends his eyes and ears to the path of anyone whom he loves.... He hears the prayers of those who call on him; he comes momentarily from afar to him who calls out for him... He lengthens and shortens life, and he adds something extra to the destiny of those whom he loves....

(from Leiden Amonshymnus--Restoration Period, after the Amarna Disturbance)

Before human minds were ever enabled to think about
equality or about equal human dignity,
some "Greater-than-Human Reality"
has taught the notion of "equality" for humankind, has
shown intentional love, and has imprinted such love onto
human memories--nowadays explained vaguely as the
accomplishment of "egos" and "instincts."
Any portion of love or value that mortal-kind regenerate
for themselves, by their own volition, lasts
less than a lifetime.

(Author Comment)

7

Other Ancient Egyptian Theologies

This chapter will introduce four ancient Egyptian theological systems, beginning with those of Hermopolis, Memphis, and Thebes. Our discussion of the Theban system, which represents New Kingdom theology, will also include a brief digression into the Amarna episode.

Amarna theology will be considered here in a subordinated manner, intentionally. Of all the ancient Egyptian monotheisms mentioned in this book, the Atonism of Akhenaton is perhaps the least significant. It nevertheless needs to be included here, because Western scholars have propelled it into prominence for the wrong reasons—and certainly to the detriment of our overall understanding of ancient Egyptian religion.

The Theology of Hermopolis

The ancient city of Unet in Upper Egypt, "Hermopolis" in Greek, is known as the home of an Ogdoad of gods.37 This Eightfoldness of divine creative personages, apparently in competition with Heliopolitan theology, came to be structured as four pairs of male gods with female partners. First is Nun, the primeval water, which co-exists with Naunet. Second, Huh, or spatial infinity, is matched with Hauhet. Third, there is Kuk, or Darkness, matched with Kauket. And fourth, Amun, in his Hiddenness, is matched with Amaunet. Some sources name instead Niau and Niaut as the fourth pair.

At some point in time, the priests of Hermopolis must have felt confident enough to challenge their Memphite competition. They moved what Memphite theologians incorporated under the names of Nun and Naunet into their understanding regarding the God-head, Ptah.

---

[37] Most commentators on Hermopolitan theology draw from Kurt Sethe, "Amun und die acht Urgötter von Hermopolis," *Abhandlungen der Preußischen Akademie der Wissenschaften* (1929: 4).

The Thebans on the other hand claimed Amun, and possibly by implication also recognized the Hermopolitan Amaunet as the spouse in union with that same hiddenness.

Early Hermopolitan documentation is scarce, and the personages of an Ogdoad are mentioned first in a Coffin Text.[38] In any case, it is difficult to tell which of the three cults—Hermopolis, Memphis, or Thebes—first tried to absorb one or both of the others. For as little as is known about the Hermopolitan cult, the possibility cannot be ruled out that Memphite or Theban theology were indebted to it.

The Theology of Memphis

A brief glance at the theological system of Memphis is essential for a larger perspective on religious trends in ancient Egypt. Our source is the famous Shabaka Stone, an eighth century BCE copy, or summary, of an alleged older text. For Memphite theologians, the name of the God of gods was Ptah. Whatever this Memphite god was before his imperial ambitions became apparent, whether or not he was Lord of Memphis or only of that city's artisans, remains unclear. We know that at one point in the history of New Kingdom theology, someone contemplated the great Ptah of Memphis, and doing so beheld again the All-God of Egypt.

Some scholars have projected the Shabaka Stone theology back in time to the beginnings of Egyptian history. This leap into the past, beyond 3 millenia BCE, was suggested by the fact that Memphis had been Egypt's first capital city. It served as residence for Menes, the founder of the First Dynasty. But such a generous historical backward projection leaves insufficient scope for the Heliopolitan system to develop and become better established by comparison. Heliopolitan theology dominated ancient Egypt at least by the time the great pyramids were built (2589 to 2504 BCE. During the reign of the Hyksos kings (1720-1540 BCE), the cult center at Heliopolis was still regarded as primary, in Lower Egypt.[39] Still later, during the reign of Ramses III, its budget far exceeded

[38]Hans Bonnet, *Reallexikon der Ägyptischen Religionsgeschichte* (Berlin: Walter de Gruyter), 1952; and Adolf Erman, *Die Religion der Ägypter* (Berlin and Leipzig: Walter de Gruyter), 1934, 5. Much of the Egyptian data for this survey section have been gleaned from Sethe and Bonnet, and from others mentioned earlier. 39 Cyril Aldred, *Akhenaten, King of Egypt* (London: Thames and Hudson), 1988, 237.

that of temples in the capital city of Memphis. The center at Heliopolis may finally have been destroyed by Cambyses, the Persian.[4] All of this, taken together, may recommend the reign of Tuthmoses I (1494-1482 BCE as a time for the formulation of the prototypical Shabaka Stone theology. This would have been a time when Memphis again had come to be the capital of Egypt. It would have been a reasonable moment for priests of Ptah to have made their bid for primacy among the theologies and cult centers in the land.

Shabaka Stone theology, as it has been preserved, constitutes an obvious usurpation of Heliopolitan theological claims. But even at our present level of historical uncertainties, the Shabaka text may serve as a good sample of the larger Egyptian process of theological and political reasoning.

Memphite priests introduced their god Ptah as having existed prior to Atum, as well as being greater in scope. Ptah completely absorbed into himself the chaotic mystery of Nun that all along, and though undefined, had been presupposed for the entire Heliopolitan process of divine procreation. The duality composed of Ptah-Nun or Ptah-Naunet—it was recorded—begat and generated the Heliopolitan Atum. In Memphite perspective, the god Ptah was considered to be "the heart and tongue of the Ennead" as "the one who gave birth to the gods."[41]

Whether Memphite or Hermopolitan priests were the first to seize on the Heliopolitan weakness of an undefined first Nun is now difficult to assess. In any case, at Memphis as well as at Her-mopolis, the category "Nun" was doubled by encapsulating the entire Heliopolitan system of theological meaning in the chaotic wrapping of the cosmos. For the evolution of Nun, its capacity was expanded to absorb within itself every other Egyptian Theo-logic. Prior knowledge on the part of Memphite theologians about the political importance of the Heliopolitan Ennead, with Atum as Godhead, may be assumed. This awareness is reflected in the most conspicuous Shabaka Stone passage:

---

40 Bonnet, *Reallexikon der Ägyptischen Religionsgeschichte,* 543ff.

41 John A. Wilson, trans., in *Ancient Near Eastern Texts,* ed. James B. Pritchard (Princeton, NJ: Princeton University Press, 1969), 5 (48). Subsequent quotations from the Shabaka Stone text are taken from pp. 4-6 of this source as well.

"There came into being as the heart and there came into being as the tongue something in the form of Atum."(p. 53)

This sentence must be one of the cleverest theological pronouncements ever devised. It bristles with priestly ambition and soft diplomatic fur. Memphite priests may have wished that the tradition of Heliopolis would disappear from the face of the earth and make room entirely for their own. However, it is significant that on account of such wishes, they never dared to deny the existence of Junu's Godhead. They simply told their Memphite story a little bigger; that is, big enough to absorb the Helipolitan theology within their own. The Shabaka Stone text sets the tone for Memphite theologizing. "Something in the form of..." means that Atum is not someone just mighty enough to worry about. His "centrality" has not been denied, of course. That would have been un-Egyptian. His name was simply absorbed by a prior and apparently larger Ptah-Nun-Naunet trinity.

All creative power, in Ptah theology, can be traced by concrete symbolism, as thought and as word, all the way to the heart and the tongue of the God. The claims of the Memphite God of gods were thereby expanded to include all living creatures under the variety of Ptah's intimate *ba* manifestations, that is, as thought-sparks of his *ka* that by emanation became visible and audible as *ba*:

The mighty Great One is Ptah, who transmitted [life to all gods], as well as (to their *ka)*, through this heart, by which Horus became Ptah, and through this tongue, by which Thoth became Ptah. Thus it happened that the heart and tongue gained control over [every other] member of the body, by teaching that he is in every body and in every mouth of all gods, all men, [all] cattle, all creeping things, and (everything that lives, by thinking and commanding everything that he wishes.) Indeed, all the divine order (lit. "every word of the god") really came into being through what the heart thought and the tongue commanded. Thus, the *ka* spirits were made and the *hemsut* spirits were appointed, they who make all provisions and all nourishment, by this speech.

Those among us within the Abrahamic traditions, who have spent some time wondering about "creation" as a result of divine command —as it is narrated in *Genesis* 1—or those who have contemplated the nature of the divine logos in *John* 1, will recognize this Memphite text as an obvious antecedent. And indeed, this Memphite story of creation tells us something about divine behavior that we have come to expect.[42] And so, Ptah was satisfied, after he had made every thing, as well as the divine order.[43]

But more is implied in this Memphite theology, and some of it shows the less comfortable side of Egyptian religion. This overplus is the factor of hyper-domestication. As far as it mattered to his human inferiors, the person and will of an Egyptian pharaoh coincided nicely with the will of the supreme God of gods. Ptah's creative thoughts and words and the judgments of a deified pharaoh were one and the same thing, even though they each supposedly operated at different levels of divine emanation. As a result, the king's claim to authority over the lives of his subjects was absolute. Memphite theology rationalized the authority and power of its deified pharaoh rather sternly:

Peace and death was given to him who has sin. So were made all work and all crafts, the action of the arms, the movement of the legs, and the activity of every member, in conformance with (this command which the heart thought, which came forth from the tongue, and which gives value to everything.... Thus, justice was given to him who does what is liked, and injustice to him who does what is disliked. Thus, life was given to him who has peace, and death was given to him who has sin.[44] Thus were made all work and all crafts, the action of the arms, the movement of the legs, and the activity of every member, in conformance with (this) command which the heart thought, which came forth from the tongue, and which gives value to everything.

The function of imperial theology, as constitution and justification for Egyptian hyper-domestication, becomes entirely clear as the list of Ptah's founding activities is enlarged. A reader of these theologically

---

[42]Even if the most recent copy-date of the Shabaka Stone (Eighth Century BCE) is assumed, the text is still a few centuries older than the corresponding Hebrew priestly source of Genesis 1.

[43] Or, "and Ptah rested, after he had made everything, as well as every word of the god." Paraphrased: "as well as every divine creative command."

[44] For American usage, Wilson's "injustice" probably should be translated more freely to read "punishment," or "justice" in the sense of "judgment."

rationalized sentences ought to keep in mind that whatever this creative God of gods was given credit for, some reigning Horus-Falcon-King felt called upon to own and to manage.

(Ptah)... has formed the gods, he has made the cities, he has founded nomes, he has put the gods in their shrines, he has made their bodies like that (with which) their hearts were satisfied. So, the gods entered into their bodies of every (kind of) wood, of every (kind of) stone, of every (kind of) clay, or anything which might grow upon him, in which they have taken form. So, all the gods, as well as their *ka* units gathered themselves to him, content and associated with the Lord of the Two Lands.

Shabaka Stone theology is historically significant for two good reasons: (1) for illustrating ancient Egyptian ways of theologizing, of how Atum-oriented theogony was recast into Ptah-oriented theogony, and (2) for showing the transition from an orthodox generative theogony to a cosmogony based on the creative divine word, logos, or command of God. The first of these reasons pertains to the history of ancient Egyptian religion, whereas the second affects our understanding of subsequent counter-currents against the Egyptian hyper-domestication religion. The second aspect casts fresh historical light on Hebrew religion and on such later universalisms as Judaism, Christendom, and Neo-Platonism. The transition from Atum-oriented to Ptah-oriented theogony, most probably, was the concern of city-based schools of priests that vied with one another for the attention of Egypt's religiously contained population.

Memphite theology really added nothing new to the conceptualization of Egypt's basic theogonic process, that is, nothing new concerning the Godhead who emanates his essence down to an outer boundary with more visibility and therefore less reality. Nothing was really new about the concomitant soteriology either. The primary bone of contention was not the basic structure of Enneadic monotheism or process theology; rather, it concerned the question of whose city deity might be politically exalted and magnified to lend its name to the unnameable Godhead of Egypt—and which city, by extended reasoning, would bestow the God's mandate on the ruling king as a legitimate son of Ptah.

The priestly cult center that was able to rationally embrace all other Egyptian theologies could aspire to become the cult center of the empire. Its high priest could become the first minister of the state cult. In such a high priest's divinely favored city, the nobility could calculate from that fact, mythologically and ontologically, their chances of eligibility for divine-royal status—for the eventuality that near the top a vacancy, a political weakness, should occur.

However, Heliopolitan theology has been a longstanding tradition, that for centuries and millennia was able to embrace and to contain within itself all rival cults and theological alternatives. To capture the religious life of all of Egypt, the Shabaka document had to be stretched, to absorb in itself everything that ever was thinkable about Atum, the All-god.

The primary weakness in the Heliopolitan theogony was that it ascribed the name of Nun to chaos—that it ascribed any name at all to that "Nothing." If Nun was really of no consequence whatsoever, then it should have remained nameless. Names are nesting places—i.e. handles—for fresh ontological configurations. This is so because it is linguistically impossible to talk about nothing, or about Nun, without somehow suggesting its presence as a "something." Moreover, "some thing" that happens to appear as a First, in time, is already pre-positioned to become a First in rank as well—sooner or later.

Theologians at Heliopolis named the Nun and then left it undefined and orphaned, to be seen as a next-to-nothing kind of chaos. The Hermopolitan theologians grasped at this weakness; they talked about Nun and proceeded to help discover its gender-opposite Naunet. Why should a First that multiplies have been single? And why could a freshly defined Nun, which enwrapped a creative Ennead, not have been somehow pro-creative to begin with? The priests of Ptah therewith enabled themselves to own the Egyptian theogony at a point where the Heliopolitans began their story. They wrapped all first manifestations of the All-Father into that which they already knew to be their local Ptah. As a consequence, and from the start, their reformulations implied political and cultic sovereignty for Memphis. They reduced the Heliopolitan All-God, his Trinity and his entire Ennead, to a smaller aspect of the larger story. All that was needed then, to begin their God-story, was the divine name that they owned. They thereby could fill the cavity that existed in their theological vocabulary. Or shall we refer to it as vocabulary "of their political theory and ontology"?

Mythologically and symbolically, the Memphite theology first shifted its emphasis from an ejaculation metaphor to a spitting metaphor, which by itself was no radical shift. Some Heliopolitan priests had done as much. Heliopolitan priests refined their spitting metaphor to mean exhaling forth the essence of Shu—thus breath, air, and life in general. As an extra hint, they had Atum emit an audible moan or "cry."

Memphite theologians, in principle, subscribed to all of this. They merely added the specific notion that the breath of their Godhead, Ptah, resounded with voice and with distinct words. In addition, they insisted that these divine words were vocalized as creative commands—implicitly on behalf of the first capital city of Memphis.

Gone was the soothing flow and divine emission of living water which, in Egypt, was experienced concretely as the regularly overflowing Nile—gone with a few stylus scratches. In Hebrew it was replaced with narrated creative commands of Yahweh which, somehow, coincided with the daily commands of some anointed king. All the while, for thousands of years, back in Egypt, pharaohs continued to sit on their thrones as eternally begotten sons of God, speaking divine commands.

The Godhead named Ptah has created specifically with the application of his logos (Word), and this, in accordance with Memphite theology, included the king's royal commands. For all practical purposes, and for the pharaoh's subjects, the logos of the Godhead and the logos of the ruling God-king were indistinguishable. In break-away Hebrew tradition, the first creation story in the book of *Genesis* begins with divine command as logos. This divine command of creation was issued in the context of Yahwistic rebel-theology. It was introduced without the need of having to legitimize the commands of a sitting deified human king.

Regarding the major differences between Hebrew and Egyptian monotheism, our assessment distances itself from commentators like Henri Frankfort who, for instance, has sharply distinguished between theological immanence and transcendence. Frankfort saw "immanence" as a factor that reduced the quality of ancient Egyptian religion. Thus, even while he recognized Amun-Ra as an otherwise "supreme and universal God, known within the scope of Egyptian polytheism," Frankfort remained more impressed by a divinity who thrones as a cosmic monarch, above and beyond earthly events. All the while, he recognized a positive tendency toward theological transcendence in what he praised as Ptah's "spiritual" method of creation by thought or word.[45]

Comparisons and evaluations of the type that Frankfort has offered, obviously, are based on a double standard. After all, the breath (Heb. *ruach*) blown as wind into Adam's nostrils by the Hebrew God, was it any less material than the Egyptian air of Shu? Were the creative commands of the Hebrew God, in *Genesis* 1, more spiritual than the commands of Ptah? Or were the words that came from the heart and the tongue of Ptah more spiritual than Atum-Shu's still mostly wordless breathing? Is a sovereign transcendent God less material when, for contrast, his influence addresses human minds that remain encased in flesh and bone?

It is time for historians of religions to become reconciled with Planet Earth and its materiality, upon which, and by which, we all live and move and have our being. Historians cannot afford to sympathize only with so-called "spiritual" half-religions that appear to be in tune with post-philosophical Indo-European dualism—or with so-called "atheistic" revisions of the Judeo-Christian vocabulary.

Several centuries after the book of Genesis had been edited for the last time—after the Seven-Day story of creation had been included—Christians broke away from their Hebrew environment. One of the major Christian narrators, John, began his gospel account with a wonderfully poetic logos-cosmogony. In the prologue to his gospel, John carefully avoided allusions to *logoi* (in plural), which could have made it easier to include human kings who harbored northern dualistic orientations in their propaganda schemes. On the contrary, he identified the creative Word of God with a Counter Son of God. This divine Son was sent into the world, specifically to enact a parody of light on the legitimized predator roles of Horus-Falcons, on princes who ruled Egypt and derivative empires by force, as princes who ruled by spreading fears of Darkness and Death. These rulers conquered their realms as predatorial beasts, by violence. They maintained slavery and spread gloom.

---

45 Henri Frankfort, *Ancient Egyptian Religion: An Interpretation,* (New York: Harper and Row), 1948, 22f.

The Christian retention of the ancient logos idea, to refer to the creative Word of God, was part and parcel of the prophetic rejection of imperial hyper-domestication theology. Instead, it signified free-for-all universal salvation, manifest in the dawning of the Kingdom of Heaven.

More remains to be said later in this book about the slippery slope between Egyptian grand-domestication religion, as that ancient ontology slid toward its Christian antithesis. But before that history can be told in greater detail, it is necessary to re-examine outbreaks of Hebrew "fire" and reflections of Hellenic "wisdom" along the larger Egyptian boundaries of "light and gloom." Only, let it be said, that against the background of Egyptian theology it no longer can be said that the Christian religion was merely, or even primarily, a compliant offspring of general Semitic religion, or of Judaism specifically—or that it ever was "spiritual" in conformity with Frankfort's dualism.

Introduction to the Theology of Thebes

The city of Uaset, which was named after a province by that name, is on record since the Middle Kingdom. Occasionally, it has been referred to as "Southern City" or as "City of Amun." The historical references to the god Amun cannot be traced farther back than the Eleventh Dynasty in Thebes. But we know that the cult was well established during the Twelfth Dynasty (1991-1786 BCE). Was this god in his first Theban manifestation a modification of the god Min? The head-dresses of Amun and Min are similar. Or did awareness of him begin with Amun-Amauet as a theological branch of the Hermopolitan Ogdoad? Or was Amun claimed rather spuriously by political Hermopolitan theologians?

The resistance and liberation movement against the Hyksos occupation of Lower Egypt proceeded under Ahmoses I, from Upper Egypt and Thebes (Eighteenth Dynasty, 1567 BCE). With this important event, the hidden god Amun—manifest in history—ushered in Egypt's "New Kingdom" era. In that process, the All-God known as Amun was established as Egypt's supreme patron, liberator, and sovereign. Egypt always tried to be a Kingdom of God. The Amun cult was seen historically, by minds that have begun to think internationally and that were inspired by an upsurge of anti-Hyksos and anti-Habiru national pride.

The Amarna Interlude (1370 BCE)

Amun's hegemony was interrupted briefly during the fourteenth century by a religious "reform" attempted by the pharaoh Akhenaton (Amenhotep IV).[46] This king hoped to institutionalize a narrowly defined monotheism, centered on the solar deity. "Aton" as sun deity and focal point of fascination is known in Egypt since the beginning of the Twelfth Dynasty. It became frequent during the reign of Amenophis III, Akhenaton's predecessor.[47] At the reform king's new capital Amarna, this brand of sun worship was institutionalized. Had Akhenaton succeeded in spreading his reform cult, he possibly would have tried to purge most of Egypt's ancient prehuman flux transformational-ism—together with much of its monotheistic process theology that was predicated on emanation.

Akhenaton's worship of Aton featured Ra theology in a restrictive mode. Cyril Aldred, finding fault with Petrie's interpretations of the typical Amarna depictions, calls attention to the fact that the rays of the Aton "do not give life to all persons, but bring its breath only to the nostrils of the king and queen."[48]

Indeed, Amarna hymnody makes that same point. Anyone who ponders the king's beautiful hymns, composed specifically for the royal worship of Aton, discovers in them more than religious devotion and poetic beauty. Had these stanzas been written by someone of low status, their theological tilt would have remained of little concern. But authored by, or ascribed to, an Egyptian king who claimed Son of God status for himself, the narrow scope and self-centeredness of these hymns, do evoke suspicion.

Their narrowness must have raised apprehensions among all Amun theologians in Egypt at the time. In none of Akhenaton's hymns is God ever approached as one who would stoop low enough

---

46 The liberation of Lower Egypt under Ahmoses I, from Semitic occupation, gave rise not only to anti-Semitic feelings in Egypt. Within a few centuries, it appears to have begun echoing as Hebrew anti-Egyptianism under the semi-legendary figure of Moses. The latter bore a plain Egyptian name that could have been ascribed for contrast, and in opposition to, "Ra-Meses."

47 Aldred, *Akhenaten, King of Egypt*, 239. 48 *Ibid.* p. 111.

to bless someone other than his chosen and beloved son, the pharaoh Akhenaton himself, together with Nefertete, his beautiful spouse. In fact, the entire wonderful world of Aton's creatures is said to have been created for the express pleasure of this king. No allowances were made in Aton liturgy for any concern in the land that did not concern this pharaoh personally. There also is no evidence that, preoccupied as he was with the religious legitimization of his divine-royal authority, this king was capable of recognizing anyone else's needs. The closing stanza of his Great Hymn to Aton is sufficient to expose the narrow vision of this would-be reformer:

Figure 13. The Pharaoh Akhenaton, Egyptian Museum. Photos and composition by the author.

You are in my heart. There is no other who knows you,
Only your son Neferkheprure, Sole-one-of-Ra,
Whom you have taught your ways and your might.
[Those on] earth come from your hand as you made them,
When you have dawned, they live. When you set they die;
You yourself are lifetime, one lives by you.
All eyes are on [your] beauty until you set,
All labor ceases when you rest in the west;
When you rise you stir [everyone] for the King,
Every leg is on the move since you founded the earth.
You rouse them for your son who came from your body,
The King who lives by Maat, the Lord of crowns,
Akhenaten, great in his lifetime; (and) the great Queen

whom he loves, the Lady of the Two Lands.
Nefernefru-Aten Nefertiti, living forever.[49]

Akhenaton's monotheism—if such selfish usurpation of God's created world by a single human ego deserves this appraisal—reveals, if nothing else, the loneliness of a hereditary and beleaguered grand-domesticator. It exposes his monotheistic solar theology as a feeble attempt at trying to become an absolutist divine Sun-king. To accomplish his goal, he had to rid himself of the religious checks and balances that, in the course of Egyptian history, came to be used to humanize government and to safeguard at least some of the interests of common people. Akhenaton, as pharaoh, wanted to shake off the largest "check and balance" that weighed on him: the Theban cult of Amun. This cult was represented by Amun temples throughout Egypt and beyond, and it had the support of many people. No doubt, Akhenaton would rather have ruled Egypt under a God who created the entire world just for him.

Thebes: The Return of Amun (Amon)

The religion and priesthood of Amun outlived Akhenaton's attempt at royal entrenchment, and Egypt probably was better off as a result of this king's failure. This is not to say that Amun's Thebes-based priesthood was the first of its kind in Egyptian history that stood apart from, or against, the Egyptian God-king. It appears that very early, at Heliopolis, Egypt had an imperial cult center that stood in something like a check and balance relationship to the royal seat at Memphis. The dichotomy of Thebes and Amarna was only a more recent example of the ancient hyper-domestication tensions and conflicting check and balance arrangements. The general emphasis that ancient Egyptian cult centers placed on funerary proceedings, underscores the dynamics of religious balancing.[50]

---

[49]Mriam Lichtheim, *Ancient Egyptian Literature,* 2 (Berkeley: University of California Press, 1976), 99.

[50]Donald B. Redford, in *Akhenaten, the Heretic King* (1984), judged the king's fascination for the sun disk Aton as constituting "atheism;" he read Horemheb's subsequent "Edict of Reform" as an indictment of Akhenaton. It lists what went wrong in Egypt during the reign of Akhenaton (p. 225). However, atheism was not necessarily the foil to Akhenaton's monotheism. Horemheb probably would have labeled "atheism" any religion that disagreed with his own theology. At stake in pharaonic religion was first the ruler's mandate. Divine endorsements, required to stabilize the social order, were not all known to justify his mandate at the outset.

After all, funerary rites are excellent occasions to celebrate the balancing of a royal strongman who willfully and violently might have pushed ahead too far during his lifetime.

Kings gained leverage and power whenever a neighboring political entity flexed its muscles. Heroic citizen defenders, of necessity, were lured into reinforcing their lord's hyper-domestication scheme by self-interest to increase their defense and protection. Then, once a strong leader dared to raise his head above the limiting norms of religious traditions, he also had no other choice but to seek greater organizational stability. He was obliged to do so for his own personal safety, as well as for the fulfillment of his divine-royal ambitions of hyper-domestication, greed for power, and authority.

It shall not be suggested here, in any shape or form, that good priests always kept bad kings in check. Balanced institutions generate their own share of ambitious and corrupt people. Nevertheless, that a zealous and jaded ruler eventually was checked by the Amun cult which appears to have represented a wider range of people—as the history of the Amun cult suggests—is in itself historically significant.

Before Aton and after Aton, in ancient Egypt, flourished the cult of Amun (Ammon). During Akhenaton's reform years, the cult of Amun was forced underground. Nevertheless, as seen from the perspective of Theban theology, the military and iconoclastic measures of Akhenaton never could inflict real damage on Amun. After he had removed the name of Amun from his own coronation name *Amen-hotep IV*, the reform king ordered that inscriptions of the name Amun be erased from temples and public buildings throughout the land. But he could never touch and remove the real name of the God who, as all the God's faithful admirers knew, was kept hidden from everyone. The All-God continued to hide his name under his cover name "Amun." It simply meant "the Hidden One."

The Leiden Papyrus

Amun theology, after Akhenaton, is nicely expressed in a document stored at a museum in Leiden. A quick reading will reveal at least one of the heights to which the pseudonym Amun was exalted in Egyptian awareness during the New Kingdom. Not only were priests of Amun active in their temples throughout the Egyptian empire, we can infer that their cult of the hidden God also responded better to the existential aspirations of greater numbers of Egyptian people, or at least with more personal attention than the Aton cult implied. In contrast to royal snobbishness, legitimated by Aton at Amarna, the relevance of Amun's mystery and hidden-ness, is noteworthy for all humans and human status levels at Thebes.[51]

Like all imperial gods in Egypt's past, Amun accounted for, and embraced, all there is. He was the power of growth in vegetation. But this God of gods also stooped to lower social levels. He stood by mortals throughout their lives and in their hour of need. Earlier in Egyptian religious history, such lowly functions had been left to lesser local gods. In the New Kingdom, such benign concerns for mortal humanity had become part and parcel of the general grace and demeanor of the supreme hidden God of gods. Amun became known as one who "drives away evil and illness"....

He is Amun who saves whom he will, and be it from the netherworld.... He lends his eyes and ears to [protect] the path of anyone whom he loves.... He hears the prayers of those who call on him; he comes momentarily from afar to him who calls out for him.... He lengthens and shortens life, and he adds something extra to the destiny of him whom he loves.... Amun's name, when called upon, is mighty on the waters; the crocodile has no power when his name is spoken; the wind changes, and the storm subsides when one thinks about him.... He is better than millions for him who keeps him in his heart, and with his name a single one is mightier than hundreds of thousands; the truly good protector ... is the irresistible [one in battle]. (66f.)

Amun's indebtedness to earlier imperial theologies is evident in many ways. And yet, earlier Egyptian theologians never have come up with a better description of the All-God:

He who has given shape to himself, his form is unknown, that beautifully shimmering (hue of) color which has become a beautiful but

---

[51] The subsequent discussion of Amun theology is based primarily on this Leiden Museum source. Quotations in English were translated from Adolf Erman, "Der Leidener Amons-hymnus," in *Sitzungsberichte der Preußischen Akademie der Wissenschaften 11* (1923): 66f, 70f, 73. Erman has assigned this document to the Restoration Period of Amunism, after Akhenaton (p. 81).

secret form—the one who gave shape to himself and who did create himself.... The eight gods were your first manifestations. Before them you alone hast been.[52] Your body was made secret to the ancients, you, who hast hidden yourself as Amun, as the first among the gods. You assumed the form of Tenen (primeval Hill) to give shape to the first gods of the primeval era.... The Ennead together, (the Nine) were in your members; in your form were all the gods united. Your first form by which you have begun was Amun—namely, he who hides his name from the gods.... When Ra arose in the sky, to rejuvenate himself again, he, Amun spat forth ... to create Shu and Tefnut to be joined. (70f). Atum at Heliopolis became Amun at Thebes.

The Godhead's hiding, together with the obscurity of his name and his general compassionate involvement in human affairs at every stratum in human history, is highlighted by a number of characteristics that scholars customarily have reserved for the God Yahweh of the Hebrews. The Israelite schema concerning the one-ness of their God was spoken somewhat earlier by Egyptian worshippers of Amun:

Amun is one! (He) who hides himself from the gods.... whose nature is unknown.... His nature is not recorded [or displayed] in sacred scriptures; he cannot be described and taught. He is too mysterious for his power to be laid bare; he is too great to be even asked about, too immense to be perceived. One would fall dead suddenly, in fear, if one were to pronounce the god's mysterious name, unknown to everyone. Not even a god can call him by his name... because his name is secret. (73.)

The All-God of ancient Egypt, in essence, has always been invisible to human eyes. Over the millennia, he has been referred to by various names. But "Amun" never was thought of as being the God's real name. It simply meant "the Hidden One." With Amun's actual hiding, his name took on additional meaning during Akhenaton's purge. By trying to obliterate the name "Amun" from all public monuments in the land, this king contributed to actually strengthening the cult of Amun—by demonstrating how he could not erase the name of this hidden deity. The status of Amun was magnified during the Amarna Period, rather than diminished. The irony is that Akhenaton

[52] The eight gods of Hermopolis, perhaps? They could as well have been the eight subsequent manifestations of the Godhead Atum, in Heliopolitan theology.

initially needed to purge a reference to Amun even from his own mandate and coronation name—which was *Amen*hotep IV.

Meanwhile, a dynamic holy Trinity was acceptable to Theban priests as easily as an Ennead was deemed by priests at Heliopolis (p. 32). The difference between polytheism and monotheism becomes here a rather insignificant issue. Human minds understand, what little they do understand, by way of grappling with and comparing the pluralities they find in this world. To finite analytic predator minds, a plurality of ineffable greater-than-human manifestations will occasionally appear real—to the extent that such unity still underwhelms its beholders religiously, as well as mathematically.

Arithmetic comes to the aid of ontology and of systematized science. Sooner or later a greater-than-human reality, conceptualized, insists on being recognized as an ineffable Singular. Trying to insist on the almightiness of a divine unity—as in the case of a sorely needed god of war. Getting overpowered by death also tends to recommend monotheism. This posture enables Homo sapiens to deal with reality more easily by counting as far as One. By contrast, Atum, Shu, and Tefnut required counting to Three, and the full Ennead permitted lengthening the God-story to Nine. Centuries before monotheism dawned in ancient Israel, Theban religion has been insisting on the singular unity of Amun. And in the Leiden Hymn to Amun, a path was cleared to count logically as far as Three, while thinking One—theologically as well as politically:

Three are all the gods, Amun, Ra, and Ptah. Aside from these is none. He who hides his name behind the pseudonym "Amun" is Ra at his head, Ptah at his body. His cities on earth are eternal: Thebes, Heliopolis and Memphis, forever (p. 73).[53]

Quoted from a religion that was pronounced dead millennia ago, this Trinitarian proclamation still resounds vibrantly alive. It radiates confidence, magnificence and awe. To some extent, it even appears politically transparent.

The ancient Israelite monarchy displayed Theban Amun-temple architecture at Solomon's temple in Jerusalem. At both the Theban

---

53 Inasmuch as thinking in ancient Egypt was believed to happen in the heart, mental functions of the deity likewise were credited to happen within Ptah himself.

and the Jerusalem temple, the hidden God lived in a recessed and hidden Holy of Holies chamber.

Judaism, with its Schema, "Hear or Israel, the Lord your God is One," generated most of its priestly authority by reducing theological and political wiggle-room to a single integer—One. All the while, the politically sagacious priests of Amun, at Thebes, sharpened the *f-stop* from the "One" to numbers "Thee," "Eight" and "Nine."

Early on, the Christians focused their theology with an arithmetic of Three. Eventually they needed to add an extra step, or *f-stop* and include a fourth name along their scale of faith. Some recognized Mary, Queen of Heaven, as a replacement for Isis—who apparently had been missed.

The excessive northern "spritualization"—of thinning out the entire concept of Tefnut into a Holy Spirit—has left the larger feminine Tefnut-Nut-Isis dimension of reality under-represented in early Christianity. The question, of whether the three members of the Christian Holy Trinity are a person, three persona or aspects, integers or fractions, was left for future mathematically inclined theologians to argue. Regarding the nature of greater-than-human reality, no satisfactory human conclusions have ever been reached mathematically, neither by way of remaining stuck at One, nor by counting to Two, Three, Four, Eight, Nine, or farther.

Part Two:

Hebrew Holy Fire and Smoke

The God of Fire

*...appears to have been recognized by humankind
between three million and one million years ago.
The first alpha shaman who dared to liberate Fire,
for it to live among and to interact with
humankind, surely became an instant semi-divine
celebrity. Early covenants and mandates were
obtained in the presence of this divine epiphany,
by the hands of first shamanic mediators,
by priests of Fire.*

8

Levites, Prophets, Patriarchs and Kings

The Monotheism of Moses

The ancient nation of Israel commemorated its escape from Egypt as the moment of its birth. Its Exodus, we are told, was inspired and accomplished with visions of fire. First there was the fire of God's holy presence that the supposed Levite-Egyptian aristocrat Moses saw when he noticed a bush aflame in the desert. Then, concerning Israel's Exodus from Egypt itself, we are told that:

> The Lord went before them by day in a pillar of cloud to lead them along the way, and by night in a pillar of fire to give them light. (*Exodus* 13:21)

The backdrop for Yahweh's covenant with Israel, his issuance of divine laws in mediation through Moses at Sinai, was introduced and draped by divine fire as well:

> And Mount Sinai was wrapped in smoke, because the Lord descended upon it in fire; and the smoke of it went up like the smoke of a of a kiln, and the whole mountain quaked greatly (*Exodus* 19:18).

Some Bible stories hint that before they were written on animal skins, narratives credited to the man Moses might have been filtered through several centuries of oral tradition. The narratives got filtered through the creative minds of multiple generations of storytellers. The present shape of the Moses stories may not have been finalized until seven or eight centuries after the events that are narrated. Like premium wines, so also stories in various linguistic environments or "yeast cultures" will ferment and get better with age. Surely, the God of ancient Israel made plenty of time available for Torah stories to improve, to settle and to get a little clearer.

All the while, it is not the primary purpose of this book to either prove or to refute textual roots. Many scholars are laboring on these tasks. Our goal calls for a broader orientation. We hope to detect a few patterns of Egyptian context, influence and aggravation, that could have affected Israelite, Judaic or Levitic religious and political reasoning. Gaps among meanings in historical narratives often become loaded with arbitrary generalities—to the chagrin and discomfort of historians who think their craft establishes certainties.

Ancient historical source materials often do not provide a clean demarcation between actually experienced and politically desired events. But even while portions of the historical landscape remain shrouded in clouds of the political dialectics, the nature and flow of the Hebrew rivulet, of religious and political faith that drifted from the shores of the Nile, through Palestine and along Mediterranean coast-lands, still can float some reasonable ancient connections and contexts to the surface. There may still be found stretches of time from which clearer patterns of historical data can be skimmed.

The Story of an Egyptian Hebrew

Apart from Hebrew scriptures themselves, we have no evidence that an Egyptian-named man, Moses, the leader of Israel's Exodus who appears in books that anciently have been ascribed to his very authorship, has ever lived as an author or as a central personage in Hebrew history, or both. Not many authors manage to die and centuries later publish their story of departure. Such a feat was long thought possible, and the man Moses is said to have accomplished it. We also do not know how much actual history we can ascribe to the Exodus Event itself. Self-serving cult documents are insufficient to establish historical certainty. Over the course of thousands of years, countless points of fresh rationalization can creep into ancient narratives. It is necessary to look sideways, past the general track of narrated sequences, to glean more information from other complexities in Hebrew literature, concerning habits of story-weaving and from along tracks that archaeologists may have been able to expose to daylight.

The composition of literary texts itself remains a historical datum that begs to be understood. It is not enough merely to distinguish certain plots in ancient texts to be either certainty or fiction.

A full historical inquiry hopes to discover motivations and aims. Exaggerations were written to impress. An ancient document, sponsored by a king or a dynasty can scarcely be free of political goals or intentions. It will be necessary to weigh metaphors within the context of their own claims and contexts. People do not write fiction simply because their elders taught them to write. There were practical reasons why some story plots begged to be enhanced with "How things happened as they did" or "Why things could not have happened differently." For educating Homines sapientes, and for effective teaching, story plots needed to be kept relevant and be maintained within familiar patterns of contextual reality.

In the course of a career that included collecting oral religious traditions, worldwide, this writer has noticed that storytelling happens everywhere along the rim of a living socio-political landscape. Cryptic reporting, metaphors and profitable exaggerations are interrelated. Goal-directed preaching and political propaganda are present in all formal teaching. Whether or not the heirs of an ancient literature appreciate their inherited plots, all texts ask to be scanned for historical depth as adjustments to paroles and slogans. In oral traditions, stories are remembered and retold for timely relevance, not to celebrate bygone storytellers.

Oral traditions are rivulets that flow, and they change directions. They add and drop story content rather easily. This author has seen ancient myths change shape from one shamanic Navajo Indian raconteur to another—within the same oral tradition and the same clan of shamans—driven primarily by a desire to communicate something relevant. Innovations were appreciated. Oral scientific traditions, as well, get altered from one scientific report to the next, depending on how much understanding one's apprentices or competitors are able to demonstrate. An inquirer, who understands the context at a Kindergarten level, can expect to be given answers that resonate at his or her level of cognition.

Improving a story for better communication is a rational process in itself. It provides hints about the momentary cultural context. Analogies and exaggerations are part of the normal process of communication. Imagine, for a moment, how Albert Einstein would have explained relativity to ten-year-olds. Political and religious analogies, or metaphors, are being told at various depths to revise or to steer alternative political and/or religious opinions.

Ancient or foreign traditions can only be understood in light of elaborate historical contexts, with the help of historical reconstructions and narration. The practical intentions of ancient scribes, for their readers, can only be inferred with broad hindsight.

Independent of what modern scholars regard to be good practice, for separating religious subject matter from secular politics or economics, in actual processes of living and reasoning, a variety of perspectives must be brought to fit together as coherent knowledge. Similar concerns can be negotiated in both, the languages of religion as well as in the languages of politics. Facing greater-than-human realities and targeting smaller tasks or situations are both necessary for survival. The general "meaning of life" that individuals are wresting from ordinary living must also include insights learned during emergencies. Rationalized memories, supporting hopes and strategies for survival, of mutual encouragement and of shedding fears, are as important as finding nourishment and shelter.

The epic of Israel's Exodus from Egypt, as recorded in the book of *Exodus,* begins with introductory events of a time when the "People of Israel" were not yet slaves in Egypt. In a wider historical context, this epic also refers to a time when these people were not yet a united group. Later scribes composed the story of how somewhere along the bank of the Nile River a Levite baby-boy was set out in a reed basket. The baby was found and adopted by the pharaoh's daughter, who raised him as her child in royal surroundings, and presumably gave him his Egyptian name, "Moses."

Inasmuch as a similar exposure of a baby, in a reed basket, has been ascribed to the first Mesopotamian imperialist, Sargon of Akkad, the literal historical weight of the Moses story will have to be adjusted downward—tentatively and independently of the political significance it had for the royal House of David, centuries later. I am now inclined to classify this story as a strategic political novella. Was this story told first to establish the credentials of Moses as a great hero of Sargon's stature? And if so, why would later Israelite scribes have wanted to rationalize the Egyptian-ness of a man known as royalty with an Egyptian name, forthwith presented as a look-alike Akkadian-style hero? Was he an Egyptian? While the story tells about the birth and the early months of a Moses-child in Egypt, it also leaves a large question-mark hanging over the biological relatives of this man.

The hunted outlaw, Moses, was escaping Egypt. He was accepted by tribal oasis dwellers who accepted him first as an in-law and then as a leader. He was rumored to be someone who had been raised along the margins of the Egyptian imperial court and who has blended in. Such considerations may never have been offered to answer real historical questions. They could as well have been musings about how the Israelite self-identity has gotten embellished, later in Palestine, with a tale of how a Hebrew trickster has managed to play God and outwit superstitious Egyptians.

The story explicitly tries to link the man's birth to his activities later in life when as a leader, stirred by God, he managed the escape of a group of enslaved Hebrews. Telling the personal story of Moses was not the primary reason for telling the Exodus narrative. The primary character, the man Moses, was made to disappear at the end of the narrative under rather obscure circumstances, even more mysteriously than he had been introduced into the story.

However, the larger story plot of the Exodus was given meaning a few centuries later, in Palestine, where a group of people celebrated their escape from Egyptian slavery as a divinely managed event. To a high degree, this narrative exudes political strategy, reasonable propaganda, and quite obvious religious legitimization for assembling unite-able tribes into a monarchy.

We are told that Moses, at a mature age, one day observed a Hebrew man being beaten by an Egyptian overseer. Moses sided with the underdog and killed the Egyptian supervisor. In fear of punishment he fled to Midian, an oasis in the Sinai desert, to the east. A priest named Jethro took the Egyptian fugitive into his home and gave him one of his daughters in marriage. She bore Moses two sons.

One day, so the narrative continues, while watching the animals of his father-in-law, Moses saw an unusual sight: an "angel of fire" burning from inside a bush. Miraculously, the fire did not consume its branches. Ever since his flight from Egypt, Moses may have wondered about his obligations toward the Hebrews who still languished and suffered back at an Egyptian labor camp. His thoughts might have been fueled by the memory of his violent act. To justify his murder of an Egyptian official, the man Moses was prone to react eventually. He was divinely challenged to upgrade his status from being a common fugitive from Egyptian justice to becoming an honest liberator of slaves, in political exile.

But let that be as it may be. From the burning bush Moses has heard the voice of God, and this voice informed him of the divine intention that Hebrew slaves should be freed from the fetters of Egyptian hyper-domestication. Then and there, God commissioned Moses to approach the elders of these subjugated Hebrews in Egypt, with a saving proposition:

You and the elders of Israel shall go to the king of Egypt and say to him, "The Lord, the God of the Hebrews, has met with us and now, we pray you, let us go a three-day journey into the wilderness, that we may sacrifice to the Lord our God." (*Exodus* 3:18

The implied reason for which God enlisted the services of a leader, who was familiar with proceedings at the Egyptian royal court, is rather transparent. Moses's strategy was to hoodwink the pharaoh with a ruse of citing religious obligations. Moses, and elders from among the Hebrew slaves were to request a furlough from work, on the pretext of having to perform religious rites to their God who, as Seth, dwelt in the Sinai desert by Egyptian reckoning. The pilgrimage pretext is refreshed with typical novella-like naivete, when the pharaoh gave permission for a portion of the people to leave. Moses rejected a partial Exodus and insisted that all Hebrew slaves were required, by their God, to go on this pilgrimage together. But why would a real pharaoh have agreed to half an Exodus to begin with?

In Hebrew opinion, the stated objective of doing religious service in the Sinai desert was amply substantiated later, as the Exodus epic unfolds. The people's service to their God, who dwells outside Egypt, was intended to last for all times. With the hindsight of tradition, it had to be that way, or else Moses could be accused of having paraded before the pharaoh, telling a strategic lie.

Apparently, Moses (or at least his narrator) held some initial hope for a diplomatic solution, to the end that a degree of religious freedom for slaves could be negotiated with an Egyptian pharaoh. And if ever on earth there was a man who could negotiate religious privileges for slaves in Egypt, it would have had to be someone like Moses who understood Egyptian imperial management and how slavery was rationalized theologically. Such a spokesman for minority rights would have had to be familiar with Egyptian theology, as well as with implied political theory. He would have known that these were the same thing. He would have had to be acquainted with the ways of Egyptian as well as with Hebrew religion. And he would have had to know how to leverage the differences that existed between them.

Yahweh as Amun

After we are told by the primary narrator how God has introduced himself to Hebrews as "Yahweh *(YHWH)*" in *Exodus* 3:7-8, apparently another hand wrote in greater detail (*Exodus* 3:9–15), perhaps for readers who were unfamiliar with the God's manner of referring to himself with a word symbol that was not a name. We are told in this Levitic narrative that the designation "Yahweh" was ascribed to the God of the Hebrews at a crucial point in their history, precisely in preparation for their Exodus from Egypt. If Moses was really an "Israelite," why did he need to ask the God of Israel for his name? Was it something that needed to be mentioned specifically for communication with Hebrew slaves in Egypt? Or was it intended to unify them, later, with Israelites who never were in Egypt? In any case, the first question that a thoughtful Levite priest would have needed to answer, hailing from Egypt or Midian, concerning the divine name is conveniently put into the mouth of the man Moses who, all told, asked God as directly as he could have asked:

If I come to the people of Israel and say to them, "the God of your fathers has sent me to you," and they ask me, "What is his name?" What shall I say to them? God said to Moses, "I Am Who I Am"—Yahweh. And he said, "Say to the people of Israel, 'I AM has sent me to you.'" (*Exodus* 3:13–14

Devout readers in later Judaism avoided reading the letter configuration YHWH aloud, because it signified the unspeakable name of God. Here it seems as though, somehow, the ones who followed Moses out of Egypt primarily understood the original lesson of Egyptian Amun theology, that the name of the hidden God is not to be pronounced—on penalty of death. According to what else their Egyptian leader Moses probably knew regarding this sacred dictum—that no human being knows that name anyhow—his Hebrew followers therefore needed not have worried excessively. It was a straight-forward Egyptian theological detail.

Earlier, in Chapter Seven of this book, in the context of Egyptian theologies, we have shown what an Egyptian aristocrat around the time of Moses could have learned about Amun. It was not possible to pronounce the supreme God's real name. Not even the lesser gods, who were divine manifestations of angelic rank, who surrounded the hidden essence of Amun, knew the Hidden One's real name. The chances of ordinary humankind ever getting to know and to be able to pronounce the real name of God—to the extent that he resembled Amun—were equally remote. The word symbol YHWH, or I AM WHO I AM, was not a name. If anything, it would have been an acronym that amounted to God gently telling Moses off. The Holy Name is not for you to know!

The Exodus story narrates the story of Moses, as a leader of Hebrews, as someone who has been born to Hebrew parents and who lived the early decades of his life as an Egyptian aristocrat in royal surroundings. If the second part of the written story is accepted as a historical possibility, and I see no reason why it could not be, it follows that this man, Moses, also must have been well versed in traditional Egyptian political theory. Throughout Egyptian history, the disciplines of Political Theory and Theology were one and the same.

Theology, at a deified ruler's court, was the elevated and divinely empowered style of communicating about politics and government. Moses, the aristocrat—or whichever Levite later told this story about Moses to Israelite and Judaic peoples—appears to have understood this aspect of contemporary Egyptian Amun theology.

Startled by a spectacular fire and an anonymous divine call, Moses asked for assurance that he would be able to finish the job, which long ago he had begun with an act of violence. Even though he asked his question on behalf of Hebrew elders who lived in Egypt, he needed clarity for himself. He needed to shore up his self-confidence and to fortify his authority and impact.

The Egyptian-educated potential leader still needed to be convinced of the feasibility of his assigned task. He found himself caught up in an interesting dilemma. Could he, as someone who knew Amun theology well, convince himself actually to obey the call of a God who allowed Hebrew migrants to be enslaved in the first place? Was he really a match for the supreme Hidden One who sustained the hyper-domesticators of Egypt? If Moses were to obey his call, could his own faith withstand the challenges and disappointments of the daring Exodus stratagem which he contemplated?

Furthermore, if this Hebrew God who commissioned Moses had actually told him his real name, could he have executed all his strategic moves with confidence?[54] In Egypt it was the hidden-ness of the All-God's name and his nature that established Amun as the greatest imaginable power in the universe. Could Moses have faced priests of Amun, or the Egyptian pharaoh, on behalf of a God who acted less powerful and mysterious than Amun? Or by doing theology the Egyptian way, could Moses have faced Egyptian opposition on behalf of a God who carelessly squandered his mystery? If unto human minds Yahweh wished to challenge Amun, then as a minimum he needed to watch his own manners.

But then, "Yahweh" is not a name, as "Amun" in Egypt also was not a name. For human minds to perceive a superficial theological sameness between two unnameable configurations of reality is not overly difficult. Both are mysteriously hidden and could therefore be identical. The Egyptian root of Amun is *imn,* which denotes being hidden. During the New Kingdom, Amun was known also as "He who abides in all things" (*Der in allen Dingen bleibt*).[55] How great is the distance from this theology to a perspective on an I AM, or on an I AM WHAT I AM, or on an I WILL BE WHAT I WILL BE, or HE CAUSES TO BE?

Hans Bonnet rejected the idea that a close similarity existed between these two theologies. Concerning the Egyptologist Kurt Sethe, he remarked that the latter "dares to suspect that Yahweh was shaped after the model of Amun." (see Bonnet, pp. 31f)

Obviously, Bonnet's judgment is based on a rarified lexical interpretation of "Yahweh," which appears informed more by Hellenic philosophical dualism than by the Moses religion as it functioned. Is pure spiritual transcendence really the most important aspect of Moses's monotheism? Is a God who disguises his presence in the

---

54 This line of reasoning, of Yahweh theology confronting the Egyptian context of Amun theology, is relevant even in the extreme case of denying the historicity of Moses or his exodus from Egypt. If the Exodus epic was composed in Palestine, in confrontation with Philistine-Canaanite traditions, along the Egyptian cultural frontier, then, the influence of the Egyptian imperial theology would have been officially present, just the same.

55 Sethe, paragraph 217–230, in Bonnet, *Reallexikon der Ägyptischen Religionsgeschichte,* 31–34.

fire of a burning bush, in a cloud or in a pillar of fire, really transcendent in the Hellenic sense of transcendent Platonic Ideas or of "spirit" in English? This writer suspects otherwise.

Inasmuch as a strong influence of Indo-European dualism on Yahweh theology during the Period of Judges and the early Monarchy seems doubtful, one nevertheless must assume a strong basis of Semitic-Canaanite religiosity for all those Hebrews who dwelled in Palestine. As we shall have occasion to suggest shortly, most of the Israelite tribes may never have been to Egypt—although all of them would eventually have become involved with the Egyptian-Philistine-Canaanite frontier. The actual exposure of Levites to full Egyptian culture and religion would, of course, have depended on the actuality of their sojourn there. It seems in any case useful to weigh the impact that Egyptian Amun theology could have had on the larger Israelite confederation, via Moses and his fellow Levites. For any Egypt-educated leader, the hidden-ness of Amun's name was a prerequisite for any faith in One Almighty God. An Exodus event and a Torah tradition, attributed to Moses, became the historicized focus for Israelite unity. We mention this Egyptian-Hebrew encounter to call attention to the widely neglected political dimension of religions.

And yes, there were significant differences between Yahweh- and Amun-oriented theology. From the Hebrew perspective, the respective cults of these supreme deities engaged in mythological wrangling over the outcome of the Exodus episode. Each of these two hidden almighty deities sponsored different units of people, and for both units of people their respective theologies were a hat size too large to fit their actual lives. Amun theology emphasized the freshness of divine breath and living water, in continuity with Shu's function at Heliopolis and with the blessings of the fertile Nile. This was a function that Yahweh appears to have assumed only later, apparently in northern Israel. With stories of the Elijah cycle, in *1 Kings* 18. The Hebrew Yahweh of desert wanderers finally established himself as an authentic giver of rain for agriculture.

Yahweh theology, at least the Levitic strain that traced its origins to the Sinai area, emphasized much more the fire of God's sternness and wrath. In Egypt, by comparison, this degree of severity was accounted for by the lowest Enneadic hypostasis known as Seth.

In proportional perceptions of greater-than-human configurations of reality, what else could one have expected? A people who dwelled all their lives in the lush and fertile Nile Valley naturally would experience more of the All-God's Shu aspect. A people who roamed on prairies and in deserts struggled daily to survive fierce heat and drought. The Midianites who harbored Moses would naturally have experienced more of the fiery aspect of the Egyptian Seth. A man like Moses would have been aware of the differences. He is said to have lived at both places long enough to have learned about such matters.

A new and far more significant difference between Yahweh- and Amun-theology emerged in the story pertaining to the Exodus struggle itself, especially at the Israelite side. YHWH became the scribal designation of the God of gods after a time when he made a special effort to liberate a select group of Hebrew people from bondage to Egypt. For the history and evolution of religion, this means that a new kind of God-of-gods awareness was introduced into the world. And the new Hebrew God-of-gods theology stood in conflict with imperial hyper-domestication that traditionally signified reigning with the God of gods imperially.

Yahweh, the God of Moses, distinguished himself not as a god who sponsors a different system of hyper-domestication, but by liberating from slavery a hyper-domesticated people.

The God who revealed himself to Moses, by the very act of his revelation, has introduced himself as being greater than his imperialistic presence in Egypt, that Moses was familiar with. The God of Moses no longer endorsed a human deified emperor for his keep—for the maintenance of his state cult. He was a God who forbade sacred images that back in Egypt were still prominently set up in temples. He forbade all divine images, apparently because in the hands of priestly and aristocratic hyper-domesticators they were utilized as levers of human control. In contrast to Egyptian deities, who also blessed artists and sculptor-priests, the God of Moses apparently had entrusted his cult to a more sublimely specialized class of scribes. It appears so when judged by the written legacy that Hebrew scribes have produced over time. But of course, everything organized under a hyper-domesticator remains corruptible, nonetheless.

The God of Moses was Lord of the entire world and, at the same time, also acted as savior of a people who had fallen victim to hyper-domestication (civilization). During the development era which followed their Exodus experience, this God, with interference from reactionary prophetic exhortations and foreign invasions, has enabled them to resist some internal hyper-domestication abuses and has kept claimants of actual divine authority in check. Enthusiasm for Yahweh may have disallowed and prevented some features of hyper-domestication from becoming overly savage—notwithstanding King Josiah's reform massacre.

Yahweh as Amun-Seth

Before leaving the monotheism of Moses to itself, in order to watch how its gospel of slave liberation enlivened Palestine and lands beyond, it may be a fitting occasion to also consider a few things about the Egyptian Seth aspect, as these were brought to relate to differences for the Yahweh-Amun theology of Moses.

In its Heliopolitan orthodox setting the divine Ennead, which includes Seth, represents a series of hypostases that emanate from a single source, Atum. During the New Kingdom, the Amun theology that Moses had learned was still the full heir of the orthodox Egyptian God-story (i.e. theogony of generation and emanation mythology). Therefore, the theological reasoning of Moses can be expected to have been contrasted not only about essential attributes of the hidden Godhead, Amun, but also about the Egyptian God's desert heat emanation impersonated by Seth, the god of death. As a desert god among the Egyptians, Seth was also known as a god of foreigners, thunder, lightning, and earthquakes. On a monthly cycle, Seth in his cosmic dimension was deemed responsible also for injuring and darkening the poor eye of Horus, or Atum—the moon.

We are told that Moses spoke to the pharaoh "in the name of the God of the Hebrews" (*Exodus* 5:3). To an Egyptian pharaoh, this meant "in the name of Seth." Of course, the Hebrew narrator happily proceeded to exaggerate the status of Moses an extra notch, at the expense of a supposedly very superstitious pharaoh. All this is understandable. The story about Moses and the Exodus was told to amuse Hebrews, not Egyptians:

The Lord said to Moses, "See, I make you as God to the Pharaoh; and Aaron your brother shall be [as] your prophet." (*Exodus* 7:1)

It is uncertain how much historical weight can be given to the ten plagues in the Exodus story. With the exception of the last, they all can be explained in terms of ordinary natural or environmental imbalances. It must also be acknowledged that, allegedly, all nine proved to be ineffective for softening the pharaoh's hardened heart.

The initial ruse, of needing to make a three-days journey into the Sinai Mountains range, to fulfill religious obligations under the threat of divine punishment, may only have been the cover to hide a shrewder plot. What halfway intelligent pharaoh would not have been able to see through the superficial part? And yes, the story tells how the pharaoh hardened his heart—as could reasonably be expected.

Perhaps the real goal or subterfuge, from the outset, was to nag and to wear down the pharaoh to a point where he no longer would pay close attention. Repeated rumors to the effect that these slaves were about to leave could have been intended to mollify the direct diplomatic requests, of Moses, with an accumulation of trickery. Repeated unsubstantiated buzzes could have given the impression to the effect that Moses and his slaves would never think of leaving without the ruler's official consent. Such a subtle strategy could have given the escapees the needed lead-time before a pharaoh would seriously have taken note when it finally happened. Of course, these are mere speculations in reference to the style of double subterfuge by which political problems in Near Eastern lands are sometimes still resolved today. We do not really know how much of the rational diplomacy of Moses has resonated instead, and has been paraphrased later, in King David's politics. The fortunes of Levitic priest/scribes, of the people of Moses, were not especially favored by the dynasty of David.

In any case, the tenth and special plague attracts our attention as the pivotal point in the Exodus story plot. All of Egypt's firstborn sons, we are told, were slain by an executioner angel of Yahweh. It is high time to rethink this story plot from the hypothetical point of view of a combined Hebrew-Egyptian mindset, such as was implied for the man Moses. The God who killed the firstborn sons of the Egyptians would have been Seth to the Egyptians, the god of desert dwellers. Furthermore, on the Egyptian side, the color and appearance of Seth, and of all his evil deeds, was bloody red.[56] On the Hebrew side, the

---

[56] Compare Erman, *Die Religion der Ägypter*, 37–39.

Moses tradition accented the role of Yahweh with manifestations of red-hot fire.

Egyptians traditionally experienced unease in the presence of Seth. Their perception of this lowest Enneadic hypostasis, in Egyptian tradition, has constituted the weakest point in the political-religious structure within which an Egyptian pharaoh was obliged to operate. Even if critical historiography refuses to accept the tenth Exodus plague as a real event, and even if the celebration of Passover is to be understood as a historicized ancient communal herder sacrifice of firstborn animals, both of these themes may together still represent a raucous diplomatic confrontation. They hint at the diplomatic leverage that Moses could reasonably have applied toward the Egyptian royal court. As a minimum, this story allows the inference that a Hebrew scribe and storyteller later, who was officially associated with the Davidic dynasty, was capable of piercing and hurting the imperial Egyptian pride at its core.

As noted earlier, when in ancient Egypt a pharaoh died, the god Seth was known to have killed him—to have reduced or transformed him into the condition of an Osiris corpse. From the Hebrew perspective, in the Exodus story, Yahweh upstaged the Egyptian perception of Seth. Instead of waiting to kill an elderly and ripe Egyptian pharaoh, Yahweh-Seth killed the firstborn prince. This means he killed the very person who during his next enthronement—during his ceremonial rebirth as Horus—was meant to become the divine ruling pharaoh. The Hebrew storyteller knew Egyptian civilization and tradition well enough, how they functioned and what could halt them.

Egyptian mythology knows the ruling pharaoh as Horus and as the avenger of Osiris. The ruling king supposedly was the Falcon who mutilated Seth during their battle. According to Egyptian tradition, however, the victory of Horus over Seth was never decisive.[57] While they struggled, Seth and Horus seriously mutilated each other. Both divinities needed to be healed by Thoth. This meant that after their struggle, when he chose to do so, Seth was again in a position to strike a blow against the next Horus-king of Egypt. Everyone knew that ruling pharaohs, when they suffered death, were dispatched by

---

[57] See *Ibid.*, 74.

Seth to be transformed into an Osiris deity. In the course of time, the god Seth habitually defeated all the ruling Egyptian Falcon deities. He transformed each of them back into the shape of his brother, an Osiris corpse.

To the extent that Moses spoke authoritatively to the pharaoh, in the name of a God who behaved as Amun and Seth combined—or as the Hebrew narrator would mockingly have it, at the level at which Moses himself could impersonate that kind of a God—the pharaoh was given a plausible reason for why the Hebrew people should be let go. People who belonged to this dangerous God of the desert could not be held captive in Egypt indefinitely, and not with impunity. Moreover, it was reasonable to think that people owned by Amun-Seth would want to appease this dangerous God on his terms, by undertaking a pilgrimage to the God's own desert places where, according to Egyptian perception, he lived. The struggle ensued between Yahweh and the pharaoh of Egypt, over the question of whose Hidden God really owned these Habiru slaves.

It is quite possible, therefore, that a diplomatically astute Moses could have assured the pharaoh that an appeased Yahweh-Amun-Seth would stop plaguing Egypt. The presence of a narrative with ten plagues, which now dominates the larger Exodus epic, suggests that at one point such threats of plagues could indeed have been made. However, the clinching plot of the Exodus narrative, which subsequently could have given credence to a preceding series of diplomatic plague threats against Egypt, was Yahweh-Seth's final killing of the Egyptian Horus-to-be—that is, the ruling pharaoh's firstborn son. For good measure, so it came to be written, the Hebrew God has killed all the remaining first-born sons in all Egyptian houses not marked with (Sethian) red blood. This reads like scripture providing hyperbole, written by scribes riding high on Pegasus—while that champion horse of poetry itself was somewhat high on oats.

The initial diplomatic bait that a man like Moses might have offered to the pharaoh is nevertheless coming into focus. In exchange for letting the Hebrew slaves serve their God in his distant desert, the land of Egypt would be spared the typical calamities that a foreigner's god, like Seth, would have been able to inflict. Positively stated, Moses has offered diplomatic conditional blessings to Egypt.

But the diplomatic positivism of the deal offered by Moses was overshadowed in the narrative when subsequent Hebrew storytellers got carried away, celebrating their "superior" escape. For good measure, and with much glee, they celebrated all the punishments that their mighty God could possibly have brought down on those Egyptians.

The death of the pharaoh's firstborn son, in historical realism, may be considered an extra step further. If, as the biblical story plot suggests, Moses actually approached the Egyptian pharaoh representing the equivalent of Amun-Seth, and if we consider how at some point during these confrontations Moses would have become angry, then a conditional curse laid on the Egyptian crown prince, by the godlike Moses, could have been a logical next amplification. The story is that the king's firstborn son actually died and that, in a subsequent state of grief, the disparaged pharaoh ordered the Israelites to get out.

Was this story the product of Hebrew wishful thinking? Was it all generated by Levite priests to anchor an ancient herders' butchering ritual in the bedrock of Palestinian and Canaanite political intrigue? Was it told to establish and commemorate Israel's unification, as liberation for their special covenant with God? Possibly, yes to all. But then, if such thinking was possible for Hebrew minds at all—and the existence of the story testifies to the fact that it was—then it also is conceivable that a desperate Moses could have unloaded on the pharaoh's son a conditional "curse," or "cause," of death. With his Sethian mission, an impatient Moses could have cursed the entire sacred Egyptian tradition of royal succession. A strong Amun-Sethian curse, spoken within hearing range of the lad, and unloaded onto the crown prince, could conceivably have brought a sensitive royal heir to his deathbed.

The Hebrew storyteller seems to have remembered that Moses acted like a god! Because the curse was conditional, only the pharaoh himself could have removed it by letting those Hebrew slaves go. Thus, in consideration of Egyptian religious beliefs at the time, and in light of experiences that had accrued for Moses over the years, the basic steps of the Exodus would appear to have been undertaken in accordance with well-reasoned propaganda and strategy.

In all likelihood, Yahweh's commission for Moses, given at the site of the burning bush, was no more than a turning point from theory to practice. While he lived at Midian, Moses had years to ponder Egyptian weaknesses, as well as Hebrew points of leverage. He probably would still have personally known some key people at the court. He would have known their religious and psychological strengths and weaknesses. And he would have been able to exploit these.

Still another question may be asked regarding the Hebrew Exodus, about what meanwhile could have happened at the Egyptian side. Was a divine curse really sufficient to scare and to kill a crown prince? Was it enough to create confusion, by which Moses and his people could escape? Or were other death-dealing measures resorted to in combination, perhaps, with some inside help at the court? Could Moses have lent a helping hand in the Passover plot by sending a human angel of death into the pharaoh's house? But then again, bodily inflictions may not have been necessary. Curses sometimes were taken seriously in those days. Could the original Exodus plot indeed have been that simple?

Maybe, or maybe not. Or perhaps simpler still. The exact nature and historical sequence of events elude those of us who live more than three millennia later. Perhaps the major Exodus plot is as simple as re-translating "passage through the Red Sea" as "wading through a Sea of Reeds"—a swampy area where reeds grew. Nevertheless, the religious-political affinity that would have existed between Moses as an Egyptian-educated aristocrat, and as the prophet of Yahweh whom in Hebrew literature we have gotten to know as lawgiver, still can be surmised in broad outlines. With help from the general history of religions, it may be possible to arrive at fresh hypotheses, perhaps with improved historical probabilities beyond what so far has gotten published.

God and his Created World

Even though the Exodus religion historically and foremost represents a reaction against Egyptian civilization and its schemes of hyper-domestication, its theological tenets come into better focus when they are seen as having emerged from under the influence of those same oppressive conditions. All messages and realizations of anti-theses are evoked by prior theses, toward which they are honed in response and against which they testify.

Religious reforms probably never changed everything as effectively as the heirs of those reforms would have liked to believe. To comprehend ancient Israel's religious and political fate, we must try to understand the backbone of their God-story in its entirety.

According to the two Hebrew creation stories, in *Genesis,* taken together, God created the world by divine word and command, and then he gave life to Adam from his own breath. No essential element in either of these story plots can be classified exclusively as Hebrew or Semitic. Many centuries earlier, perhaps in a first round while educating inexperienced children or semi-experienced juveniles, the oldest Egyptian texts have explained the generative emanation process as Atum's spitting. They told of the Godhead as blowing forth his breath (Egyptian *Shu*). Considerably later, but still some centuries before a Hebrew stylus wrote *Genesis* 1, Memphite theologians explained that same creative emission, or spitting, in terms of spitting forth words and giving creative commands—thus in terms of *logos* theology.[58]

A word of caution, stated already in Chapter Seven of this book, must be repeated here. From the late point in time from which we now are viewing these records, the logos modification may seem like an immense improvement. But examined over an ancient time perspective, it appears as though this refinement could as well have been a superficial choice of analogies. Already in Memphite theology, that same "improvement"—Creation by Command—has added up to an unbalanced theological statement, and therefore constituted a mixed societal blessing. If the Memphite theology ever was adopted unilaterally, it has given Egyptian kings undue power without sufficient checks and balances. Kings were the ones who issued most of the so-called "divine creation" or "elimination" commands that inferior Egyptians were obliged to accept—including their own deaths.

---

[58] The Shabaka Stone of about 800 BCE alleges to be a copy of an earlier text. But even if its later date of copying is accepted, it still antedates the Hebrew source, which generally is estimated at 550 BCE or later.

For the sake of human dignity it was necessary, in Egypt, to also retain the older and more universalistic Heliopolitan Atum mythology, including the phallus and hand metaphors. Every male or female, high and low, was able to participate in this dimension of divine creative emanation—including imitational masturbation. A measure of elementary divine status, of basic equal rights for all people, could so be inferred more easily from the older stratum of Heliopolitan Atum mythology. This means that basic human rights could be rationalized more easily under the older Heliopolitan biocosmic theogony than from the advanced logos model of Memphis.

On the other hand, after their liberation from exile in Babylonia, Hebrew scribes recorded their account of creation in surprising harmony with the Egyptian Memphite mythos of creation by logos (ca. 500 BCE), perhaps. They mentioned a full sequence of divine creative commands. At that time, they felt safe enough to do so without worrying about political checks and balances. The Judaic scribes could afford to subscribe to a creation by command theology, because during their Babylonian exile, they and their people had no power or responsibility to keep a deified hyper-domesticator in power—or in check. The priestly scribe and his readers, in Babylon, were free to celebrate the notion, that their world was created by full and genuine divine command. At the same time, they could afford to be unconcerned about whether their texts might endorse theocratic dictatorship.

The second Hebrew creation story, the creation of Adam from a lump of clay and divine breath, apparently belongs to a more primitive literary stratum of Egyptian and Hebrew thought. Moreover, creation by divine breath is itself an old notion that antedated the ancient Egyptian idea of creation by Shu—beginning with a child breathing at a butterfly, perhaps, or a concerned shepherd blowing air into the mouth of a newborn lamb. Inasmuch as breath is an essential function for all higher forms of life, this notion of soul, as air and divine breath, could have gotten first narrated at any imaginable time or anywhere on the globe.

Most of our schoolbooks today overemphasize the dependency of ancient Israelite religion on Semitic Mesopotamia. We are told that Abraham and his ancestors roamed there, and that the Mesopotamians and Hebrews have flood stories in common. But these schoolbooks generally were written from a post-Exodus bias, which is to say, from the anti-Egyptian perspective in which much of the Torah has been cast. Historically speaking, the vague human memory about original floods may go back as far as snow-melts and sea levels rising at the end of the Ice Age, some ten millennia ago. Certainly, these ancient memories also included annual inundations of floodplains along Egypt's River Nile.

Before our fresh historical assessment evokes unnecessary concerns, I might hurry to add that in light of slavery in Egypt, which preceded Exodus and *Torah,* such anti-Egyptian sentiments could well have been justified. They probably were as justified as, earlier, the Egyptian anti-Semitic resentment against Hyksos invaders could be justified. Indeed, all tribal and later national sentiments, could at one time or other have contained chips of historical pragmatism. But then, should historians of today remain obliged toward hatreds that festered, and were kept alive in books, the holiness of which depended simply on the fact of having gotten old? Should their memories turn out to be mankind's greatest curse?

Is the polytheistic theological comedy of the Mesopotamian flood story, the Enuma Elish and its Gilgamesh Epic, really as relevant for elucidating its Hebrew counterpart as it generally is made out to be? Is it really important to know how capricious gods drowned Mesopotamians when we also know that the All-God of Egypt inundated the Egyptians habitually every year? Flood stories among floodplain civilizations, and in this world of manifest limestone strata and fossils, are numerous and widely spread. And religiously speaking, most of these flood stories are of little consequence.

Are creation stories not infinitely more important for understanding Near Eastern domesticator cultures and religions? After all, creation stories are what have legitimized domestication—the ownership of land, of animals and seeds. They represent primary scripture for orderly sedentary living. They furnish "title" to all kinds of possessions that had been created by a recognized divine Creator, by whom they then could have been "sold" or given in trust to humankind in exchange for share offerings or sacrifices.

In sharp contrast with the Egyptian "breath and logos" cosmogony, the burlesque Mesopotamian tradition informs us how the creator-god, Marduk, did his creating in grotesque opposition to logos. He drew his sword and cut the goddess Tiamat into two halves. Her upper half became Heaven and her lower half became Earth. Marduk's words of creation, that accompany this deed, add up to a curse. Even the wind (breath) that he sent represented a negative force over against Tiamat. Marduk, an ex-hunter deity, wielded forces of death, rather than the positive life essence of Shu. Thereafter, human beings were created from the blood of a criminal deity named Kingu, to serve the gods. This myth clearly was told to function as a justification for the enslavement of humankind—for hyper-domestication.

All of this adds up to a Mesopotamian cosmogony of the Hesiodic hunter-herder-warrior variety. Hesiodic warrior theology will be discussed in greater detail in Chapter Eleven. Creation by weapon, by sword or knife, is a very ancient theme of theologicial hunter burlesque. It is a theme cultivated far and wide among the mal-adapted progeny of male scavengers and hunters. Some groups of that progeny remained part-time hunters. Some became head-hunters and cannibals; still others became herders and aristocratic pioneers of civilization —fulfilling their dreams of evolution and mob adaptation. And never mind Hesiod, who put into the hands of the Titan Cronos a "sickle" to blackmail farmers.[59] His tale was recited, nonetheless, by bards who entertained the Greek aristocratic equivalents to our mens clubs or military veterans associations.

Creation by weapon was the mythological basis for people who scorned the planters' origin mythology, that elaborated on sexual generation. At the point in history where we have now arrived, it looks as though those horse-war-and-glory poets, of the Homeric and Hesiodic variety, have told their epic tales of castration intentionally to mock the unheroic priests of the sedentary variety, those who were disposed toward cultivating fields and educating farmers. Hesiod's castration story, and Marduk's slicing of Tiamat into halves, were satire on generative creation theogony. One should note the contrast between these warrior and hunter jokes—those told to amuse audiences of cutthroats, of nostalgically orthodox hunters and warriors —and those of birthing mythology on the Egyptian Geb and Nut.

It must be acknowledged, of course, that some violence appears in Heliopolitan theology at the lowest level of Enneadic emanation. Seth would kill the Osiris-to-be, and the next Horus would avenge his

---

[59] See the summary presentation of this mythology below, in Chapter 11.

father Osiris. This much violence was admitted by Egyptian priests for a number of reasons: (1) to maintain pharaonic dynasties, (2) to assert the divine ruler's power over life and death, and (3) to explain the king's own death and transformation into an Osiris deity who then returns, homeward in the direction of union with the Godhead. Violence imposed by an outside divine agent would further help rationalize the death of those "ordinarily immortal" divine pharaohs.

While the theme of creation by weapon has been mentioned here in reference to Mesopotamian Marduk mythology, one ought to point to a related blemish in Hebrew scripture. In the second creation story, in *Genesis,* an embarrassing fragment from a weapon-and-knife origin story has survived. Raw material obtained and utilized by the Creator, for the creation of Eve, had been one of Adam's ribs.[60] Of course, we know that this peculiar story resulted from a linguistic mix-up, and intentionally in jest. This episode of creation implies some sort of surgical cutting up of the first man's body. This fragment of Mesopotamian knife mythology, in the history of Hebrew theology, has been more of an embarrassment than an educational blessing.

Against Hyper-domestication

Civilization, if seen here in the long-range context of human evolution, and from the perspective of the history of religions, represents a state of cultural achievement wherein the arts of domestication—of mining, settlement, herding and planting—have been overdone to also include the enslavement (herding and owning) of humankind.

---

[60] See, for instance, the rabbinic tale that intentionally makes light of this story plot by way of elaborating why women must wear perfume: Eve's basic substance was a rib, an organic substance that spoils easily, whereas clay, the substance of which Adam had been made, keeps indefinitely. See Louis Ginzberg, *Legends of the Jews,* 34ff.

[61] The Sumerian words for "living" and for "rib" are homonymous; they are both written as *ti*. Thus, the Babylonian goddess Ninhursag was referred to as Ninti. Accordingly, the Life-giving Goddess was nicknamed "Rib-Lady." In *Genesis* 2:21–22, Eve is that Rib-Lady, while in *Genesis* 3:20 she is referred to more correctly as Mother of the Living. See Don C. Benjamin, "The Adam and Eve Story" (1990, and the S. N. Kramer translation, of "Enki and Ninhursag: A Paradise Myth" in James P. Pritchard, ed., *Ancient Near Eastern Texts,* 37–41.

Hyper-domestication is a human effort, put forth by ambitious folk who progressed beyond the mere domestication of plants and animals to also control fellow humankind, groups of people, together with their gods. Militarism, slavery, exploitation, castration, cannibalism, head-hunting, as well as human sacrifice, are crowning activities that resulted from purportedly glorious "grand" domestication schemes. On that account, imperialistic grand-domesticators who have become oppressive are more adequately referred to as hyper-domesticators. By contrast, movements of universal salvation are popular rational reactions against systems of hyper-domestication that have become abusive. They are natural reactions to conditions evoked by hyper-domestication, seeking balance. Reactionary movements can be universalistic and optimistic, in the sense that their adherents focus on more generous types of superior configurations of reality. In the ancient Near East, this meant allegiance to a deity that was kinder and greater than some powerful emperor's God of gods. The imperial type of God-story has all too frequently been tweaked to legitimize conquest, violence, and terrorism.

Seen within an expanded historical horizon, it was no accident that several movements of universal salvation—including later Judaism, Christianity, and Islam—were born between the very fangs of the two oldest civilizations in the Near East, between Mesopotamia and Egypt. Of course, we must allow for the fact that by the time these universal-isms were taking shape, Egypt was dwarfed by Rome, and Mesopotamia was over-run by Persia.

Nevertheless, changing of the guards among grand-domestication systems still drives home the point that long after aggressive aggregates of culture or civilization have been ravaged for decay, their threatening specters and religious codifications may linger. A case in point is *Second Isaiah* which eight centuries after the semi-legendary Exodus, still evoked the scarecrow of slavery with its escape from Egypt. It was invoked to persuade people to leave Babylon. The specter and conquest of Cyrus of Persia, has upset Nabunaid's Babylonia. Still today, in the Near East, ancient Persian might resonates within the Shiite-Persian identity vis-à-vis lands where now the Sunna prevails. Likewise, the tribal Hebrew notion of Davidic messiahship—which was cultivated in excess to weaponize King Josiah's violent Reform—still today incites portions of Christianity to violent reactions.

Founders and reformers of universalistic salvation religions, obviously learned much about theological structures and organizations from the grand-domesticators under which they were raised, whose dogmas they were taught, struggled with, and subsequently hoped to defeat. On that account they reacted against established imperial monotheisms by transcending their older theologies. To subjected masses, universalistic reform monotheisms offered the vision of a more reasonable and kinder Mighty God to subjected masses, one who would sponsor more of life than what older imperial orthodoxies were willing to tolerate under previous deified managements.

A grand-domestication system that became "hyper" and oppressive, could be challenged. But reforms could only be risked if the existent hyper-domestication establishment could be coaxed into a better world-view and be overwhelmed by a more benign greater-than-human reality. Before people can risk to live with less violent behavior, they need to believe and to see first that the world could indeed be managed with less violence, and guaranteed by a kinder greater-than-human reality or divine authority.

Humans on Planet Earth are offspring of primates, and primates are good imitators. Moreover, humankind is *Homo sapiens, Homo religiosus and Homo imitates,* all in one. We imitate whatever superior realities we encounter. We approximate, surpass and try to own anything we think we understand. As we fail to dominate a supreme reality, we admit its superiority only with hesitation. As a rule, we fail to recognize evidence of greater-than-human reality anywhere among the residues of analyses which we deem less-than-human.

Concerning the culture and religion of ancient Israel, it may be said that into its cradle were tossed the hopes as well as the frustrations and warfare of both ancient Near Eastern civilizations. From Mesopotamia, presumably, the Israelites inherited their passion for herding. After suffering slavery in Egypt, Levites emerged with their dreams of divine imperial stability and better-than-human kings. But in real life, all Near Eastern city states were administered by mortals themselves entrapped by hyper-domestication thought. Their safety and survival depended on the support of mighty gods, on the piety of people who revered these gods, as well as on broken relationships between people and their gods. Political variability was implicit in polytheism. But religious relationships with any deity could always be corrupted by the human ego. Therefore, no cult can be respected absolutely.

From among the Hebrew patriarchs, Abraham was said to have been in closest contact with Mesopotamia, and from thence his independent herder mind, supposedly, was enabled to listen to God afresh in matters regarding human sacrifice. Tradition has it that he used to roam as a successful herdsman over a wide territory, and that he insisted on his semi-nomadic independence. His domain has been traced to the vicinity of Hebron.[62] By contrast, Isaac stood in closer contact with the Egyptian frontier in the region presently known as Gaza. The domain of the patriarch Jacob, at the dawn of Israelite history, was centered on Bethel even while much of his life story has been linked directly to Egypt. Tradition has it that he and his family took refuge in Egypt, from a lengthy famine. A son of Jacob, named Joseph, is said to have risen there to the rank of a viceroy in the service of some Egyptian pharaoh.

Centuries later along that story's time-line, an Egyptian aristocrat named Moses was destined to give Israel its less ambiguous and more universalistic monotheism. Ostensibly, this Egyptian Levite leader was initially schooled in imperial religion and political theory. Still later, the royal house of King David, at Jerusalem, utilized Levitic Yahweh religion. David established it in synthesis with the local Canaanite cult of El Elyon which had pre-existed when Salem was still called "Jebus" and while the local Canaanite cult was administered by descendants of Melchizedek.

Stories that narrate the lives of patriarchs, associated with Abraham, describe conditions that could have existed some eight centuries before the Israelite and Judaic monarchies were founded. Therefore, by reading these ancient stories one must, with an eye focused on history, take into consideration the apparent motivations of narrators and scribes who first might have told and recorded them, starting perhaps as early as the tenth century BCE. Some of these scribes undoubtedly were obligated to prior priestly traditions and were put on the royal payroll on account of their skills. Most biblical scribes wrote and expanded their scriptures perhaps more than half a

---

62 People in Anatolia (Eastern Turkey) insist that their Sanli Urfa is the Ur where Terah lived and Abraham was born. Haran is situated about 44 kilometers southeast of Sanli Urfa, just north of the Syrian border. Whether this version is based on an ancient literary tradition, on ancient or on modern interests of tourism, this author cannot yet judge.

millennium after David. The story of a brief encounter between Abraham and Melchizedek, narrated in *Genesis* 14, reflects rather clearly the concerns and ambitions of King David some eight centuries later. It rationalizes and justifies David's political scheme of ruling Israelite tribes from the seat of a Canaanite city that he had taken. The Abraham story also was utilized to justify King David's installation of the native Canaanite priestly family, the Zadokites, to administer the cult of Israel's God Yahweh, and the Canaanite El Elyon as one religion. The literary tradition concerning Moses and Yahweh was introduced by Levite priests.[63] Other episodes in patriarchal story cycles, pertaining to God's covenants with patriarchs and kings, serve similar goals of cult synthesis and nation-building.

The Abolition of Human Sacrifice

One Abraham story, in particular, holds great significance for the Hebrew patriarchal contribution to what was to become the religion of ancient Israel (*Genesis* 22). Storytellers remembered their first patriarch for having accomplished a radical reform in Near Eastern religious attitudes. Abraham considered for a while, and then by the grace of his God he wavered and abolished the practice of human sacrifice. He meant to sacrifice his firstborn son, but at the decisive moment he substituted a ram that his God had provided for the occasion. He sacrificed the ram as a substitutionary payment to God, who, at that moment returned Abraham to a more ancient herder ritual of animal sacrifice. But, of course, the scriptural record is more ambiguous than that. In all likelihood it was the original scribe who already made it a point, and subsequent Jewish and Christian commentators vied with him and among themselves, to rationalize Abraham's initial willingness to sacrifice the life of his son. Allegedly, the God of Abraham wanted to "test the faith" of his

---

[63] It probably is an oversimplification to reconstruct the ancient history of Israel's religion in terms of only two priestly houses, Levites and Zadokites. A more thorough reconstruction would have to account for Libnites, Hebronites, Mahlites, Mosesites, Korahites, and possibly even the Aaronites as separate priestly lineages. See J. Maxwell Miller and John H. Hayes, *A History of Ancient Israel and Judah* (Philadelphia: Westminster Press, 1986), 112f. Among relevant passages concerning Levites and Zadokites may be mentioned *2 Samuel* 5:8–10; 8:17; 15:24ff; and *1 Kings* 2:35.

devotee, which means that God tested the man's willingness and readiness for mindless obedience.[64] In the absence of sufficient historical perspective, still, the Danish philosopher Kierkegaard has exaggerated this so-called "faith" of Abraham into a full-fledged trans-rational existential "leap of faith."[65]

In historical perspective, it is difficult to see how any interpretation of the Abraham story could be farther from the mark than the one offered by Kierkegaard. Abraham's decision was no leap of faith. Abraham walked every mile of his way to Moriah rationally and ethically aware, step after step. Over-domesticators everywhere, and in their times, have understood rationally well, why they sacrificed humankind. All their motives had to be justified religiously and rationally, with a posture of humble obedience to superior necessities and circumstances. It is a well-known fact that the practice of obeying orders, religiously, has generally been an alibi of tyrants and hyper-domesticators who, for the sake of personal justification, posed intermittently as servants, or emanations, of some higher greater-than-human authority.

In the context of an inter-religious dialogue, one ought to keep in mind that, according to some Muslim interpreters, the son who was about to be sacrificed was Ishmael, not Isaac. But, inasmuch as our present discussion focuses on the historical record of human sacrifice as an aspect of general hyper-domestication, and of ceremonial butchering, the fact that Abraham avoided sacrificing either of these sons, and the fact that Abraham did not become an ordinary grand-domesticator, appears far more significant than any other benefits that might have accrued to the estate of either survivor.

The good news here is that both second-generation patriarchs, the favorite son of Judaism and the one favored by Islam, have survived the supposed "faith" of Abraham. The world is a better place for the fact that this old supposed faith was abolished more emphatically,

---

64 For the original moralized story, see *Genesis* 22. Also, the New Testament's Epistle to the *Hebrews* shows the Christian continuation on that theme.

65 Soren Kierkegaard has argued that Abraham was willing to sacrifice Isaac for God's sake, because God required this proof of faith. He rationalized this faith posture of Abraham as the teleological suspension of the ethical, see "Fear and Trembling: A Dialectical Lyric by Johannes de Silentio" (1843), trans. Walter Lowrie, in Robert Bretall, ed., *A Kierkegaard Anthology* (Princeton, NJ: Princeton University Press, 1946), 116–134.

still, by later universalistic prophets and reformers. In this manner, the peoples who practice religion in the evolutionary shadow of Abraham are thereby challenged by their God to love and to let live. Anyone who stays in the vicinity of a potential grand-domesticator for a while, will see enough of him, showing his hand and disclosing what is on his mind. All along, a potential grand-domesticator will have listened carefully to divine revelations that promised to advance his personal cravings and his justifications for power.[66]

A grand-domesticator, even someone like Abraham who only was tempted to become one, will sooner or later demand his reward from the God whom he serves faithfully and inhumanely. The sacrifice of one's own love for family and kin—and one's own precious rationality to boot—goes against the drift of life that is made manifest in the processes and directionality of nature. Presumably, life with all its mysteries and riddles is, in the first place, intended to be lived! Thus, both types of sacrifice, of rationality as well as of love for kindred, seem to call for personal rewards from an Almighty God. At the very least, they bestow extraordinary status and justification. And behold, the ears of Abraham indeed heard the rewarding voice of God swear an oath:

I will indeed bless you, and I will multiply your descendants as the stars of heaven and as the sand which is on the seashore. As your descendants shall possess the gate of their enemies, and by your descendants shall all the nations of the earth bless themselves. (*Genesis* 22: 17-18)

Multiplication and patriarchal blessings, as heard by Abraham or as composed later by an Israelite scribe of the royal dynasty, or

---

[66] For a more systematic discussion of grand-domestication, over-domestication or hyper-domestication see our layout in Chapter One. In addition, years ago, I noticed that for most readers, a rational historical grasp of the need for sacrifice is extremely difficult. I have therefore rewritten the epic of Abraham and Isaac as a simplified libretto for a musical piece, with choir, to which Jonas Nordwall has added an organ accompaniment. Our musical presents the same issues, that the present book offers in prose reasonings, in a somewhat softer and less confrontational medium. See Karl W. Luckert and Jonas Nordwall, *Peace of Abraham, a Musical Narrative,* Triple-hood, 2014 edition. For a comparative essay on that same subject matter, see also "Gaia, El Elyon reject Human Sacrifice," Chapter 18, in Luckert, *Stone Age Religion at Goebekli Tepe,* 2013 (available also in German, Turkish, and Chinese translations).

poetry written in hope of getting on a king's payroll, are only wrappings of the divine promise.[67] Possessing the city gates of competitive enemies, this is the real pearl of hyper-domestication which even good folks like Abraham, who are tempted to become grand-domesticators, desired to win. Yes, there is temptation hidden in this story after all. But it is the temptation of hyper-domestication which later Israelite scribes, perhaps eight centuries after Abraham, no longer could discern critically within the royalist dream-world they had fallen into.

How has the Abraham story received its traditional "divine faith-testing" motif? Any reflective educator surely can remember occasions that readily answer this question. It is highly unlikely that Israelite scribes, who transcribed their favorite faith-answers for posterity, actually wanted their students to consider performing human sacrifices obediently in the future—living, as they did, already under a somewhat kinder deity. In contrast to the actual practices in surrounding cultures, it was rational resistance to tradition, not blind faith, that Abraham's religion implied.

If confronted with the difficult theological question as to why God would have demanded such obedience of Abraham, Hebrew rabbis could not very well have said that their story's supreme patriarch might have misunderstood God, or worse, that their God was arbitrary. If these scribes really had wanted to dwell on the horrible notion of human sacrifice, or if their sheltered guild of scribes still knew much about why formerly human beings were sacrificed, they at least would have concocted some impressive proto-Levite rationalization for such a sacrificial ritual.

As it was, however, old Israelite teachers simply took the shortest and easiest path to finish off their lesson. And they did so as a people who knew themselves specially chosen by God and redeemed from hyper-domestication after the tradition of Abraham and Moses. They sidestepped the problem of God's right to arbitrariness. This would have been too difficult to handle by the minds of average faithful disciples. Instead, these teachers steered their discussion to

---

[67] Capturing city gates from enemies certainly is not an integral part of universal salvation religion. Raiding cities requires losers and can, therefore, not be universalized. Compare here also Jacob's self-interest and bartering, in *Genesis* 28: 20-22, as a prelude to becoming prosperous.

school-room level ethics, that is, to the grand-domestication aspect of theology that could directly be applied to enforce obedient student behavior in a teaching situation.

Every teacher is caught up to some degree in the exercise of grand-domestication. And if an available story happens to teach discipline along with its memorable subject matter, and if thereby it promises to make teaching easier, not many educators will resist endorsing an authority that will get them effectively through another day of instruction. As all people in a king's entourage had to do, and as most scribes did, so also later generations of students were expected to practice obedience as if they were blindfolded by nature.

The basic plot of the story remains that Abraham became a different kind of religious supplicant, one who did not sacrifice his son. All those who propagated this story about Abraham knew, with all their rational faculties intact, why they wanted to remember precisely the faith of this patriarch and, at the same time, disregard the similar and much stronger faiths of grand-domesticators in the ancient world who, in fact, have actually sacrificed their offspring and relatives.

In its historical context, the Abraham story carries the full rational weight of entry into a new universalistic salvation theology. The saving message that made this story worth remembering, and that made it worth retelling especially among firstborn sons, was the result that Abraham did not sacrifice his son, and that by his God's own generous waiver, he was able to substitute a ram. The implied futuristic theology pointed to a kinder God of gods. It pointed to a new revelation of the God of gods—to the effect that the divine appetite no longer includes a grand-domesticator's hunger for power over human lives or flesh.[68] Whether the appetite of the real God actually ever included the craving for human flesh, beyond the possibility of human misunderstanding, is a different kind of question. It does not belong into our present discourse.

Among the civilizations that thrived alongside the early Judaic monarchy, it was still deemed possible that an appetite for human

---

[68] The theological breakthrough reflected in the Abraham story does not mean that human sacrifice in particular, or over-domestication religion in general, were completely eliminated as a practice in ancient Israel, or for that matter in Judah. For flagrant exceptions, see *Judges* 11:31ff, *2 Kings* 16:3, and *Jeremiah* 7:31.

flesh and blood could be a genuine divine attribute.[69] But be that as it may, by preferring ordinary domesticator food, the God of Abraham, in tune with plain domesticator needs, was more archaic and more humane, was less of a hyper-domesticator and therefore less "civilized" in the imperialistic sense.

From the perspective of a civilized ruler, or of a high-priest at the time, the implied theological reform of Abraham meant a step backward. Pressured by God, Abraham recoiled from progressive over-domestication sacrifice. He retreated to the simpler primitive animal sacrifices of orthodox hunter- and herder-folk. "Retreat" is the primary characteristic of religious behavior—and it becomes manifest in space as well as in time, toward simpler living.

Of course, a complete turning away from complex civilization or from thinking hyper-domestication thoughts, a return to simple domestication, was impossible even for Abraham. No human conscience and no religious repentance from aggressive behavior, neither penitent somersaults nor spiritual reorientations, will ever completely turn back the clock of evolution in a people's progress toward cultural complexity. Hands continue to grasp, teeth continue to bite and gnaw—and minds remain addicted to analysis. Humankind hastens along its progressive, unsustainable forward path.

With the help of exciting distractions, such as the Greek Muses or such as religious rites may introduce, the fruits of aggression and progress can be de-emphasized and kept in check for a while. In some societies, such fine arts of diversion are sometimes welcomed by reformers as being "cultured" or "civilized." But as we examine the entire flow of time, grue-some excesses cannot be ignored. The hyper-domesticators' practice of enslaving and sacrificing human victims has become a historical reality for priestly executioners, zealous reformers and revolutionaries. The reputation of a God on whose tables hapless human victims were once sacrificed, by virtue of the hungry God's acceptance according to priestly rationalization, has become ontologically fixed in

---

[69]Consider, for example, the sacrifice of a young man excavated in 1979, seven kilometers south of the great palace of Knossos. The proceedings of the sacrificial rite were interrupted by an earthquake and subsequent fire, some 3,700 years ago. See Yannis Sakellarakis and Efi Sapouna Sakellarakis, in National Geographic Vol. 159, No. 2 (February 1981), 204–222. See also a discussion in Chapter 18, in Karl W. Luckert, *Stone Age Religion at Göbekli Tepe*, 2013.

the minds of later devotees.[70] As a God who has shown an appetite for human flesh, his cult can be accepted or abandoned. But the historical fact of such a cult cannot be erased easily from the slates of time.

Consequently, those who retreated with Abraham to a simpler mode of behavior, and who began to sacrifice again old-fashioned domesticators' animal sacrifices, discovered that their sacrificial victims could no longer be presented in accordance with simple ancient domesticator logic. Before grand-domestication was practiced, firstborn sacrificial animals were given as share offerings, in payment for domestic herds. This transaction was done to legitimize human ownership of breeding herds under a God who, previously, had made and owned the animals —who created and allotted (in effect "sold") them to humankind in exchange for share offerings.

The first offerings, or share offerings, of body parts of felled animals that hunters paid to their divine hunting dogs and other tutelaries—to shift the weight of hunters guilt unto partner-gods—were amplified by domesticators with staging ceremonial butchering feasts. Domesticators sacrificed whole firstborn animals to pay for subsequent litters, or for whole herds. After these, ordinary animal sacrifices of domesticators were magnified by hyper-domesticators to pay still mightier sponsors with the more valuable currency of human lives—to justify owning herds of human slaves. Surrounded for context, by hyper-domesticator ambitions, the revised religion of someone like Abraham, of sacrificing again animal victims of lesser value, acquired its more pleasant and somewhat redemptive reform meaning for humankind.

In the shadow of Abraham's temptation, in light of his new faith, sacrificial animals inevitably became "substitution" offerings for humankind. Animal victims had to be given, henceforth, as substitutes to redeem prospective human victims whom grand-domesticacator cults had doomed to be sacrificed to the deity. Because of this new substitutionary function, it is not warranted anymore to classify

---

[70] Consider the "Ransom Theory" of St. Anselm, reasoned on hand of the sacrificial cult of Old Testament theology. It implies a more archaic, a more cruel and weaker deity, on the defensive. A God who is obligated to the Devil to pay ransom, or must satisfy higher requirements of justice, definitely does not measure up to the "Almighty God" or to the loving "Father of Jesus Christ."

either Abraham's religiosity or the three faiths of Judaism, Christianity and Islam, which descended from it, as nostalgic returns to primitive domesticator religion. It is the case that the human spirit, looking out for itself, for co-existence and universal human concerns —after having almost gotten stuck in hyper-domestication ontology and ambitions—was compelled to retreat temporarily to older ritualistic primitive-isms of animal slaughter and sacrifice. The drive for refinement had to start anew to obtain fresh inclusive world perspectives, energy, motivations and momentum.

Of course, all this religious retreat attitude happened by necessity. Greater-than-human configurations of reality have a way of limiting human ambitions, impacting human goals at every step. Their presence and reality cannot be ignored for long by mortal minds. All the while, religious retreat responses may be deemed rational as long as they do not suppress unnecessarily but, rather, assist in the task of balancing human life for survival.

9

Priests, Monarchy and Reform

Linguistic research and recent archaeological surveys have taught us to approach subjects like the "Exodus" and "Joshua's Conquest of Palestine" with some reservations. The linguistic configuration in *Deuteronomy* and *Joshua* comes from a few centuries later than the supposed events, and the linguistic age of Joshua's Conquest do not match the archaeology of cities that allegedly were destroyed. Moreover, settlements are mentioned that were built several hundred years too late to support the story.[71]

For a while, motives in the Joshua epic appeared to correspond best to the grand-domesticator ambitions of certain kings like Josiah (641–610 BCE) or Hezekiah (ca. 727–699 BC) of Judah, both of whom apparently attempted religious-political reforms. They dreamed of a restored and a reunited Israel, of one supposedly ruled by members of the House of David. It appears that kings and their scribal collaborators produced historical fiction. They embellished Joshua's Conquest of Palestine which, in their days, had happened already several centuries in the past. Information garnered from *I* and *II Kings* and *Chronicles I* and *II* has led a number of archaeologists to change their views.

Much of what was written about the kings David and Solomon, or about the entire Davidic dynasty, might have originated as political fiction. "Propaganda" would today be a more familiar street name for this genre of writings. Apparently, envious dreamers from the small Southern Kingdom of Judah, have hyped their story of the

---

[71] See Miller and Hayes, *A History of Ancient Israel and Judah*, 60f and 71f, concerning thirteenth century BCE city destructions. "Conquest cities" like Arad, Heshbon, Jericho, Ai, and Gibeon yielded no archaeological evidence of Late Bronze Age occupation, much less of destruction by war.

Davidic dynasty, in competition with the more successful Kingdom of Omri, in northern Israel.[72] The Omride dynasty existed from 886 to 835 BCE. Their palaces have been excavated at Samaria.[73] Almost no palace ruins of the Davidic dynasty have yet been found at Jerusalem. To some historians it appears as though much of that dynasty could have been a fantasy on parchment. According to earlier interpretations, supposedly, during the time of Joshua all Israelite tribes invaded Palestine as a united group. With the direct help of God Almighty they took the land that, supposedly, the one and only Creator-God had given them. Nevertheless, it now appears that most of the people who belonged to the ancient tribes of Israel were already in the land when Levite wanderer priests could have arrived there from Midian to propagate their Exodus narrative and to formalize the Passover ritual. The tribal territories apparently were already claimed, and this could be a good reason why the tribe of Levi had no territory allotted to it (see *Deuteronomy* 10:9).

---

[72]According to Silberman and Finkelstein, the literary magnification of the Davidic Dynasty began in earnest perhaps after the Omrides at Samaria had been defeated by Tiglath-Pileser III, Shalmaneser V, Sargon II, and Sennacherib and after the northern leaders had been deported to Assyria and have there disappeared into the general population. Though, Judah likewise was later conquered and its people were deported to Babylonia, a remnant of their leadership was given a chance, by Cyrus of Persia, 539 BCE, to return to Jerusalem and to rebuild. One of the more incisively written textbooks for the current discussion is *The Bible Unearthed: Archaeology's New Vision of Ancient Israel and the Origin of Its Sacred Texts,* by Neil Asher Silberman and Israel Finkelstein (2002). At some point in biblical history it appeared as though Judah, with its Davidic Dynasty, was the only entity left to inherit the divine covenant. The historically "over-rated" royalty of Judah was then given a chance, to return to Jerusalem to record a sparsely known heritage and dream history, on parchment.

[73] Numerous other studies have been written to "unearth" (i.e. excavate) the Bible or to illuminate the archaeology of the so-called "Jerusalem Monarchy" and the "Divided Kingdom" periods. For my first edition of this book (1991), I relied heavily on Maxwell J. Miller and John H. Hayes (1986). Other pathways for entry into the larger subject matter have since been produced by Amihai Mazar (1990), Suzanne Richard (2003), Avraham Faust (2010 and 2012), and more. A textbook anthology widely read in Christian theological schools—*Ancient Israel's History: An Introduction to Issues and Sources*—has been published by Bill T. Arnold and Richard S. Hess, at Baker Academic (2014). Additional contributors to this volume are James K. Hoffmeier, Samuel Greengus, Lawson G. Stone, Robert D. Miller II, Daniel Bodi, Steven M. Ortiz, James K. Mead, Kyle Greenwood, Sandra Richter, Brad E. Kelle, Peter van der Veen, André Lemaire, and David A. deSilva. I thank James Moyer and John Strong for several of these bibliographical suggestions.

All the while, priests did not ordinarily refuse ownership of land if they could help it. Moreover, it seems as though the Levite cult of Yahweh, once upon a time, was centered on a portable tabernacle tent, and within that tent was kept a chest that contained a few sacred mementos from their assumed escape from Egypt. But more important than the sacred portable chest, for the Israelite confederation of tribes, has become the annual ceremonial commemoration of the Exodus event itself. Both of these symbolic happenstances were initiated by Levites.

As priestly mediators between God and humankind, Levite tribesmen celebrated their tradition of escape from Egyptian hyper-domestication. Their God of gods favored Hebrew slaves over other denizens of the mighty Egyptian empire. These people roamed as Hapiru when they settled at their first place of refuge, at the Midian Oasis on the Sinai Peninsula. From there they moved into the hill country of Palestine to interact with Israelite tribes. "Hapiru" was the Egyptian and Mesopotamian designation of foreigners and nomads, rebels and outlaws. It referred to people who lived and moved between these two large systems of grand-domestication and who generally managed to slip away from the control of either. The label "Hapiru" appears to have given rise, later, to the positive self-designation "Hebrew." The story tells about how twelve tribes of Israel were united into a kingdom, under David (ca. 1000 BCE) and how King Solomon, David's son, expanded the kingdom. For their part, some Hebrews in Palestine (in "Philistine Country") referred to themselves as the tribes of *Yishrahel*—a name that seems to have meant fighters, resisters, or partisans of El (their Lord God).[74]

The Levites first created and told the narratives of Israel's Exodus epic. These people might be designated the first "priestly cheerleaders" of a magnificent, romantically hyped pastoralist confederacy of *Yishrahelite* rebel groups. Their Exodus commemoration and annual Passover celebration remained anchored in memories of patriarchal pastoralism. It was associated in part with the Sinai Peninsula as their Holy Land. They cultivated thoughts and sacrificial rituals that made the historical rationalization of their united Yahweh religion possible.

---

[74] The author gratefully acknowledges this probable etymology as a suggestion of David Wucher.

Associated tribes subscribed to the Levite story and to their ritualized feast days, and in time, they all learned to commemorate their "joint" miraculous escape from Egypt as united tribes of Israel. But what precisely could have been the historical common experience, the empirical basis for their joint ceremonial commemoration that made it possible to think about such a unity of tribes?

Up to the time of King David's monarchic experiment, at Jebus, he was the chieftain of a prowling band of men who sold protection to vulnerable refugees and settlers—this was the general pattern by which, in their transition from Stone Age hunting to domestication and hyper-domestication, many early kings established themselves. The tribes that later became Israel initially fought separately. They fought for survival along the northern Egyptian frontier, sometimes with and sometimes against the Philistine and Canaanite city-states of the Gaza area. Sometimes they fought among themselves (cf. *Judges* 12), and their descendant priestly scribes historicized those evolving encounters.[75] They recast the ancient herder custom of sacrificing lambs into a historical epic. They avoided the charge of writing untruths by giving all credits for their words to God Almighty. Having so been accredited, all responsibilities for human obedient responses and beliefs became then the problem of God. In this same process, the herder rituals that they adopted from the culture stratum of ancient patriarchs, in opposition to Egyptian hyper-domestication schemes, has cemented these rebel tribes ideologically into a more uniform trend.

The apparent "historical" books in the Bible—Judges, Samuel and Kings, in conjunction with recent Near Eastern archaeology—give us fresh oblique clues regarding the early history of Israel. During Israel's formative years, the Philistine kings in the region ruled Canaanite city-states that over previous centuries had adopted a general pattern

---

[75] They "historicized" in the same sense as the Exodus epic was made the central theme of state and cult—as a conveniently agreed-upon foundational event in history. Exodus and Passover were celebrated by Hapiru refugees from Egyptian-Philistine-Canaanite city-states. These literary creations emerged from ritualized and romantic herder nostalgia, as at the time these were being adopted to contemporary reality. Yishrahel rebels, and refugees, escaped to freer semi-pastoral lifestyles in the hill country. They made virtue of necessity by way of idealizing the lifestyle of their distant pastoral patriarchs, reinventing themselves in the process.

of Egyptian culture. Concerning the ancient Israelites, the biblical sources tell of a first leader, Saul, who was anointed grudgingly by the priest Samuel for the purpose of leading Israel's defense against surrounding kings. His kingship was intended only for the duration of military emergencies. The general anti-monarchism on the part of Yahweh'spriests reflected what all along had been the way of tribal herdsmen who led a semi-nomadic existence. They continued to insist on their inheritance of nomadic independence.

Some of King Saul's Philistine-Canaanite opponents were well organized city-states along the northern Egyptian cultural frontier—organized under established aristocracies. During most of Israel's formative centuries, these city-states increasingly refused to heed the wills of weakening Egyptian pharaohs. Nevertheless, for the Israelite tribes to stand up against the organized might of Philistine city-kings required a more stable military policy than King Saul could deliver on the part-time short leash that Samuel, the priest, was willing to justify in the name of the anti-monarchic Yahweh.

Saul, as a part-time Israelite king, succumbed to pressure from Samuel. As a result, under the might of Philistine kings and under the presence of his rival David, King Saul's dynasty crumbled. David, for a while joined the Philistine opposition, though, also in the eyes of these allies he appeared like an untrustworthy partner. King David's private fighting force consisted of Hapiru rebels and refugees, some of which had come directly from those hyper-domesticated city-states, and from established Hapiru tribal bands in the hill country of Palestine. Back in the hill country, David, while organizing his own rival Yishrahel tribes, succeeded in deploying their military potential. Some Philistine city-kingdoms fell before him. How much of David's success was later invented in his honor, is difficult to infer from the wider historical context that presently is emerging. In stark variance with the Conquest narratives in *Joshua* 1–11, one finds in *Judges* 1:27–33 a list of seventeen Canaanite cities that the Israelites had been unable to take. According to *2 Samuel* 8, David finally defeated and subdued these remaining Philistine-Canaanite cities. But even this amount of credit, ascribed to King David, appears to have been an overstatement in light of *1 Kings* 9:16. There one learns, that it was the pharaoh of Egypt, who controlled the Canaanite city of Gezer, who gave it as a dowry to his daughter when she became a wife of King Solomon. Solomon's monarchy, so it appears in hindsight, was an Egyptian-style scheme of hyper-domestication. Small wonder, therefore, that the temple that Solomon built in Jerusalem was given the floor-plan of a typical Egyptian temple of Amun. During the formative years of the Israelite monarchy, the Levite cult of Yahweh had become a rallying symbol for the young nation. During Israel's formative centuries of rebellion, against the Egyptian-Philistine frontier, the revolution under Yahweh made it possible to build and orchestrate a semblance of inter-tribal unity and cooperation.

But what could have been the common experience among the Israelite tribes that made the joint commemoration of Passover and Exodus a meaningful and unifying symbolic act? In light of freshly attained historical context, a reconstruction can now be attempted in a more straightforward manner. All these tribes held memories in common—about shared sufferings under grand-domesticators, with resentments toward their former Egyptian-Philistine overlords and other such hostiles. They achieved a measure of unity on the basis of their Passover-Exodus celebration, which symbolized the sentiments of underdogs escaping Egyptian hyper-domestication, which was their common enemy.

Whether one actually escaped in an Exodus from the Nile Delta, led by Levite leaders such as Moses and Aaron, or whether one escaped Philistine-Egyptian city states to join Yishrahel rebel tribes in the hills, or whether one merely participated in David's victory over some of the city states—in any of these situations, one had prevailed against the general Egyptian influence and "bondage."[76] The plot of the Levite Exodus epic, which celebrates Yahweh's victory over Egyptian task-masters, was eventually established as cult-epic by the dynasty of David. It happened while this dynasty was also taking credit for Israel's actual liberation from contemporary Egyptian systems of hyper-domestication. It should be kept in mind

[76]Although arguments concerning motives, over ways and means of Israel's revolution, have not been completely resolved and the historical synthesis remains incomplete, a general consensus appears now to recognize Egypt's former overlordship over the Philistines, whose domains they authorized. For the beginning of this debate, see Norman K. Gottwald, *The Tribes of Yahweh* (Maryknoll, NY: Orbis Books, 1979), 410ff. It should be kept in mind that still during the reign of Solomon, it was within the power of the Egyptian pharaoh to give the city of Gezer as a dowry to Solomon, as his son-in-law.

that ritualized playacting is a powerful method for mobilizing collective thinking and political allegiances, especially among minds caught up religiously in celebrating joint survivals. *Homines sapientes* may be a misnomer for creatures who, in fact, are *Homines ludentes*—people that play together. And for coordination, the staging of communal religious pageants, contests of strain, suffering and endurance have always been of paramount importance. As an effective means of unifying people, play-acted religious rituals remain more vibrantly important than all historicized heroic propaganda, intuited by salaried scribal minds, combined.

A small analogy from the author's personal experience may help explain this acculturation process. A typical immigrant to America sooner or later gets drawn into celebrating a version of American Thanksgiving—or as a minimum, into watching Thanksgiving pageants. Like the Jewish Passover, so this American national holiday is celebrated in exchange for divine blessings, for security and for title to the land. Our American epic about pilgrims who arrived on the Mayflower is remembered annually and nationwide, with interdenominational Thanksgiving celebrations. The covenant with Manifest Destiny is sealed with a festive meal that includes sacrificial turkey as an American stand-in for the biblical sacrificial Passover lamb.[77]

The American turkey, as a latter-day substitute for the Jewish Passover Lamb, has redeemed the wanderings of many timid Eurasian immigrants who came to the American shores. It has translated their wanderings into divinely blessed pilgrimages. Rites and celebrations appear to be the real means by which national epics have become motivators of communal aspirations.

---

77 While in actuality the notion of sacrifice is maintained in a very superficial manner, the original idea of a real sacrifice still shows through the quaint practice of having the president of the United States pardon a turkey, in jest, to permit the animal to survive. The meaning of Sacrifice is thereby reduced, jokingly, to the level of a judicial sacrifice. I expect that in a nation that is trying to avoid official religion, this levity will someday beg a more serious question about the link between ancient sacrificial cults and the practice of capital punishment. American Christians know well enough that Jesus Christ was executed as a victim, in a Roman judicial sacrificial procedure.

A Levitic priestly storyteller, roaming three millennia ago in the domain controlled by David, could assist in embellishing and amplifying the Judaic-Israelite national epic of the Exodus and thereby win patriotic standing for himself and for his wandering tribesmen. Samuel, a priest of Yahweh, resisted monarchy as long as he could. The first two kings, Saul and David, as Israelite and Judaic warlords, both needed to justify their grand-domestication mandate with claims of having been anointed by that same influential anti-monarchic priest (*1 Samuel* 10 and 16).

There in the hill country, east of the Philistines, was a small settlement of Canaanite people. Their city was known as "Jebus." David, a Judaic organizer who commanded his own band of warriors, took over this place and named it "Salem" (City of Peace). Today, some of the now anonymous offspring of Saul's "ten lost tribes" among Yishraelite partisans of El, and some very self-conscious offspring of David's Judaic-Benjaminite alliance, are struggling with each other over this region that, meanwhile, has become known as "Jerusalem."

At some point King David fetched and brought home the sacred Ark of the Covenant, that used to be kept in Samuel's shrine at Shiloh. David was a wise politician who understood religious symbolism. He recited poetry and sang psalms in the proximity of God, to enthuse. The portable shrine of Levitic Yahweh-ism was known to contain souvenirs from the Exodus event. At Salem the chest was placed in a makeshift tabernacle tent. In the former Canaanite city, the presence of this chest legitimized David's claims to the entire Levitic Exodus tradition. David installed the Canaanite Zadok, a priest of El Elyon (God Most High) who, then, alongside Abi'athar the Levite—whose people had brought the Yahweh tradition—jointly maintained the Yahweh/El Elyon religion (*1 Chronicles* 15:11 and *1 Kings* 2:26). Solomon later banished the Levitic co-pontiff Abi'athar from the region—for having earlier supported the coup attempt of Absalom, (*1 Kings* 1:22, 26). Zadok was the high priest who remained in charge of the Yahweh/El Elyon religion.[78]

Understandably, the political and militarily successful David also wanted to build a lasting temple of stone; perhaps he so hoped to fortify

---

[78] Zadok apparently was a man of the local Jebusite, i.e. Canaanite, family of priests that descended from a priest-king, Melchizedek. A later source, 1 Chronicle 24:3 and 12:27–28 sought to explain away David's synthesis of Canaanite and Levitic religion by assuming that Zadok was a Levite. See also *Genesis* 14: 18–20 and Footnote 63, here-in.

his political grasp as a step toward to grand-domestication. But the rebel ethos of the Israelite tribes, by the justification of which David had won and organized his "kingdom," apparently would not yet permit him to go that far. The prophet Nathan, at one point had given King David permission to build a temple, but he quickly reconsidered and came forth with God's revised order to desist (2 *Samuel* 7). Temples of stone, managed by priestly officials of a royal estate, do compromise a deity so managed, to a point where its priests appear to preside over hyper-domestication. But the God of recently liberated Hebrews would not yet tolerate his own incarceration in a stone structure built by a potential grand-domesticator, at least not yet. It seems as though religious purity does not seem to have been a factor. The alliance between the prophet Nathan and Solomon appears politically suspicious.

David and his appointed priests therefore had to make do for a while longer with a nomadic herders' tabernacle tent. Whether this Levite tent-religion was actual history, or whether it represented nostalgic transitional fiction that helped break the boredom of scribal priests in Babylon, so far only their God knows for sure.

Another one of David's grand-domestication schemes concerned the organization of military force. He conducted a census of "valiant men" throughout Israel, that is, a registration for military conscription (2 *Samuel* 24). It is said that David confessed his guilt and accepted the responsibility for having ordered this census. Yahweh's verdict, along with the rationalization of an epidemic that was on hand, was enunciated by David's own court diviner.

Religiously inspired roadblocks of this sort were placed in the path of Israel's first king by anti-monarchic men of God who first ceremonially, and later prophetically, continued to interfere by the ethos of their Yahwistic rebel tradition. Obstacles of this sort defined the perimeters beyond which the Yishrahel-ite ethos would not permit the ambitions of their anointed kings to venture.

Under Solomon

According to the story, it fell to Solomon, who rose to the throne with help of the prophet Nathan's plotting, to build Jerusalem's first temple of stone and to bring the Yahweh cult under his royal control (*1 Kings* 6). Within a solid temple court, the presence of God could be meticulously maintained by priests who were on the royal payroll. The ground-plan of Solomon's temple itself was laid out according to Phoenician-Egyptian models; it accommodated a "Holy of Holies" recess inside, as also exists in Egyptian temples of Amun.[79] Thus, King Solomon took his Israelites away from their fixation on Exodus and Freedom—back to conditions where a hidden mystery, such as Amun or Yahweh, could be owned, managed, and royally exploited.

The difficulty with a magnificently organized temple cult was the fact that a God, who accepted the maintenance of his cult from the hands of a human king, became himself dependent on the generosity and ministrations of the human hyper-domesticator. In this manner, the divine-human relationship of dependence was reversed. This is the typical outcome whenever the religious behavior of common folk falls under the control of grand-domesticators who undertake to intersperse religious demeanor more gloriously at their own level of status. Ordinary domesticators were so, as a rule, hyper-domesticated together with their livestock and together with the tribal gods who earlier have supported freedom.

According to the story, during the reign of Solomon, the Israelite kingdom competed in superficial splendor with the glories of Egypt and Mesopotamia, and for a while, his royal cult allegedly surpassed theirs. Solomon's royal scribes collected wisdom literature in their king's honor, boasting about his wisdom. But inasmuch as the existence of a Solomonic kingdom has so far not been archaeologically proven, one must allow for the possibility that this king's splen-dor may have been a political invention—for competing with the Omride dynasty at Samaria, up north. His wisdom was claimed to have been greater than the wisdom of all the sages of Egypt (*1 Kings* 5, 10). The fact that scribes of his dynasty resorted to such boasting in competition with Egypt, smacks of a measure of defen-sive indebtedness of some of Hebrew culture and religion to that civilization, at least indirectly. Their competitive boasting would not have been necessary if Egypt had not presented a challenge to their self-esteem. Also, let us not forget that this Israelite king was married to a daughter of the Egyptian pharaoh (*1 Kings* 3:1).

---

79 Commentaries ordinarily cite the affinity of Solomon's temple with Phoenician prototypes. But similar floor plans, with Holy of Holies chambers, were customary also in Egyptian temples of Amun, Egypt's One God—whose name, like that of Yahweh, could not be spoken. See, for instance, the Middle Kingdom core of the Temple of Amun-Ra, at Karnak. See also Casson, *Ancient Egypt*, 120ff.

But Israel's political and religious identity was sustained, all the while, by its Exodus tradition, by its religious fervor and partisanship—thus by the combined early Mesopotamian and the subsequent Hapiru herder and warrior traditions that resonated in competition with Egyptian grand-domestication. The Davidic upstart dynasty was not yet supported by a time-tested and balanced organization. Schools of loyal scribes and officials, with guilds of artisans and other groups of citizens on which Mesopotamian and Egyptian civilizations relied during their centuries of stability—all such cultural advances were still in their infancy during Solomon's reign. He needed to import Phoenician craftsmen to build his temple. Only his militaries appear to have been safely organized. Nevertheless, Solomon's grand-domestication system, with an imbalance of exploitation-oriented "power and order," could not last.

According to the biblical record, when Solomon died, in 922 BCE, the northern tribes of Israel broke away from Judah. They refused to serve Solomon's son, Rehoboam, who stoutly promised to continue the police-state management of his ambitious father. The northern tribes refused to accept forced labor any longer or to pay the king's excessive taxes. They seceded to form their own "Israelite" kingdom under Jeroboam I (*1 Kings* 12). The two kingdoms, Israel and Judah, existed alongside each other until Sargon II of Assyria defeated Samaria in 721 BCE. So reads the southern version of the story which, one may suppose, Northerners knew differently.

Josiah's ruthless conquest of the northern Israelite realm, and the "Reform" (of 622 BCE) during which he slew all northern priests at their sanctuaries, was duly legitimized with the celebration of a Levitic Passover commemoration. A detailed account of this event is narrated in *2 Kings* 23. Then, as a result of Nebuchadnezzar's sweep, which enforced the Babylonian policy of integrating the Near East, Josiah's dynasty disappeared soon afterward. The southern monarchy of Judah held on a little longer, into the Sixth Century, when in two deportations most of its people were sent into exile to Babylon as well—in 597 and 587 BCE. Survivors of the southern kingdom, Judah and Benjamin, eventually returned from their exile in Babylon, while another group of Judeans who had fled in the direction of Egypt, who dragged with them the prophet Jeremiah (*Jeremiah* 43:1-8), left no written records. Near the first cataract, traces of their descendants may have been found.

Exiles in Babylonia, and even their distant offspring long after their dispersion by the Roman Empire, have continued to celebrate their liberation from slavery in Egypt. Thanks to the art of writing, the scar acquired from ancient Egyptian hyper-domestication will never heal entirely. When in 539 BCE Babylon fell to Cyrus the Great, Palestine came under Persian hegemony. With permission granted by Cyrus, and by later Persian rulers, Judaic exiles were permitted to return to Jerusalem with a charter to reestablish again a Judaic state.

Alexander in 336–323 BCE drove the Persian overlords from the area. He and his heirs justified their rule of the Near East as cultural colonizers and "saviors." Then in 168 BCE the small state of Judah, in rebellion against their Greek overlords, became independent for a while under the Maccabees. But after having become radicalized through revolution against the Greeks, the Hasmonaean priest-kings themselves quickly lapsed into methods of tyranny and hyper-domestication.

The period of Roman domination, beginning in 63 BCE, was marked by repeated brush fires of Judaic rebellions. Their hope of ever getting another independent Judaic state was smashed by Roman might during the first century CE. The dispersion of religiously bonded Jewish people, which followed, lasted almost two millennia.

Only during the Twentieth Century, after extreme persecution and Holocaust, and after World War II, have Jews of the Jamnian tradition returned to Palestine in large numbers. Meanwhile America and the Western world continue to linger in the shadows of easily exploited Judeo-Christian ambiguities, such as original sin, collective guilt, and ancient divine promises. These trans-historical obscurities, taught and believed, have in turn disturbed the American dream of keeping religion essentially distinct from political reasoning. This fuzzy logic today, Fall of 2020, has precipitated what may be the most severe political crisis for democracy. Within the spacey drift of fuzzy historical conceptualization, people in this Judeo-Christian stream appear unable to abandon their habit of playing political games by uploading their burden of undefined "religion," of "original sin" and "collective guilt," on one another.

At the Christian side, it was the Roman imperial guilt accrued for the Crucifixion of the Savior that had been internalized and spread to be born by Christian believers in common. The role of the Roman Empire in Christ's execution, could not be promulgated openly while

Constantine was actively engaging Jesus Christ as his favorite Roman Deity of War. By endorsing the imperial scheme of grand-domestication, Jewish, Christian and Roman religious notions became intermingled. Hyper-selfcritical piety and undefinable reasons for penitence, anywhere, does weaken or extinguish any onsets of democratic egalitarian reasoning. Christians in the West, right now watching a generation of new Israelite pioneers wondering, while at the same time they are trying to accept the Bible for themselves, as their own holy almanac of divine promises of God. In response, Jews appear apprehensive for losing control over their own national epic to outsiders. In return, Christians continue to resent, periodically, how half of their accepted Word of God, half of their Bible, continues to rank them a notch below the Chosen People —as Gentile Christians, seemingly forever.

Two millennia ago the founders of Christendom—John the Baptizer and Jesus of Nazareth—both depreciated the significance of Abraham. Nevertheless, in Christian soteriology the status of this ancestor has continued to rise, fertilized apparently by printed bibles. The heavily political Abraham stories have ended up, in Christian hands, getting marketed as printed Words of God.

Less than six centuries after Christendom began moving away from Judaism, the prophet Muhammad, founder of the religion of Islam, began tracing his personal ancestry back to the family of Ishmael. The religious significance of the Abraham figure, amidst controversies and scuffles among Jews, Christians, and Muslims began to swell. They all learned to argue their salvation in terms of political aspirations, as privileges, covenants, divine promises, mandates, including divine titles to real estate.[80]

---

80 The News of today, July 7, 2017, is that UNESCO has declared the Mosque of Ibrahim, (Abraham) a "Palestinian World Heritage Site." This international honor was then strongly criticized by officials of the present state of Israel: they alleged that this designation negates the "deep" Jewish ties to the biblical town Hebron with its ancient shrine, presumably housing the burials of Abraham and other patriarchal figures. Bones of contention are trace-able to three millennia ancient events that no-one can precisely remember. The narrated Abraham events could have happened eight centuries before they were inscribed as story. Oral traditions, and not even written events or genetic traditions, can vouch for historical accuracy over such stretches of time.

Abraham is revered today by Jews, Christians, and Muslims competitively, with almost equal intensity. However the status of this ancient story character, as a man chosen by God, fluctuates according to the value attributed to his divine covenant or mandate. Three millennia ago Abraham, as patriarchal personality, was already the product of an eight centuries long evolution of story telling. He was utilized by King David as a central political symbol for the monarchy which he hoped to unify and to legitimatize religiously.

Along every military front in the Near East, still marking Twenty-First Century conflicts, the name of Abraham is being blessed for victories or blamed for the carnage it inspires and helps rationalize. Present-day "descendants" tend to regard Abraham's name as being significantly greater than the names of other people's forebears. Genres of stories in founded and ancestral religions carry within themselves their own genes for blessings as well as for corresponding contrasts and curses.

Both, blessings and curses, duly recorded onto processed animal skins, are suitable to hustle followers, descendants and/or adopted heirs from places of persecution and suffering into additional trappings of oppression. There, confrontations that happened long ago do tend to resurrect old grudges and inflame long extinguished pains. They memorialize ancient wrongs to help reclaim long abandoned titles to real estate. All this happens upon far-flung masses of land that growing oceans constantly are trying to separate farther. The speed of Earth expansion is too slow to keep members of the human species from battling each other under their increasingly contaminated skies and on their spreading oceans.

10

Universal Monotheism and Messianism

An early trail of universal salvation religiosity, in the Near East, has gotten introduced with stories about Abraham. It became visible early on in ancient Israelite religious history. This legendary patriarch has been credited with having escaped the central temptation of hyper-domesticated civilization, of sacrificing a human victim. This feat implicitly credits him with having abandoned the ancient theology of hyper-domestication.

Hebrew, or Hapiru reactionary universalism became politically significant during the Davidic monarchy, when, with the Exodus and Moses stories the Egyptian God of gods was getting challenged. The God of Hebrews, of a people who were enslaved by Egypt, began revealing to them and to their offspring that he prefers them to be free. With Amun, the "Hidden God of gods" theology was established in Egypt to legitimize imperial grand-domestication or "civilization" for the Egyptian King of kings. Egyptian imperialism later was being challenged by Hebrew liberation theology.

Nevertheless, the theologies of Abraham and Moses cannot yet be counted as "universalism." The Moses Reform was only the beginning of a movement in this direction. Limitations to the universalism of Moses were, as such limitations always are, circumscribed by historical conditions of culture. In their quest for liberation, ancient Levite slaves acquired fresh questions that they needed to raise religiously. While arms and military organization remained out of reach, they needed divine encouragement. Thereby the God, who in his mercy has liberated them from slavery, continued to support them during the aftermath. It goes without saying that the mundane concerns of the fledgling Moses cult of liberation also led the theological universalism of the founder figure back onto a return path of hyper-sensitive exclusivity. Over the longer run, the defensive entrenchment of will and ego could scarcely be avoided.

It is a fact in the history of cultures and religions that any God while he is expected to serve as a war deity, to lead his people as a "Lord of Hosts," has of necessity ceased to function as a universal or almighty Lord of the world. The insistence that a Lord of War nevertheless is a universal almighty deity has so far led only to fanatic warfare. To prove the truth of the victors' theological fixation implies the extermination of enemies. Thus, war campaigns that insist on the universality of a sponsoring deity, can only lead to calamity either for the believers or for their enemies. They lead to losses at least on one side of the confrontation. Either way, the universalistic outlook is eclipsed. People conquered by an "almighty war deity" are left to turn to an alternate theism, or to atheism.

In Chapter Seventeen, below, we find how **Jesus Christ, when he was utilized by the Emperor Constantine as his God of War, could nonetheless be retained in the Christian creed as universal Savior—but only as Son of the Father and within the larger Holy Trinity.**

Under David and Solomon

Two or three centuries after the fabled Exodus event, the Hebrew Lord of Hosts cult began to ripen to its next phase. "Yahweh Sabaoth" was foremost a deity of war. He was invoked to sponsor a grand-domestication system. During the reigns of David and Solomon, a monarchic system reached its zenith quickly. While living under these two kings, heirs of the Israelite rebel tradition gloried in their united monarchy briefly, as in something that was divinely established. The abrupt split of the early kingdom into northern and southern portions (Israel and Judah), severely dampened the monarchic euphoria. Their division resulted in hostile literary exaggerations.

The Moses tradition remained an internal contradiction within both Israel and Judah. With an anti-hyper-domestication Exodus tradition—a Passover and Liberation celebration at their centers, both kingdoms remained riddles and aggravations unto themselves. One must, of course, annotate this perception. Only the hostile perspective of the Southerners has survived in writing. At best, our total understanding of ancient Israelite history is off center, and at its worst, and more likely, the cultic depravity of the Northerners is a projection. The writings of Southerners appear driven by envy, over not having achieved glories of state that could match those in the North. To illustrate their confrontation, we need to point only to their most conspicuous bone of contention—the Canaanite cult of the bovine.

Considered mythically and symbolically, the famous calf sculpture that the first Levite high-priest, Aaron, has set up in gold for worship (*Exodus* 32), and the ones which Jeroboam is said to have set up at sanctuaries in Bethel and Dan (*1 Kings* 12:28), surely have served Canaanite nuances similar to those provided by the twelve calves that have supported a bronze basin at the Jerusalem temple (at least on parchment, in *1 Kings* 7:23–26 and *2 Chronicles* 4:2–5). All the complaints about the apostasy of Northerners, by Southern kings and their prophetic and scribal supporters, must be evaluated in light of the fact that, ordinarily in this world a sheer loss of hegemony breeds resentment and bad blood. It happens in the presence of revered greater-than-human realities as easily as it does among discrepancies in humanistically historicized narratives.

Modern rationalists frequently dismiss ancient conflicts over cultic behavior as irrational thinking, and they include in this judgment all religious behavior to boot. But such evaluations usually fail to see the rational and political significance of socialized religious symbolism. In our introductory chapter, we defined general religion as retreat-oriented behavior. Accordingly, in politics and society, the predictability of religious behavior implies, that whosoever bows to or retreats together with others from under communally acknowledged greater-than-human realities or dangers, can be relied on in emergencies and in battle. Dependable comrades share similar breaking points—that is, points at which it makes sense to either continue fighting, and points at which people can quickly agree to retreat together. In post-theistic and secular political ideologies, swearing oaths of unity to a national emblem, or to a flag, supposedly serve the same function of validating or sealing historical allegiances, covenants, or reformations.

Back in the early literature of the Israelite monarchy, one finds the kind of flattery that was customary at grand-domesticator courts everywhere: May the King have a long life! May his dynasty last forever! And in a complete relapse into the Egyptian-style hyper-domestication, the zealous prophets of Yahweh themselves participated fully in idolatrous adulations. The prophet Nathan, who personally had been scheming to have Solomon installed as David's successor, is said to have gone so far as to attribute divine son-ship to his favorite prince. These words of a "Man of God" resounded as if spoken by God himself:

"I will be his father, and he shall be my son... I will not take my steadfast love from him... and your house and kingdom shall be made sure forever before me; your throne shall be established forever." (2 *Samuel* 7:14–16)

The priestly poet who composed the Second Psalm recited this same message even more daringly—as an unabashed grand-domesticator's breaking and dashing, poetically sublimated. This poet impersonated the voice of God:

"I have set my king on Zion, my holy hill." I will tell of the decree of the Lord: He said to me, "You are my son, today have I begotten you. Ask of me, and I will make the nations your heritage, and the ends of the earth your possession. You shall break them with a rod of iron, and dash them in pieces like a potter's vessel." (*Psalms* 2:6–9)

Born ever so gradually of court flattery and carried on the wings of poetry, a gradual transformation could be observed in Israelite grand-domestication etiquette and liturgy. The internal politico-religious contradiction, between form and content, began to squirm and to stir with utmost strain on human consciences.

Any reader of the Psalm just quoted, will invariably be impressed by the extreme exaggeration in that metaphor. How can a metaphor of battle blaze a path beyond itself and beyond present political realities—aesthetically? To contemplate the possibilities of this process of artistic magnification, one might suggest an alternate step for this increase of sublimation. One need only experience it under the wonderful musical umbrella which George Friedrich Handel has constructed in his inspired oratorio, *The Messiah*. There the atrocious smashings and the dashings do sound rather wonderful.

As much as I would miss the wonderful embellishments of Handel, I sometimes also wish that these *Psalm* lyrics, about smashing and dashing had never been intuited or composed by a human mind —or credited to a Deity of War that posed as God Almighty.

Isaiah and Micah

In the poetic prophesies of Isaiah (Eighth Century BCE, royal etiquette and court flattery rose to the demands of dynasty and throne. Scholars have suggested that this noteworthy "messianic" passage may originally have been recited while celebrating the ascension of King Hezekiah to the throne of Judah:

"For unto us a child is born, to us a son is given; and the government will be upon his shoulder, and his name will be called "Wonderful Counselor, Mighty God, Everlasting Father, Prince of Peace." Of the increase of his government and of peace there will be no end, upon the throne of David, and over his kingdom.... The zeal of the Lord of hosts will do this. (*Isaiah* 9:6-7)

Even after making allowances for a generous amount of court flattery, this passage in *Isaiah* no longer fits very well the coronation of a human king. These words of poetry soared too high, so as to leave any kind of human Hezekiah mired far behind in the dust of the planet. As a result of having transcended their mortal subject matter, such words actually have ceased to be court flattery. Carried on the wings of superlatives and metaphors, such exaggerations, in Homo sapiens minds, were miraculously transposed from preposterous flattery into more rationally acceptable "prophesy." Resounding as direct echoes, as words from the mouth of God himself, in whose eternal presence they were composed, such words would continue to circulate among human worries and fortunes as ambiguous and graciously revealed divine promises of increase and greatness. Had they not been understood as promises, spoken directly by God, such words of human poetry would forever need to be pilloried for communicating dishonest pandering and deceptive invention. Of course, if the newly installed king really had been Mighty God, then their emperor-worship and political flattery would have gotten harmonized.

But as it was, the prophet Isaiah abandoned the hope of expecting very much from a mortal contemporary king. Prophetically, therefore, he proceeded to celebrate instead an ideal king, one whose arrival could realistically only be hoped for in the future. Looking away from the present king on the throne of Judah, the prophet has permitted his train of thought to start afresh with a newly born baby boy who, in a manner of speaking, at the moment, was still "out of this world." If we accept the suggestion of some scholars, that this text represents enthronement liturgy from the days of King Hezekiah, then it is possible that the meaning of the quoted passage could have gotten amended—after disappointment had set in about the king's defeat under Sennacherib of Assyria.

In any case, Isaiah no longer had in mind an ordinary human king, one that would disappoint again. He anticipated a king who was no less than an aspect of Mighty God himself. Thus, beginning with

Isaiah, pro-monarchic prophets have gradually shifted their political enthusiasm toward a sublime trans-monarchic Kingdom of God.

Micah was a younger contemporary of Isaiah. He, too, projected the focus of his hope forward into the future. But he also looked back into the past and to the possibility of starting afresh with a royal childhood. With a new start, he humbly and ambitiously began to re-envision Davidic history from scratch, beginning at Bethlehem where the boy who became King David was born.

> But you, O Bethlehem Eph'rathah, who are little to be among the clans of Judah, from you shall come forth for me one who is to be ruler in Israel. (*Micah* 5:2)

Hananiah and Jeremiah

The Judaic experiment with grand-domestication began to disintegrate after the death of Solomon. It came to an end early during the sixth century BCE when King Zedekiah, of Judah, put in his lot with an Egyptian coalition against Babylonia's rising king, Nebuchadnezzar. At this important junction in the history of Judah, one does find two prophets hurling opposing revelations on behalf of God.

Hananiah, in past-present-future tense, spoke in support of joining the Egyptian coalition: "Thus says the Lord of hosts, the God of Israel: I have broken the yoke of the king of Babylon" (*Jeremiah* 28:2). The prophet Jeremiah, who regarded revolt against Babylon to be folly, replied with ridicule and later with a more serious counter-prophesy:

> "Thus, says the Lord of Hosts, the God of Israel: I have put upon the neck of all these nations an iron yoke of servitude to Nebuchadnezzar, King of Babylon."

To strengthen his statement further, Jeremiah accused Hananiah of telling a lie, and for emphasis, he placed a curse of death on him. Beyond the art of court flattery, such was the style of royal advisement in those days. Unfortunately, King Zedekiah took hold of the wrong divine promise, and thereby chose a curse.

Nebuchadnezzar destroyed Jerusalem and its temple; he wasted the land and deported most Judaeans to Babylon. There, over some fifty years, perhaps, they were given an opportunity, to get weaned away from the dream vestiges of a Davidic monarchy.

When Jeremiah's attempt to influence his king's foreign policy failed, he declared old religious covenants null and void, including the one that was believed to have existed between God and the Dynasty of David. And while contemplating Israel's situation, he hastened to reject also the covenant that Moses had mediated between God and Israel. Jeremiah saw the old covenants ripe to be replaced with the dawn of a new era of personal religion—of personal salvation, in a universalistic context. The new covenant implied a complete change of human nature—so complete, that it amounted to a new creation.

"Behold, the days are coming, says the Lord, when I will make a new covenant with the house of Israel and the house of Judah, not like the covenant which I made with their fathers when I took them by the hand to bring them out of the land of Egypt, my covenant which they broke.... But ... I will put my law within them, and I will write it upon their hearts; and they will be my people. And no longer shall each man teach his neighbor and his brother, saying, 'Know the Lord,' for they shall all know me, from the least of them to the greatest, says the Lord; for I will forgive their iniquity, and I will remember their sin no more." (*Jeremiah* 31:31–33)[81]

The Second Isaiah

The end of captivity for the Jews in Babylonia came with poetic fanfare. An admirer of the eighth century BCE prophet Isaiah, an unnamed poet now known only as Second Isaiah, tagged an appendix to the old scroll. It was later portioned off as *Isaiah* 40–56. The fact that he got away with this feat suggests that he was a scribe rather high up in the rabbinic hierarchy, and that his message was deemed proper. His long poem exploded with fervor about the wonderful saving event that had just occurred—an event that he himself had been able to witness and to decode.

The person who wrote *Second Isaiah* can be identified as a poet; this much is certified by his style of writing. But he also must be recognized as a priest and prophet. The prophesy of Second Isaiah opens with a chant for comfort. Its words speak as though they were chanted by a Council held in Heaven and it was addressed to the Judaic survivors of nearly fifty years of exile—that is, sixty years for victims of an earlier

[81] See also *Jeremiah* 32:38–40 and *Ezekiel* 11:19. A similar new relationship between God and people was also anticipated in *Hosea* 2:20.

deportation. The substantial reason for his freshly offered divine comfort is included at several points throughout the poem: God has sent his Messiah (his Anointed) to conquer Babylon and to set his chosen people free. Never mind if that Messiah of Yahweh happened to be a Persian conqueror who did not seem to know much about the God of the land of Judah!

> Thus, says the Lord, your Redeemer, who formed you from the womb: "I am the Lord, who made all things"... who says of Cyrus, "He is my shepherd, and he shall fulfill all my purpose;" saying of Jerusalem, "She shall be built," and of the temple, "Your foundation shall be laid." "Thus, says the Lord to his Anointed, to Cyrus, whose right hand I have grasped to subdue nations before him and ungird the loins of kings, to open doors before him. (*Isaiah* 44: 24-45:1)

The phrase "whose right hand I have grasped," in *Second Isaiah*, corresponds to a similar phrase on the *Cyrus Cylinder*, a cuneiform record inscribed by Babylonian priests of Marduk. It shows the priests of the Babylonian high-god equally enthused, welcoming this Persian imperialist as their savior. It appears that Cyrus had saved the Babylonian cult of Marduk as well. Indeed, he has saved all cults in the land from the hands of a Babylonian revisionist king, Nabonidus.[82] This invading Persian imperialist, Cyrus, was also given credit for having liberated numerous divine statues belonging to various city cults in the greater Mesopotamian realm, and also for rebuilding their regional sanctuaries.

All this does not mean that our poet from Judah necessarily got his phrases from the priests of Marduk directly; rather, it means that both priestly sources apparently obtained similar messages from Cyrus's own generous edicts. All the while, it is obvious that Persian propaganda, in Babylonia, was informed and advised by priests of Marduk who, unabashedly, collaborated with Cyrus in governing their city-state. One may suspect that they already have collaborated in Cyrus's takeover of the city.

Some portions of *Second Isaiah*, for example Chapters 44 and 46, contain explicit ridicule of Mesopotamian polytheism. Their hostile posture has, superficially, kept many scholars from considering the poet's actual indebtedness to Babylonian religion. However, a historian who wishes to attain a realistic perspective must assume that a reasonable Judaic poet, during his fifty years of exposure to

---

[82] See Pritchard, ed., *Ancient Near Eastern Texts Relating to the Old Testament*, 315f.

Babylonia, could not have helped but to do some serious reflecting on the Marduk religion. A curious Judaic unemployed priest, a priestly rabbi of sorts, could not have helped but wonder what the Babylonian Akitu rites (the New Year festival) were all about. Important to Babylonian religion and statecraft, these rituals were as central as Passover had become for Judaic and Israelite traditions. Some Akitu rituals were public and could easily be observed in the open.

The exit of the Babylonian god Marduk from his temple, and his return, were an integral part of the ceremonial procedures. Moreover, the functions of this Babylonian chief deity were closely linked with the fortunes of the king who knew himself to be commissioned by this God. In Babylon the king played a key role in the divine-human drama of suffering and redemption. The king was dethroned and deprived of his insignia. He was humiliated to the point where the high priest of Mar-duk would pull him by the ears, strike his cheeks, and extract a confession to the effect that he had not sinned against the Lord of the lands, had not been negligent in serving the God, and had not destroyed Babylon.[83] Later, the face of the king was struck once more, to draw tears from his eyes as a good omen for water and fresh growth on the land. All this had to be duly enacted in order to renew the land and the year, thus to renew space and time and begin another round of Mesopotamian balance and prosperity.

Jonathan Z. Smith has commented on the negative confession in this Babylonian ritual as an "incongruity."[84] He has done so, allegedly, for the purpose of stimulating discussion and gaining an entry into this archaic text. If anyone would have destroyed Babylon, he reasoned, it was foreigners when given a chance. Rhetorically he asked: "What native king of Babylonia ever contemplated or was guilty of destroying or overthrowing Babylon, smashing its walls or neglecting/destroying Esagila?" Nevertheless, the *Nabonidus Chronicle* and the *Cyrus Cylinder* suggest otherwise.[85] Collaborators with Cyrus, priests of Marduk, accused the last king of the Babylonian dynasty, Nabonidus, of having done

---

83 Henri Frankfort, *Kingship and the Gods* (Chicago: U. of Chicago Press 1948), 313ff.

84 Jonathan Z. Smith. "A Pearl of Great Price and a Cargo of Yams: A Study in Situ- ational Incongruity," *History of Religions,* 16:1 (1976): 1–11.

85 See Prichard, *Ancient Near Eastern Texts Related to the Old Testament,* 305ff, 315ff. For more regarding the Decree of Cyrus, see also *Ezra* 1:1-11.

just that. In an empire where the central seat of power frequently was moved from one convenient capital city to another, the protestation of "having not destroyed Babylon and Esagila" appears to have included also the meanings of neglect and abandonment.

In light of a wider religious-historical perspective, the priestly inquest during a Babylonian Akitu rite, therefore, need not be written off as a situational incongruity. Any high priest of Marduk who felt responsible for the God's cult, and for balancing Babylonian culture and empire, would have regarded both ritualized instances of slapping the king as being proper—and even as reasonable and necessary. Often in history, cities and states have been ruined from within by follies committed by their own leaders (cf. the USA now, in 2020).

Governments always have been two-edged swords, one edge to cut inward and the other to cut outward. One may see in the Babylonian Akitu tradition an archaic system of political checks and balances which the priestly cult was able to impose on the king's ambitions as a means of delimiting the God's otherwise generous legitimization of royal ambitions. We all know that hyper-domestication powers, everywhere, have tended to become absolute when left unchecked. Millennia were needed to fine-tune this blessed incongruity, and judging from religious-political arrangements elsewhere in history and society, all these balancing measures probably never really worked well, or endured as long as the priests might have hoped.

Also please note, that this paragraph on realism is being written in the year 2018, in the USA. Every generation of friends of humankind, has to scheme anew, as masters of ceremonies and *homines ludentes*, to balance manners of survival—of harmony versus power, of cultist retreat-dancing against the aggressiveness of raw state. Every generation needs to invoke greater-than-human reality anew, to affirm sanctions that keep selfish leaders from compiling privileges, from amplifying privileges and turning them into absolute rights.

Religious rituals were established, in the past, to prevent even benevolent dictators from taking the lead in schemes of self-aggrandizement. In 586 BCE, citizens of Judah went into exile with the Deuteronomic knowledge that God rewards good behavior and punishes the bad. They had been taught how to interpret divine punishments as evidence of guilt and sin. Throughout their exile in in Babylonia, they were haunted by the very same question that Job has asked of God: "What is my sin?" They wondered whether, collectively, they were guilty of something more than than peoples who were not exiled. And so, at the end of their sojourn in Babylonia, their Second Isaiah answered these questions by way of insisting that suffering, although at some point it may have been a punishment by God, was nevertheless also the kind of thing that God himself was enduring. Suffering was to be understood as a necessary prelude to redemption. The poetry of *Isaiah* 53 celebrates the notion of divinely sanctioned and redemptive suffering. The questions that the poet has raised are all typically Judaic, and they have been raised by the Second Isaiah's own experience of deportation and exile. His answers drew heavily from the rational core of Babylonian religion itself.

During the cult rites of that religion, the statue of the god Marduk was made to disappear temporarily from the land of the living.[86]

The debate still continues about whether in Babylonia the God Marduk actually was thought of as a "dying and rising god," as deities of that type have been categorized by Sir James Frazer.[87] Indeed, reconstructions of the full Akitu sequence must rely on bringing together Mesopotamian documents from several strata of culture. But in addition, I suspect, that our debate has relied far too heavily on variances between Christian and Jewish interpretations. According to the Christian tradition, dying and rising taken together are reasonable divine attributes, whereas historians of Jewish provenance, with their take on what was respectable Semitic religion, tended to regard such notions as constituting obsolete hyperbole. But be that as it may. Even if Marduk's temporary disappearance during the New Year's rite is not really death, the king's suffering, prefigured by disappearance of the national deity, demands by itself some kind of theological parallelism, to maintain Babylonian imperialism, or at least a justification for the priest's assertive behavior. The simplest motive of why a high-priest should have struck the king, appears to have been the assertion of Marduk's authority over the king. Beyond that, a king to be struck during

---

86 See Frankfort, *Kingship and the Gods*, 321ff.

87 See, for instance, "A Pearl of Great Price and a Cargo of Yams," in the previous reference to Jonathan Z. Smith. Footnote 84.

annual reinstatement appears justified, and can still now be best explained by referencing such rituals to the exemplary behavior and nature of the supreme deity—to delimit the arrogance of human egos, of rulers and subjects alike.

But again, be that as it may. We must not allow ourselves to be distracted by emotive meanings that "death" or "resurrection" carry variously among reasoned traditions. What in the realm of the immortal gods, or at the level of a God of gods, could dying possibly mean? Certainly, it meant not death in the final tragic human sense.

And together with these considerations, the existence of the text in *Second Isaiah* 53 is itself a Judaic-Babylonian datum that needs to be reckoned with. For Exile history, such data definitely outweigh their later Christian as well as later Jewish usage and meaning. The question of whether Marduk should be classified as a dying and rising deity is really beside the point. The central purpose of the Akitu drama was that divine roles and royal roles be kept at balance. For the duration of a safe ritualized interval, of renewal, the risk was taken for these roles to be re-affirmed—only to be interrupted ceremonially and thereby be restored afresh.

God and king together have "suffered" and have put forth an effort, as it were, for the redemption and renewal of Babylon. After Marduk re-emerged from his mausoleum, the king of Babylon once again could sit on his throne and govern. And so, in full accord with Babylonian soteriology, the "Servant Israel," in *Second Isaiah*, suffered and was "cut off from the land of the living."

The poet considered him dead and proceeded, accordingly, to dwell on what could still be salvaged from this situation. Thus, with an application of Babylonian soteriology and logic, the poetry of Second Isaiah progresses from death to reemergence and to new life. The poet knew that his message may indeed have sounded incredible to fellow Judaic ears, and he said so:

"Who has believed what we have heard? And to whom has the arm of the Lord been revealed? For he grew up before him like a young plant, and like a root out of dry ground; he had no form or comeliness that we should look at him, and no beauty that we should desire him. He was despised and rejected by men; a man of sorrows and grief. Surely, he has borne our griefs and carried our sorrows; yet we esteemed him stricken, smitten by God, and afflicted. But he was wounded for our transgressions, he was bruised for our iniquities; upon him was the chastisement that made us whole, and with his stripes we are healed." (*Isaiah* 53:1-5) [88]

But then, the Second Isaiah communicated the will of his God not as it pertained to Persian interests in Babylonia, but as it affected him as one of God's specially chosen servants. His immediate goal was to persuade his fellow deportees to accept the God-given opportunity and return home to Jerusalem. He either did not see, or chose to overlook, the strategic pragmatism that motivated Cyrus to participate in the New Year rites, that is, to participate strategically in divine suffering. To Second Isaiah it did not appear politically suspicious. Yet, even the poet's own words were a strategic recitation to motivate people to return to Judah.

As far as the Second Isaiah was concerned, Cyrus of Persia, as a Messiah of God, invaded Babylonia for the sole purpose of liberating God's special people. The Second Isaiah experienced this saving event as if it were new light and a first insight, sent to him by God directly. Then, while he was still at it, he proceeded to decode the riddle that God had been putting to Judaism by way of their Deuteronomic theory of suffering. The identity of the Suffering Servant in *Second Isaiah* is dual and triple.

One may identify in this text at least two different Servant figures. A first "Servant Israel" signifies the people of Judah going into exile. This Servant died by the very fact of having been exiled. But then, after the "burial" by exile, of the Servant Israel, "alongside the wicked and the rich" of Babylonia, followed a rebirth of the liberated and freshly prospering Servant Israel.

The second Servant, Cyrus, getting struck ceremoniously, gave to Second Isaiah his saving insight. The liberation of his people from Exile, demonstrated by Babylonian royal ritual, finally made sense of

---

[88]The evidence is somewhat indirect and contextual. Upon taking over Babylon, Cyrus sacrificed sheep, offered incense, and "constantly prayed to the gods, prostrated on his face" (*Verse Account of Nabonidus*). The priests of Marduk further wrote concerning their God, that "he scanned and looked through all the countries, searching for a righteous ruler willing to lead him"—i.e. Marduk, in the annual procession—see the *Cyrus Cylinder*. Both documents are published in Pritchard, *Ancient Near Eastern Texts*, 312-316.

his own predicament. So he personalized: the Babylonian sovereign accepted punishment from God, while God liberates his own prophet and people. The first Servant Judah died at the moment when exile was decreed by Nebuchadnezzar; the second was born when freedom was approved by Cyrus.

Second Isaiah was open-minded and ready to learn from Babylonian religion about the will of his own God. The role of Cyrus vis-à-vis Israel corresponded, in Babylonian terms, to the role of the god Nebu who himself liberated the God Marduk from the confines of his netherworld mountain. All the while, looking at it from the view-point of Israel's sovereign God, the prophet saw neither Marduk nor Cyrus emerging together from their netherworld captivity. But from the point of view of Israel's God, he saw the new Israel being reborn instead. Thus, for him the larger scenario looked as follows:

For a brief moment I forsook you, but with great compassion I will gather you. In overflowing wrath, for a moment I hid my face from you, but with everlasting love I will have compassion on you, says the Lord, your Redeemer. (*Isaiah* 54:7–8)

The epiphany of a Persian messiah has introduced into the theology of Second Isaiah a new Servant figure, named Cyrus. His mission is closely fused with the fortunes of the second Servant. This figure was introduced on the strength of Judaic Messianism and Babylonian New-Year ritualism, revealing the implicit Babylonian gospel of redemptive divine suffering. Its introduction into the scriptures of Judaism had far-reaching consequences for the distant future—as for the larger world. The writer of *Second Isaiah* called for a re-enactment of the Exodus, whereas the immediate result could be counted only in small numbers of people who were willing to return to their Judaic homeland.

Beyond these meager results, Judaism later produced under Ezra and Nehemiah much the opposite of what the universalistic Second Isaiah had hoped for. For their own safety the Judaic rebuilders pulled back, defensively, into clannish parochialism against the remnants of their Samaritan-Israelite kin who had not been taken into Exile.

The universalistic motives expressed by biblical writers of the Post-Exilic period, such as are reflected in novellas like *Ruth* and *Jonah*, reveal the postures afforded by a generous minority. But the fact that these texts, too, were collected and recopied is sufficient proof that some scribes or teachers persisted in laboring for a humane and universalistic outlook.

It must be said that the universalism that was contained in *Second Isaiah* itself, with all its international openness, still contained some selfishly focused nationalistic blotches. Here and there the poet-turned-scribe appears to be unduly patronizing toward other nations. The strong identification of Israel, with Cyrus as a Gentile messiah and conqueror, generated some tragic opinions:

For you will spread abroad to the right and to the left, and your descendants will possess the nations and will populate the desolate cities (54:3).... Behold, you shall call nations that you know not, and [in response] nations who knew you not shall run to you, because of the Lord your God, the Holy One of Israel, for he has glorified you (55:5).

Hyperboles are words that can bless, can curse, and even kill. Second Isaiah, unduly impressed by Cyrus the Conqueror, as special Messiah of God who startled many nations, while being praised as Savior of Israel's exceptional status, of the foremost Chosen Servant-Nation of God, still dreamed the dream of Joseph (compare *Genesis* 37). In the end, Second Isaiah still taught the theology of a "tribal" and "petty" Almighty God. This tribalistic over-stated piety not only propagated a distorted view regarding Gentile peoples and other nations, but also instilled an exaggerated latent martyr complex whenever other nations appeared unduly blessed by the otherwise logical impossibility of being ruled by their tribal "Almighty God."

The derivative Christian notion, of an idolized ethnic "Apple of God's eye," piously garnered from *Zechariah* 2:8, necessarily invited vultures from near and far to peck precisely at this divinely favored eye of a foreign God. The Christian exploitation of *Second Isaiah,* of pre-empting the sufferings of the Servant figure to refer exclusively to the sufferings of Jesus Christ—has aggravated deadly competition between two almost universalistic sibling faiths. It has heightened the irritability and vulnerability of Christian and Jewish egos alike. It has conceptualized Judaic tribalism to persist in its diaspora of a sanctified and stubborn exceptionalism. At the same time it has saddled vast stretches of Christendom with its scriptural fixation on a similar divinely uploaded competitive identity.

What in prophetic poetry began as special grace and encouragement, for unity and divine proximity, has become a predecessor of secular reactionary nationalism. It turned into naive nationalism as it was being remodeled from its religious context of righteousness into a tradition of theological favoritism. The prophetic lure of partiality and love, as it was being claimed by God's favorite human herds, has driven Judaism and Christianity to go a tragic step too far in the direction of exceptional-ism, of arrogance and self-conceit.

And so, for example, during the Holocaust under German National Socialism, there have emerged two nationalisms, one seeing itself as "elected by God" and the other insisting on having been "selected by Nature"—both were emboldened by heroes who were steeped in post-Versailles anger during moments of worldwide economic desperation. We saw the younger grip the throat of the older. All human cultural achievements, all sciences, thrive on taking away —or being given from among the possessions of God, regardless of whether or not such properties are presently owned by a sovereign Father God or rest contained in the embrace of an extremely masochistic or inert Mother Nature.

Judaism and Christianity represent two ancient attempts at universalistic salvation religion; and both are more provincial than either of them likes to think of itself. Both abide in almost complete ignorance about each other's full culture and history. And thus, they repeatedly predispose themselves to new opportunities for conflict. Islam meanwhile has come onto the same scene. It participates in the same scuffle of competitive egos, mobilized as if for an almighty God with similar human-like zeal. Nevertheless, a historian must try to remain collected. By sixth century BCE Jewish standards, the universalism of Second Isaiah was remarkable and radical. Salvation had come to his people by a Persian grand-domesticator, perceived to be the Anointed of God—of the God of gods, of all the peoples whom he liberated.

Such historical realism, apparently, was not yet ripe among exiles in Babylonia two-and-a-half millennia ago. Wold-wide it appears out of reach still today. Instead, something else has happened. The very introduction and presence, of a treatise like *Second Isaiah*, within the thought-stream of Judaism, after a period of incubation, was destined to break forth with a fresh and a different kind of political as well as religious Messianism, presenting a radically different kind of internationalized anointed Savior, with a different religious repertoire and aim.

A new era of salvation, of redemptive divine/human suffering was ushered in—a reversal of defeatist gloom by a faith in resurrection and in victory over death. An ancient religious notion, that previously had been cultivated mostly to justify hyper-domestication, was transformed by divine grace into a Good News story for the offspring of imperial victims.

During the early Christian era, hyper-domestication could here and there be shamed and softened. And no, the Christian movement did not begin with dumbing down victimized peoples for easier management. Rather, it began with defeating the ontology of hyper-domestication with fairer, straight-forward antithetical argumentation. The imperial political theater was thereby deprived of its own faith concerning the power of imperial "Deification" and "Resurrection"—of its victory over death by the mighty. The new gospel of liberation began in Judea where religious faithfuls knew how to argue with their God Almighty. During the centuries that followed, their insights penetrated and flooded the Roman Empire. Roman culture and living conditions gradually were given another rhythm. In some ways the empire changed.

And thereby, for the rest of the world, our manner of reckoning with politics and history has switched BCE onto an alternate current—onto something uncommon, so that it now resembles our present "Common Era," (CE).

General Theological Orientation

The theological emphases of the Christian New Testament, and of the early Church Fathers, signified a broad breach in the dike of Judaism. The rupture enabled a rivulet of Hebrew thought flow outward into the larger estuary that was the Roman Empire.

The movement carried a distinct theology and soteriology--a combination of Hebrew Messianism, sustained by memories of King David and Cyrus the Great of Persia. It was structured by Egyptian-style, Graeco-Roman Trinitarianism, and it entailed Numenology and Mariology.

This emulsion flowed like a transfusion of thought. It became orthodox Christendom. The Christian strain of Trinitarianism brought the time-tested ancient Egyptian themes of divine emanation, and of political resurrection theology to the surface and therewith gave shape to Western Civilization.

Part Three:
Northern Scions,
on Southern Rootstock

The Other Ontology

With some Distortions of Hindsight, or Foresight, the history of ancient Greek philosophy reads like a millennium of nostalgia facing both ways--back to Pharaonic Theocracy and forward to Christianity.

Greek Philosophy represents an adjustment to Egyptian imperial mythology and ontology--not unlike the Hebrew prophetic response that, eventually, has blossomed into Christian "Kingdom of Heaven" enthusiasm--thus, a reaction to theocratic and imperial hyper-domestication.

Egyptian "Neo-Platonism" has shaped the rational milieu for what in Western Civilization has softened and cushioned the physical scientific caricature of the world which sciences have been trying to create. The new phenotype of Egyptian religious ontology was reborn in its new form of organized Christendom. It has helped to emulsify the chips and debris of technological analysis toward fresh degrees of complexity and possibilities.

11

From Mythology to Philosophy

Environments in which Philosophy grew

Information in this part of the book, which focuses on Greek philosophy and its roots, is presented in the reverse order of its discovery. Some decades ago, in a seminar, I was explaining Heliopolitan theology to a group of students. At one point during the discussion I found myself grasping for a better analogy, and I heard myself say: "It is somewhat like. . .? Like, Neo-Platonic ontology!"

As I heard these words spoken, they came as a complete surprise to me. At that moment, it has been more than a quarter century since I had read the *Enneads* of Plotinus. Back in those early years I searched for eternal philosophical truths, and I never wondered where or how Plotinus might have learned what he knew. In our a-historical pursuit of philosophy, back then, we were easily led astray by the sheer weight of words and names. We generally were satisfied with reaching and grasping what Plotinus supposedly taught as "New Platonism." Nomenclature provided cover for the inadequate historical curiosity we cultivated back then. But after having confirmed that Plotinus and his teacher Ammonius were both native Egyptians, who came to Alexandria to learn and to share, it became necessary to ask how two intelligent Egyptians could have converted to a non-existent Greek "New-Platonic" philosophy.

The reason for mentioning this incident, pertaining to this writer's sub-conscious indebtedness to "Neo-Platonism," is not to explain how that which is here being written about the ancient Egyptian theological heritage is merely the embellishment of a historical incident, of decades ago. Rather, it is to show how a small insight into Neo-platonic beginnings, in Egypt, now continues to generate questions we might ask about "Neo-Egyptianism."

At a later occasion, after I had written most parts of *Egyptian Light and Hebrew Fire,* I began to wonder how strange my fresh exposition of the *Enneads* must appear to readers who, all along, have been told that the philosophy of Plotinus is an elaboration on Plato. Such an astonished audience would have included practically everyone I knew in the field of academic philosophy. According to the teachers whom some of us shared, Plotinus, as founder of Neo-Platonism, was a "new Plato." He just *had* to be a product of the ancient Greek Socratic and Platonic fraternity of aristocratic wise men. I therefore resolved that my essay, demands a summation of the teachings of Plato—for contrast and comparison. But then, in as much as Plotinus was quoting sentences not only of Plato, but also of other Greek philosophers, a broader view on the formation of Greek ontology appeared to be called for.

A series of surprises followed in quick succession, and each of these would have demanded that my book be expanded sideways to the size of a multi-volume encyclopedia on subject matter that momentarily did not hold my primary fascination. Not only did portions of Plato's dialogues, such as the *Timaeus,* derive their elementary ontology from ancient Egypt, so also did the writings of other Greek wise men before Plato. The only way to do justice to the prehistory of Plotinus's so-called Neo-Platonism was to call attention to traces of Egyptian ontology in the bequests of other philosophers.

It goes without saying that a short general bibliographical acknowledgement of this sort can only be preliminary and hypothetical. Future historians of philosophy, and historians of religions together, will need to reexamine the larger panorama of Hellenic philosophy in light of the ancient Egyptian connection. In the course of time, we surely will end up with a wider scope for the history of Greek philosophy. Future historians will need to come up with better summaries of subject matter than I am trying to survey.

The Hellenic philosophical tradition affected the structure by which thinking about Christian theology would be done. This result happened primarily by way of Neo-Platonism which, as we now know, enabled a home-coming of Greek philosophy to neo-Egyptian ontology. The history of ancient Greek philosophy now reads like a millennium of nostalgia facing both ways, back to ancient Egypt and forward to Christianity—though, most philosophers would prefer to sidestep Christian history and go directly to their Enlightenment Period.

Greek philosophy was the transition from Egyptian mythology to Enlightenment reasoning, similar to how the Hebrew prophetic tradition has evoked Christian "Kingdom of Heaven" enthusiasm that politically led to Christianized imperialism and to later democratic reductions.

The beginnings of Greek philosophy, of Christian doctrine, Gnosticism—plus an assortment of mystery cults that flourished during the period that has gotten named "Hellenism"—all together were ancient Egypt's maternal gifts to Mediterranean and Western Civilization. Egyptian "Neo-Platonism" summarized the evolving rational milieu for which the evolving Western world—with its phenotype converting to Christianity—brought together various layers of divine ontology. The Council of Nicaea and the writings of St. Augustine may be studied, profitably, as benchmarks along the path of this confluence of traditions. The essential Greek prerequisite, that early Christianity and Neo-Platonism had in common, was the fact that both were communicated and their proponents wrote in Greek. After the exploits of Alexander the Great, eastward, Greek has become the lingua franca of the Near East.

In one of his dialogues, the philosopher Plato narrated a playful discussion on mythology, carried on by Socrates and Phaedrus in the shadow of a tree. The latter of the two seemed to remember that it was "somewhere about here, that they say Boreas seized Orithyia from the river?" Socrates acknowledged that this indeed was the tradition. But then he came up with a surprise. The notorious Athenian gadfly, who stood mentally poised to expose the foolishness of any Homo sapiens he met, refused to demythologize this tale or its divine characters. Instead, he became introspective and mused about his personal priorities:

I cannot as yet "know myself," as the inscription at Delphi enjoins, and so long as that ignorance remains it seems to me ridiculous to inquire into extraneous matters. (*Phaedrus* 230a)[89]

Introspection on self-knowledge, and on the pursuit of philosophy, this Socrates has mentioned as his immediate goal in the *Phaedo*,

---

[89] See E. Hamilton and H. Cairns, eds., *Collected Dialogues of Plato.* Princeton, N.J., Princeton University Press, 1963.

placed on a somber common denominator (see 67c–e). He was there contemplating his own impending death, informing us how his dying has all along been prefigured dualistically in his life-long pursuit of philosophy, as a process of "differentiating his soul from the body." In an earlier instance, speaking from a less ultimate point of view, Socrates insisted on balancing the Apollonian advice of "know thyself" with the dictum of temperance, "nothing in excess" (*Protagoras* 343a–b). Notwithstanding all this, Socrates and his companions approached such religious-philosophical introspection, ethics and temperance on rather individualistic pretexts. Philosophy was pursued by small circles of students and associates under a single tutor. The subject matter of their study was, therefore, generally restricted to the teacher's own musings about his personal ethics or his general soteriology (his theory of salvation and ontology).

Philosophical quests traditionally have engaged small numbers of elitist minds who were motivated and sustained by equally elitist egos. Moreover, those few minds rarely contemplated their subject matter beyond a stretch of time that would have reached farther in time than what could be scanned by the two generations that were present when an influential teacher assembled his group of students.

Knowledge and truth were conceived in moments of intuition—at moments that were anticipated while traversing lengthy tracks of formal reasoning. Mental journeys tended to be dedicated to an a-historical exploration of statically eternal structures, conditions, and meanings. Personal quests for intuition, at abstract levels of conception, seldom brought much enlightenment or consensus to people who needed to struggle for survival in competition with multitudes of competitive beings.

With some glimpses of hindsight, cast on the entire history of Greek philosophy, Apollo's dictum of "know thyself" now beckons to supplement philosophical introspection with a measure of historical delineation. The expanded Apollonian dictum becomes for us "know thyself as one knower among others." Know thyself as a changing participant in a larger changing trend of learning; and know your own tradition as a dribble that trickles alongside, and interplays with other traditions of knowing! Not all traditions of human wit are "philosophical" in the Socratic sense; nevertheless, all historical introspections on this subject matter calls, as a minimum, for a brief introductory historical sketch to Greek philosophy.

While dwelling still nearer to the fountainhead of their inherited tradition, and while pondering a-historical ideas at leisure, Socrates and Plato had great difficulty seeing just how much their own critical habits of reasoning were still dependent on an ethos rooted in mythology. Thinking of themselves as intellectual reformers, Greek philosophers generally disliked the Greek mythological substratum of more ancient metaphors and modes of sharing. In addition, they were largely unaware of the motherland of mythology that led them into philosophizing. While philosophers were aware of the evolution of sounds and shapes in their Greek vocabulary, they regarded the meanings of their words to be far more firmly set than the evolving structures of any language could ever support.

Socrates and Plato would have been surprised to learn how their philosophical analytic habits, as distinguished from ontological contemplations, were still akin to the destructive habits of herder-bandit-warrior-ancestors who, mounted on horseback, had pushed out from the Eurasian plains some centuries earlier. They would not have been any less astonished to learn how their aristocratic talents of analytic reasoning themselves have evolved as mental substitutes —for the predatory aggressiveness of their intrusive ancestors.

The analytic physical breakdown of prey and environment, by predators and hunters, has gradually and over millions of years been enhanced beyond the basic necessity of mere chewing and digestion. The exaggeration was accomplished most effectively by aggressive male members of the genus Homo who, in the course of millions of years, reinvented themselves as scavengers and tool-using predators.

An updated Apollonian dictum of "Know Thyself" challenges individual lovers of wisdom, to get to know the entire evolution and history of cultures and religions, seriously in light of recent anthropological and archaeological discoveries. Of course, as circumscribed as the personal task of philosophical introspection may be, it always has been a good point to begin.

Inter-cultural and inter-religious understanding can only be successful in connection with prior introspection into one's personal, philosophical, and religious positions. Minds grasp to understand by seeing contrasts and similarities. Thus, a student who impatiently rushes toward understanding another culture, or its concomitant religion, may still lack the wherewithal for detecting meaningful historical distinctions. Without historical depth and details, without an awareness of time and the fact that all things and their designations change, divide or reunite, any of our cultural trends, our philosophical orientations and religious conversions will fail to come into focus. Neither will the corresponding perspectives of other people enter the translation range of our mental mirrors. We must begin our introspections afresh, back at points where the proponents of Indo-European glory advise us to begin—with early Indo-European epics and myths, perhaps.

Hesiod

Centuries before Greek philosophers and scientists began to reduce divine functions to abstract aspects and categories, and to impersonal principles—nay, even before classical Greek sculptors began to incarnate old divinities in charming bodies of wood or to weigh them down with the inertia of stone—the poet Hesiod penned theogony (story of gods). His powerful myth was destined to provide ethos for practically anything philosophical or scientific that previously had been achieved for Western civilization.

The mythic event of a divine son, Cronos, castrating his Father Uranos (Sky or Heaven, at the bidding of Mother Earth), goes a long way toward explaining how Oedipus complexes thrive in societies afflicted with scruples of patrilineality, under gods who themselves needed to rise up against their fathers. It exposes problems inherent in aristocratic succession. And it may even provide still older clues about elementary tensions that shaped relationships between parental and offspring generations within the Mammalian class.

But in addition, this *Theogony* of Hesiod also exposes the roots of Western philosophy, of Western science and Western culture. It reveals ancient existential reasons as to why, in spite of the presence of philosophy, new religious movements have become popular. Seen from the angle of Greek history, the dualistic Greek philosophers, Socrates and Plato, and to some extent even Aristotle, added little more than footnotes to the seminal Hesiodic god-story of castration—to this archetype of progress among Western domesticators. Philosophical advance and scientific progress required legitimation. It entailed awareness of the archetype of "progress," drawn from a still virile god-story that rationalizes life in an emasculated cosmos, managed by humankind. It behooves us to refresh our memories concerning this important tale and to contemplate afresh its central plot. We are being taught, at the dawn of Greek literature, that Earth was primary and Heaven was secondary:

Verily at first Chaos came to be, but next wide-bosomed Earth, the ever-sure foundation of all.... And Earth first bare starry Heaven, equal to herself, to cover her on every side, and to be an ever-sure abiding place for the gods.[90]

The mythic narrative of how Mother Earth subsequently gave birth to hills and nymphs; to Pontus, Oceanus, Coeus, Crius, Hyperion, Iapetus, Theia, and Rhea; to Themis, Mnemosyne, Phoebe, and Thethys; to Cronos, the Cyclopes, and finally to Cottus, Briareos, and Gyes —moves on speedily to a divine plot. The mythic incident, as has been hinted already, has produced far-reaching results in the mental development of not only ancient Greeks, but among all who were born into Western civilization later.

For of all the children born of Earth and Heaven, these were the most terrible, and they were hated by their own father from the start. He would hide them all away in a secret place on Earth as soon as each was born and would not suffer them to come up into the light, and Heaven rejoiced in his evildoing. But vast Earth groaned within, being straitened, and she devised a crafty plan. She made the element of gray flint and shaped a great sickle and told her plan to her dear sons. She spoke, cheering them, while she was vexed in her dear heart:

"My children, gotten of a sinful father, if you will obey me, we should punish the vile outrage of your father; for he first thought of doing shameful things." This she said; but fear seized them all, and none of them uttered a word.

But great Cronos, the wily, took courage and answered his dear mother: "Mother, I will undertake to do this deed, for I reverence not our father of evil name, for he first thought of doing shameful things."

This he said: and vast Earth rejoiced greatly in spirit, and set and hid him in an ambush, and put in his hands the jagged sickle, and revealed to him the whole plot.

---

90 Hesiod, "Theogony," in *Hesiod, the Homeric Hymns and Homerica*, trans. G. Evelyn-White (Cambridge, Mass.: Harvard University Press, 1977), 87, 89.

And Heaven came, bringing on night and longing for love, and he lay about Earth spreading himself full upon her. Then the son from his ambush stretched forth his left hand and in his right, he took the great long sickle with jagged teeth, and swiftly lopped off his own father's members and cast them away to fall behind him.[91]

Herding, Farming, Banditry

In contrast to the indigenous Egyptian civilization of sedentary valley farmers, the Greek cultural heritage received its primary impulses from Euro-Asiatic herders and antecedent hunters. During much of its early history, it appears, Egypt was sheltered from these northern movements of nomadic herder peoples. It was, however, obliged to adjust and respond to impulses from Mesopotamian sedentary presences. In later times, especially after the arrival of Eurasian horses in Egypt with the Hyksos, and after the expulsion of the same, Egyptian militaries were lured, in pursuit, to expand northeasterly in the general direction from which the Hyksos kings with their horse-drawn chariots had come.

For the sake of a broad overview, the time when ancient Israel and Judah emerged in the Near East may be studied elliptically by beginning with two very diverse cultural foci. Egyptian civilization and religion, with a Hebrew-Mesopotamian reaction, may be viewed as the original range for the biblical story to unfold. Hellas, to the north, contained older strata of Indo-European herder culture from the prairies of western and central Asia. A significant segment had also been moving west and south into Mediterranean coastlands early on. The Philistines arrived in Egypt by sea, about 1150 BCE, and in collaboration with the Egyptian imperial "New Kingdom" they occupied land along the eastern Mediterranean shore. Biblical narratives locate them there, and today the land still is named after them—"Palestine."

These people, in all likelihood, were seafaring remnants of the Mycenaean civilization, from the general area centered on today's Greece. The Mycenaean civilization was dissolving by about 1200 BCE. Culturally, these Philistines seemed to have blended in with the larger population of Canaanites and "other nations."

---

[91] *Ibid.*, 91, 93.

Nomadic cultures, whether they arrived in Egypt as warriors with horse-drawn wagons from the northeast, or whether they arrived in Egypt later with ships along the Mediterranean coast, were heavily preshaped by their lifestyle as herders. It all happened after the last Ice Age, when hunters began to evolve into owners and domesticators of animals.

Significant groups of people adhered tenaciously to the older Neolithic ways of full-time hunting. They transformed themselves gradually into warring groups of human hordes who bested their progressive herder neighbors by using their hunting weapons to "domesticate" both herders and planters who had become sedentary. Human "herds" became sedentary, together with their livestock. Swaggering bandits and warriors were the forebears of royal and imperial hyper-domesticators who whipped human herds—into civilizations. In Egypt and elsewhere, civilization had been evolving based on irrigation-driven agriculture. The evolution of early Egyptian civilization from totemism ownward we have sketched already in Chapter Three, above.

When Central Asian herders succeeded in domesticating horses, they were electrified by the power and speed of their subjugated animals. When herders perfected the art of riding on horseback, warfare became fiercer and could never be the same again. When Asiatic horse breeders brought their animals to the sedentary cultures in the Near East, those settlers were energized by cavalry-incited militarism. An equine-inspired cultural dynamic was set in motion, one that pulsated clear into our twentieth century. World War I was still ignited by it, and World War II erupted among its embers only to be continued with variants of so-called "horse-less" armored carriages. I personally may have witnessed one of the last cavalry battles in Western history, in 1945, just about two kilometers from my boyhood home. Horses and artillerymen were being killed by motorized artillery from an invading army still farther away.

Nothing in this broad overview conflicts with Colin Renfrew's postulate of a prior westward expansion of agriculture into Europe by carriers who spoke a proto-Indo-European language. Settlers of the LBK (Linear-Band-Keramik) culture arrived in Europe over seven millennia ago, from the Near East. On the steppes of Eurasia, an equine-generated cultural expansion might later have "exploded" and have forced additional westward movement onto fleeing dislodged farmers.[92]

The appellation "cowboy," in its modern Western sense, may not be entirely appropriate for labeling the entire scavenger-hunter-herder-bandit-warrior mentality, brought into bloom by Euro-Asian horsemanship; in this book we nevertheless will use this term occasionally.[93] Cowboys may be as close as a modern Western reader might ever get to the primitive Asiatic horse-oriented megalomania of a Genghis Khan and to the milieu of swagger that he exuded. The term "cowboy" enables us to think about the commoners ancient Egyptian agriculture in contrast, or as a foil. The ancient land of Egypt contained many sedentary farmers who would rather have been left alone by grand-domesticators and by empire builders, to plant their fields, to domesticate animals and raise families.

Earlier in this chapter, we learned from Hesiod's *Theogony* some interesting aspects of the behavior of traditional Greek cowboy-rough Titan gods. And we recognize that our quoted portion points only to one act of violence among others mentioned in Hesiod's story. Prior to the cosmic castration incident, Father Sky has tormented his offspring. Then Cronos, to whom the cruelty of castration has gotten ascribed, was defeated and imprisoned by his own son, Zeus.

What ought a historian make of this grand array of conflict mythology? Should one agree with the philosopher Plato, who suggested in his *Republic* that storytellers like Homer and Hesiod should be censured for having told lies? Plato himself went so far as to propose an effective method for silencing their literature forever. According to him, their literature contained only lies.

There is, first of all.... the greatest lie about the things of greatest concern... how Uranos did what Hesiod says he did to Cronos, and

[92] Colin Renfrew, *Archaeology and Language: The Puzzle of Indo-European Origins.*

[93] The author's assessment of horseback riders and violent cowboy culture, in the 1991 edition of Egyptian Light and Hebrew Fire, needs to be illuminated differently now, while considering the evolutionary progression of hunting, domestication, hyper-domestication and warfare, based on more recent archaeological data. See the author's Göbekli Tepe (2013) publication.

how Cronos in turn took his revenge, and then there are the doings and sufferings of Cronos at the hands of his son. Even if they were true I should not think that they ought to be thus lightly told to thoughtless young persons. But the best way would be to bury them in silence.[94]

Here is how Plato envisioned this silent burial. First, the audience should be restricted to a very few. A pledge of strict secrecy should be required. On top of that, a large sacrifice should be given; not just "a pig, but some huge and unprocurable victim."

Needless to say, Plato did not want those stories repeated, neither then, nor ever. He was convinced that these were lies and that the gods never waged war or did other cruel deeds. Plato knew that humankind naturally strives to imitate and to surpass their gods. He was afraid that people who hear these stories might want to believe and begin to imitate the alleged violence of the gods. Indeed, the philosopher was right on. Humankind—offspring of ape-like primates—have, as a rule, imitated, usurped, and tried to absorb into themselves whatever of All-Might appeared greater.

Originally, these myths were told to glorify and to justify hunter-herder-bandit styles of violence.[95] Moreover, this epic tradition was so strong and highly revered that in Central Asia it has survived to

---

94 Plato, "Republic" 377e–378a, in *Collected Dialogues.*

95 This suggestion is based on personal impressions, obtained during extensive travels in search of oral literature. Fantasies and fiction about violence, in Homo sapiens minds, kindle and justify violence for actual life. Sane minds will com-prehend the concerns of Socrates and Plato only after mustering the courage to view the violent productions of our Western entertainment industries somewhat realistically. Those industries pretend, that anything they produce contributes to education and to the improvement of culture. Nevertheless, unbalanced violent fiction, and love of lethal weapons, can only educate for Civil War. As long as our teachers are encouraged to utilize the effectiveness of audio-visual technology, to render their ordinary class-room lectures more understandable, those same means can also be used to introduce violence. Hands-on video games, practicing battle strategy, are even more suspect. Battlefields welcome many types of players. For example, why would a Russian KGB-remnant organization have ever wanted to support a citizens' National Rifle Association in the USA—which initially had been thriving on the romantic patriotic dream of defending their democratic civilization? Certainly, some hostile agents have noticed America's sentimental Achilles' Heel—namely, our "Son-of-a-Gun" romanticism of the old American Wild West and our capital-driven happy-go-lucky gaming media. Surely, profit-driven free media are insufficient protection against democratic patriotism that has gone treasonous. Media are ready tools to mobilize whatever resonates with the emotive "consumer souls" of their audiences.

to this very day. Castration and killing were skills in the repertoire of herders and horse-riders. Bards like Homer and Hesiod peddled their warrior theologies among would-be warriors and aristocrats for entertainment... in an environment that recently in America would have corresponded to our veterans club culture. Seen comparatively, these rowdy ancient Greek tales functioned as equivalents to our blue movies which, during the 1950s, ushered in an era of porn profanity. But then, because Hesiod's and Homer's epics were done well, as works of art, they became regular schoolbooks for ancient Greeks who were learning to write. Hesiod alone should probably not be blamed for the existence of his craft, nor perhaps even for the existence of an epic tradition. His level of violent humor surely was a time-honored inheritance already when prehistoric hunters met at sacred coves, along their road of becoming marauding Eurasian horsemen.

For a broader historical perspective on this hero-horse-and-glory religiosity of Homer and Hesiod, we do well when we compare them to an Indo-European tradition that might even be older than theirs. We do have antecedent Hittite texts, perhaps over a thousand years older. And these may have been derived from still older Hurrian sources. The first God of Heaven of the Hittites, Alalus, was killed by Anus, and Anus was defeated by Kumarbis. We are told that Kumarbis bit off the manhood of the vanquished god and swallowed it. Inside his belly, the phallus of Anus grew into the Hittitite stormgod. After he was born, this storm-god proceeded to defeat Kumarbis at the instigation of Anus who, understandably had remained angry and sore about his loss.[96]

Seen from the Hittite angle, Hesiod's version cannot necessarily be evaluated as an improvement. The severed members of Anus matured into the Hittite storm god, a counterpart to Zeus. By contrast, things that were cut away from Uranos, according to Hesiodic mythology, were defeated more severely by being transformed into their sexual opposite, the female Aphrodite, goddess of love. One may surmise that for Hesiod, personally, the mode of disposal of Uranus's virility was probably irrelevant. The transformation of Uranus's manhood into Aphrodite was a convenient method of disposal—it almost

---

[96] See Albrecht Goetze, "Hittite Myths, Epics, and Legends," in Pritchard, *Ancient Near Eastern Texts*, 120ff.

certainly signified a chauvinistic obscenity; or, put in evolutionary terms, an early outrageous masculine "tale of abstraction."

If from the land of the Hittites, about that time, we had traveled east across a mountain range, we could have come across some Aryan tribesmen who were in the process of descending southward onto the Indus civilization. Aryan gurus, centuries later in the *Rig Veda,* still ascribed similar cruelty to their chief warrior deity, Indra —such as smashing Dasyu fortifications which, thereupon, aborted their darker-skinned inhabitants, as pregnant women would have aborted if so struck.[97] This is a genre of still raw theological burlesque, produced by hunters turned herders and bandits, and by nomadic warriors thereafter. They became hunters of humankind, which is, men who at heart remained predators that killed and butchered. As domesticators and hyper-domesticators they knew how to castrate, how to seek out weaker sedentary planters and to rob their livelihood. By the systematic perfection of their banditry they became aristocrats and rulers. They told tales of creation of cosmic scope to ridicule the softer procreation- and generation-oriented mythology of sedentary peoples, whom they enslaved.

The task of fair historical interpretation is always difficult. Whenever in history one sees someone score as a great hero, glamorous enough to where, as hero, he can afford to build palaces and other noteworthy monuments—monasteries, temples, churches, or mosques for apparent atonement—his most cruel deeds have already been done. As a rule, the scribes and historians arrive at the scene just in time for the whitewash—to be paid royally for their labor. For understanding religions historically, we must therefore watch for clues to data regarding aggressive cultures vis-à-vis the thoughts of common people who ended up suffering. To also detect shortcuts to the minds of horse-and-glory warriors—with their shabby mythology of violence, their entertainment epics and artistically meritorious styles of recitation. We must keep an eye on history and on the larger context of human pursuits during their evolution.

---

[97] See Karl F. Geldner, *Der Rigveda* (Cambridge, Mass.: Harvard University Press, 1951) 1,101,1 and note; 2,20,7; 4,16,13. The Dasyu victims of the Aryan god Indra were worshipers of the cosmic serpent Vrtra. They also were identified as phallus worshipers, as in *Rig Veda* 10,99,3.

As we have explained religion in our introductory chapters, the initial intent of genuine religious awareness is to balance the scope and functions regarding some life-sustaining cultural necessities vis-à-vis greater-than-human realities, and to soothe worries regarding the future that threatens to overwhelm. By way of reinterpreting whatever bits of knowledge are in circulation, organized religions establish resolutions for dealing with greater-than-human problems. They offer fresh relationships with greater-than-human authorities under new extra-ordinary circumstances.

Poets as Reformers

As strange as it may seem, the predecessor poets of Homer and Hesiod, in their time, were actually spreading some "starter yeast" for religious sentiments, of a weak sort. They initiated the long process of converting actual bloodthirsty bandits and warriors into spoiled aristocrats who, in time, would listen to stories of heroism in the form of clever poetry rather than perform the cruel deeds themselves on an actual battlefield.

But of course the poetic approach, of reforming cutthroats by artistic sublimation, works exceedingly slow. On that account, Hesiod's solution was deemed no longer sufficient or considered decent by Plato, to be admitted into his design of an ideal republic. Belief in a personal God or gods, to the extent that such faith is maintained piously, may indeed facilitate honest humility. But to the extent that belief in God or gods has gotten organized in support of aggressive schemes of hyper-domestication, it also could be mobilized to justify tyranny and war-mongering.

All peoples on earth, at one time or another, have wrapped themselves into religiously rationalized blankets of legitimization. "As it was in the beginning [in God's greater-than-human order], is now, and ever shall be [in human behavior]." This is not only a Christian liturgical formula. It is the logical structure along which all cultures of *Homines sapientes* have rationally evolved, albeit often unnoticed by the people themselves.

Where does all of this leave ancient Greek philosophers with their conflicts among influences from the ethos of hunter and herder culture and the mental dispositions of farmer civilizations? In Greek society, philosophers functioned approximately as prophets did in Hebrew society. Of course, Greek philosophers were different from the Hebrew prophets who spoke or wrote in ancient Judah and Israel. They had no first Egyptian imperial deity from under whom, in their Greek political settings they needed to escape—such as the Hebrew memory had to rationalize in relation to their Exodus tradition. Greek polytheism did not need to upstage a strong monotheistic theology or deny the reality of what might have been lingering of an ancient Egyptian imperial Godhead.

Nevertheless, Greek philosophers were squaring off with their own Hellenic hyper-domestication residues, just the same. Had they spoken like Hebrew prophets, Greek philosophers probably would not have lasted very long in that still rough-and-tumble polytheistic environment. In their social context, where learners still gloried in the youthful ethos of ancient heroes, Homeric cutthroats still were considered to be not only necessary, but also were expected to appear aristocratic and noble—if not divine. Before a Poet or Reformer can communicate something meaningful to an audience, he or she must first be in tune with the language spoken and must himself be shaped by the present generation of listeners and learners.

Ammonius Saccas and Plotinus

The reconciling doctrine which Ammonius Saccas and Plotinus have been teaching to first students of so-called Neo-Platonism, at Alexandria, was older than the teachings of Plato or Aristotle, and older even than those of Thales and Anaximander--and certainly older than the logic by which Christian bishops reasoned at Nicaea. It was Egyptian orthodox Emanation Theo-Logic, old enough to have helped deify Egyptian pharaohs. It was ancient enough to nourish Greek philosophies in their infancy, with almost two millennia to spare.

12

Greek Philosophy

Philosophy as a Movement for Change

It must be acknowledged at the outset that Greek philosophy is not entirely Greek. Its origin was in Miletus, Ionia, in Asia Minor, a harbor city which at the time was the primary trading partner of Egypt. This should give us a clue. But trade in material goods is not our concern here, and the identities of carrier storytellers cannot be traced. We therefore seek our evidence of Greek indebtedness to Ionia more generally, in ancient Egyptian similarities themselves. Common sense opinions, at the basic axiomatic level, can be carried from harbor to harbor by ordinary folk. No direct exchange of leading thinkers between Egypt and Ionia was necessary for transmitting basic ontology; though, surely, there also were astute scholars traveling. Regarding Greek philosophy, we must distinguish its method from its content, its analytic habits from its axiomatic ontological content and context. The analytical habits of philosophers, by and large, were the indigenous end-product of ancient Greek predatory warrior intellect. Seen in an evolutionary perspective, their "analyses" represent the mental sublimation and perfection of ancient material hunting and butchering skills. There will always be a difference between the knife of analysis and the subject matter to which that knife is being applied. Meanwhile, traces of Egyptian religious context can also still be found in the Homeric epics.[98]

No matter how much Greek philosophers disliked Hesiodic mythology later, their own method of inquiry and thought was all the same conditioned by its very same aggressive cowboy ethos. This

[98] Garth Alford, in a still unpublished paper titled "Elysion—a Foreign Eschatological Concept in Homer's Odyssey," furnishes convincing linguistic proof that links the Greek "elysion" to the Egyptian "fields of rushes." In addition, Kjell Aartun, working along the paths of Cyrus Gordon and Rudolf Macuch, recently demonstrated linguistic continuity between ancient Crete and Egypt of four to five thousand years ago. See Lyn Ryne, "The Faistos Disc—Norwegian Researcher Unravels Ancient Mystery," *Norway Now,* no. 6. (1990):12. All this suggests the possibility of a flow of ideas into Hellenic culture from the south.

ethos contained the herders' notions of castration and the skills of hunters to kill and to butcher, with flint weapons and scraper edges.

Castration, in its raw physical form, is a procedure that domesticators, especially herders, knew how to inflict on some of their animals to control their breeding and to render them more tame. In Hesiod's *Theogony* we obtain a glimpse of how this skill was magnified by raconteurs to justify the neutering of animals and men. Even the high-god Uranos (Father Sky, Heaven) was singled out as prime victim for having been given this treatment. As in the course of human evolution, domestication progressed to the level of hyper-domestication—of enslaving humankind—we find that divinely mandated despots would guard their harems by stationing castrated eunuchs. When eventually this severe degree of hyper-domestication called for additional legitimization, imitating the celibate Uranos of Hesiod became an activity of virtue, of praising God as Pure Spirit by voluntary castration. The very predicament of Heaven (Uranos) could so be mobilized itself for "spiritual," aesthetic, or intellectual endeavors—theological, philosophical, as well as for scrupulously advantageous scientific precision.

Up to this point, we have sketched the prehistory of Hesiod's myth in relation to herder life. What follows next, as history of Greek philosophy, will be the sequence of Greek rationalizations, concocted on behalf of self-sublimation. Almost an "eternity" before Hesiod recorded the story of Father Heaven's castration, Stone Age sculptors at Göbekli Tepe buried phallus images of this universal male, deep into the Earth to magnify fertilization. After Hesiod, Greek sculptors transfixed the high-god's progeny into concrete and inert bodies of wood and stone. The happenstance, that gods themselves have gotten entrapped in static and compromising human postures, by the skill of human hands, proved damaging to their reputation in the longer run. In addition, ingenious playwrights paraded the old Hellenic gods as inert compromised images, lined up like assemblies of enslaved prisoners to everyone's delight.

Finally, when the time was ripe, philosophers arrived. These men occasionally quoted the old names of Hellenic gods with an air of piety. But all the same, the Greek divine names that they spoke no longer were linked to anything in the greater-than-human dimension. Living deities no longer participate in abstracted ontology. Analysis and abstraction are the mental equivalences to physical killing, butchering and castration. For instance, that which survives of a Creator, after philosophical abstraction, no longer is a personal deity. It is reduced to a static philosophical principle of "creativity."

Accordingly, the realm of "Platonic ideas" has been conceptualized as an eternal but nevertheless static dimension of greater-than-human reality. About Aristotle's Prime Mover we are told that everything moves because of him, but he himself is the Unmoved Mover (*Physics* 5). The First Mover has no limit or magnitude and is situated at the circumference of the known world (*Physics* 10). Aristotle ruled out the possibility of having a Prime Mover create movement by either pushing or pulling. In his Metaphysics he therefore derived motion in the universe from the fact that the Prime Mover remains "an object of desire" on account of which other entities move.[99] This finally implies that the First Mover is not only unmoved by anyone else, but that in actuality he may be impotent and unmoving on that account. Thus, all the famous Greek philosophical systems that Western sciences subsequently have borrowed, may be suffering from the Hesiodic castration syndrome—which is, from the analytic fallout of the Hesiodic "Uranos Predicament."

Of course, our Greek philosophers were not that negative toward all the gods. It would have been impossible, hoping to reform their culture from the platform of an all-out atheism. Greek philosophers also have appropriated, perhaps unknowingly, the ontology of ancient Egyptian monotheism—at least in its degraded form as monism. What do we mean by "degraded form"? This question calls for a brief digression and explanation.

Human rationality moves like music. It can shift from one key to another or slide from one octave to the next, up or down, depending on a composer's inspiration, instrumentation, or cultural habits. The language of experiential religion can, accordingly, be translated into languages of theology, philosophy, science, and/or technology. Where personalized ontologies decay, there the threshold of religious experiences moves and invites fresh archetypes and vocabulary.

---

[99] See W. D. Ross, *Aristotle: A Complete Exposition of His Works* (Cleveland: Meridian Books, 1959), 95f, 175ff.

The energies of genuine religious experience begin to fade naturally, by the yeast of rational theology. This happens inevitably, because Homo religiosus is a Homo sapiens as well. Analysis, an innate aspect of reasoning by an imitative apish mind, corresponds to teeth and digestive acids in a predator's physical body. Teeth and digestive acids together perform elementary analysis, that is, a break-down into smaller subject matter—while food substances are reduced to feces. Systematic theological minds, in like manner, break down the subject matter of religion—gods and God—by way of identifying divine "functions," abstracting "aspects," or assigning "attributes" to what, originally were encountered as whole divine personages.

Thereafter, processes, aspects, and attributes of larger configurations of reality are reduced by philosophers to the size of more easily graspable and more manageable abstractions. Monotheism thereby becomes monism, and polytheism becomes pluralism. Sped along by analytic cutting and reasoning, the products of systematic or analytic theology continue to be degraded into philosophical abstractions and thinkable principles. What used to be greater-than-human realities can so be approached without having to show respect or defer to them. By its very human-centered approach to subject matter, philosophy therefore initiates movement in the direction of atheism.

Philosophies eventually decay into sciences that contemplate "variables"—thus, principles and substances are trimmed to be smaller, more precise and more manageable. Justifications for excesses or human needs become "defense mechanisms" and humans, as such, learn how to think of themselves as machines. They promptly expect their doctors to be "technicians." Scientific disciplines easily decay into short-sighted technologies, or into industries that inflict unnatural endings. Thereby they disturb balances among natural forces. The usefulness of man-made artifacts and compounds are measured in short spans of time—they are subject to mortality and fads. Everything man-made crumbles into ruins, requires larger landfills or litters the oceans.

With fresh conceptualizations of World and Nature, and with fresh caricatures of greater-than-human reality, with residues of divine grace or chance quanta of luck, the process of analytic decay may be given an opportunity to reform itself and begin anew with a fresh vision of greater-than-human reality. Thus, inherent in Greek philosophy was not only the possibility of analysis toward decay, but also an opportunity for invoking positive contributions. Fresh seeds of redemption and reform, and rational religious retreats toward divinely balanced common sense also were possible.

Religious retreat from aggressive analysis was implied when Ionian philosophers paused long enough to think about substance (*apeiron*) as something "divine"—divine in the holistic Egyptian sense. The Ennead-ean stream of life, or Atum's seminal emission, is what Anaxagoras fell back on when he envisioned Anaximander's *apeiron* as being full of "seeds." That same theology of fertile flux and flow, that initially may have been contemplated along the shores of the living River Nile, still echoed from the philosophy of Heraclitus when he saw reality as being alive and flowing. Plato returned to that same Egyptian theology when, in the *Timaeus,* he summed up his description of the cosmogonic process as God generating an "only-begotten universe."

Eventually, that same theology of redemption was dawning when Aristotle struggled to overcome Plato's dichotomy—his invariable "Realm of Ideas" versus "living objects of sense experience." With his graduated theory of "form and matter," the philosopher Aristotle succeeded in constructing a metaphysical ladder halfway between Platonic dualism and the ancient Egyptian path of holistic emanation, of overflow and radiation—with multiple smaller steps of analysis.

Greek philosophy eventually won its skirmishes against the old wea-ponizing legitimation cults. It left behind on the battlefield, for decay, the reputation of heroic hyper-domesticators. It also abandoned in its wake the ancient burlesque myths that glorified killing, castration, slavery, and other bad hyper-domestication habits that stuck mired in satire and disdain. Greek philosophers arranged for fresher and more cautious rapprochements with Egyptian dynamic monism. As they went, they labored to disenfranchise hyper-domestication.

Beyond this, perhaps without really knowing or trying, the philoso-phers of Greece redefined common-sense contexts and thereby opened the path to a fresh monotheistic vision. The conceptual decay of mono-theism into monism was not irreversible. Analogically speaking, dual-ism "hunts" the wild animal, suspends and splits it into halves. Monism kept arithmetic at bay and enabled contemplation of that same "animal" alive and whole again. And behold! Greek philosophy subse-quently found a new mythological home in the Christian religion—new reasons for its ancient Egyptian heritage and ontological scaf-foldings were discovered.

Philosophy from Thales to Anaxagoras

The history of Greek philosophy begins with the sixth century BCE in the seaport city Miletus, along the Western coast of Asia Minor. At the time when the first teachers of science and philosophy appeared in that Greek settlement, the city had already become the most prosperous trade center in all of Hellas. A significant portion of the city's trading capacity was developed with the help of Phoenician middlemen.

The Milesian city-state maintained its own colonies. Some of these were located along the eastern shore of the Black Sea. At the same time, Miletus obtained a strong trading foothold in Egypt. After they regained independence from Assyria, pharaohs of the Twenty-Sixth Dynasty (663–525 BCE) built a strong mercantile fleet. Their primary trading partner during this renaissance was Greece, and Miletus was the seaport most frequented. Inasmuch as Ionia had early on fallen under Lydian and Persian hegemony, the subsequent Persian takeover of Egypt, under Cambyses, did not unduly disturb the Miletus-Nile connection.

It is with a sense of irony and embarrassment that I, a staunch admirer of Greek civilization, have had to acknowledge that Greek philosophy well-nigh had its beginnings outside of Greece itself. Had it not been for political unrest and the migration of refugee scholars to the Greek mainland, where Athens enjoyed a quick blossoming under Pericles (460–429 BCE), the flame of Greek philoophy could as easily have been scattered abroad among other Greek colonies, and farther west. As it was, philosophy flourished but for a few generations in Athens and, perhaps, already had passed its climax with the death of Socrates.

Greek philosophy's final and most enduring flower, Neo-Platonism, grew and blossomed at a place similar to the environment in which the Greek quest for wisdom itself began—namely, in a peripheral Greek settlement. Though "Platonic" by appellation, Neo-Platonism was conceived in Egypt, in the afterglow of ancient Egyptian culture and religion. It took on form in a more direct and a more intimate relationship with Egyptian theology than even the beginnings of philosophy in Ionia had taken form. Neo-Platonism was taught by two Egyptian wise men, Ammonius and Plotinus, in Alexandria, which was a Greek colonial city on Egyptian soil.

Alexandria was surrounded by the heritage of ancient Egyptian mentality and religiosity. The founders of Neo-Platonism understood the basic tenets of their ancient Egyptian heritage still better than Greek colonizers had been able to anticipate.

Thales

Thales (ca. 624-548 BCE) gained great renown in Miletus for a number of scientific and technological accomplishments. He is remembered especially for having correctly predicted the year of a solar eclipse, which happened on May 22, 585 BCE. Diogenes took great pains in telling us, secondhand, how most writers described Thales as a genuine Milesian who belonged to a distinguished family. All the same, we read in *Herodotus* (1:170) that his ancestors were Phoenicians.[100]

Historical documentation that would trace some of Thales's education to specific other places along the eastern Mediterranean is not available; nevertheless, for a family with Phoenician ancestry, some such connections may safely be assumed. All the while, it may be surmised that a man of Thales's intellect, living in a leading Mediterranean port city, would hardly have remained ignorant of Mesopotamian and Egyptian thinking. Unfortunately, we have only scant information about the cosmogony that formed the back-drop for his philosophy. What little we do have, however, matches nicely the remnants that have survived among the teachings of his successors, Anaximander and Anaximenes.

Aristotle considered himself distantly related to the philosophical tradition that was begun by Thales. He credited Thales with having been the first thinker who postulated a "material principle" as underlying the nature or substance of all things. For Thales this principle is water, and for this reason… the earth rests on water. (*Metaph.* A, 983b, 6ff). [101]

We can spare ourselves the remainder of Aristotle's commentary, by which he gave his own oblique rationalizations as to why the wise Thales might have reasoned the way he did. However, to the

---

[100] W.K.C. Guthrie, *A History of Greek Philosophy*, Volume 1 (Cambridge: Cambridge University Press, 1962), 46, 50. My summary overview on Greek philosophy is heavily indebted to W.K.C. Guthrie.

[101] *Ibid.*, 45, 55f.

delight of this historian of religions, Aristotle showed himself in that treatise not entirely insensitive to mythological and theological modes of description. Surely, Thales would have been amused by his proponent's casual references to Oceanus, Thethys, and Styx—unless, of course, these references permitted also some kind of overlap of these divinities with an original Egyptian Nun or watery Chaos. But it looks as though the larger context is fairly clear. Aristotle tried to give historical depth to his own discourses, and he invoked the wisdom of Thales as a convenient early Greek historical benchmark.

This is not to suggest that Aristotle was wrong in his overall assessment of Thales's analytic temperament. One may very much suspect, however, that in this particular instance, Aristotle appealed to the wrong mythology. The Egyptian myth of Atum, rising from Nun, an earthen hill that rose from watery Chaos, matches Thales's world portrait far better than anything that could be gathered from incoherent plots in Greek mythology from which Aristotle attempted to scrape meaning. The Greek myths of Hesiod and Homer were already approaching incoherency, and they were ill suited to furnish monist ontology for orderly scientific breakdown. Greeks no longer had coherent mythology with which Ionian philosophers could have demonstrated their skills of analysis.

Anaximander

Anaximander (ca. 611–546 BCE) is remembered for having elaborated on the cosmogony of Thales. Like his teacher, he assumed a singular homogeneous and living substratum of reality, something unlimited:

... it is neither water nor any other one of the things called elements, but the infinite is something of a different nature, from which things arise, to that they return of necessity when they are destroyed; for they suffer punishment and make reparation to one another for their injustice according to the order of time, as he says in somewhat poetical language.[102]

---

[102] Milton C. Nahm, ed., *Selections from Early Greek Philosophy* (New York: Appleton-Century-Crofts, 1962 [1934]): Simplicius, *Phys.* 6r; 24, 26.

Here we have arrived at a crucial point in early Greek philosophy, namely, at Anaximander's vision of the cosmogonic process whereby the ordered world had supposedly come into being. This process is a separating out, brought about by an eternal motion in the *apeiron*. All things come from and return to the *apeiron*, from the infinite or boundless substratum of the universe. The discourse simply moves between scientific and religious questions. Of special interest is information on Anaximander, provided by Theophrastus, as originally given by Eusebius:

He says that at the birth of this cosmos, a germ of hot and cold was separated off from the eternal substance, and out of this a sphere of flame grew about the vapor surrounding the earth like the bark around a tree. When this was torn away and shut off in certain rings, the sun, moon, and stars came into existence.[103]

Thus, instead of a somewhat concrete First within the cosmos, e.g. the Egyptian chaos, as the water to which Thales referred, Anaximander has returned to the more vaporous and less tangible concept of Nun. From within it he derived the world and then the sun, moon, and stars. All these emanated from the center successively, contained within rings of fire. Indeed, in the orthodox Egyptian context, these fiery emanation rings provide a rational pattern for visualization. Atum was the central primeval Hill-Sun from where all lesser realities came. Successive emanations, spewing from the Hill-Sun center, puffed forth as rings of fire, like a playful smoker might blow smoke rings that float and emanate.

Anaximander thought of these emanations as some kind of a "seed" substance. This metaphor can be linked with the Heliopolitan prototype of Atum's seminal emission which appears in the earliest strata of Egyptian texts. There the Godhead's emissions are fire or the light of Ra. Thus, the elements of water, earth, air, and fire, about which the Milesians reasoned "scientifically" or "philosophically," can be identified still as distinct divine realities that, in Heliopolitan theology, were present as Nun, Atum, Shu, and Ra, respectively. The dynamic link between Atum and Ra, earthy hill and ecstatic fiery emanation, is in the later generation of Enneadic gods depreciated from Shu to Geb—which is, down to Father Earth.

---

[103] D. K. A. 10, in Guthrie, *A History of Greek Philosophy*, 89f.

Egyptian paintings of the Heliopolitan hypostasis of Geb and Nut sometimes depict stars as decorations along the arching body of the sky goddess. Stars were places in the sky where light bursts broke forth and became manifest. Moreover, Anaximander's allusion to the cyclic return of all things to the original substratum, along a sequence of emanated worlds, personages, or things, conveniently matches the generational and soteriological cycle of the Heliopolitan system.

Anaximander's notion of justice and injustice, within the cosmological process, had been judged and adjusted in Egypt by priests of Tefnut/Mahet about a millennium and a half earlier than Anaximander's speculations were written. Mahet was the same personal determinant who also put in order the remainder of the cosmos. She was the ancient goddess Tefnut, renamed. She represented order in cosmology as well as justice and righteousness in the sacerdotal monarchy. In ancient Egypt, these two realms were fused. Thus, terminology taken from jurisprudence in Anaximander's case was not poetic license, as Simplicius suggested. These concepts were carried to Ionia as aspects of Egyptian theological and political theory: the singular homogeneous and boundless substratum, the All-Being that Anaximander deemed divine. Aristotle affirms that all those ancient philosophers, who did not postulate other external causalities, such as Mind or Love, assumed the divine nature of the *apeiron*:

> ... and this they say is the divine, for it is immortal and imperishable, as Anaximander and most of the writers on nature call it. (*Phys.* 203b, 6.[104]

Thinkers who have not distinguished Mind or Love, as agents independent from the apeiron, assumed that motivational energies resided within. Thus, any way one turns it, Anaximander's primal substratum of reality remains analogous to the Egyptian Godhead's emanation. Egyptian theology thereby lured and aggravated Hellenic analytic minds into a new millennium of mindful "civilized" breakdown—analysis—and reflection.

---

[104] *Ibid.*, 87ff.

Anaximenes

Anaximenes was a younger contemporary of Anaximander who is remembered for having advanced an alternate cosmology. Like his elder dialogue partner, he also embraced monistic Egyptian ontology. In this case, in the tailwind of Amun theology of the New Kingdom era, the Egyptian Godhead continued to keep his name hidden. Accordingly, the elder Anaximander contemplated a "nameless" *apeiron*. By contrast, the younger Anaximenes boldly identified the unbounded primal substance as air or breath:

Anaximenes of Miletus . . . calls it air and says that it differs in rarity and density according to the different substances. Rarefied, it becomes fire; condensed, it becomes first wind, then cloud, and when condensed still further, water and then earth and stones. Everything else is made of these. He, too, postulated eternal motion, which is indeed the cause of the change (Simplicius, *Phys.* 24.26, A5).[105]

Appreciative philosophers, such as W.K.C. Guthrie, have done what can be done to preserve Anaximenes's theory of rarefaction and condensation as something philosophically reasonable, honorable, or scientific.[104] After all, a co-founder of Greek philosophy and Western science deserves to be remembered with respect. It is not our intention in this book to detract from what already has gotten attributed to ancient thinkers for contributions along their historical trails.

However, on behalf of Egyptian predecessors to Ionian philosophy, it is necessary to insist that a millennium and a half earlier, some Egyptian minds have concluded that Shu, present as air, was sufficient to account for the plethora of Atum's masculine emanation. This tendency is clearly traceable in the Coffin Texts and has been delineated earlier in this book. It should be remembered that Shu was life-breath and also was understood, more concretely, as representing Atum's seminal emission; he continued the creative "spitting" that was begun by Atum.

Ancient priestly minds indeed have envisioned Atum's seminal emissions, or emanations, as radiating outward from an invisible center toward a periphery that had greater visibility and mass. Thus, it would not have been at all difficult for them to accommodate

---

[105] *Ibid.*, 121.

Anaximenes, referring to this emanation process and then, in the direction of greater visibility recognize some kind of thinning out.

And, inversely, anyone who now reconsiders the theophany of the Sun-god Ra, or an Egyptian soul's funerary ritual for its return journey in the company of the Sun-god, will also understand that these ancient Egyptian thinkers were able to reason homeward, that is, about processes of "refinement" or about the "rarefaction" of visible substances—thus from the environs of the atmosphere back toward purer fire, light and truth. These considerations lead toward the conclusion that Anaximenes, as much as Thales and Anaximander before him, still "lived, moved, and had their being" in Egyptian cosmology—as does anyone today who, somehow, still understands this phrase among the words of the Apostle Paul, in the New Testament.

Pythagoras

Pythagoras (ca. 570–? BCE) was a philosopher from Samos, an island facing the Ionian coast. We do not know how highly he thought of his three Ionian contemporaries. Probably not overly so. But we do know that he shied away from their general tendency of objectifying aspects of the larger divine order materialistically. Instead, he regarded numbers to be the key to understanding the universe and its contents. For this basic scientific insight, the modern world owes him thanks.

Ethnologically speaking, nouns and names have in the course of human evolution come into use to keep track of individual beings or things, people and animals, and even gods—and so to interact with them. Somewhat later, the addition of numbers enabled humankind to keep track of accumulated possessions and to claim them more easily and impersonally as property. A human mind that applies numbers self-interestedly, can objectively claim many things as property without ever having to know their individual names or true characteristics. Numerology was devised as a tool for achieving objective control. Numbers expedite management of soul-less things. That is, they enable possessive extraction from the greater whole of reality, or from the environment.

In the actual struggle for victorious human survival, numbers have been applied to many things. Once numbers were assigned, they helped sustain the illusion that all things numbered are indeed rightfully manipulated by finite human hands. As numbered entities, things can be owned and manipulated. The utilization of numbers equips a rational creature with its sharpest mental claws, with a tool for "analysis to be made easier." By means of faceless digital labels, a human mind can snatch objects as "properties" from what beforehand belonged into the domain of greater-than-human configurations of reality. All the while, the human conscience is kept tranquil under the euphoria of being mathematically correct, proving that the protagonist is intellectually (i.e. actually) in charge and thereby a justified owner. Economics, by extension, is therefore an art indebted to mathematics—is a mental-magical web of monetary abstractions.

Nevertheless, extreme analytic or scientific "progress," in its reliance on rationality, sooner or later also requires its opposite for achieving a living balance—namely, a religious retreat posture. Accordingly, the Pythagorean predatory mental abstraction of the universe, its division into coordinates and numbers, demanded for balance the more holistic faith in a harmonic cosmos. The mathematician's ego of Pythagoras withdrew into an aesthetically conceived larger harmony—into "music of the heavenly spheres." This mental realm is a perfect home for fictitious numbers to dwell. There he found his refuge—survivable balance and existential comfort.

Pythagoras and his religious brotherhood repented from the mathematical sins that weighed on them. First they tried to balance their aggressive numerology by living ascetic lives. It appears as though some greater-than-mathematics reality—the God of Cosmos and Numbers—has scared the Pythagorean mortals back into more restricted domains. While their ennobled minds remained preoccupied with escaping their mortality, with their intellectual souls intact, they contemplated Music as essential activity of the Spheres.

Whereas Milesian thinkers evolved their analytic claws—their brain-tipped teeth—to break down the divine visible cosmos into smaller impersonal and manageable segments, or elements, the Pythagoreans dedicated their minds to perfecting the ultimate mental fishing net of mathematics. Thereby they became aggressively successful. They also became religiously estranged and vulnerable.

As frightened *Homines religiosi*, the Pythagoreans were destined to evolve for their mathematical "science" a matching religious posture

—a "*con*-science." This step necessitated among them a more balanced personal eschatology that could save them. Practicing initiation rituals and pursuing rites of purification, they intuited how their souls initially had gotten caught up in a process of transmigration and reincarnation. This religious posture was what, on a personal level, furnished a mode of balance and atonement for their mental ambitions and existential estrangement.

Comparative historians will remember, that in India this was the time when sons of priests began to doubt the *Vedas* as well as the efficacy of their grand-domestication cult of sacrifices. This also was the time when aristocratic warrior sons expressed their dissent more adamantly, when throngs of dropout hippie-monks refused to be fascinated any longer by ceremonial spectacles of bloody power-grabs. Instead, they opted for pious meditation. Their new religious ways, their yoga discipline and their philosophical contemplations, were henceforth defined against the backdrop of *samsara*, that is, against the cosmic process by which entangled souls transmigrate after death. The souls of those who died anticipated successive rounds of reincarnation in compliance with the law of *karma*, for repeat opportunities of penance and purification.

It is quite possible that Pythagoras has been directly touched by Hinduism. His doctrine of transmigration and reincarnation points in that direction. It is even possible that, along with religious tenets, some of his geometry and mathematics could have come from India as well. Physical as well as mental development and corresponding religious retreat behavior, tend to leapfrog each other in rational evolution. On the other hand, some of what is now known as Pythagorean mathematics may also have been inspired by funerary edifices in Egypt.[106] But even at that, Pythagoras, with his Hindu-like ontology and religion, appears to be the least Egyptianized among ancient Greek philosophers.

Heraclitus

Heraclitus (ca. 540–480 BCE lived in Ephesus, a short distance from Miletus, the cradle of Greek philosophy. His ontological inheritance

---

[106] A spark of practical trigonometry could easily have dawned on Protagoras from the direction of Egypt, as he may have contemplated and inquired about the ever-so-conspicuous triangular surfaces of the pyramids.

was the same general Ionian-Egyptian monism which we detected already among the first Milesian philosophers. Historians of philosophy, thus far, have not been very successful in linking Heraclitus to any known school. On that account, many of this man's aphorisms have been interpreted on the assumption that he was a haughtily independent obscurantist, a poet and fabricator of riddles.

Surprisingly, however, when approached from the direction of an ancient Egyptian ontological heritage, the aphorisms of Heraclitus make at least as much sense as—if not more than—any of the fragments that survived from the teachings of his Ionian contemporaries. A good place to begin is the following concise summary of Heraclitus, by Diogenes Laertius:

> . . . fire is the element; all things are exchange for fire and come into being by rarefaction and condensation ... All things come into being by conflict of opposites, and the sum of things flows like a stream. Furthermore, all that is, is limited and comprises one world. And it is alternately born from fire and again resolved into fire in fixed cycles to all eternity.... Of the opposites, that which tends to birth or creation is called war and strife, and that which tends to destruction by fire is called concord and peace.... Change he called a pathway up and down, and this determines the birth of the world. (*Book* 4, 9, 8-12).[107]

The sequence of emanations that Diogenes attributed to Heraclitus begins, one can easily see, with the radiant fire of Ra the Sun-god. Along the downward path of condensation, fire transforms into moisture; moisture condenses into water, and water congeals into earth. The return path leads along the same sequence in reverse. Anyone who has contemplated our Figure 11, earlier, will have no difficulty recognizing here the same basic orthodox Egyptian U-turn pattern.

We also are told by Heraclitus that "the sum of things flows like a stream." He could as well have said that it flows like the seminal emission of Atum. The fixed cycles here, of course, do not refer to sequential disappearances and reappearances of entire divine hypostases or bodies. Rather, they are comparable to sectional swirls or

---

107 Heraclitus, "Fragments" in Nahm, *Selections from Early Greek Philosophy*, 89–97. All subsequent quotes from Heraclitus are from this source.

eddies that become visible here and there along edges of the total stream of life, of being and becoming. As soon as one considers this broader ancient Egyptian perspective, the task of explaining some of Heraclitus's *Fragments* is made much easier. For instance, what should one make of this?

[The earth] is poured out as sea, and measures the same amount as existed before it became earth (*Fragments* 23).

This cosmogonic moment pertains to the turnaround point at the lower end of the emanation process. The stream of All-Being was made visible to us already when moisture is precipitated into water. It was made more solid after water congealed into earth. And all the while, the mass or energy of the divine emanation remains constant. For the broader Egyptian context, one should note how in the more distant mythological past, Atum, as the ontological center of All-Being, arose as a solid hill from amidst Nun, which remained watery chaos. All the while, the total *ka* essence of Atum has remained constant.

Human souls are caught up in the outward emanation-flow as much as they get caught up in the homeward current. Thus, the question may rightly be asked: How is it that souls ever appear in material bodies? Any adult parent who ever has participated intimately in the procreational process of reincarnating a soul, and has reflected on it, knows that *Fragments* 72 explains it as well as can be: "It is a delight to souls to become wet."

Here is how grandfatherly and patiently Heliopolitan priests might have explained the Heraclitean puzzle to us, had we visited them in the heyday of their religion. Consider the experience of prospective parents. First, they detect "fire" in each other's eyes; then they sense "moisture" welling up inside, and externally they exude sweat. Invisible sparks of their ecstatic *ka* souls—reflected as gleams in their eyes—swim onward in the aforementioned waters to mingle and to fuse. Amidst those fluids, in time, evolve and grow tangible human beings, as visible *ba*. How and why? "Because it is a delight, for *ka* souls to become wet."

Of course, in the opinion of a Hellenic lover of wisdom, of the stature of Heraclitus, "a dry soul is wisest and best," or as viewed by a homeward-bound soul, from a less personal beam of light that radiates from the greater Atum-Ra and All-Being, "a dry beam is the wisest and best soul" (*Fragments* 74f), which of course refers to "the purest *ka*." All this simply means that closer to the divine source of souls, at the hypostasis of rarefied light and fire, even an individual human soul sparkles brighter. At that refined level of Sun and fire, a *ka* soul is less passionate, less visible, less wet or messy.

What is the intelligence that steers all things in and through all things? Or what should the creative Godhead be named? Religious Greeks have named him Zeus, whereas contemporary wise men in Egypt, of the Theban persuasion, would have refused to ascribe any name at all to Amun, the Hidden One. A similar gnosis concerning the real name of the Godhead speaks from *Fragments* 19: "It is willing and is unwilling to be called by the name Zeus."

When Heraclitus spoke religiously about successive emanations of the Godhead, about gods in plural form, he considered some of these to be gods in relation to other hypostases that were less than they. Thus, whichever is higher can be thought of as "dying" when its dignity is being compromised—is being lowered beneath a fellow equal or reduced to the level of a lesser substance or entity. In turn, an entity at a lower level dies when it surrenders to be mystically absorbed by a higher one. All this happens in full accord with the orthodox U-turn pattern of Egyptian theogony and soteriology. Of course, our wise man from Ephesus, as a diligent student of Egyptian priestly riddles, knew how to say all of this more profoundly and succinctly:

Gods are mortals, men are immortals, each living in the other's death and dying in the others' life. (*Fragments* 67)

Having thus commented on only a few samples near the core of Heraclitus's ontology, it may no longer be necessary to puzzle about the famous *Fragments* 41, 42, or 81 at the usual elementary level: "In the same rivers we step and we do not step; we are and we are not." It means that now we are, and then we are different. Not only is the river going in and out of existence for us from one moment of perception to the next, but we also are becoming other kinds of beings by the time our minds and wills have adjusted to step into any river again. We concurrently exist in two modes. "We are (this) and we are not (that)"—determined by our own homeward movements, perspectives and positions, within the larger two-way stream of life, of All-Being, which itself is flux.

Parmenides

Parmenides (ca. 515–456 BCE) began his philosophical inquiries with the Pythagorean brotherhood at Elea, in southern Italy. Under the spell of Pythagoras, he fell heir to a more shamanic perspective on Egyptian ontology. Nevertheless, he became known in the history of philosophy for his alleged insistence on the permanence of all being, permanence defined vis-à-vis Heraclitus's fascination for flux and becoming. After reexamining both philosophers, Parmenides and Heraclitus, from the perspective of a postulated common Egyptian ontology, this alleged difference will now need to be reconsidered.

Parmenides's insistence on the permanence of being appears to be no more than a semantic echo from his Pythagorean days when, in mathematical language, he habitually dealt with abstract and fixed principles. These eternal principles supposedly govern an equally fixed and impersonal system of numerology.

Our chances for understanding either Heraclitus or Parmenides have been severely impaired by subsequent interpretations generated by their latter-day progeny, by generations of materialistic philosophers and scientists. In the course of their respective hermeneutical fate, the integrity of Heraclitus was partially protected by his own obscurantism and love of Egyptian riddles. On the other hand, the bequest of Parmenides, reviewed positively by historians of science, was thereby severely distorted. If Parmenides had a weakness, it was the fact that he took his contemporaries too seriously. He invested altogether too heavily in the language of Milesian positivism.

Parmenides's religious-metaphysical poem, "The Way of Truth and the Way of Opinion," was defended and fortified by his well-intentioned student Zeno before the Athenian tribunal in the very presence of Socrates himself. It was defended against a wrong set of nonreligious questions and upon a battlefield already objectified by others. Its religious-ontological and epistemological message was permitted thereby to dissipate in the dry dunes of analysis. Instead of recognizing the conclusions that Parmenides had reached, religiously—and his existential lesson from the depth of what he called his "mental paralysis"—philosophers exploited incidentals to be able to imagine All-Being for themselves as something inert, as something impersonal or dead. By this distortion of Parmenides's philosophy, the predatory minds of budding scientists hoped that All-Being might become a fair and easier target for experimental control and utilization.

There is no essential conflict between the teachings of Heraclitus and Parmenides. Both men describe the same All-Being from different momentary human perspectives. To enable adequate comparison and contrast, we must refocus on Heraclitus one more time—for the duration of a paragraph, perhaps.

As a living and a changing mind, Heraclitus has dwelled conceptually within the All-Being. Knowing himself as becoming, he participated in the All-Being's larger process of change and becoming. Heraclitus was fascinated by the dynamics of finite living, and apparently, he also enjoyed swimming and swirling about, among the currents and eddies in the larger stream of life and being. All the while, he was reconciled to his humble destiny of being a small changing bubble of thought, or hype, in the larger mind of the All-God. Like Socrates later, who appealed to the dictum "know thyself," so Heraclitus, with a similar haughty sense of aloofness, despised those who seemed unaware of a rational need for introspection and sense of finitude. Greek philosophers have, as conspicuous leaders have in other cultures and situations, generated a contradiction between maintaining their inner egos and the external profiles of their public egos. In the case of Greek philosophers, one should keep in mind that their love of wisdom was an aristocratic brand of soteriology and was shared with minds of similar haughty temperament and status.

By contrast, the mind of Parmenides had temporarily wandered off on a trans-human shamanic journey, estranged and severed from its own axioms and ontology. Temporarily, the philosopher Parmenides was able to imagine, and to achieve, some sort of fleeting focus on objectified All-Being. And momentarily this reality, I dare say, appeared to his playful analytic predator mind as a perfect sphere—it appeared to his playful kitten mind as an inviting ball of yarn. At that point, Parmenides had not yet learned how All-Being could play possum, that is, how it could feign death when confronted by an analytic predator-mind that had been impressed unduly by its own powers of objectification.

Such objectification implied mental fixation and abstraction—thus, fixation similar to castration or killing a victim. Parmenides "hunted" and objectified the All-Being. The All-Being played possum.

We must ask the pivotal question: how did Parmenides achieve his temporary state of trans-human objectivity, which led to the illusion that nothing moves? And what exactly happened when the All-Being played possum toward him? His poem points to a rational method of usurpation on the philosopher's part. He assumed a posture as if to absorb into himself all imaginable motion and commotion. No wonder, therefore, that all-being apart from himself seemed motionless by comparison! We must, by all means, take the relativity in his testimonial seriously.

A goddess who, we might assume, was herself born from within the divine All-Being—someone like Isis or Athena—took Parmenides for a ride. She took him out on that same kind of glorious ride that, in the concrete material world, could easily have resulted in the destruction of cities and of fellow humankind. Parmenides traveled on a war chariot drawn by horses and guided by the sun-ray daughters of Father Helios.[108] Entering the Egyptian realm of Ra's splendor, our philosopher tells how he left behind "retributive Justice" (compare, Mahet), holding her key at the gate between darkness and light. Parmenides traveled onward with his personal guardian goddess as on a shamanic-philosophic trance journey. His divine female guide kept for him "horses and chariot straight on the high road."

Amidst this personal visionary motion and commotion, and always in hot pursuit of enduring ontological glimpses, Parmenides was destined to learn his first ontological lesson about the All-Being. He experienced relative motion between observer and observed. From his fast-moving point of view, in a chariot somewhere out there in nowhere, Parmenides looked back and, objectifying all the while, beheld the All-Being. In this manner, he distinguished the "abiding essence of persuasive truth" from ordinary "men's opinions in which rests no true belief." And the all-abiding essence of persuasive truth being mirrored and held, and fixed as abstract concept in the mind of this man Parmenides, showed no sign of motion.

---

[108] The entire discussion of Parmenides from here on will follow the text given in "The Way of Truth and the Way of Opinion," in Nahm, *Selections from Early Greek Philosophy*, 113–121.

Meanwhile, Parmenides completely overlooked the fact that he himself was still contained within that same, now conceptually fixed and abstracted, All-Being. And this fact, suddenly, invalidated the entire logic of his motion-packed trance journey. Not knowing where and to whom this was happening was his tragic mistake.

Such forgetfulness, in the presence of the less forgetful gods, shows off human finitude with unforgiving severity. And it may safely be assumed that Parmenides's sun-maiden escort, his enlightenment mistress, succeeded by her divine flirtatious demeanor in dulling the otherwise sharp wits of this philosopher. Comparatively speaking, it seems worthwhile to contemplate how in our world even ordinary sun rays do occasionally bequeath similar paralyzing strokes, on even less philosophically active human brains.

The first lesson taught by the goddess seems simple enough. "Whatever is *is*." Everything could have been well, amidst the splendor of all that light, had Parmenides not overvalued his own sense of sight and mental light. Had at the moment his mind been capable of interfacing with other sense data, such as touch, sound, taste, and smell, he could have heard and smelled that his imaginary horses, and the chariot containing his own presence, were still part of a swirl of sensate memories within All-Being. But as it was, in his state of super-visionary hype and voluntary sensual deprivation, the mirror-bubble-words in Parmenides's own thought-process were mistakenly perceived capable of comprehending All-Being.

In the same way as formerly, during mathematical trance, the realm of numbers became statically fixed for Pythagoras as All-Being —and as happened to the "Realm of Ideas" when it became static for Plato (and/or Socrates)—so in this instance the mind of Parmenides tried to hold on to All-Being as an objectively mirrored replication. An objectified replication no longer lives, appears, or moves independently real. The mental habit of stunning or freezing world portraits, by objectification, has become commonplace among the scientific descendants of this philosopher. Objectification, as a human trick, serves foremost the justification for experimenting with, or for controlling, docile less-than-human things.

But let us not do unto Parmenides as his own friends have done to him —friends for whom his now motionless tongue is sufficient proof that, indeed, he must have taught the immobility of all things. This is no way to treat an ancestor whose legacy of words still speaks almost as clearly as do our own contemporaries. We gladly grant him the ability to explain greater-than-human configurations of reality, among some other "things":

Therefore, thinking and that by reason of which thought exists, are one and the same thing, for you will not find thinking without the being from which it receives its name. Nor is there nor will there be anything apart from being; for fate has linked it together, so that it is a whole and immovable. . .. (117:94–99

What can then be said about the nature of All-Being? Of its existence? Its multiplicity? Its immobility? Its completeness? Its homogeneity and unity? Has Parmenides really intended his words to be useful for the positivistic conquest of God and World, as if these could be treated like inert corpses? Midway during the statement just quoted, while he contemplated last movements or twitching, Parmenides achieved a very sharp focus of introspection on his own habit of objectification toward All-Being. He felt the gentle movement of Fate, actively "linking together" into an immovable whole—not "immobility affecting All-Being," as commentators on Parmenides frequently try to tell us. Instead, he reflected on his own weak "thinking" as it collided with All-Being. There is a tremendous difference between the two readings: a difference of life and death for Parmenides, as well as for All-Being.

Parmenides's personal thinking, after recognizing itself as a process happening in the All-being, became instantly disabled as an independent agency. As soon as his objective thinking had come into contact with the living presence of All-Being, it felt like a kiss of death. His analytic thoughts struck in unison, demonstrating their usual effectiveness as if they were serpentine venom.

We come to the crucial point. Inasmuch as Parmenides perceived both sides, the philosopher's thought process and the All-Being as having become immobilized together, the poor man had no way of knowing anymore which of the two had fallen victim to the other. Nor on the basis of his testimony can we find such knowledge.

In its paralyzed condition, the dazed mind of Parmenides was barely able to finish the remainder of his poem. The man was reduced to finishing his discourse with an admitted play on empty names and words. I shall continue Parmenides's statement, quoted earlier, by repeating its closing phrase for the sake of better continuity:

So that it is a whole and immovable. Wherefore all these things will be but a name, all these things which mortals determined in the belief that they were true (pp. 117: 99-102).

Parmenides's first lesson has stunned his mind. How so? Did this happen because he gazed upon objectified reality? Of course not. Rather, his mind was immobilized because he contemplated All-Being as if it were an objectify-able reality. His self-centered pursuit could not help but overload and shorten out his mental circuits. For a moment he still noticed himself gazing on the whole of All-Being, and by doing so he discovered that he himself was missing in that objectified one-and-only realm of being. Under these conditions, how could he or anyone else ever truly know whither or whether he or someone else was actually gazing?

Gazing on All-being from a constantly changing distance, as from a moving celestial war chariot, happens to be a dangerous undertaking. The philosopher's sharp mind suddenly sensed that it had fallen as victim to its own predating self, into mortal danger. For a supposedly immortal Greek mind to get into that quandary was reason enough to become fearful and to freeze.

Having caught itself AWOL (Absent With-Out Leave from the All-Being, arrested by his own conscience, the mind of Parmenides accepted for a moment its own death sentence based on the datum of its sheer absence.

To translate this simple assessment into philosophically more respectable terminology, one might summarily say, that Parmenides's hype of his own epistemology, which claimed for itself the status of ontology, was what did him in. What he gave us was no longer full legitimate ontology, but analytic debris.

It may be useful to recall how for similar reasons a man named Moses, who had come under the spell of Egyptian wisdom long before Parmenides's time, had learned that Man shall not see the hidden God and live (*Exodus* 33:20). In Parmenides's case, this meant that he who saw All-Being without seeing himself included, is by his own logic doomed to collapse into non-being and immobility, that is, into an apparent state of not being in there. Or still more precisely, his mind chose for itself a content of fixed notions—thus, static, unmovable, and unverifiable non-being.

Fortunately, the goddess who initially had lured him into estrangement from the All-Being let Parmenides down gently. While "trustworthy discourse" on the All-Being went blank in the philosopher's mind, as a confessing finite mortal, Parmenides was instructed to learn instead more about "these things which mortals determined," thus, about opinions presently uttered in the languages of mortals. Pure monism was too much to ponder; Parmenides was given dichotomies as second-best. What humans can determine are word-fragments wrapped in still older language. Human languages are evaporating into oblivion, along with their most favored over-sized and over-used words, replacing them with initially unknown syllables and uploading them with connotations that humans determine.

On the one hand, there is an ethereal flame of fire, fine and rarefied, everywhere identical with itself and not identical with its opposite; and on the second hand, opposed to the first, is the other principle of flame-less darkness, dense and heavy in character (118:116-121).

With the extremities of ethereal fire and heavy darkness having so been placed safely out of the reach of human hands and minds, Parmenides proceeded to describe the range of emanating hypostases in space. He became fully aware that between his "one hand" and his "other hand" there extended the divine body of the All-Being. This body existed, as circles of rarefied fire, nearer to the center. Toward the outer periphery, it appeared increasingly mixed with darkness. Thus, according to the afore-mentioned quotation the All-Being is surrounded by "the second principle" of solid darkness.

In accordance with this dualistic conceptualization, some of Parmenides's specifics do now follow and match nicely the Egyptian overview of emanation with which we have already become familiar:

The smaller circles are filled with unmixed fire, and those next to them with darkness into which their portion of light penetrates; in the midst of these is the divinity who directs the course of all (118:125–130).

The divinity who "in the midst of these" directs the course of all, is the Godhead of orthodox Egyptian theology. In as much as this divinity still "directs," it is being acknowledged here to exist outside the realm of the personal inertia of Parmenides. Only the Egyptian gender awareness is reversed here to accommodate Greek Hesiodic theography, which is manifest in the primacy of Gaia over Uranos. What else can one expect of a rational man who thinks under the spell of a goddess! For him it was a "She" who devised first love.

Elsewhere, in a more intense confrontation, we are given a hint that Parmenides might have thought of this central deity as Fate. In our present context, it does not really matter, because we know, specifically, that this was the deity that devised love. She served the same first creative function by Atum's hand. And she was active in the creativity of Shu, Tefnut, and Isis in ancient Egypt.

Parmenides has returned from his poetic trance journey on the high road, so it seems, reconciled to Egyptian ontology. He was ready to humble himself by learning less important notions about "the wandering deeds of the round-eyed moon" (the eye of Horus). He contemplated "the sky (Nut) surrounding all, whence it arose, and how necessity took it and chained it so as to serve as a limit (Tefnut and Nut) to the courses of the stars." The writers of ancient Egyptian Coffin Spells were better at describing these kinds of things than Parmenides was. But he was a Greek who introduced Egyptian wisdom to his people, second-hand. He did the best he could.

An interesting comparison remains to be made with Parmenides's "cosmos devoid of motion." As the hyperactive biblical warrior Joshua is said to have seen the sun stand still (*Joshua* 10:13), so, too, the mentally hyperactive Parmenides saw the All-Being motionless during a few moments of visionary trance. Thus, faced by ultimate greater-than-human reality, let us all get used to hyperbole!

Finite beings who stop short of pari-nirvana must return to paradises of a lesser kind. Parmenides returned smack into orthodox Egyptian ontology. And there, in this cosmos of unitary emanation, of flowing from light toward collision with darkness, moving between visibility and invisibility, Parmenides moved about. From there he lived and he died and rose. Or, as an Egyptian wise man might have said it—there he has had, he has, and he will have his being. His own moments of transient perception have had only temporary effects on him, and even far less on All-Being.

Human minds are caught up, together, in the singular universal process of emanation—evolving and diversifying all the while. Animal instincts still illustrate the root modes learned by evolving, while having all together adapted and suffered each other's impacts. Like most advanced predators on this planet still do, so humans also tend to chase and to fetch what previously has been perceived as trying to escape. To hunt, to catch and to kill, appear to be standard responses not only in the world of some animals, but still also among human offspring for whom ideas have become their prey. For the human mind—"with, and toward us" in theoretical analysis, an intelligent All-Being has played possum.

The most typical experience of getting stunned and of "freezing" was experienced by human ancestors when, suddenly, they were confronted by greater-than-human (divine carnivores. The ancestors of Parmenides have survived long enough to get stunned by darkness and non-being—to communicate their experiences to their offspring, just enough for them to learn and to think philosophically.

The Pluralists

For better or for worse, the philosophy of Parmenides and of his defender Zeno has left the impression on analytic minds that the All-Being is motionless and passive. Whereas such a conclusion would have been in line with Hesiodic "castration theology," it would have been unthinkable, if not blasphemous, in the original context of Egyptian monotheism. As much as some later Greek philosophers protested the works of Hesiod and Homer, to the effect that these poets have slandered the gods by ascribing scandalous behavior to them, men like Socrates and Plato could still continue to think of themselves as true children of the great Mother Earth.

The scandalous behavior of Cronos got sublimated into archetypal methodology for doing Greek analysis and science. It was Cronos who first immobilized and neutered the All-Father Uranos. It was the popularized version of Parmenides's analytic philosophy that, applied the Hesiodic "sickle" to All-Being. Hesiod established the mythological archetype for subjecting all of reality to philosophical and scientific analytic treatment. Philosophers do mental analysis, and scientists legitimize material analysis by experimentation.

Predators, by nature, cultivate their minds and learn how to do more extensive and thorough analysis. As a rule, they shun potential victims that lie still. Most predators prefer the challenge to hunt victims that are still afoot. They love to pursue and kill with lively excitement. They rise to the challenge and will not rest until they are exhausted or their victims are felled, torn apart or "butchered" for consumption. After traditional prey animals became over-hunted, hunting continued. The victims were human domesticators who kept and owned herds of domesticates. Even the gods who ruled domesticators were conquered and managed by orthodox hunters for whom life without hunting had become pointless. Hunting animals evolved into warfare by which progressive hunters "herded" humankind.

With the upper half of the Greek cosmos having been neutered by storytellers like Hesiod, the keen predator minds of the first Ionian philosophers aimed their analytic curiosities toward a theology that at the time was being carried abroad from Egypt and was still somewhat alive. Greek analytic thinkers dealt with the Egyptian reality with mixed success. Parmenides attempted to extract from All-Being all movement including his own moving self. He failed as he himself was sorely missed in his own ontological inventory.

Heirs of Parmenides in celestial chariots, not knowing themselves in context and in relative motion, distinguished motion from All-Being. It took several generations of Greek philosophers to explain this absence of motion in All-Being, alongside the obstinate apparent presence of motion, experienced daily by the senses. The prime years of Greek philosophy were spent on resolving the disparity between permanent being on one hand, and flux or becoming on the other. Egyptian theologians easily would have diagnosed debates of this sort as the futile life-and-death struggles of mortal humankind within the larger process of world-emanation. The Egyptian hidden All-God was, after all, beyond the reach of Cronos's sickle, as he also remains out of reach to the scalpels of later analysts. Latter-day mortal Titans are too small to apply their Hesiodic tools of surgery along the entire soft underside of the self-emanating All-God.

Historians of religions, who nowadays concern themselves with the larger evolutionary process, will have no difficulty seeing in the classical philosophical discourses an intellectualized repetition of ancestral hunters' guilt. Pluralistic philosophers and scientists, within the tradition of Parmenides, have repeatedly reenacted the moments at which ancestral primitive hunters stood, after stately animals had just been felled, and have contemplated the stillness that they inflicted on the carcass. Not many new events happen in the world of predators, under Helios!

After Parmenides, the experience and rationalization of life and motion no longer needed to distract philosophers from their contemplations—especially not of those who came to be classified as pluralists, such as Empedocles, Anaxagoras, Leucippus, Democritus, Epicurus, and Lucretius. Upon misunderstanding Parmenides, these men sought ways to distinguish, to analyze, to divide, or otherwise labor for the demise of All-Being. Mental butchering feasts of analysis could be staged; old chariots were pushed aside; free technological progress and large-scale warfare were free to surge.

Empedocles

Empedocles (ca. 493-433 BCE could detect in Parmenides's All-Being no longer any traces of divine life. He no longer could see, and much less enjoy, those mysterious ancient qualitative mutations from one wonderfully overflowing hypostasis to a next. Since the onset of Greek philosophy, early divine manifestations that have appeared in historical time were conceptually distinguishable from their source, as well as from one another. Former divine manifestations had gotten reduced to stationary "roots," that is, to root elements of fire, air, earth, and water. Though the elements have been depersonalized and abstracted, it is not difficult to recognize the first three as original manifestations of the Egyptian Godhead. Hellenized they had become named "remnants" of three former Egyptian living hypostases—Ra as fire, Shu as air, and Geb as earth. By the same procedure of analytic sorting, an inert liquid had been abstracted from the vivacious seminal flow of Atum. A purified impersonal element was postulated instead. It was water.

Empedocles's attempt to valorize abstracted aspects, by identifying them with old deities of the Hellenic tradition, obviously endangered all the gods which can be contrasted or compared with each other. The gradual demise of older gods, as human concepts under analysis, is unavoidable. Ontological equations and less understood subject matter will all get absorbed into what is deemed simple and can be comprehended or dealt with easily. Look at this:

Hear first [of] the four roots of all things: bright Zeus, life-giving Hera (air, and Aidoneus, earth, and Nestis who moistens the springs of men with her tears). And a second thing I will tell thee: There is no origination of anything that is mortal, nor yet any end in baneful death; but only mixture and separation of what is mixed, but men call this "origination" (*Fragments* 33–34).[109]

This halfhearted attempt by Empedocles to revitalize his basic categories, his root elements, by linking them to Greek polytheism seems almost pitiful. Even monotheism, for analytic hunter minds, defaults into monism—which is to say, into a worldview according to which human minds are fulfilled by what hands might do. All modes of depersonalization and of human progress, are accomplished at the expense of eventually extinguishing the living mysteries of animals, men, and gods along with stiffening the living All-God himself. After primitive hunters have killed a prey animal, after butchering and analysis, there was nothing else to do but to eat meat and be satiated —and formally to accept enduring rest as their own destiny. All hunters, analysts, and conquerors come to rest, eventually, to endorse the manifest destiny of their victims with their own lives.

In Empedocles's fourfold world, what accounts for life or motion? What, or who, does the mixing and the separating of elemental roots? As efficient causes for this process Empedocles mentions Love and Strife. But beyond personal beings, who themselves thrive as aggregates, what are Love and Strife? Set in an almost Buddhist context of origination, as efficient causes, Love and Strife turn out to be mere relics of what once upon a time used to be the living Mars and Aphrodite. These gods have become abstractions which, for mobility, now depend on a new set of motivators. They have fallen into the hands of a philosopher who, as linguistic undertaker and manager, understands how to ascribe or how to withhold, "efficacy" from whatever he acknowledges to be an aggregate of reality.

Anaxagoras

Living circa 500–428 BCE, Anaxagoras was an older contemporary of Empedocles, and he responded to the younger. He, as well, denied the ontological status of "coming into being" and of "perishing." The general pattern that he saw in the universe resembled the one that Empedocles had already postulated. But to him a set of only four elements, mixing and separating, seemed overly simple and crude.

---

109 Empedocles, 101 "Fragments" in Nahm, Selections from Early Greek Philosophy, 128–144.

He therefore postulated a creative Mind that disseminated an infinite number—and watch this!—of first principles or "seeds."

Over against the Egyptian heritage, we can recognize instantly the antiquity of this idea of Anaxagoras. Procedurally, he disagreed with Empedocles's dissolution of four hypostases of the Godhead into four separate elements. But then, as a remedy to this depersonalization of reality, he hurried to return to basic orthodox Egyptian process theology. The stream of All-Being still could be explained by him best as an infinite number of seeds, flowing, joining and separating—as if it all happens still within the un-nameable Egyptian Godhead's seminal flow. Nevertheless, the focal meaning of this metaphor has meanwhile been widened from zoology to include processes in botany.

Anaxagoras derived his ontology of seeds from his assumption of emanation, traceable to the land of the Nile.. But his aim was not to establish an Egyptian cult. On the contrary, he contributed to Greek philosophy and made his intellectual progeny ever more curious about what kind of distinct small seed particles actually did exist within the All-Being. Increasingly smaller seeds were just waiting to be discovered by humankind, almost as if begging to be manipulated.

The remaining pluralists, the Atomists Leucippus, Democritus, and Epicurus, need not be discussed to provide additional perspective for this book. Their contributions lead farther in the opposite direction, away from our interests in the history of religions field. Once the principles of division and subtraction were applied in philosophical methodology, scientific analysis with predator teeth, appetites and scalpels continued scavenging off the bones that remained.

Philosophical debates thereafter engaged analytic "scientific" questions, about how much smaller the first principles, atoms, or seeds needed to be imagined for free manipulation and eventual experimentation to begin. As long as they were imagined large enough to still remain visible, reasoning could proceed quantitatively. Whenever they were too small to be seen, philosophical discussion continued just the same, on the basis of degrees of projected qualities. Qualities could be quantified along abstractly numbered arbitrary scales. For down-to-earth industry and for the applied sciences, pluralistic thinking was a blessing. It provided countless pieces and fragments that could be gathered, owned, modified, and brought under control.

The numerology of religiously timid Pythagoreans came to serve philosophers and scientists quite well—after the same manner in which plain counting-skills had already been useful earlier to ambitious illiterate domesticators and to the hyper-domesticators who proceeded to enslave them.

Socrates, Plato, Aristotle

For the purpose of only showing the dependency of Greek philosophy on ancient Egyptian ontology, or of sketching the history of Greek philosophy, one could stop at this point and cease to explain things further. The continuity of subject matter between the Egyptian parental ontology and the beginnings of Greek philosophy, has been displayed sufficiently. Anyone who wishes to reexamine this overview need only revisit portions of this treatise comparatively.

But then, Greek philosophy not only had its history, it also has contributed to the future. Socrates, Plato, and Aristotle have become the most famous philosophers of classical Greece. And then, beginning with the first century CE, students of philosophy in the Graeco-Roman world were destined to interact increasingly with another glow of Egypt-inspired practical rationality that had been escaping, as a spark of *ka* from Hebrew Fire. It was the Christian religion.

Athenian analytic rationality, such as that of Plato, Aristotle and of their successors, squeezed the life juices from the remaining grand-domestication religiosity within the range of Hellenistic influence. The cultural landscapes were left barren, to dry and to ignite fresh brush fires for fresh religious life to sprout. The brush fire of Christian "Kingdom of Heaven" enthusiasm, a Hebrew-Egyptian spark of faith, swept through the Graeco-Roman lands. It illuminated and reshaped the rhythms of life beginning at urban centers and spreading further into the country sites. What became Neo-Platonic philosophy and soteriology, what between the First and Third Century CE spread from Alexandria, played a significant role during the institutionalization phase and for the intellectual structuring of what has become orthodox Christendom.

Socrates

The principal representative of Greek philosophy in Athens, Socrates (ca. 469–399 BCE), made famous by Plato, needs to be mentioned only in passing. The fact that this discussion will pay less attention to Socrates than to some of his Ionian predecessors may appear unbalanced. However, the motive for this abridgment is not to deprive Socrates of his rightful place in the annals of intellectual history. Nor has it here been our aim to write a fresh historical sketch of Greek philosophy or to revise the biographical sketches of those remembered as having been philosophers. All these tasks have been done more thoroughly by W.K.C. Guthrie and others.

Our aim merely is to show enough of ontology, cosmogony, and cosmology to expose the ideological continuity between ancient Egyptian thought and what in Ionia and Athens has become "philosophy."

In his younger years, the man Socrates, like most progressive minds of his time, was attracted to the study of natural science. This implies that he still concerned himself seriously with the implied Egyptian/Ionian ontological inheritances already sketched in this chapter. But by the time Socrates became acquainted with the younger Plato, his social conscience had matured to a point where he preferred to dwell on questions of ethics and on socio-political implications. His mind was pre-occupied with all problems that have perplexed hyper-domesticated civilizations.

Socrates placed his hope on the honest confrontation and cultivation of logos, thus, on the direct rational search for truth. Of course, this is not to say that in his discussions he failed to appreciate a certain amount of humane playfulness. He knew that for some people he had the reputation of being wise; but he also knew that his knowledge was quite deficient. According to his own musings, he did not even know enough about his own self.

The philosophical method of Socrates was designed to educate potential leaders for a still youthful and confident Hellenic civilization, for one that was not yet far removed from the nomadic hunter-herder-bandit stratum of cultures that a little earlier, on the prairies of Eurasia, developed a taste for horsemanship and adventure. The glow of ancestral excitement still sparkled in the eyes of Socrates and his friends. Their confidence in the positive power of intellect, and in its applicability for ordering or governing human society—or for re-inventing society while they were at it—drew from the wellspring of that same positive fighting spirit of people who earlier roamed on the steppes of Central Asia.

The confidence that Socrates placed in the ability of human reason knew few bounds. It remained unshaken to his death. To steer the Hellenic virgin intellect in the direction of a rational and humane political order, Socrates baited young aspirants with puzzles and enduring existential questions. He lured them into membership of his intellectual aristocracy. Admission into that circle of philosopher friends had to be earned by duels in rational discourse.

People from lower social strata, whose struggles and menial labors have kept their spirits numb and humble, had little appreciation for Athenian philosophers or for the progeny of young wise guys who hung out with the older ones of their kind. Yes, Socrates's methods of intellectual engagement inspired bright young men of leisure to intellectual competition, self-confidence and the perfection of mental skills. But these same habits quite easily alienated average folk. The philosophers' haughtiness inflicted intellectual defeats on slower-witted people. Their embarrassments festered and mutated to resentment. Enough Athenians disliked Socrates in 399 BCE, when the death sentence was proposed at his trial. And the motion was passed.

A "Plato" Preview

The primary aspect of the philosophy of Plato (427–347 BCE) that needs to be sketched here is his famous theory of "Ideas." Quite likely, he learned this theory from Socrates himself. We also will offer some statements from the *Timaeus* to provide clues regarding Plato's cosmological orientation. The theory of Ideas is central to Plato's system and harmonizes well with thoughts in the *Timaeus*. Moreover, with this theory, he achieved a position of compromise between Parmenides's supposed insistence on permanence and Heraclites's emphasis on life as flux. Accordingly, Platonic Ideas "are," whereas objects in the realm of sense experience still are caught up in a process of "becoming." Data obtained pertaining to objects of sense experience are known to fluctuate and change. They only share or participate temporarily in the Intelligible World—in the realm of permanent Ideas—to the extent that human minds have become aware of them. While considering the Socratic/Platonic theory of Ideas from the point of view of a nominalistic and process-conscious epistemology, a somewhat critical perspective is called for. All-inclusive plurals or universal ideas, named, taken and abstracted from their concrete associations in the visible world, whenever these were committed to memory and fixed as word symbols, have been admired as Platonic Ideas. They are habitually envisioned by finite minds and, necessarily self-serving, they become fixed in human memory as being eternally stable and valid. Finite minds will grasp at anything that promises an opportunity of owning an aspect of eternity.

In contrast to the Ideas, which in human memory reappear as permanent or as fixed, the living world that is experienced by the five senses appears naturally transient, changing and therefore less dependable. Mortal eyes and hands that insist on owning the help of eternal gods—if such is possible—can never be fully satisfied.

Plato intuited his universal Ideas as realities that transcend sense data. He regarded them as realities that participate in, and abide in, still greater units of reality. Of course, he presumed that universal Ideas were more than just inert, static, or memorized symbols. His Idealism insisted that Ideas participate in, and emanate from, the most permanent type of realities. Moreover, all objects of sense experience, that come into or drift out of human awareness, do "participate" in eternal Ideas. In this context, at lower levels of intensity, "Ideas appear" to human minds and thereby become thinkable. Even sensations can thereby become meaningful, because they participate in meanings that emanate from the higher and more enduring Platonic Ideas, which themselves abide in still surer relevances. This hierarchy of ever greater Ideas ascends to where it culminates in the most inclusive trinity of Goodness, Truth, and Beauty.

Within the domain of human contemplation, these three inclusive top Ideas can be utilized and reasoned with, metaphorically speaking still further, to ever larger accumulations of stable generality where then, formally and logically, they can be thought of as sharing, or as participating in the greatest singular reality. The most inclusive and supreme, lastingly fixed sum of all goodness, truth, and beauty within the *summum bonum*—comprises the supreme GOOD. Call it GOD, and you got theology with an "O" to spare.

Looking back at Plato through the eyes of his younger contemporary Aristotle, the older philosopher's ontology of eternal Ideas appeared unsatisfactory. It could not explain adequately the realm of motion and sense experience which, to Aristotle, appeared more real than to Plato. In response to this deficiency, Aristotle introduced his own doctrine of no less than four distinct causes—material, formal, efficient (i.e. motive), and final causes. Could one, five, or a hundred distinct causes, perceived monotonously by analysis, have gotten Aristotle's universe better into motion under the auspices of his Unmoved and Unmoving Prime Mover? It seems doubtful.

Every historian of philosophy, sooner or later, will face the fact that the world of every Greek philosopher, in the footsteps of Hesiod, have tended to tear reality apart along the same lingual seam. They cut a gash between Heaven and Earth, between Being and Becoming, between a standard of reality grasped by reason in eternal memory, and the realm of temporarily throbbing life and sense experience—between ultimate reality and theory.

Plato in the *Timaeus*

The most elaborate textual source for Plato's cosmology is a dialogue named after its primary speaker, Timaeus. It generally is agreed that this person Timaeus, who in the dialogue converses with Socrates, speaks as a proponent of Plato himself and so expresses the writer's own ideas. The dialogue format of Plato, in the *Timaeus*, was the philosopher-playwright's convenient device for exhibiting a number of weak hypotheses without having to risk his personal reputation as an author. Theogonies and scientific cosmologies from different periods or perspectives could so be given a voice in Plato's treatise.

Whether Plato's speculations in the *Timaeus* are believable anymore, or whether today they should be discarded, is of no great concern for a historian's task. We are here interested in exploring the traces of Egyptian religion in Plato's ontology. Posterity has made use of the Timaeus in a variety of ways. The so-called Middle Platonists and Neo-Platonists, in Alexandria, favored the *Timaeus* for what modern philosophers have come to regard as its weakness—for its voracious variety. The loosely structured treatise enabled Neo-Platonists to roam within the sphere of Greek philosophy and, at the same time, dip into the anonymous ever-bearing substratum of Egyptian theology to their hearts' content.

Christian theologians naturally preferred the *Timaeus* over other Platonic writings. In the dialogue's underlayment of Egyptian ontology, they discovered a natural affinity with their own christology and theology. After all, Christendom was born within, and overtaken by, the same Alexandrian-Hellenistic ancient Egyptian theological groundswell that later also helped transform Porphyry and Saint Augustine. Both men embraced the Egyptian process theology under the guise of a religiously "neutral" philosophy. Each did so for different reasons, of course. With its amazing openness to an unidentified ancient ontology that has puzzled students of Plato from early on, the *Timaeus* has provided materials for building a rational bridge of rapprochement from Platonic philosophy to Christian theology.

Egypt Romanticized

The major dialogue in the *Timaeus* is introduced by a quaint secondhand tale, and that tale is traced to an old priest who served the goddess Neith, in Sais, Egypt. The tale's significance, however, rests not on what Plato permitted Timaeus to say about Egypt. In light of the fact that the Egyptian priest has only shared historicized Athenian smugness, his tale appears almost negligible. It presents fantasies about the fabled glory of ancient Athens, of nine thousand years earlier and a thousand years before the city of Sais itself was supposed to have been founded.

Such a tale, obviously, amounts to a round of self-congratulation among members of the Athenian philosophers club. Moreover, the Egyptian goddess Neith was deemed significant only to the extent that she could be identified with Athena. By the same token, Plato's knowledge about the Nile being Egypt's never-failing savior, and about the fact that Egyptians know stories about many floods, is of the superficial type that could have arrived in Greece as the gossip of any traveler or trader.

Nevertheless, the intellectual dependency of Greece on ancient Egyptian tradition is implicit throughout this introductory tale. The assertion made by the very old Egyptian priest, to the effect that in comparison with Egyptian sages, "Hellenes are never anything but children" who "in mind are still all young" (*Timaeus,* 22b), is not contested by Socrates in the course of the dialogue, nor by anyone else. Although specific evidence of Plato's familiarity with Egyptian culture and religion seems to be absent, the reader is nevertheless left with the distinct impression that, according to Plato's own estimate, Egyptian wisdom preceded Greek *sophia*. And this fabled Egyptian "prehistory," in all likelihood, was amplified for what the character Timaeus was expected to communicate on behalf of Plato.

The Cosmogony

Even though he was introduced as an astronomer, Timaeus quickly comes around to one of Plato's own central concerns: the distinction between Parmenidean "being" and Heraclitean "becoming," or eternal Ideas vis-à-vis objects of sense experience:

First then, in my judgment, we must make a distinction and ask, what is that which always is and has no becoming, and what is that which is always becoming and never is? That which is apprehended by intelligence and reason is always in the same state, but that which is conceived by opinion with the help of sensation and without reason is always in a process of becoming and perishing and never really is (*Timaeus* 27d–28a).[110]

The method by which the universe was created is explained at the outset. A generative process is assumed, which, although mentioned repeatedly, is never questioned throughout the dialogue: "The creator made this world of generation" (*Timaeus* 29d). And, when the creator framed the universe, "he put intelligence in soul, and soul in body ... the world came into being—a living creature truly endowed with soul and intelligence by the providence of God"(30b). The original universe is and was invisible, but it "contains in itself all intelligible beings, just as this world comprehends us and all other visible creatures" (30c–d). Timaeus calls the realm that includes all intelligible creatures the "One only-begotten and created heaven" (31b) and thereby he specified the divine method of generation as having been "procreation," essentially. True to the pre-Socratic tradition of Greek philosophy, Plato gives precedence to the "biological" nature of this living and only-begotten

---

110 Hamilton and Cairns, ed., *Collected Dialogues of Plato,* 1151–1211. All translations from the *Timaeus* are quoted by courtesy of Princeton University Press.

universe, over and above the need for clarifying astronomical structure. Ontological concerns predominate here over bare cosmological questions. Plato's relational density scale, relative to the four elements of his "biophysics" echoes, so to speak, from Heliopolitan theology as well as from traditional Ionian philosophy.

"As fire is to air so is air to water, and as air is to water so is water to earth" (*Timaeus* 32b). The universe is a creature, spherical in shape, and soul diffuses from its center throughout its body and represents "a circle moving in a circle." As far as soul is concerned, "in origin and excellence," it or she "is prior to and older than the body." The creator has formed within her the corporeal universe (*Timaeus* 34a–c; 36d). And "when the father and creator saw the creature which he had made moving and living, the created image of the eternal gods, he rejoiced" (37c).

The actual arrangement of sun, moon, and planets in orbits around the earth was made by God for the establishment of time: "The sun and moon and five other stars, which are called the planets, were created by him in order to distinguish and to preserve the numbers of time... he placed them in orbits ... in seven orbits seven stars." The moon was placed in the nearest orbit circling earth, next the sun, then the morning star and the star sacred to Hermes (*Timaeus* 38c–d). Against these moving stars, for contrast, "the fixed stars were created to be divine and eternal animals, ever abiding and revolving after the same manner and on the same spot" (40b).

Timaeus—the Interlude

Two very interesting paragraphs follow here (*Timaeus* 40d–41a). Timaeus pleaded *agnosia* with regard to knowing something about the folk wisdom to the effect that one "must accept the traditions of the men of old time who affirmed themselves to be the offspring of the gods—that is what they say—and they must surely have known their own ancestors." Subtle irony here is transposed, rhetorically and without wasting an extra word, into mild satire: "How can we doubt the word of the children of the gods?"

It appears as though Greek gods are mentioned next simply for good measure—Oceanus and Thethys as children of Earth and Heaven, along with Phorcys (god of the sea), Cronos, and Rhea; and

Zeus and Hera. Together they seem almost as foreign to the cosmology of the *Timaeus* as the arbitrary insertion of an American Indian "Earth Diver" origin myth would have been. These paragraphs represent no more than a courteous bow in the direction of ancient Greek mythology. Plato hurried on to get to what earlier we already have identified as orthodox Egyptian ontology.

Toward a Hellenic Tefnut

Earth herself is first introduced as "our nurse" (*Timaeus* 40b). It appears as though Plato is careful here, so as not to present her as a potential equal partner of God the father. Earth, however, is definitely situated opposite of Heaven, along Plato's invisibility/visibility scale. This reading is supported by the fact that later, at 49b, the "receptacle" or "nurse of all generation," or "mother" (50c-d) embraces the entire creation, not only the earth.

Along the larger cosmic scale the receiving principle is Mother, whereas the source and wellspring of all being is Father. The entire creation is the creator's generation of offspring. If there had been no castration plot in Hesiod's Greek Theogony, it would up to this point be conceivable that this portion of Plato's vision of the universe could be traced to some kind of Greek Father Heaven and Mother Earth mythology. But as the case happens to be, Plato's statements rest squarely on the Egyptian basis. We may suspect that he had an inkling of this. Why else, with all his Athenian pride, would he have Egyptian-ized this dialogue from the outset with an irrelevant tall tale about Athens and Sais? The road back to Hesiodic theogony, or into general Indo-European dualism, was efficiently blocked for Plato, by himself. The first Mother he had in mind resembles far more the invisible and universally receptive Tefnut than Hesiod's concrete Mother Earth:

> ...the mother and receptacle of all created and visible, and in any way sensible things, is not to be termed earth or air or fire or water, or any of their compounds, or any of the elements from which these are derived, but is an invisible and formless being which receives all things and in some mysterious way partakes of the intelligible, and is most incomprehensible (*Timaeus* 51a–b).

This Platonic statement would almost certainly have passed earlier, at Heliopolis, as an adequate description of Tefnut and her matching polarity in relation to Shu. The amazing thing is that Plato does not even stop at this point of rapprochement to Egyptian orthodoxy. He does not let this postulated invisible mother dangle, so to speak, from his Platonic heaven of eternal "Ideas." Instead, Plato assures us that fire inflames her from time to time, that water moistens her, and that her motherly substance becomes earth and air (*Timaeus* 51b). She indeed is the full Tefnut, Atum's receptacle "hand," and the All-Mother of the Heliopolitan universe.

Pythagorean Numerology

Traces of the Pythagorean significance of numbers, and geometric structure, are frequent in Plato's *Timaeus*, especially in sections 43–44 and 53c–57d. In all likelihood, Plato had his theory of Ideas already in place by the time he exposed his mind to Pythagoreans in southern Italy. Moreover, their numerological key to the cosmos could be accommodated easily into his own broader view. For Plato, the invisible world of Pythagorean numerical abstractions became simply another dimension, a register or stratum, in the greater expanse of eternal Ideas.

The pragmatic continuity between numbers and words has already been alluded to in the preceding chapter, in the section on Pythagoras and his place in the history of Greek philosophy. Ciphers and numbers correspond in their function to nouns and names—but they differ from nouns and names in that they have been subjugated more severely by the human mind and will. Numbers are faceless names or words, deprived of personal or individual characteristics, reduced and thereby "grasped" more easily, possessed and manipulated because they could be manipulated as impersonal labels.

"Number-Ideas" do match Platonic Word-Ideas quite nicely. But they also furnish greater confidence for human assertiveness vis-à-vis the cosmos; they furnish authority to control, more than Word- or Name-Ideas can provide. Inasmuch as numbers can help us reduce greater reality configurations to manageable "things," they also contribute significantly to shoring up our otherwise finite philosopher and scientist egos, along with our claims to properties.

In the same manner in which "numbers" in Plato's mind have become fused with "ideas," so both of these were deemed to fuse in the mind of God. Therefore, "when the world began to get into order ...

God fashioned them by form and number... as far as possible the fairest and best, out of things which were not fair and good (*Timaeus* 53b).

Souls and Salvation

The creator has delegated to his first-generation offspring, to immortal gods, the task of creating mortal animate beings on earth. But before assigning this task, the creator himself made a great number of immortal souls, equal in number to the stars (*Timaeus* 41a–e). Lesser gods then created mortal bodies, and into these they incorporated the immortal souls that God had made. Not being the creation of a single father throughout, the unions of immortal souls and mortal bodies are temporary arrangements. Moreover, the immortal principle of reason is thereby assigned the task of transforming or sublimating the mortal portion, or as Plato writes, "to draw in its train the turbulent mob of later accretions of fire, air, water and earth" (42c).[111]

The immortal soul, guided by reason, is thus given the task of achieving some kind of victory over the sensate and irrational dimension of a human being. For its reward, the soul is returned to its better and original divine state.

But then, perhaps in combination with the presence of Pythagorean number mysticism, Hindu notions about *samsara* and *karma,* fueled by the philosophers' intellectual elitism, might have introduced into the *Timaeus,* and left Plato, with a rather twisted notion concerning soteriology for the whole of humankind:

He who lived well during his appointed time was to return and dwell in his native star, and there he would have a blessed and congenial existence. But if he failed in attaining this, then at the second birth his soul would pass into the body of a woman, and if in that state of being he did not desist from evil, he would continually be changed into some brute who resembled him in the evil nature which he had acquired (*Timaeus* 42b-c).

---

111 The soteriology alluded to here may be understood as a reversal of direction, a reversal of the creative descent of the soul, as hinted by Wordsworth in "trailing clouds of glory we have come from God, who is our home." However, Plato's return journey, here, does seem more like "trailing billows of fury and weight."

Timaeus—the Summary

A quick glance at Plato's concluding sentences in the Timaeus will help place his larger conceptual framework into the Egyptian-Hellenic perspective which we already have exegeted in this treatise:

We may now say that our discourse about the nature of the universe has [come to] an end. The world has received animals (living beings, mortal and immortal, and is fulfilled with them, and has become the visible animal containing the visible—the sensible God who is the image of the intellectual, the greatest, best, fairest, most perfect—the one only-begotten heaven. (*Timaeus* 92c.

If contemplated for its ontology and structure, from the greater to the smaller, this summary statement recognizes an Intellect-God who is the greatest, best, fairest, and most perfect. No doubt, Plato associated this Intellect-God with his entire realm of Ideas; that is, he associated them at some point prior to where distinctions are made among strata and levels of these Ideas. So far, so good. But are the sensible and the intellectual manifestations of God, together, not called "the one only-begotten heaven?" Separately as well as jointly, either of these strata implies a supreme begetter who exists beyond the static and sterile realm of Platonic Ideas.

One may doubt that Plato knew very much directly about ancient Egyptian theology. But from the living or divine cosmos that he sketched he garnered significant matching similarities. This living and divine cosmos also was presupposed by most among his Greek predecessors in Ionian philosophy. Whenever the inertness of his abstract eternal Ideas disappointed him, Plato, like everyone else, was forced to think of the remaining cosmos as being nevertheless alive. In this manner, the philosopher ended by assuming a Godhead who could beget intelligent as well as animate offspring.

Of course, such a conclusion, obtained while reasoning from data of the Creator's offspring, becomes ontologically inverted. In the context of concrete existential living, the philosopher Plato, like everyone else, comfortably inferred the greater cause from the presence of numerous lesser results; then, he told his tale of deduction forward from the greater cause to lesser effects. What human mind can be faulted—and by whom?—for exhibiting tautological habits that are necessitated by finitude!

The visible universe that Plato contemplated was a god—that is, a cosmos revealed by a higher invisible Intellect-God and the Creator of Souls—thus, a creator situated within his own process of begetting, among his own Begotten. That visible universe conceived its animals with all the implied philosophical-zoological ambiguity: "Of the divine, he himself was the creator, but the creation of the mortal he committed to his offspring" (*Timaeus* 69c). So much for Plato's theory of creation and evolution!

Subsequent Gnostic prophets and teachers, especially those inclined toward Persian dualism, made much of Plato's ever so slight Hesiodic severance between God and his mixed mortal offspring. Plato's profane metaphor portrays God as mixing immortal souls with lesser elements, as in an ordinary mixing bowl—or as if arbitrarily he had been wrapping souls into lesser elements from the outer dimensions. The unity that existed between the Godhead and derivative humanity, implied by the Heliopolitan concept of emanation, seems to have gotten broken by Plato's abbreviated metaphor.

"Conception," amidst the Intelligible and Sensible realms, can be understood philosophically as "conceiving ideas." At the lower level of sense-objects, the same word means the bodily conception of offspring. Both denotations refer to the same process of divine emanation—to procreation as "conceiving concepts as well as bodies." The presence of this dual meaning, in English, may be appreciated as homophony that leaked from our Egyptian-Platonic heritage, all the way into our remote Germanic English language.

Aristotle between Earth and Heaven

Half a generation after Plato, the philosopher Aristotle (384–322 BCE answered Socratic queries and issues in his own learned manner. Aristotle was dissatisfied with the Hesiodic gash that Plato, his mentor, seemed to have accepted as a line of separation and distinction across his entire ontology, between the static reality of eternal Ideas (of a neutered Father Heaven) and the realm of transient sense experiences (upon the living and fertile Mother Earth).[112]

---

112 In presenting Plato's ontology we have, for obvious reasons, relied heavily on his most Egyptianized dialogue, the *Timaeus*. In other Platonic dialogues, the dichotomy of Ideas versus objects of sense experience is made more explicit. Aristotle's contrast must be appreciated in the larger context of Plato's writings.

With the healing hand of a physician, Aristotle arranged Plato's Ideas along the vertical dimension of a hierarchy. He arranged them as convertible "forms" that, individually could be seen getting imposed on convertible stratified "matter"—that is to say, in the world of visible entities. A higher "form" (formerly a Platonic "idea") contains within itself Aristotle's "next lower form, as its matter."

So, for example, an entity such as a "chair" constitutes subject matter (i.e. content in relation to the larger form "furniture" whereas "chair" at the same time also provides shape or form to the "wood" which it contains. Thus, in the next context with the lower order, "chair" becomes form, whereas "wood" is matter. Furniture, chair, and wood are interrelated hierarchically, participating as matter in a next higher form. Each "form" embraces a next lower form as its "matter." They may thus be distinguished as participating at different levels of reality—to different degrees of actuality, vis-à-vis potentiality. But as form and matter they are interrelated. Levels of reality are knitted together in a hierarchy from the highest to the lowest. Pure matter, the lowest, is pure potentiality, whereas pure form, the highest, is actuality. In Aristotle's astronomy, these designations are applied to various spheres of a single geocentric universe. A single cosmic hierarchy of beings ranges thus from matter and earth, here below, all the way up to pure actuality, the formal Prime Mover.

With this stairway of forms and matter, Aristotle has attempted to cut or to subdivide the primary cut-line of ontological severance, the line that separates Plato's realm of Ideas from his realm of sense-experience. This cut corresponds to the old gash of mythology, by which Cronos cut apart Heaven and Earth—and thereby, Aristotle has subdivided the cut into many smaller and less gruesome incisions. His conceptual stairway is adjusted by assigning attributes of "potentiality" for matter and of "actuality" for form. It extends from the material earth to the perimeter of the universe, the Prime Mover.

This famous student of Plato nevertheless was unable to heal the Uranos wound by applying his analytic method. By substituting many graduated analytic cuts (or steps), even the best analytic mind cannot subdivide a larger cut back to its former state of uncut wholeness. A human mind can imagine how to divide or subdivide a larger wound, hypothetically, into smaller wounds. But in real life, any wound treated in this manner enlarges—at least for the duration that predator minds gnaw at it, analytically. Analysis happens to be a function and an innate habit of Homo sapiens. Analysis is the mental derivative of physical functions, originally performed by teeth and acidic alimentary tracts.

Aristotle showed his Hesiodic "mental hand" even more in his questionable science of astronomy than by way of his metaphysics. His model of a perfectly circular universe had Earth at its center, representing the lowest level of matter and of "potentiality" at the same time. Earth is encircled by energy spheres which all, like the Earth, contemplate in succession some next higher moving celestial body, as from some higher epicycle or orbit of motion. Inasmuch as Greek philosophers disliked infinite regress, it seemed reasonable that there should be a farthest circling sphere, which has no concretely moving celestial aspect to it but which, nevertheless, could be contemplated. Beyond that outer sphere, and extending beyond, abides the Prime Mover.

Even though everything else moves beneath him, and on account of him, Aristotle assures us that the divine Prime Mover himself is an Unmoved Mover (*Physics* 5). This First Mover has no limit or magnitude and is situated at the circumference of the Eudoxian-Aristotelian universe. Aristotle ruled out the possibility of having the Prime Mover create movement by either pushing or pulling. Thus, for his metaphysics, he derived motion in the universe from the fact that the Prime Mover remains an object of desire. In accordance with their desire, all other entities are moving.[113] This finally implies that the Mover God not only is unmoved by anyone else, but also is not moving toward or away from anyone.

As a mental First Cause who himself is here thought of as contemplating after the stationary fashion of an armchair philosopher, and who exists beyond the planets and any offspring subject matter, this kind of First Mover demonstrates no physical motion himself. Being pure form and mind, he only can contemplate motion. He thinks about motion unencumbered by the uncertainties displayed at the lowest matter-laden Earth or by her physical rhythms of commotion and by her productivity.

---

113 See Ross, *Aristotle*, 95f, 175ff.

Centuries before philosophers pondered matters abstractly, Hesiod's Hellenic Sky Father had mythologically, or "metaphorically" if you like, lost his ability and his desire to be an active participant in creation. The celestial inaction of Aristotle's First Cause of the universe, of the Prime Mover, resembles remarkably well the condition of Hesiod's violently retired Father Sky. At least since the days of Hesiod, the Greek Father-god of Heaven no longer had actively been able to affect the productivity and the life of Mother Earth, nor life upon her. Contemplation of celestial motion that leads to responsive motion on Earth in Hesiod's as well as in Aristotle's worlds, happens from desires awakened in the lower regions.

All the while, a dynamic Earth still moves and continually renews her landscapes and generates fresh life. She produces mortal nourishment for mortal offspring. In contrast, the anciently castrated Hesiodic Father Sky, the Unmoved Mover in the mind of Aristotle, could only contemplate the motion to which his own potency no longer can contribute. His energy appears to suffice only to contemplate what, apart from his Non-Motion, his potency still can afford. The epistemological fact of the matter is that in the self-sufficient philosophical perspective of Aristotle, the human activity of thinking could begin to see itself, conveniently, as the self-caused cause of all motion. Thus, modeled after the contents of a human mind, Aristotle's most distant celestial reality is thereby merely meant to be comprehended by human ideas. Motion at its purest, sheer form and actuality, has been refined and reduced philosophically to the purity of pure thought. Indeed, only a divine mind, and just barely yet a philosopher's mind, can imagine such purity of thought as it happens to occur in "unmoving" ideal Prime Motion.

Eudoxus of Knidos and Aristotle

Of course, there is more to Aristotle's story than a Platonic education and Hesiodic mythology. Aristotle also learned a few things from the astronomer and mathematician Eudoxus of Knidos (ca. 400–350 BCE), a teacher who once went to Egypt and shaved his head. He lived with Egyptian priests for sixteen months to learn from them.[114] One can assume that a man of the caliber of Eudoxus, while under-

---

[114] Diogenes Laertius, VIII 86–89, in Martin Bernal, *Black Athena* (New Brunswick, N.J.: Princeton University Press, 1987), 103, 108, 514.

going such inconveniences, has sought out Egypt's most prominent thinkers to make his efforts worth the while. Unfortunately, we can trace the teachings of Eudoxus only indirectly by way of the imprint they have left on Aristotle. Whatever value there can still be attributed to the joint geocentric astronomy of Eudoxus and Aristotle, two and a half millennia later, will eventually be limited to points that their lessons might have added to Western intellectual history.

Based on what already is known about Egyptian theology, it should not be difficult to envision how something like the geocentric astronomy of Eudoxus could have been concocted in Egypt. Nor should that feat have appeared unreasonable to a Greek materialist who dabbled in Egyptian theology. All he needed for a starter was the orthodox theology of Heliopolis. When astronomical observations are added to emanational Atum theology, the Eudoxian astronomy comes into focus by itself. It focuses together with Aristotle's metaphysics of "forms and matter" which was extrapolated from that same hybrid of emanation astronomy. Against the Egyptian theological background, surprisingly, even Aristotle's astronomy begins to make some sense. Heavenly bodies move as they can be observed, and creative thought-power can, still in participation, be traced back through levels of emanation to a distant Atum-Shu-Mahet-like source. A semblance of harmony between Egyptian theology and Greek scientific reasoning has, apparently, been achieved by way of recognizing and climbing the broadest stairway of emanation.

But there is also a problem lingering in the Eudoxian geocentric astronomy. It is being contemplated in relation to its orthodox Egyptian setting. Heliopolitan ontology, with its Atum-Ra or with its first Hill-Sun manifestation, was not only geocentric, it was heliocentric as well. By contrast, the cosmology of Aristotle and Eudoxus was only geo-centric. Eudoxian astronomy lacked the flow and motion of the Egyptian model, according to which both motion and intelligence emanated jointly from the same source and direction. Motion, in the Heliopolitan god-story, was accounted for with the central Godhead's seminal emission. It happened as solar radiation, as spitting, and later in Memphite theology through the speaking of commands.

The Greek mythical-philosophical background, however, which had inherited Hesiod's castrated and immobilized Father Sky, and which assumed that motion was usurped by Earth, by her son Cronos and by her remaining progeny, blocked for Eudoxus and Aristotle the full Egyptian two-way path of reasoning. For them Egypt's larger mythology of fertile emanation has gotten blocked. Without some concrete mythological dynamic for conceptualizing greater-than-human reality, the abstract foam of analytic philosophy and science—devoid of mythic-ontological purpose and ethos—evaporates from human experience as linguistic foam and fury.

Egyptian Metaphysics in Aristotle

Let us nevertheless appreciate for a little while longer the positive side of Aristotle's thought. What made him want to heal the Hesiodic wound? We may never know the full answer to this question. Long before Pascal's ditty was being recited—to the effect that the heart has reasons of which reason does not know—the "heart" of an Egyptian thinker had reasons of which Greek minds initially understood little. But Greek minds nevertheless were attracted, alternately and occasionally, by thoughtful Egyptian "hearts."

We must therefore restate our question: Was Aristotle's metaphysic of Form and Matter, perchance, also philosophy born of an Egyptian heart? If Aristotle's starting point is seen as confrontation to Plato's ontological dualism, then we can truly say that in response, Aristotle would have set out on a path of reasoning that led back toward orthodox Egyptian holistic process theology. The challenge of reconciling his philosophy with Eudoxian-Egyptian astronomy might have moved him to think along the line of this implicit rapprochement. Even though Aristotle ended up building a metaphysical and linguistic stairway of Forms and Matter—with many steps for matching progressions of his linguistic classifications—he nevertheless managed to restore at least some sort of cascading stairway that resembled the larger Egyptian "water-fall" of emanation.

Inasmuch as Aristotle characterized Earth and Matter together as potentiality, and the Prime Mover as static pure form of actuality, he insisted implicitly on some form of emanation, from Heaven on high all the way down to the dark Earth. Thus, the primary difference that remained between Aristotelian and Egyptian cosmology was the assumption that, for him, the First Cause of Motion was no longer located at the center but at the periphery of the universe.

Aristotle's First Cause of Everything was expanded along the periphery of his known world. The philosopher reached this conclusion while also accommodating the approximate whereabouts of the impotent Hesiodic Uranos, as a mythic model for his Prime Mover. But then, even if no real energy was emanating from Aristotle's Prime Mover, the latter's sheer presence harbored at least thoughts of motion that lower spheres could imitate—perhaps by way of showing some pity for his lameness. The retired Sky Father remained a disinterested distant model—thus, only a vague phantom of the original active Egyptian Godhead, Atum. The spheres of the universe moved, undriven by an Unmoving Mover—perhaps by sheer awareness and pity, in memory of the First Cause of whom the offspring have lost sight quickly after their own reflexes began to kick in.

Eureka! All activities of rational thinking have thereby gotten captured, for safekeeping. They were made available to human minds alone.

It appears as though with his ontological stairway of "Forms and Matter," which he has modeled in part on the structure of Eudoxian astronomy, Aristotle struggled to repair his Hesiodic estrangement with an incomplete glimpse of Egyptian soteriology. The nostalgia that is present in the lower planetary spheres, toward their distant Prime Mover who, as Pure Actuality only motivates mentally and without actually moving anything.

Not even the most generous cosmology is capable of engendering a trustworthy soteriology. The final step of reconciling Greek philosophy with its ancient Egyptian root ontology—that could begin healing the Hesiodic wound—was left to two other men with Egyptian connections. Both were Egyptians living in Alexandria and they were marginally recognized as "Greek philosophers." They were Ammonius Saccas and his student Plotinus. Ammonius is arguably the most mysterious figure in the history of philosophy, and he was known in Alexandria as "the Porter." The menial work of guarding an entrance door and welcoming guests, apparently, enabled this founding father of so-called "Neo-Platonism" earn a livelihood while, alongside, he ushered his inherited Egyptian ontology into the widening corridor of Western Christian thought—along the margins of groups of philosophers.

A Parting Smile for Eudoxian-Aristotelian Astronomy

It happened during my last year of undergraduate work at the University of Kansas, in 1961; our staunchest Professor of Philosophy concluded his explanations regarding the astronomy of Aristotle by allowing himself some unexpected levity: "It is easy to see why Aristotle did not become famous for his astronomy."Applause for the always resulate and somber professor was assured. And ever since that day, when reminiscing on this lecture, I too, have permitted myself a non-philosophical smirk of amusement.

A "geo-centric universe" in the aftermath of Galileo and Copernicus, today, no longer appears ipso facto funny. I am now inclined to take back some of my improper smirks.

Projecting the Earth into the center of our known universe is an obvious convenience for modern physicists who, with the help of the most advanced telescopes, including satellite telescopes, choose to plot the position of our Planet Earth at the center of the universe. To human eyes, ever unable to detect black matter, the universe will always appear like a sphere. With the formation of a universe within essentially a spherical Big-Bang, the radius of our universe will always need to be projected like a ray of light in any direction into which from here we choose to aim our telescopes. Compare Neil Turok, *The Universe Within: From Quantum to Cosmos*, House of Anansi Press, 2012.

For drawing their circular map of their universe, Eudoxus and Aristotle probably could have done much worse than choosing the Earth with its obelisk at the temple of Heliopolis (Junu) as their center. After our newest understanding of the still hypothetical Big Bang event, which supposedly began to open our universe, the dark Atum Mountain and the orifice from which the bright Sun-Deity Ra issued correspond, essentially, to the same Heliopolis in present geographic space. Did Eudoxus and Aristotle possibly sense the identity of their chosen Geo-Center with the Circumference of their Universe?—of a center exploding outward, toward larger circumferences?

13

The Neo-Egyptian Philosophy of Plotinus

Plotinus conceptualized the Supreme Divinity as a trinity that manifests itself in three hypostases: as the One, as Mind, and as Soul. Prototypes of these hypostases can be recognized in the history of Egyptian thought first, as the three divinities who make up the Heliopolitan Ennead: Atum-Ra, Shu, and Tefnut-Mahet. In the philosophy of Plotinus, these correspond to the One, Mind, and Soul (compare Figure 12). To designate and to get his three hypostases to flow, Plotinus had recourse to a number of synonyms. Inasmuch as some of these designations will occur frequently throughout this chapter, they shall be introduced in summary form here, at the outset.[115]

Plotinus in Brief – "The One"

The One is unknowable, beyond evaluation, and transcends our concepts of ordinary being. It is also called the Transcendent, the Infinite, the Unconditioned, and sometimes Father or the God. What can be predicated about its existence is only that non-existence would be a wrong ascription. The One also is beyond thought, because thought implies analytic distinctions, and analytic distinctions, in turn, imply the presence of parts and thereby the possibility of deficiencies and imperfections.

---

[115] For this summary, I have availed myself especially of the translator's "Extracts from the Explanatory Matter in the First Translation," in *Plotinus: The Enneads,* trans. Stephen MacKenna (New York: Pantheon Books, 1962), xxi-xxxiv. In addition, I remember with great fondness an old professor at the University of Kansas during the late 1950s—Professor of Philosophy, Clifford Osborne, who was the first to explain Plotinus to us—though, without linkage to Egypt.

Plotinus in Brief – "The Mind"

MacKenna translates "nous" most often as Intellectual Principle. It also is given as Divine Thought and Universal Intelligence, or as the first something of which existence can be predicated. It is the Act, the Offspring, as well as the still unseen "Image" of the One; it is a Mediation with the unknowable One. Its function is to know. Nous or Mind is the highest something knowable or approachable by human minds. In that sense, it also may be named Spirit or Supreme Soul.

Together with the Divine Mind, with Divine Intellection, or with the Divine-Intellectual-Principle, plurality has its beginning alongside complexity and multiplicity. Mind is the Intelligible Universe or the totality of Divine Thoughts. The content of the Divine Mind, in Greek philosophy, corresponds to Plato's "Realm of Ideas."

Like the One from which they emanate, so also the Platonic Ideas themselves are real beings, eternal originals, archetypes, and intellectual forms of whatever exists in the lower spheres. The Intelligible Universe extends to, or encompasses, all particular minds and intelligences that—metaphorically speaking and unseen—are the images, representations, phantasms, or reflections of the invisible Universal or Divine Mind. All the graduated degenerate beings, as they emanate from the One down in the direction of lowly matter, which happens to be the faintest presence of Real Being, are nevertheless more realistically present, concurrently, as archetypes or Platonic Ideas. They are still within the realm of the hypostasis of Divine Thought.

Divine Intellection works two-directionally. Downward (i.e. overflowing outward from the center), it generates creative power that dis-plays thoughts with increasing degrees of visibility. Upward (and In-ward), it contemplates its own invisible core, the One. The presence of the Mind-Hypostasis affects appearances along its own path of descent. Along that path, Mind generates "real being"—among presences and traces that fade downward, toward the next hypostasis.

Plotinus in Brief – "The Soul"

The lowest hypostasis of Plotinus' trinity is *psyche* or Soul, the All-Soul, Universal Soul or Soul of the All. After the manner in which Mind is an emanation of the One, Soul is the continued emanation of the One and Mind together. The Soul's outward flow is an extension of the larger range of Mind. Its High-Soul aspect contemplates the Intellectual Principle or Mind, up-stream, whereas its Low-Soul aspect may be visualized downward, as the effective Logos or Creative Word of the Universe.[116] The Low-Soul aspect generates body for its temporary home. However, by its embodiment, the physically embedded human soul also experiences a desire to return home. Nostalgically, a soul contemplates and retraces its path homeward, first toward the Intellectual Principle for getting closer, and then to merge again into the One.

The All-Soul, which is downward and outward oriented, with its creative outward flow, along its Low-Soul dimension, still remains involved with its High-Soul dimension by way of upward contemplation. In the downward or outward flow, soul is the cause of all visible forms and movements. It is the cause of the visible cosmos and world, of everything that humans can encounter by their five senses. The All-Soul comprises all outward emanated as well as homeward-bound instances of Low and High Soul, together.[117]

Thus, the Plotinian trinity is being emanated in three hypostases. Within these hypostases, a singular stream of generative creativity or vitality flows outward from the One, all the way toward meon or matter, which shows off the outer edge of Real Being in general, and of Soul in particular. Along this outer edge, souls or elements of the All-Soul and All-Being, curve inward unto themselves to initiate a counter current that begins to flow homeward again to the One. For conceptualization, utilizing the metaphor of light, it may be helpful to visualize the outward flow as generation and the homeward flow as nostalgic contemplation. It happens along a luminous and shiny spectrum that ranges from all light to complete darkness. In this spectrum, the One functions as the source of all light—of light so bright that the human eye is unable to distinguish content. The One transcends all human faculties and

---

[116] It is truly amazing how the continuity of meaning between Atum's seminal emission, attested to in the Pyramid- and Coffin Texts and the creative words of Ptah, have been maintained by this late Neo-Egyptian philosopher-theologian, Plotinus. High Soul corresponds to *ka,* and Low Soul corresponds to *ba*—as in the Heliopolitan and Memphite theologies, shown earlier in this book, Chapters 3-6.

[117] Or, in orthodox Egyptian language, all sparks of *ka* as well as all lower apparitions of *ba.*

and knowledge. At the lower or darkened end of the spectrum, Soul as Real Being fades into sluggish materiality by way of becoming visible, creating body and residue. Soul, at its lowest or outermost extremity stops just short of disappearing into non-being.

What, in the larger context corresponds, then, to the hypostasis of Mind? It is present along the intermediate portion of the total spectrum, extending from the unknowable One, down to visible Soul. The contents of Mind are invisible; but they do become knowable.

If radiation of light, as it affects mortal persons, is to be used as a metaphor for our discourse, then intellectual enlightenment at the level of mind transcends, and corresponds analogically to the enjoyment of visible light rays in the lower realm where some involved souls have become visible. At the outer reaches of their "radiation," souls become involved in sensate bodies. Moreover, in this lower realm, the experience of light is brought within the range of vision by "shadows" of darkness and non-being. Souls at that level, are enabled to sense the purer light rays of luminous bodies with which they themselves have become involved, in contrast with the shadows of non-being.

Thus, whereas for Plotinus there are three hypostases, there is only one source, one essence, and one movement that along its outer reach curls back unto itself, defensively. There is only one reality, one God-head, one process. All of being, All-Being, which comprises this process, is considered good. From a transient human perspective, the absence of detectable being, the happenstance of void or non-being, can only be experienced or described as apparent evil. In this context, the word "evil" is not a substantive. For Soul this word indicates merely its downward and outward emanation or its estrangement. If the soul were able to continue further in the direction of matter and non-being, presumably, it could vanish forever. But this will never happen. Soul is a manifestation of All-Being. It will adhere to Being itself and return, sooner or later, homeward again, toward its source .

Samples from the Sixth Ennead

The extant writings of Plotinus are fifty-four essays that have been gathered by Porphyry into six Enneads—six volumes containing nine essays each. It is clear that initially these essays were not written to make sense sequentially. Any one Ennead, and even portions within each of the six Enneads, may be approached as independent units.

Individually, and taken together, all of them attempt to explain a single reality. They represent variations on a single theme, on the All-Being and its emanation.

This book has limited aims and therefore provides commentary on only two Enneads. The Sixth Ennead will be utilized here as a wide-angle lens, to assist our focus on the larger ontology and total process. The Fifth Ennead will be consulted for a more specific view on Plotinian trinitarianism.

To begin our readings somewhere in the Sixth Ennead, we take a hint from Emile Brehier, who in a lecture titled "The Orientalism of Plotinus," delivered in 1921–22, suggested that "the fourth and fifth treatises of the Sixth Ennead . . . can be easily read without any reference to Greek philosophy."[118] Similar observations can be made regarding other Enneads. In any case, we present here a brief commentary to treatises that Brehier already has singled out.

An Egyptian Clue in VI,4

A discussion of the omnipresence of Soul, in the fourth treatise of the Sixth Ennead, concludes with statements that could easily pass for meditations on ancient Egyptian funerary liturgy:

As for the entry into the World of the Shades, if this means into the unseen, that is its [the soul's] release; if into some lower place, there is nothing strange in that, since even here the soul is taken to be where the body is, in place with the body... (Enneads VI, 4, 16).[119]

This afterlife anticipation offers comfort for the time when funerary rites must be performed for deceased mortals. What follows after these words of assurance reintroduces a dualism of souls, which is not foreign to Egyptologists, namely, a distinction of the authentic soul (the *ka*) and an image soul (the *ba*). Elsewhere, Plotinus has identified these as High Soul and Low Soul. But what about the dissolution off the body? So long as the image-soul has not been

---

118 Emile Brehier, *The Philosophy of Plotinus,* trans. Joseph Thomas (Chicago: University of Chicago Press, 1958), 111.

119 For this sketch of Plotinus's philosophy, the new Armstrong translation has been consulted, but quotations, nevertheless, have been chosen from the freer translation of MacKenna, for easier access for non-specialist readers. See *The Enneads, by Plotinus,* trans. MacKenna (New York, 1962). Quoted with the permission of Faber and Faber Ltd.

discarded, clearly the higher will be where that is; if, on the contrary, the higher has been completely emancipated by philosophic discipline, the image-soul may well go alone to that lower place, while the authentic passes uncontaminated into the Intellectual, separated from the image "but nonetheless the soul entire."

Let the image—offspring of the individuality—fare as it may, the true soul when it turns its light upon itself, chooses the higher and by that choice blends into the All, neither acting now nor extinct (*Enneads* VI,4,16).

The true soul (*ka)* ascends and it returns to blend with the All, while approaching and seeking its future in its past, in the direction of the One. Following death, the high soul's former association with a soul, the soul-generated body, the body's condition as corpse, and even all ghostly or prehuman flux *ba* apparitions remain behind to disappear eventually from the shadow-play with Non-being. Body and corpse never were more than temporary images. After light is withdrawn, no reality is left in what used to be a shadow-figure. The authentic *ka* energy seeks, reunites and blends with divinity, the *ka* of the All.

An Egyptian Clue in VI,5

Looking for a moment at the culminating sentences of the fifth treatise in the Sixth Ennead, which Brehier has mentioned as reflecting an extra-Greek origin, we find the same theory of soul. Only non-being, we are told, is abandoned as the authentic High-Soul travels, purified and whole, toward the still higher hypostasis of Mind, and from there to the One.

. . . you become an All. No doubt you were always that, but there has been an addition and by that addition you are [you were] diminished; for the addition was . . . from non-being. It is not by some admixture of non-being that one becomes an entire, but by putting non-being away.

Visibility and apparitions result from turning away from All-Being, and from looking toward its opposite, non-being. Plotinus moved on to illustrations concerning general folk religiosity. It must be kept in mind that he did not rationalize here the existence of lesser gods, as if he were pursuing theological apologetics. On the contrary! The philosophy of Plotinus becomes more relevant for making its basic enets agree with popular religion. Apparitions of less popular gods happen under well-known circumstances, as Plotinus concedes.

The gods, "in many guises seek our cities;" but there is "That Other" whom the cities seek, and all the earth and heaven—Him who is everywhere self-abiding and from whom derives Being and the Real Beings [i.e. Ideas] down to Soul and Life, all bound to Him and so moving to that unity which, by its very lack of extension, is infinite (*Enneads* VI,5,12).

One cannot help but be impressed by the summary statement of the seventh treatise. The emanation process of the All is there explained as a sequence of dependent hypostases:

Soul dependent upon Intellectual-Principle and Intellectual Principle upon the Good, all is linked to the Supreme by intermediaries, some close, some nearing those of the closer attachment, while the order of sense stands remotest, dependent on soul (*Enneads* VI,7,42).

Inasmuch as no attribute is thinkable pertaining to the Supreme Good—inasmuch as it extends beyond ideas and attributions—all relationships and dependencies must be explained from the perspective of lower hypostases. Sense experience happens in the domain of soul. Then Soul is dependent on Intellectual Principle or Mind, whereas Intellectual Principle is dependent on the Good or Supreme One. Envisioned objectively, the continuum that from the One extends down and outward to some lowly sensate soul has, in the Enneads, repeatedly been characterized as emanation, radiation, or flow. The beginnings of this conceptualization of the total dynamic process can be traced to ancient Heliopolitan mythology.

Does not the previous passage also have reference to Plato's supreme Idea of the Good? Indeed, it seems so. But would this mean that Plotinus borrowed his total ontological vision from Plato's Dialogues? The more one contemplates the words of Plotinus in their Egyptian context, the more obvious it becomes that the word "Good" was used here to communicate the orthodox Egyptian notion of the Godhead—of Atum, Ptah, or Amun—to Greek minds. The writings of Greek philosophers, together with their specialized philosophical vocabulary, were for Plotinus foremost a tool for dialogue. Quoting from them, he was able to communicate with the intelligentsia of Graeco-Roman colonial culture. Thus, although

Plotinus shared his basic Egyptian ontological orientation in the context of Greek philosophies, the latter philosophies appear to have been of limited use to him.

Samples from the Fifth Ennead

Greek ontology is built largely on nouns. Platonic ontology, in particular, has contributed to this idolatry of nouns by its habit of elevating some nouns to the status of eternal Ideas. Generalities were thereby promoted to infinity. Plotinus's ontology, we now see, has not been shaped mostly by contemplating static nouns and Ideas—which Platonic philosophy permitted to lounge inertly (as Osiris lay inertly on a bier); rather, Plotinus's philosophy has been affected more by the way an inherited Egyptian theology could be paraphrased in the idiom of Hellenistic rationalism. Inasmuch as the Godhead of Egyptian orthodoxy always has been beyond the reach of human conceptualization, and as descriptive names or nouns were treated by Egyptian theologians with playful suspicion, process and verbs have become significant for Plotinus.

At the same time, verbs that describe the divine process of emanation ordinarily escaped notice among Plotinus's critics, who all along had been predisposed toward "Hesiodic" analytic Hellenism. This is not to say that Plotinus taught theology underhandedly. As far as his religious orientation is concerned, he was not even afraid of pointing to the Godhead metaphorically as an All-Father. Plotinus never hesitated to describe this All-Father's creative virility as an active process of engendering.

A crutch for the Reader: No further discussion of the basic theme is necessary at this point, except to say that on the following pages our aim will be to highlight certain significant verbs, or verbalizations, that pertain to the emanation activity of the Godhead, as a process of engendering, nurturing, saving, and retrieving the begotten. **In some quotations from the *Enneads*, here, certain verbalizations will be rendered in italics—to call attention to "process."**

Ennead V,1,1

Porphyry placed the treatise "On the Three Principal Hypostases" at the beginning of the Fifth or "theological" Ennead. This treatise is perhaps the most important among those that paved Neo-Platonism's inroads into Christendom. Eusebius of Caesarea, Augustine,

Basil, Cyril, and Theodoret—they all quoted from it.[120] Plotinus began his discussion at the level of human existence, that is, with the facts of divine creation and the soul's estrangement from God. Throughout Part One of this book, the attentive reader will have found that these were favorite propositions in the ancient Egyptian funerary cult as well.

What can it be that has brought *the souls to forget the Father,* God, and though members of the Divine and entirely of that world, *to ignore* at once themselves and it? The evil that has overtaken them has its source in self-will ... (i.e.) *desire for self-ownership ... drifting further and further they came to lose* even the thought of their origin in the Divine. (V,1,1)

The epistemology implied by these sentences describes, accordingly, the existential upward and homeward yearning of Plotinus's own estranged soul. His epistemology and ontology are the road map for his return journey home to God. His philosophical doctrines are, in fact, soteriology (doctrine of salvation).

Ennead V,1,2

After the existential position of his soul had been determined and plotted by soteriology and epistemology, Plotinus focused on his position in life as the starting point for his ontology:

Let *every soul recall,* then, at the outset the truth that *soul is the author of all living things, that it has breathed the life into them* all, whatever is nourished by earth and sea, all the creatures of the air; the divine stars in the sky; *it is the maker of the sun;* itself *formed and ordered* this vast heaven and *conducts* all that rhythmic motion ... (all these living things) *gather or dissolve, as soul brings them life or abandons them,* but soul, since it never can abandon itself, is of eternal being.

Continuing with this postulate of the soul's eternal and divine nature, the discussion which follows moves from smaller human souls to the presence of still greater souls, to such who have not succumbed to the downward lure that bewitched and estranged the souls of ordinary humankind. Without soul, in Plotinus's words, there would be only "stark body"—clay and water—or, rather, the blankness of matter, the absence of Being, and as sometimes it is put,

---

120 See Paul Henry, "The Place of Plotinus in the History of Thought," in *The Enneads by Plotinus,* trans. MacKenna (New York, 1962), xliv, note 6.

the excretion of the gods. In search of the greater Soul and to better understand its nature and power, Plotinus contemplated the heavenly system in the upward direction:

By the power of the Soul the manifold and diverse heavenly system is a unit: *through soul this universe is a God: and the sun is a God because it is ensouled; so too the stars; and whatsoever we ourselves may be, it is all in virtue of soul*; for "dead is viler than dung." This, *by which the gods are divine*, must be the oldest God of them all: and our own soul is of that same Idea nature... (it is) honorable above all that is bodily. For what is body but earth?

Plotinus still points here from the human condition to higher divinities, such as the universe, the sun, and the stars. These are deities to the extent that Soul empowers them. Of course, the statement also implies that these cosmic divinities, to the extent that they have become visible, still are somewhat tainted by matter. Plotinus does not hesitate to inject here, momentarily and for contrast, a scatological metaphor that classifies human corpses as being somewhat viler than dung. In the same impressive manner of basic speech, matter, when devoid of soul, is likened to "excretion of the gods." The metaphor of divine pro-creation is temporarily replaced with an even more vulnerable metaphor of divine defecation. One is reminded of the Heliopolitan cosmologists who earlier shifted from their masturbation metaphor to refer to "spitting."

The presence of ultra-earthy metaphors in lofty philosophical discourse provides a reliable clue to the wider range of dynamic experiential data with which Plotinus felt comfortable. Only a mind that has been nurtured in a rich mythological background can hope to achieve such broad ease with concrete infra-imagery. In the evolution of human thought, one must not forget that mythological events and figures preceded philosophical principles and abstractions. Mythological beings preceded philosophical generalities. Mythological reasoning always has been, and remains, the earthy ancestor and starting point for philosophical refinement.

Occasionally some of Plotinus's mythological background shows through his thinly woven, and worn, fabric of Hellenic philosophical discourse. Ancient deities appear insufficiently veiled by the caricature masks of abstract "hypostases." One may wonder why Plotinus ever classified the Godhead simply as another hypostasis.

Plotinus introduced hypostases for very pragmatic reasons, for the sake of communication. Hypostases are the philosophical abstractions, single picture frames and caricatures, projected unto, and emanating from, the three personae of Plotinus's supreme Egyptian trinity. Without the use of these abstractions (or shall we call them "intentional acts of memory fixation"?) the subtraction of personhood or virility from mighty divinities would have been unthinkable. Without hypostases, Plotinus could not have bested philosophers who preferred Greek intellectual analysis and abstraction.

Nevertheless, during moments of greater inwardness and honesty, Plotinus placed himself mystically inside the All that he described. This is what happened very early in the Fifth Ennead where, seeing himself situated at the lower end of the hypostasis of Soul, he introduced—as he often did—his epistemological perspective to merge it with his personal soteriology.[121]

Ennead V,1,3

The recognition of one's own soul, by faith and mind, implies upward contemplation and the rapprochement on the part of temporarily estranged minds toward God. Above Soul is situated a more divine source—is a higher hypostasis, waiting to be recognized.

Soul, for all the worth we have shown to belong to it, is yet a secondary, an image of the Intellectual-Principle: reason uttered is an image of the reason stored within the soul, and in the same way *Soul is an utterance* of the Intellectual-Principle: this is even *the total of its activity*, the entire stream of life sent forth by that Principle *for the production of further being*: it is *the forth-going heat of a fire* which also has heat essentially inherent ... sprung, in other words, from the Intellectual-Principle, Soul is intellective. It is an intellection, operating by the method of reasoning: for its perfection, it must look to that Divine Mind.

The interrelationship of source and image, of the Intellectual Principle and reasoning that enlivens Soul, Plotinus has explained with an Aristotelian type of form-and-matter regression. Had Plotinus chosen to apply his scatological metaphor this high up along his

121 He speaks from this inside perspective also at the completion of his mental journey, in Section VI.

scale of emanation, he also could have referred to Soul as "excrement" that issues from the Intellectual Principle. But, of course, Plotinus reserved his scatological process-metaphor to depict the lower transition within the overall emanation process—namely, the downward drifting of living souls into visible matter, approaching nothingness.

Ennead V,1,4

The Divine Mind, or Intellect, also can be approached by contemplating the world with the myriads of sensory experiences it offers, indirectly of course, by contemplating the archetypes of all creatures. Intelligence as such, which is unapproachable divine wisdom, unsoiled, presides over all particulars.

Thus, another paragraph of Plotinus represents a proverbial "bone thrown" to Greek philosophy that has lost touch with its own Hellenic mythic tradition. For the rhetorical purpose on hand, Plotinus's allusion to a non-Egyptian mythology, and to linguistic analysis, needed not be overly precise. His ideas certainly do not match those of Hesiod. Judge for yourself:

That archetypal world is the true Golden Age, the Age of Cronos whose very name [in Greek] suggests Abundance and Intellect. *Here is contained all that is immortal*: nothing here but its divine Mind; all is God; this is the place of every soul.

The sermonette on mystic bliss in the true Golden Age of Cronos sobered up to a description of the process of emanation a little lower from where intellect-infusion into the hypostasis of Soul happens. As there is a higher and a lower Soul, so also the realm of Mind or Divine Intellect emanates from higher to lower:

Soul deals with thing after thing—now Socrates; now a horse: always some one entity from among beings—but the Intellectual Principle is all and therefore *its entire content is simultaneously present* in that identity: this is pure being in eternal actuality; nowhere is there any future, because every then is a now; nor is there any past... and the total of all is Intellectual Principle entire, and Being entire.

Ennead V,1,5

The divine Intellectual Principle exists above the Soul. However, both Mind and Soul together constitute a single continuum. Even at the lower end, all souls stand fused as members with the higher divinity—unless estranged by deliberate apostasy. From this basis, established earlier, the upward contemplation proceeds from the Dyad of Soul and Divine Mind toward immersion in the One.[122] Inasmuch as Plotinus is here contemplating onward and upward against the creative current that overflows from the One, he tightens his conceptual net. The number of permissible attributions to deity becomes smaller. Thus, rather than letting the complicated text speak for itself, at this point, it may be useful to exegete and to paraphrase small steps and sentences:

1. The Intellectual Principle exists above the Soul.

2. Contemplating upward, the Soul brings itself closer to divine Intellect.

3. The Soul unites with the Intellect, as a Dyad, and the Egyptian question is asked: What has *"engendered"* this twofold God?

4. The Soul contemplating divine Intellect is a number quantity, or member, of the divine Dyad.

5. This Dyad of Number (i.e. Soul and Intellectual Principle) is undetermined; it represents, so to speak, the underlayment or "matter" for the Mind.

6. The Dyad is shaped in two ways: by Ideas rising within it, and by the presence of the One.

7. The Dyad in this homeward intellection is subject; the One from whom Mind emanates is object.

8. Within this current of creativity and counter-current of nostalgic intellection, the subject and its object become identical.

Thus, reunion of Soul with Intellect is achieved by the wholesome homeward yearning of individual souls. The subsequent reunion of the Dyad (the Twofoldness of Intellect and Soul together) with the complete One is a process of a more advanced mode of intellectual homeward contemplation. In a diluted mode, at a lower level, this extended type of philosophical contemplation and homeward yearning is just being begun by souls, with their incitement.

---

122 The conceptualization of Mind and Soul together, as a Dyad, follows time-honored orthodox Egyptian conventions. See in Part One the references to Ruti, the Lion Pair, that is, Shu and Tefnut.

Ennead V,1,6

With this Section, Plotinus completes the sketch of his contemplative homeward journey; he anchors himself again in cosmogony and theogony. Wrapped in the receptive Dyad—as animal souls are wrapped up in bodily living—so as a sharp-witted mystic, Plotinus contemplated the Intellectual Principle or Divine Mind. He pondered the question of his own mind's relatedness to Divine Mind:

But how and what does the Intellectual Principle see and, specifically, how has it *sprung from* that which is to become the object of its vision? The mind demands the existence of these beings, but it is still in trouble over the problem, endlessly debated by the most ancient philosophers. From such unity as we have declared the One to be, how does anything at all come into substantial existence, any multiplicity, dyad, or number? Why has the Primal not remained self-gathered?

The contemplative soul of Plotinus, on its journey, reaches its happy goal. He lays aside philosophical objective description and then, humbly, as a soul knowing itself already enveloped in the Dyad (the Twofoldness), he prays religiously and as humbly as perhaps few philosophers who followed in Plotinus's steps have dared to do:

In venturing an answer, we first invoke God Himself, not in loud word but in that way of prayer which is always within our power, *leaning in soul towards Him* by aspiration, alone towards the Alone. But if we seek the vision of that great Being within the Inner Sanctuary—i.e. self-gathered tranquilly, remote above all else—we begin by considering the images stationed at the outer precincts, exactly at the moment when the first *image appears*. How the *Divine Mind comes into being*, this must be explained.

A few additional statements, generated by this prayer, do complete the sketch. Everything moving needs an object toward which it advances—motion is relative to a goal—and motion cannot be ascribed without such a goal. Movement is an attribute of the second hypostasis. But then again, how does multiplicity result from the Supreme Immovable One? Plotinus answers that it must be happening through "circum-radiation." The creative emanation from the static and unchanging Supreme One "may be compared to the brilliant light that surrounds the Sun (as it is being) *ceaselessly generated* from that unchanging substance."

With the static process of The One's creativity, thus defined as circum-radiation, Plotinus would have been set to narrate the story of his journey in the outward and downward direction, traveling on or trailing the rays of creative radiation. He could have dwelt on the Mind reaching out to become radiantly manifest as Soul, and from there he could have flirted with matter and surfed along the shadow play of Non-being. But true to orthodox Egyptian theology, having once invoked the narrowing metaphor of solar circum-radia-tion, like Atonism, Plotinus quickly returned to the larger metaphor of creation as begetting, in honor of the total Atum-Ra:

. . . *all that is fully achieved [matured] engenders*, therefore, the eternally achieved *engenders eternally* and eternal being. The offspring is always minor . . . of the Divine Mind. *The offspring must seek and love the begetter; and especially so when begetter and begotten are alone in their sphere*; when, in addition, the begetter is the highest Good, *the offspring is attached* by a bond of sheer necessity, separated only by being distinct.

While this statement has resolved for Plotinus just about everything that physicists have come to define as force or physical gravity, the philosophy of Plotinus was first and foremost soteriology—never a fatalistic resignation to low or lowering blind forces. Theoretical philosophy for him was the handmaiden for emancipated living; it never was an end in itself. It therefore seems safe to say that what held Ammonius and Plotinus together, for eleven years of intimate study, was their mutual preoccupation with soteriology—the orthodox Egyptian version of salvation.

Ennead V,1,7

Plotinus began Section Seven with an exhortation to himself and to his readers: "We must be more explicit." It is significant that although he described his soul's entire journey homeward to the One, he referred to Hellenic mythology only once—to the Golden Age of Cronos (V,1,4)—and very imprecisely at that. After he promised to be more explicit, he added no more than ordinary commentary. He simply undertook to rationalize the sketch of his homeward journey in greater detail, which for Greeks meant to have recourse to philosophical jargon and understood generalities.

If Greek philosophy had been Plotinus's actual starting point, why would he not have begun with Greek philosophy and ended his treatise with some kind of rationalization or concluding synthesis? The answer to this question is straight forward, indeed.

Plotinus has given us Egyptian religion, theology dressed in Hellenic philosophical vocabulary. His Greek philosophical and linguistic cover, with his occasional nods to Platonic philosophy, sufficed to hold the attention of a few Greek-speaking students of philosophy. From his personal vantage point, his *Sitz im Leben*, Plotinus first and foremost taught orthodox Egyptian ontology and apologetics, derived from ancient imperial soteriology. During Egypt's New Kingdom era, this ancient soteriology emanated trickle-down hopes for commoners. Still later within Christianity, the "brothers and sisters of Jesus Christ" who knew themselves to be adopted children of God the All-Father, cultivated implicit notions of human equality which, with gradual secularization, then led to open revolutions against established theocracies and monarchies. Along with other universal salvation religions of the world, Christianity led humankind onto the rocky road of democratization.

14

"Neo-Platonism" Scholarship

As the name implies, "Neo-Platonism" has been studied traditionally as a natural offspring of Greek "Platonic" philosophy while taking into account a reasonable amount of stimulation from other "Hellenistic"schools. The first suggestion, that "oriental" influences might be present in the philosophy of Plotinus was offered by Franz Brentano in 1876. Thirty-eight years later, H.F. Mueller refuted Brentano's assertions. More recently, in an essay prepared for an international conference on Neo-Platonism and Indian Thought, which was held at Brock University in Ontario, Albert M. Wolters surveyed the "orientalism" controversy up to the year 1976.[123] He traced the primary stimulus for the lead question of the Ontario Conference to the Plotinus scholar Emile Brehier.

During the winter of 1921-22, Emile Brehier gave a series of lectures at the Sorbonne, which were published six years later. In his Seventh Chapter, he discussed the orientalism of Plotinus, whereby he observed that the fourth and fifth treatises of the Sixth Ennead easily can be read without reference to Greek philosophy. He concluded, cautiously enough it seems, that the non-Hellenic place of origin for these "oriental" ideas could have been India. Unfortunately, he omitted in this lecture to name any specific literary or historical points of contact. Wolters observed in his survey that Brehier's thesis has found almost no support among other Plotinus scholars.

Indicative of this mood were also the presentations made at the 1976 Ontario Conference itself. The papers remained noncommittal about specific Indian influences on Plotinus, and most presenters at the conference roamed within the safe realm of making topical comparisons.

---

123 Albert M. Wolters, "Survey of Modern Scholarly Opinion," in R. Baine Harris, ed., *Neo Platonism and Indian Thought* (Norfolk, Va.: International Society for Neo-Platonic Studies, 1982), 293–308.

For the English translation of his lectures, Brehier wrote a new introduction. He concluded his statement with an evasive apology:

And we have deemed it legitimate and even necessary to advance a hypothesis of the relations of Plotinus to India which others who are more competent will perhaps want to investigate and verify.[124]

An additional oddity emerges from Brehier's new introduction. In preparation for his defensive finale, he appealed to a bit of historical common sense:

After Alexander, the Greeks, without doubt did Hellenize the Orient; but inversely Egypt, "the land where gods are invented," [Brehier quotes here Asclepius], stamped its powerful imprint not only upon the customs but upon the ideas of the Greeks, in spite of the efforts of the rulers of Egypt to keep the Egyptians in a subordinate state. But we have come to believe, as will be seen, that in order to render the thought of Plotinus intelligible, it will be necessary to look beyond Egypt.

Brehier has not told us whether, before writing these words, he ever searched among Egyptian sources for antecedents. Nor are we told why he abandoned searching in Egypt so quickly to hurry on to India—to come up empty-handed there as well. But then, what else could be done? The lectures by that time were several decades old, and he had to introduce, somehow, what was in hand and what was about to be printed in English. Moreover, Brehier shared with many Neo-Platonism scholars the peculiar lumped notion of a culturally coherent region named "Orient." Presumably, several centuries of Hellenistic expansion, of Greeks reaching India and Egypt, had obliterated most essential cultural differences in the far-away lands that had been traversed by Alexander's army—as if military adventurers could possibly have erased ancient civilizations to tabula rasa virgin territories.

In the case of real historical situations, considering the conservative nature of human cultures and cults everywhere, the Alexandrian obliteration of local traditions that Brehier assumes is well-nigh unthinkable. On the other hand, had the professor wanted to pursue this issue a little further, his momentary one-sentence hunch

[124] Brehier, *The Philosophy of Plotinus*, 1–12.

of an Egyptian cultural backlash against Hellenistic influence would have been realistic and almost on target.[125]

Ammonius and Plotinus

Ammonius Saccas (ca. 175-242 CE), also referred to as "Ammonius the Porter," is arguably the most shadowy figure in the chronicles of Greek philosophy. No written work of his has survived, and most of what we can infer about his philosophy must be gleaned from the teachings of his students, Plotinus and Origen, the Christian. Moreover, for information about Plotinus himself we depend, in turn, on the writings of his student, Porphyry, and concerning Origen, we learn a few things from Eusebius and Hierocles.[126]

Later students of Plotinus have remembered Ammonius as a theodiktatos, that is, as one who was taught by God. So apparently, he never studied formally under a recognized Greek teacher of philosophy.[127] Whenever he commented on writings of earlier Greek philosophers, he seems to have followed the biddings of his own mind. We know from Porphyry that his teacher, Plotinus (205–270 CE), had been the most devoted and famous student of Ammonius and had a similar habit of commenting on philosophical works.[127] As a result of knowing this, all references in the Enneads regarding the writings of earlier Greek philosophers can be read in various ways.[128] Those who

---

125 Rather than calling it "backlash," I would describe these results as "Egyptian resilience." I have been searching in oral and written literary strata in primitive traditions, and I have found, among cultures that were conquered and overrun, frequent situations wherein remnants of archaic meaning have survived. These remnant meanings could still be recorded by ethnology and brought to light "archaeologically" from among rites and artifacts of ancient culture strata. I very much doubt, therefore, Brehier's placement "beyond doubt" the opinion that the "Greeks did Hellenize the Orient" and that the homeland of Plotinus itself can be ignored for doing Plotinus research. How many minds can a band of destructive warrior-wanderers really change? Defensive entrenchments were more likely.

126 For a treatment of this question, see E. R. Dodds, "Numenius and Ammonius"and subsequent conference discussions in E. R. Dodds et al., Les Sources de Plotin, in *Entretiens sur L'Antiquite Classique,* Book 5 (Geneva: Foundation Hardt, 1966), 3–61.

127 Dean Inge, in Grace H. Turnbull, *The Essence of Plotinus* (Westport, CT: Green- Greenwood Press, 1934, 2.

128 Porphyry, "Life of Plotinus," par. 14, in *Plotinus*, vol. 1, trans. Armstrong (Cambridge, Mass.: Harvard University Press, 1978).

presuppose that Plotinus was foremost a Platonist, generally use the Greek quotations to show his dependence on Greek philosophy. On the other hand, those who approach him without this presupposition will eventually discover that even if all "borrowed citations" from Greek philosophers were removed from Plotinus's fifty-four treatises, they would still teach the same ontology.

Ammonius probably would have been amused by the credit given to him by Hierocles, in a text by Photius, to the effect that "Ammonius reconciled the doctrines of Plato and Aristotle."[129] Indeed, while approaching this elusive teacher of Plotinus, we will attempt to show how, placed against his home background in Egyptian theology, Ammonius could have generated all his commentaries without becoming overly indebted to the ontologies of either Plato or Aristotle. To say that Ammonius sidestepped the doctrines of Plato and Aristotle and winked at them in passing, probably would be more correct. Thus, to suspect that Ammonius obtained his ontology from the mythological and general religious milieu of his homeland, Egypt, would be closer to the truth. Egyptian mythology and ontology had trickled down to Ionians, to Plato and to Aristotle, from among whom other Greek wise men have then suckled mother's milk of their Egyptian grandmother—from ancient Egyptian ontology.

The fact is, no one knows exactly how much Ammonius learned from Greek masters in Alexandria. It could have been little, or it could have been a little more. In light of the dependence of Platonic and Aristotelian philosophy on ancient Egyptian ontology, which we have been able to introduce, an answer to this question no longer matters as much as it once did. The reconciling doctrine which Ammonius Saccas and Plotinus taught their first students of Neo-Platonism, at Alexandria, was older than the teachings of Plato or Aristotle, older than teachings of Thales and Anaximander—and certainly older than the logic by which Christian bishops reasoned at Nicaea. It was Egyptian orthodox emanation Theo-Logic, ancient enough to have deified Egyptian pharaohs and nourished Greek philosophy in its infancy, with almost two millennia to spare. Why, then, should someone who reviews Greek philosophies historically be surprised to find how nicely some ancient Greek philosophical notions harmonize with native Egyptian common sense—with remnants of Egyptian thoughts that earlier have engendered Greek philosophy?

---

[129] See Inge, in Turnbull, *The Essence of Plotinus.*

Ammonius remained true to a long-established tradition of Egyptian priests. He left no writings. Apparently, his students were obligated to him by some vow of secrecy not to publish their mentor's lectures. Porphyry of Tyre (233–304 CE), who became Plotinus's editor and biographer, trying to defend his own exclusive publication rights, accused Erennius and Origen of having broken that agreement.

Most commentators nowadays doubt Ammonius's authorship of two apparent non-Platonic titles.[130] The fact remains, however, that both titles can be reconciled easily with a background in ancient Egyptian theology. The first could have been a general theological treatise on an array of good gods and bad demons, as these appeared along the All-God's path of emanation. In this manner the ancient Egyptian theodicy could have been explained to Greek students—whereas the second of these treatises could have responded to the enduring Egyptian political question, about a monarch's identity with the creative Godhead, such as with Amun or with the Heliopolitan Ennead.

Inasmuch as Origen, the Christian, has surfaced in Egypt as a leading theologian, able to explain Christian theodicy meaningfully to Egyptian Christians, he may indeed have used Ammonian concepts and structure to clarify his faith in terms of basic Egyptian emanation and process vocabulary. Origen could have used Ammonius's *On Demons* to arrange gods, angels, demons, and men along the track of his trinitarian sketch of emanation. He could have used a book titled *The King is the Only Maker* to allegorize the Egyptian All-God's emanation—to think of deified pharaohs and the god Horus as precursors, and then to recognize Jesus Christ as true Son of God. Origen could have rationalized the Christian structure of the "Kingdom of God" in the context of ancient Egyptian theological and political vocabularies. This possibility makes unnecessary the judgment of Armstrong to the effect that the second of these book titles amounts to a "fulsome piece of court flattery."

---

130 According to Porphyry, the editor of Plotinus's *Enneads*, two men whom he mentioned as Erennius and Origen, published two books of Ammonius Saccas, titled *The Spirits* (i.e. Demons) and *The King is the Only Maker*. Porphyry accused these men of illicit publication as he claimed the sole rights for all Plotinus publications for himself. The timeframe that Porphyry mentions could possibly exclude Origen, the Christian. See *Plotinus*, Armstrong trans., 10; also Mark J. Edwards, "Origen," in *Stanford Encyclopedia of Philosophy*, 2014. Reference there is made to Porphyry, *Life of Plotinus*, 20, 36-45.

An identification of the Creator with the deified King of Egypt has survived, fully developed in Memphite theology, as it also was explicit in Akhenaton's haughty exclusivism. Unfortunately, because the works of Ammonius themselves are lost, more historical speculation about them could be a waste of time.

In an essay titled "Ammonius der Lehrer des Origenes," Willy Theiler followed Fritz Heinemann (in *Hermes* 61 [1926]: 1ff, believing that much of Ammonius's philosophy is still extant in written form. He postulated a line of succession that began with Ammonius Saccas and through Origen, led to Plutarch and thence to Hierocles of two centuries later.[131] We are then advised to look for the lost teachings of the founder of Neo-Platonism in the legacy of Hierocles, pp. 2ff. Theiler proceeded to reconstruct for himself an Ammonius Saccas who conveniently matched the profile of a typical Greek Platonist.

But then, unfortunately, this reconstruction of Ammonius, based on quotes from Hierocles, left the better known founder of Neo-Platonism, Plotinus, stranded "like an island in the stream of Platonic tradition," as Theiler confessed on page 42. Therefore, to examine the Theiler hypothesis, one will need to reexamine Hierocles seriously in comparison with Plotinus, in light of the revised context that I am suggesting here. Someone else, in the future, will need to do the work of fishing for similarities that might be there.

Speculative tracing of Ammonian texts over several generations of students and teachers, and across a major religious fault line, does indeed seem far-fetched—too far for comfort. However, I personally remain convinced that in the absence of the philosopher's own writings, a historical refocusing on Ammonius Saccas will fare better by first taking a closer look at the bequest of Plotinus. One may dislike the fact that Plotinus himself also has written nothing that survives. It was his editor, Porphyry—another generation removed from the original Ammonius—who eventually published the *Enneads* of Plotinus. We may note that the relationship between Plotinus and Porphyry appears to be reasonably well documented. As far as Plotinus himself was concerned, he remained a student of Ammonius for over twice the time that Origen stayed with this teacher.

---

[131] Willy Theiler, *Forschungen zum Neuplatonismus* (Berlin: Gruyter & Co., 1966.

We shall assume for this discussion that the man whom we have come to know as Origen, the Christian theologian, could have been a student of Ammonius. Beyond this questionable datum, it seems that Plotinus began his studies a year after Origen had left, about 232 CE. This means that Plotinus benefited from Ammonius's more mature years. But he also could not have known everything that transpired between Ammonius and Origen earlier. Moreover Porphyry, by his own admission was not privy to Plotinus's personal relationships and affairs.

There is a rumor about a happenstance... that a certain Eunapius has told someone... that the birthplace of Plotinus was Lyco or Lycopolis. Two towns at the time were known by that name, one in Upper Egypt and another in the Delta.

Porphyry told us that after coming to Alexandria, Plotinus listened in on the lectures of every prominent philosopher in the city at the time. He was summarily disappointed by all. Only after listening to Ammonius Saccas—also known as "the Porter"—somewhere along the periphery of Alexandrian intellectual circles, the interest of Plotinus was kindled. After Origen and a few others, including the Egyptian Plotinus, had chosen Ammonius as their teacher, it was Plotinus who remained his faithful student longest—for eleven years. Such a span of time suggests that the student was determined to absorb nothing short of the teacher's total world-view.

It does seem significant that Porphyry of Tyre was unable to elicit from his Egyptian master, Plotinus, any information about his race or his parents or his native region. It is indeed remarkable—if not almost unthinkable—that Porphyry, the man who thought of himself as Plotinus's closest friend, could have been kept completely in the dark about his teacher's family and their religious or ethnic background.

All the while, it appears as though Porphyry was in Alexandria the typical industrious "foreign student," who succeeded in provoking his master into doing more systematic dictation for publication than the master probably has actually enjoyed. Plotinus responded by taking on Porphyry as his personal "Editor in Greek." Their friendship was a pragmatic arrangement. Porphyry appears to have had a native command of the Greek language, whereas Plotinus, whose native language and thought structure were Egyptian, depended on someone like Porphyry for public communication—to make himself understood better by audiences of the surrounding Greek culture. This pragmatic arrangement of friendship endured to the end, even after the master has politely persuaded his student to take a permanent vacation.[132]

The fact that Plotinus never entrusted information about his cultural, personal, and family background to his student Porphyry need not be surprising. As an Egyptian who in Alexandria engaged in active competition with Greek philosophers, while he himself was coming from along the Egyptian sidelines, Plotinus has dedicated his life to a mission of bridging between the two cultures, to harmonize their diverging styles of thinking. He accepted the challenge to communicate effectively near the apex of the Greek intellectual society. To that effect, Plotinus needed to assure his Greek students of his Hellenic proficiency and compatibility. For that same reason, he also was obliged to quote, where possible, from the writings of prestigious Greek philosophers.

Plotinus knew quite well that if he did not do so, haughty Hellenic minds would quickly lose interest in him. Colonialist prejudices regarding the inferiority of Egyptian thought probably ran deep. Without being given proper Greek words, the Greek intelligentsia would have rejected portions of his wisdom as Egyptian superstition. Ancient Egyptian concepts, needed to be spoon-fed and wrapped in quotations of Greek wise men, to render them palatable for Greek tastes.

---

[132] In spite of Plotinus's silence toward Porphyry about personal matters, the relationship between these two men, the Greek and the Egyptian, does emerge somewhat transparent from the perspective of someone who, like this writer, has observed similar strained relationships develop between indigenous peoples and certain scientifically constrained scholars who, occasionally, solicited his advice. I myself encountered no unbridgeable difficulties with either Christian, Jewish, or Muslim fellows, with American Indian or Chinese shamans, with Communist cadres or any other partners in learning, regarding their willingness to communicate mind to mind. All that was ever required of me was to try to understand their "archaisms" as thoroughly as I was willing to understand my own parents and grandparents. As soon as people recognized me as an ordinary stray human being, entering their world as a friend, we could converse about anything we wished. Of course, one should try to sense social entanglements and avoid getting too close to obsolete personal wounds—until the doors to the "holy of holies" of their souls, would get opened freely from the inside. Scientific precision is not a substitute for empathy and friendship.

Plotinus, whose status as a teacher rested on his pretense of Hellenic competitive proficiency, had nothing to gain and much to lose by opening up to Porphyry about his non-Hellenic background. On the other hand, given what else we know about the kind and saintly nature of Plotinus, it is almost impossible to imagine that he himself was emotionally cut off from his Egyptian family. Rather, we may assume that aside from protecting his inter-cultural role for Egyptian natives, Plotinus might also have seen it as his duty to protect his Egyptian kin from less sensitive Colonialist intruders. His kindred probably needed to be protected against local suspicions that an overly close association with intrepid foreigners could have evoked.

A rather obvious clue about the Egyptian background of Plotinus's teacher, Ammonius Saccas, has been consistently overlooked by the commentators—his name. *Ammonius* was a common Egyptian name, and this fact testifies to the persistence of New Kingdom religion. The man Ammonius had been dedicated as a child to the Egyptian hidden All-God, Amun (Ammon). This means that the boy was raised by parents who, as a minimum, could explain to their curious offspring the meaning of his name and, even more likely, were able to explain to him aspects of orthodox Egyptian theology. An inquisitive lad like Ammonius, whose intellectual curiosity drove him to seek the company of foreign philosophers in Alexandria, surely has earlier also learned a few things from Egyptian wise men, back home.[133]

Thus, after considering the strong rational/mystic impulse that Ammonius was able to communicate to Plotinus, it appears that the first shadowy founder-figure of Neo-Platonism has been reared devoutly, in accordance with ancient Egyptian patterns of piety. It remains doubtful that these patterns were Christian, even though Eusebius has quoted Porphyry as having harbored suspicions to that effect.[134] What Christian parents would possibly have named their son Ammonius? Though, an Ammonius Saccas, interested in Christianity on his own Egyptian terms, remains a possibility.

---

133 Imagine, for a moment, the likelihood of a modern Egyptian lad named "Muhammad" being totally ignorant about Islam. It seems unthinkable. All the while, the hostile attitude that Porphyry held toward Christianity, would have been enough to keep any world-open Christian-friendly Egyptian teacher silent on these sympathies. Had Porphyry had real knowledge about Christianity, he probably would have noticed an affinity in that religion with his teacher's native ontology.

134 See Footnote in *Plotinus*, Armstrong translation, 10f.

Plotinus, the Egyptian boy became disillusioned with the leading Greek philosophers at Alexandria. His inquisitive mind discovered in the native pietism of Ammonius a comprehensive view of the world that sustained his own Egyptian cultural identity. In the context of his own impiety toward Greek scholasticism, Plotinus found in Ammonius Saccas a kindred spirit. A stable world-view of cosmic and theological emanation, and nothing short of that, was the home-grown ideology that Ammonius imparted to his student. And in response, Plotinus devoted eleven years of his life to studying the Egyptian wisdom of Ammonius and its rationalization in relation to Greek colonial philosophy, in the Greek idiom.

The affection that Plotinus, an Egyptian, showed for the wisdom of Ammonius, a fellow Egyptian, was probably rooted in simple folk mythos and ethos, some of which would have been judged superstitious by Greek wise men. The life story of Plotinus has all the markings of an Egyptian student finding his ontological home in his own Egyptian roots. And his searching and finding happened in dialogue and under the sway of increased Hellenistic analytic rationality.

Ammonius and Plotinus succeeded in rationalizing the Egyptian theological and cosmic notion of emanation. They expressed their thinking in the language of the Eastern Roman Empire, which was Greek, as well as in the formal wrappings or style of respectable Hellenic philosophical dialogue.

Two Egyptian scholars have intruded along the periphery of Hellenism, from along its Egyptian flank, and from there have infused Greek philosophy with an apparently "brand new" monistic ontology which, it turns out, was already several thousand years old. While a Christian influence on Ammonius has been suspected, we deem this possibility somewhat remote—even though, on Egyptian terms, such an influence need not be ruled out completely. Apparently, Ammonius was curious about any wisdom. Some such affiliation would explain why not only Plotinus's religious and family affiliations, but even the general Egyptian roots of Ammonius Saccas, might have remained hidden from Porphyry. On the other side of this coin, some Christians probably would not have been overly keen about being seen with Ammonius Saccas—even though Origen studied with him four years. While Christians probably would have welcomed this vagrant seeker to some degree, he certainly would have remained mainstream Egyptian.

Traditional dualistic Greek philosophy could not withstand the impact of an open ancient monism for very long. Nevertheless, the basic Ionian ontological presuppositions from which Hellenic philosophy evolved, from which it drew mythos and soul, had been dependent on monotheistic ancient Egyptian process theology all along.

Ancient Egyptian gods, presiding at Alexandria at the time, must have delighted in their game of creating ironies. A foreign student, Porphyry, felt moved to group Plotinus's bequest of fifty-four treatises into six sets of "enneads"—hence the title of his book. All the while, this student-editor, Porphyry, appears to have been quite unaware of Ammonius's and Plotinus's distant theological Enneadic concepts. It appears as though the ancient gods personally intervened, and have lent a helping hand to Porphyry in his choice of numerology and outline. The Enneads of Plotinus do indeed contain elaborations on the nature of the Heliopolitan Godhead, on his threefold as well as his ninefold emanation.

On the Originality of Plotinus

As the founder of a new Graeco-Egyptian philosophical school named Neo-Platonism, Plotinus has consistently been studied with regard to what he might have owed to Plato and Socrates. The presence of quotations from Platonic *Dialogues* in his writings has been weighed in as primary evidence. For example, Paul Henry mentions the most frequently cited Platonic sources.[135] Among these are the *Timaeus, Republic, Phaedo, Phaedrus, Symposium, Theaetetus, Philebus, Sophis,* and the *Parmenides*. Comparisons of Plotinus with Plato have so led to fragmented doctrinal interpretations at both sides. In this simple manner, similarities have been chalked up as indebtedness; differences have been scored as creativity and original contributions.

But such a simple comparative approach works only until new similarities are discovered elsewhere among ancient sources that hitherto were deemed outside the family tree of the Athenian philosophical school. When such sources turned out to be in a reasonable geographical location, to be historical precedents, then the possibility of indebtedness no longer can be ignored. In spite of what I have already said about handicaps on the part of Porphyry;

135 Paul Henry, "The Place of Plotinus in the History of Thought," in MacKenna, *The Enneads*, xxxv–lxx.

I will welcome him, nevertheless, to be our principal biographer for Plotinus:[136]

> In writing he (Plotinus) is concise and full of thought. He puts things shortly and abounds more in ideas than in words; he generally expresses himself in a tone of rapt inspiration, and states what he himself really feels about the matter and not what has been handed down by tradition. His writings, however, are full of concealed Stoic and Peripatetic doctrines. Aristotle's Metaphysics, in particular, are concentrated in them.... In the meetings of the school he used to have the commentaries read, perhaps of Severus, perhaps of Cronius or Numenius or Gaius or Atticus, and among the Peripatetics of Aspasius, Alexander, Adrastus, and others that were available. But he did not just speak straight out of these books but took a distinctive personal line in his consideration, and he brought the mind of Ammonius to bear on the investigations at hand.

What was the cultural and intellectual context for his "rapt inspirations"? Could a common source of doctrine be postulated—beyond the Stoic, Peripatetic, and others of which Porphyry was also aware? During conferences, what motivated his momentary requests for books authored by Platonists and Peripatetics? Were they consulted to learn and to borrow, or were they simply used to strengthen his presentations? Was his utilization of Plato's Dialogues in any way different from his treatment of other sources? And finally, was the original bequest of Ammonius to Plotinus really a method?

Tentatively admitted, in preliminary fashion, our Plotinus questions can be answered. Inspirations and revelations come from the direction toward which a receptive mind is oriented. The realm from which most of the inspirations of Ammonius and Plotinus were derived, were ancient Egyptian theology in a variety of current Egyptian shapes and rivulets.

Not so much the indebtedness of Plotinus to Greek antecedents, but much more the independence of his mind is highlighted in

---

[136] Porphyry, "Life of Plotinus," par. 14, in *Plotinus*, trans. Armstrong, vol. 1. After the emanation-oriented world-view had been cultivated through millennia at Heliopolis, no one in the ancient Near East who heard about its implied theology or ontology, within the wake of this inheritance, could avoid getting caught up in it.

Porphyry's eulogy. This happenstance begs a number of crucial considerations: Porphyry leaves no doubt that Plotinus followed his own mind. During conferences, the books from which he read were those that happened to "be available." Those momentary calls for books do suggest that these sources were exploited to help elucidate Plotinus's own perspective. Upon reflecting on his uses of Plato in the Enneads, it appears that Plotinus mined the Dialogues of Plato and the writings of other philosophers in similar ways and with similar aims.[137]

It is also quite understandable how Porphyry, a student of Greek philosophy, initially was hoping to perfect his Socratic skills. He would so have approached the philosophy of Plotinus in search of the teacher's "method." Unable to point to Socrates, Plato, or Aristotle as sources for his method, and asked to identify a source, Plotinus simply deferred to the almost unknown Ammonius Saccas. But clearly, method for Plotinus was secondary—was second to content and ontology—as surely as method had already been secondary to Socrates and to Ammonius. Methodology is sought by beginners as a substitute for content that happens to be still missing in a young learner's repertoire. Ontology, insufficiently filled or saturated with content is often stretched to be studied "methodologically," to save face. Methodology so utilized can make a little real knowledge go a long ways.

---

137 This writer suspects that personal experiences, shared languages and literatures, do carry within themselves thought-embryos and nexuses that lie scattered and run through entire philosophies and cultures. Every English "noun" or German "substantive" carries within itself the ontological question of "what is?" Even though I had never taken formal higher academic training in Germany, by the time I came to study "philosophy" at an American university, I noticed how Kant and other German philosophers, even Romantic writers, mystics and atheists, resonated a little clearer amidst other contexts and repertoires in my native German language—even when contained in the rustic religiosity of laymen. Outside the box of English literature, the results of my interpretations often turned out to be different from what fellow American students detected in English translations of those same texts.

As is the History of Christian Thought, the history of religious thought in general, so also is the entire subject matter of "religion" itself under-estimated in the sphere of education and politics. The Founders of American democracy, together with the minds that now guide our trends in education and politics, generally have ignored knowledge about religions as being optionals—as pertaining merely to superstitions of ages past. While our Founder Fathers bracketed remnants of bygone ontologies, they expected them to evaporate on their own. Thus discounting the wisdom of ancient traditions, they frequently chose to walk the paths of maximum convenience and least resistance.

Any culture that discards an aging religion, without bothering to study or to understand why it had been initiated, why it was cultivated and then left to deteriorate, or what might replace its intended societal functions, will do so at its own peril. Religions have achieved their earliest meanings by balancing societal or political strides that people have taken. Most ritualized customs, at some point in time, have served to soothe what otherwise, in brittle rationality, might have gotten torn and then festered as a wound. A bandage removed and discarded too soon will, at some point, be missed and needs to be replaced with something else. A patch placed on a wound, modified by specialists who neither understood the underlying condition nor the first healer's intent, may endanger the patient and risk failure.

Part Four:
Toward the Birth of Christendom

Overview—First Sparks of Christian Thought

...were as old as ancient Egypt, Greece and Rome, and—perhaps several millennia older. Christian Thought was born with a strong flicker of doubt about the divine status that violent imperialists claimed for themselves. Bandits, pharaohs, high priests, tyrants, kings and emperors emerged from totemic associations of Stone Age hunters. Some celebrated the deaths of their ancestors as transfer-initiations, as resurrections or rebirths for divine empowerment. Brandishing divine ancestries as their mandates, they enslaved settlers and domesticators. Thus, "fake Sons of God," as hyper-domesticators, have enslaved and dispatched humankind as if they were less-than-human property or legal tender.

Three thousand years and a few centuries, before Christian Thought was credited to Jesus Christ, the first pharaoh of Egypt, Narmer, made his debut as a divinely entitled killer and owner of humankind. Others probably preceded him by thousands of years. Three thousand years and some centuries later, a commoner woman — Mary—gave birth to an extra intelligent son who came to be known as Jesus of Nazareth, the central founder of the Christian religion. To contrast himself from "made" Sons of God who ruled as divine emperors, this man dared to mock Fake Sons of God by his own non-violent living as a Son of Man, and rumors begun spreading that he might be the real Son of God.

Jesus was born during the Reign of Augustus Octavius, an acclaimed Son of God, and he was crucified during the Reign of Tiberius, Rome's next Son of God. In time, people who followed Jesus held him to be the only-begotten Son of God—to distinguish him from the imperials who simply were "made." Increasingly more people believed the story about the Son of God who was crucified, who died and rose from the tomb. Eventually, the Jesus story blocked the path to deification for all Roman emperors. Imperial hype could not compete with the Christian story which proclaimed faith in Jesus Christ on the basis of his Death, Resurrection, and Ascension into Heaven.

Christians were not the first to mention Resurrection or Deification, or to believe in a Son of God. Nevertheless, by insisting on their equal adoptability as children of God, they implicitly competed with all rulers who claimed divine ancestry. The commotion about the death and resurrection of Jesus of Nazareth, and his defiance of imperially deified Sons of God, has not been matched or surpassed to this very day. Jesus Christ has raised human status of all his followers to the level of being adopted children of God. Christianity has thus made it impossible, for any ruler in Western Civilization to claim for himself the status of a Son of God ever again. It was the Christian faith of two millennia ago that raised humankind to the level of adoptable brothers and sisters of the Son of God Jesus Christ. Their faith has made it possible, over time, to downgrade deified emperors and to begin with inventing secular republics and democracies, based on the principle of equality.

15

The Reign of Heaven is at Hand

Premonitions in Prehistory

Two thousand and a few years ago, the founders of the Christian religion were born unto our planet. While everyone seems to be wrangling over details and precise "historical" circumstances regarding the beginnings, I shall skip some of these favorites. Instead, I will focus on conditions that made it possible, back in those days, by hearsay and gossip about resurrection, for a crucified and shamed man to rise to the apex of what was to become orthodox Christian theology.

What happened has been nothing short of an ideological realignment, one that transformed Western Civilization. Mythology and theological thought are not empty vapors rising from intellectually challenged minds. Rather, they are serious rational responses to serious problems of management that weigh on the minds of people who understand political dogma and inflictions of trauma. Two thousand years ago, at a turning point for Western history, the then three-thousand-years-old Egyptian imperial theology was still rationalizing the "civilized" enslavement of humankind. Justifications and fresh hopes for freedom needed to be rebalanced, religiously afresh, for all commoners who got caught up in the shadows of imperial civilization.

Ancient Israelite religion may indeed be explained as a distant step-grandfather of Christendom—whereas later Judaism played the role of an older sibling. I am alluding here to a sibling relationship, complete with proximities and rivalries. Key theological features identify Egyptian religion as having been Christendom's silent and long-enduring mother. At the time of her daughter's birth, the ancient Mother Egypt had already been balancing her civilization for three millennia. After having gradually slid from the hands of her pharaonic keepers into those of foreign conquerors, Egypt was managed also by Persian, Greek, and Roman God-impersonators. Some of these titled themselves "Savior" (Gk. *(Soter=Σωτήρ)*.

Foreign rulers openly resembled and imitated the Horuses (Falcons) who have ruled Egypt for two and a half millennia. Then the old mother religion of Egypt died. Nevertheless, her ancient womb and heart remained fertile and compliant, to continue incubating, centuries after her ancient empire disintegrated. Clear into our time she gave birth to cultural and religious configurations in Western lands.[138]

Christian theology and soteriology, their indebtedness to ancient Egypt, are still within the focus of Part Four of this book. At the same time, our exposition does not in the least aim at diminishing the significance of the life and teachings of Jesus, Christianity's central founder figure. And most certainly, the greater part of collective experiences and impulses among the teachings of founders—as distinguished from later systematic reasoning—have come down to us from the Graeco-Roman/Judaic ferment of post-Maccabean culture.

To understand the formative years of Christendom as a world religion, it is helpful to distinguish between Hebrew and still earlier traditions. Bold Hebrew seminal ideas were imparted to the Christian movement by John the Baptizer, by Jesus of Nazareth, by Paul of Tarsus and others. The personal beliefs of these founders, their hopes for some "Rule of God" or "Empire of Heaven," implied new ways of seeing God, as well as of defining humankind afresh as divinely shepherded people alongside the entire heavenly entourage. Angels appear especially vivid in the birth stories of John and Jesus. Their survival in literature may be taken as an indicator of how the nature of God's heavenly "empire" was understood by Jesus and his disciples, and by some of their Jewish contemporaries.

Saul of Tarsus, a student of Gamaliel, became a Christian apostle who widened Judaic Christianity to welcome converts from the larger Roman empire, from among Gentiles. His teacher Gamaliel was a famous teacher of Mosaic law, a member of the San-hedrin and of the Hillel family of rabbinic masters. It could have been Gamaliel's tolerant defense of Peter and other apostles, on trial before the Sanhedrin, in

---

138 Some six centuries after Christendom the religion of Islam came onto the world stage. For it to remain intelligible within the flow of human languages and in mental comprehension, its story, too, will need to be periodically adjusted. For best results, however, it should be restructured and harmonized within its own indigenous linguistic currents. Neither Hebrew, nor Greek, nor Latin, Arabic, English, or any assembly of other languages will ever be stable enough to maintain lasting definitions or to enable precise and durable communication.

Acts 5:34–40, that nudged his deadly serious student, Saul of Tarsus, in a direction where he could recognize his Enlightenment angel in the person of Jesus of Nazareth.

His vision of light, and hearing the voice of Jesus as Israel's expected Anointed, have enabled "Saul" of Tarsus to become the Apostle "Paul" — a messenger of Jesus Christ. Paul labored energetically to liberate Christians from the egg-shell remnants of their Israelite tribal tradition. His former teacher Gamaliel, already, appears to have been able to see through the machinations of hyper-domestication — and to make sound religious and political judgments.

Important features of the Christian religion were derived from Judaism. The memory meal that Jesus has hosted was continued by the apostles and elders of the Church after their Lord's departure. The meal was also included as an afterthought, to replace the Jewish rite of Passover, which was a celebration of Israel's Exodus and liberation from slavery. But begrudging Egypt in excess of a thousand years was long enough. Ritualistic slaughtering of lambs, initially, was an apology to the lambs themselves and then it became a sacrificial payment to God who was their Creator — by which herders atoned for owning and slaughtering livestock. Seeds and animal herds were "bought" from God or gods and they were paid for with share offerings. When Abraham stopped the hyper-domestication sacrifice of his son Isaac, God accepted the substitutionary "reduced" payment of a ram.

Abraham's ceremonial substitution of a sacrificial lamb slowed the cultural drift toward hyper-domestication. It revoked a measure of justification regarding the ownership of humankind by humans — of slavery, castration, murder, warfare, and even ownership of children by power-addicted parents. The vegetarian food mysticism of bread and wine that Jesus super-imposed on Passover, as a measure of reform, was intentionally kept bloodless. While it did not explicitly forbid acts of hunting or of raising animals for slaughter — primary activities which have empowered the evolution of human culture — it nevertheless removed the shedding of blood from the list of religious necessities. Cannibalism, warfare, owning humankind, and all rituals that in the past might have entailed the shedding of blood, have been annulled by the Savior of Christianity. Over time, not even the rite of circumcision for membership in an archaic tribe — with its surgical spilling of blood — would be needed anymore for atonement with a God who came to transcend tribalism. Neither the bleeding of sacerdotal victims, nor the felling of people in war, could attract the blessings of God anymore onto wayward hunter-warrior offspring.

Stone Age hunter cults and subsequent religions of domesticators have all sought atonement for killing and for the sin of turning flesh into meat. Ritualized atonement freed them to become human. Ancient methods of atonement required sharing portions of the substance of hunted animals with the gods who helped men hunt. Divine and human participants thereby assumed joint responsibility for killing animal "persons." Hunters paid their divine helpers with share portions of animals they butchered. Early Hebrew herders knew how to sacrifice whole firstborn animals as down-payment for animals still to be born. Prepaid siblings were expected to be born in return. The practice of sacrificing firstborns has favored maximum lifespans for the ewes. It also paved the way for an economy based on selling livestock and meat. Domesticators of plants tended to pay Creators with shares of first-fruits, for seeds and for their ownership of fields. Hyper-domesticators spun this sacrificial economy another step and paid extra for owning human slaves; they sacrificed shares for their human herds. Warfare and jurisprudence both conspire to own human lives —still today, souls are dispatched to God and to Manifest Destiny, on behalf of the Homeland. Blood spilled is being declared good; as a payment sacrifice it is being circumvented by modern jurisprudence—for instance, with ritual formulas like "May God have mercy on your soul!" Entire nations of potential equals could be forced into servitude and slavery with rituals of this sort.[139]

---

[139] In the course of human evolution, gods usually were not the causes of human consternation. They were not "invented," but rather, they were discovered and invited into the human group as creators, justifiers, or partners. They were welcome "saviors," motivated by grace toward humankind. In the course of evolution, wounds have been cut, inflicted by superior intelligence and cognition. Inasmuch as the cutting collided with "conscience," it helped us become human. Rogue primates, while they were hoping to become balanced partners among gods, learning to be "artificial" predators, could acquire consciences. With their expanding minds, they literally begged the gods to help them balance their lives. Only if one is enabled to kill and to eat with balance, free of emotions or weaknesses, can a Homo sapient afford to discard faith in a greater-than-human reality. Our next mental way-station in this evolution comes epistemologically defined: to attain a more angelic disposition, some day, unaffected by the presence of human teeth, hunger, or digestive tract. If we were to deprive ourselves of theologies, of angelic "sheep fleeces" to hide in—of consciences or the Golden Rule—what would remain of the human soul? Would we shrivel down to be soul-less machines, enslaveable by engineers? This writer happens to view with sorrow the solution that wise atheists have provided in response to quandaries of killing fellow humankind. If man really is the only measure of all things, then who is measuring what, whom, and how? Who or what notion can then save humankind from real or imagined necessities?

Homines sapientes initially have taken or purchased their "possessions" from the Creator who made and owned them beforehand. With thanksgiving and flattery they managed to ritualize their killing, and their eating of substances that were severed from fellow divinely procreated beings. They learned to justify management of their world sacramentally. Prevalent among emerging hyper-domestication cultures were practices of headhunting and cannibalism. Starved bands of obsolescent hunters easily transformed into hordes of were-wolves and warriors. Throughout the human evolution and progress, by greed and technology, there also were opportunities for common-sense religious retreat behavior, for rational re-balancing of human desires and needs.

The Christian "Heavenly Father" theology went a step beyond progress by hyper-domestication. It reduced sacrificial rituals beyond Judaic expectations. Even though the early Judaic Christians still went to worship at the Herodian temple (as in *Acts* 2:42ff), the consensus gradually prevailed that Christ died not only for the sins of killing animals, or to endorse Abraham's abolishment of human sacrifice, but it also devalued animal sacrifices in general, including initiations by circumcision. The sacramental memory meal that Christians celebrated, to replace Passover, substituted plant products—bread and wine—for the flesh of domestic lambs. To underwrite a new world order, the execution of Jesus came to be viewed as the last redemptive human sacrifice that by traditional religious thinking might have been necessary. Christians explained the death of Jesus, the Anointed, as culmination of the Abrahamic covenant.

After the death and resurrection message of Jesus Christ became standard fare, the Empire of Heaven idea continued to evolve to accommodate the churches that were getting organized instead. There is nothing unusual about this development. The "Reign of God" idea had been fluid for thousands of years. It dawned in opposition to the ancient Near Eastern empires which were ruled by deified kings—thus by Sons of God or gods. It got established, thereupon, within the prophetic "protestant" consciousness of ancient Israel. The radical Christian expectation of the Empire of Heaven, as an antithesis to mundane imperialism, began in the minds of radical Hebrew prophets and zealots who, expected a New Covenant that would abrogate patriarchal and royal entitlements. They counted on a revised and broader dispensation in the future. The teachings of John the Baptizer and Jesus of Nazareth greatly accelerated the "Empire-of-Heaven" awareness.

The new awareness can be seen taking shape in stories that prior to Christianity were current in popular Judaism. In post-exilic Judaic religion, angels populated, as well as staffed, God's heaven. Rabbinic storytellers recited stories about the patriarchal age and about slavery in Egypt, whereby they hoped to escape the gory glories of tyranny and hyper-domestication, they also still saw the messenger angels of God Almighty appear habitually in the guise of ordinary human travelers. During the formative period of Israel's monarchy, while the dynasty of David drifted into its own grand-domestication phase, God was increasingly visualized as being a Lord of Hosts, thus as a God of the army (Yahweh Sabaoth). In as much as the Godhead was hailed as a deity of war, his angelic hosts were expected to appear as a variety of warriors. As a result, the distinction between angelic warriors and Israelite human warriors often became blurred. For example, it is said that when the warrior-chieftain David faced the Philistine giant Goliath, he spoke confident words like these:

You come to me with a sword and a spear, and with a javelin; but I come to you in the name of the Lord of hosts, the God of the armies of Israel. (*1 Samuel* 17:45)

The prophet Isaiah, who still lived in the bright afterglow of the Davidic monarchy, envisioned Almighty God as sitting on a high cosmic throne. The earth was God's footstool and the entire universe his monarchy. He saw and heard God's messenger angels shout words of praise, while angels had transformed from their original military postures into performers of musical fine arts:

Holy, holy, holy is the Lord of hosts; the whole earth is full of his glory! (*Isaiah* 6:3)

In post-exilic Jewish literature, angelology reached amazingly beautiful heights. The philosopher Philo, having come under the spell of Egyptian emanation theology, in Alexandria, arranged Yahweh's angels in a hierarchy of created beings. Generous readers could easily have reconciled Philo's angelology with the so-called polytheism at Heliopolis. From our perspective, ancient Egyptian religion has been monotheism with poly-manifestations, all along. It may not matter, historically or in the final analysis, whether certain divine beings are referred to as angels or as lesser gods. Among religious faiths that have emerged from the ancient Egyptian environment, it was "functions performed" by divine personages that counted.

The primary differences between ancient Egyptian theology and the angelology from the period that Christians later identified as the Inter-testamental Period, concerned foremost the mode of divine creation and the style of divine government. The ancient Egyptian Godhead first generated divine offspring and then continued to remain internally and externally involved with his offspring. He generated the visible world, to appear from along his less visible essence. By contrast, in early Israelite perspective, the divine creator simply commanded, somewhat despotically, that creatures should exist. With that same voice he also seems to have decreed that there should exist angels to serve him as his messengers.

The theological distinction turns on the small question of what existed first in God's world. Was it the presence of servants in his divine hierarchy? Or was it the Lord's commandeering that brought everything into being, to serve him subsequently? This point may not tell much about God, but perhaps it discloses the attitude and outlook of storytellers, regarding their own bosses, servants and slaves.

In contrast to Egyptian emanation theology, Judaic apocalyptic literature presented the angels of God with a tinge of Zoroastrian dualistic confrontation. This situation can be accounted for historically, by considering Persian-Judaic relations during the Post-Exilic Period. Inasmuch as all commands, including those of the Creator, could be disobeyed by strong minds, it became necessary in Judaism to distinguish what in Egypt used to be distant emanations of God, from estranged or disobedient creatures, farther downstream.

Not only humankind, but also some angels needed to be counted among God's disobedient or fallen creatures. God's obedient angels continued to dwell in the divine realm of light, whereas the rebellious Satan and his accomplices had fallen into darkness. These two shades of angels were interacting in constant strife. Men saw their own wars mirrored in the larger cosmos which then, apparently, naturalized and legitimized their own strife. Explained on hand of the God-story, and still somewhat in accord with Egyptian polytheistic emanation logic, the dark and evil angels would have been those falling away farthest from the presence of God. They defiled themselves in unions with human maidens (*Genesis* 6:1–4). The material bottom layer of man-made aristocratic rank has, historically, been accumulated by warrior skills and weaponry.

In the Egyptian context this accumulation simply would have meant that within the general plethora of emanation, fallen angels had been drifting too far out toward Non-being. In the Jewish perspective, the behavior of these angels had evolutionary consequences. It meant that some human offspring or subsequent creatures of those estranged angels evolved into monsters. It also meant that these monsters were responsible for introducing warfare among humankind.[140]

Altogether, this summary amounts to a wonderful Hebrew diatribe on aristocratic warriors anywhere, namely, on heroes and cutthroats who were in the habit of claiming descent from totems or gods. All the while, when seen under a beam of Zoroastrian light, sideways, with stark contrasts and shadows, some of the farthest estranged angels appeared to be devils. The book of *Jubilees* 2 : 2, a late second century BCE source, identifies a number of angels as spirits (personal souls embodied in natural phenomena: fire, wind, cloud, darkness, snow, hail, hoarfrost, voices, thunder, lightning, cold, heat, winter, spring, autumn, and summer).[141] The acknowledgment of the presence of an angel of fire echoes the Torah story of Moses noticing a burning bush. But then, in a wider historical perspective, Judaic angels also do occupy a transitional position between Egyptian polytheism and the idiom of Hellenistic naturalism. They correspond to lower emanated Egyptian gods as well as to Hellenic natural phenomena—thus to natural forces named by scientists.

The changing knowledge about angelic beings has thoroughly redefined the idea of God's Kingdom of Heaven. This much is suggested in Second Enoch. It is said that during his visionary journey through ten heavens, the man Enoch has traversed space in the upward direction and has explored the entire heavenly expanse.[142] At the level of the third heaven, he found three hundred angels worshiping the Lord with "never-ceasing voice and pleasant singing" (8:8).

---

140 James H. Charlesworth, ed., *The Old Testament Pseudo-Epigrapha,* Vol. 1 (Garden City, N.Y.: Doubleday and Co., 1983, 6ff, 13ff.

141 James H. Charlesworth, ed., *The Apogrypha and Pseudepigrapha of the Old Testament,* Vol. 2 (Oxford: Clarendon Press, 1913), 13f.

142 See Charlesworth, *The Old Testament Pseudo-Epigrapha,* Vol. 1, 130ff. The contents of extant Enoch traditions cannot be dated with certainty. Nevertheless, their presence in Jewish libraries, centuries later, does indicate the general path along which angelology has been evolving.

In the fourth heaven, whenever the Lord commanded, phoenix and khalkedra birds burst forth into song (15:1). Angelic hosts here might still have carried Bronze Age weapons, but the original importance of arms certainly has been upstaged by the prominence of musical instruments. Accordingly, Enoch saw in the "middle" of the heavens:

... armed troops, worshiping the Lord with tympani and pipes and unceasing voices, and pleasant... and various songs, which it is impossible to describe. And every mind would be quite astonished, so marvelous and wonderful is the singing of these angels. (17:1)

From the sixth heaven, seven bands of archangels gave orders on how to maintain order in the world. They were informed by "the goings of the stars, and the alteration of the moon, by the revolution of the sun, and the good government of the world."

Apparently, ancient Babylonian wisdom supplied the writer of *Second Enoch* with rudimentary information about astrology. But be that as it may. It is important to note that orderliness, in the heavenly space itself, was maintained with music.

And they (the angels) make all celestial life peaceful; and they preserve the commandments and the instructions, and sweet voices and singing, every kind of praise and glory (19:3).

Angelic men then lifted Enoch up and onward to the seventh heaven, the very stairway to the Lord's own dwelling:

And all the heavenly armies came and stood on the ten steps corresponding to their ranks, and they did obeisance to the Lord. And then they went to their places in joy and merriment and in immeasurable light, singing songs with soft and gentle voices, while presenting the liturgy to him gloriously. (20:3–4)

Enoch's vision in the tenth heaven is expressed in terms of humble insufficiency. Incomprehensibility is explained no further than to the point of being indescribable:

And who am I to give an account of the incomprehensible being of the Lord, and of his face, so extremely strange and indescribable? And how many are his commands, and his multiple voice, and the Lord's throne, supremely great and not made by hands, and the choir stalls all around him, the cherubim and the *seraphim* armies, and their never-silent singing. (22:2)

Thus, along heaven's entire hierarchy, from the very face of God all the way down to the third heaven, the visionary Enoch is said to have heard God's kingdom break forth with singing and musical joy. All this constitutes marvelous background information for understanding the Jewish context from which the Christian gospel regarding the Kingdom of Heaven has sprouted, and whence it was first introduced. Even though the inter-testamental Jewish notion of the Kingdom of Heaven still contained armed soldiers—an assumption that also has been ascribed to the mind of Jesus, in *Matthew* 26:53—the divine monarchy no longer was thought of as a military regime. All the same, to the extent that the author of *Second Enoch* shared his secrets with mortal humankind, his "kingdom of heaven" idea had to be communicated to a world where some kind of soldiers were still necessary for defense and for peoples' collective safety. The important progression in Kingdom of Heaven symbolism, during the inter-testamental period, called for angels breaking forth into the world of human awareness, with singing. Eventually, in the gospel story told by Christians, angels could be heard breaking forth with singing, downward and earthward from the lower levels of heaven, all the way to the earth where their messages and songs reached the ears of lowliest humankind.

Of course, the Christian story about the birth of Jesus Christ was originally a Jewish story. It took off precisely at the point in the history of Jewish angelology that is reflected in Second Enoch. According to *Luke,* the new Kingdom of Heaven music no longer was audible only to scribes who composed pseudonymous stories about trance journeys of ancient holy men, but was heard instead by unsophisticated sheepherder folk (2:13f). Luke's introduction to the Christian good-news story, about the birth of Jesus, has made the new "heavenly kingdom" idea accessible at the level of common people. By adding angelology, Luke added nothing that was different from what was already implied in the "Reign of God" message of Jesus.

Our point here is not to teach angelology, but to put aspirations of humankind into a historical context. An announcement by God's messenger angel was heard on earth, during the night—in darkness. And a multitude of the heavenly hosts appeared from on high, radiating the glory of God that was present in heaven. It came to tingle some of the lowliest among human ears. Momentarily, the Kingdom of Heaven erupted with gentle music—explicitly, not with the thunder and violence of a heavenly army.

The reign of God has thereby been made manifest as an otherworldly, kinder regime that intruded from beyond. A gentler kind of kingdom broke into our world with the birth of a helpless baby boy. The story of this humble event, which came to introduce the new Christian universalism, has God's own messenger angel appear and announce the new world order at the level of lowly herder folk. The simple story speaks for itself:

And the angel said to them: "Be not afraid; for behold, I bring you good news of a great joy which will come to all the people."... And suddenly there was with the angel a multitude of the heavenly host, praising God and saying, "Glory to God in the highest, and on earth peace among men with whom he [can be] pleased!" (*Luke* 2:10–14). Jesus and the Kingdom of Heaven.

The Christian universalism spread into the Graeco-Roman world with time-conscious proclamations, such as the one quoted next from a letter written by the Apostle Paul to Christians in Galatia, in Asia Minor. Paul strips away hyper-domestication and brings his audience back to simpler family categories and essentials—such as Father, Son, and Mother:

But when the time had fully come, God sent forth his Son, born of a woman, born under the law so that we might receive adoption as sons.[143] And because you are sons, God sent the spirit of his son into our hearts, crying, "Abba! Father!" So, through God you are no longer slave but a son, and if a son then an heir (*Galatians* 4:4–7).

An awareness, of history being linear, has all along been a favorite concept for the rational structure of both the Hebrew and Christian traditions. Hebrew Torah mythology begins with the creation of the world and moves along linear time to visions of divine interference and election that, in due time, resulted in a people's liberation from Egyptian hyper-domestication. God's interference in history has set up a group of Hebrew slaves for a divine lesson—of a people getting liberated—unfortunately, at the time still with a mandate, by God, to inflict their round of hyper-domestication on certain others.

---

[143] Female readers in the year 2020 CE need not feel excluded by Paul's patriarchal orientation, with his emphasis on sons. As the Empire of Heaven dawns, it is any-how first the warrior cult of males that is put on the chopping block for criticism.

The Christian good-news story broke forth from Judaism during the first century CE with the weight of a cosmic-political event. It happened "when the time had fully come" and when conditions were ripe. Of course, with the benefit of hindsight, all significant events in human history and awareness do happen in *kairos*—when the time is ripe.

A man in his early thirties, named Jesus, from Nazareth in Galilee, appeared among the followers of John the Baptizer somewhere along the Jordan River. John lived an ascetic life. He led a popular Kingdom of Heaven movement that his followers joined by way of a baptism ritual. The simple rite required immersion in water, to emerge and to be reborn therefrom. Those who participated in this ritual expressed repentance from their former ways. Ritualized bathing came to symbolize some sort of preparation or anticipation of the Rule of Heaven. In light of the general Egyptian background to Jewish piety, delineated in Part One of this book, we have come to suspect that for John the Baptizer, and for Jesus, the Jordan River flowed somewhat like an extension of God's creative "water of life" after the manner in which such waters were recognized in *Genesis* (2:10ff) and in the gospel of *John* (4:10 and 7:38). It is significant that the "Fourth Gospel," John, also happens to be the most Egyptianized among the canonical gospels. All together, the baptisms performed by John the Baptizer appear to have signified an initiation into the Kingdom of Heaven, the beginning of a process of trans-formation into divine life. The water that flowed in the Jordan, for Jesus, came closer in meaning to the maternal efflux that facilitates a process of birthing, rather than the mere process of washing and purification. The Jordan River carried water of life, as anciently the River Nile was thought to have been doing.

For a less Egyptian and a more symbolic Hebrew account, we can turn to Matthew. There John the Baptizer's mission is summarized by an allegory of a heavenly monarchy:

In those days came John the Baptist, preaching in the wilderness of Judea, "Repent, for the kingdom of heaven is at hand" (*Matthew* 3:1–2).

We are given here a first historical glimpse of the man Jesus, as he appeared among followers of John the Baptizer. Like many others, so also Jesus participated in the non-conformist hippie preacher's ritual of immersion. Perhaps in accordance with his prior expectations, this experience became extraordinary meaningful to Jesus. He went up immediately from the water, and behold, the heavens were opened and he saw the Spirit of God descending like a dove, and alighting on him; and lo, a voice from heaven, saying: "This is my beloved Son, with whom I am well pleased." (*Matthew* 3:16-17)

Matthew became a disciple of Jesus, and notwithstanding the possibility of subsequent editorial adjustments in the gospel text attributed to him, it is likely that either he or a fellow disciple obtained this tidbit of information directly from their rabbi. This means that the original experience of Jesus presupposes a divine auditory revelation of sorts, which originally had been understood by Jesus in the second-and-first-person singular: "You are my beloved Son, I like you!" The narrative continues to tell what effect these very personal words of God have had on Jesus:

Then Jesus was led up by the Spirit into the wilderness to be tempted by the devil. And he fasted forty days and forty nights, and after-ward he was hungry. (*Matthew* 4:1–2)

The three temptations that Jesus was said to have resisted in the wilderness concerned (1) the avoidance of hunger and suffering, (2) antics of might and heroic populism, and finally (3) hyper-domestication ambitions on an imperialistic scale. According to this story, the tempter's allurements progressed from the satisfaction of physical hunger to craving for public notoriety, and thence to the added glamour that could lead to ruling the world with absolute power.

Jesus emerged from his wilderness ordeal with a resolution of renewed commitment to a cause that was defined earlier by John the Baptizer. The continuation is given a few sentences later:

From that time Jesus began to preach, saying, "Repent, for the kingdom of heaven is at hand." (4:17)

Even a small amount of thoughtful reading in the canonical gospels will make it obvious that the retreat of Jesus into the desert, and his temptations there, represent a reaction to his baptismal experience. Somehow, Jesus of Nazareth has heard God's endorsement of himself as being a "beloved Son." And this affirmation, in the mind of Jesus, and subsequently among his followers, became the seed idea from which the Christian religion grew—as an antithesis to the politically present empires of the world.

The existential question that drove Jesus into solitude was the logical result of divine revelation and human intuition: What does it really mean to be a Son of God? The conclusion which Jesus reached after baptism, under the sway of a straight-talking fringe-preacher named John, and during forty days of prayer and fasting in wilderness solitude, answers precisely this question.

This implies that Jesus rejected and condemned all "satanic" schemes of sovereignty. He was not going to be one of those fake hyper-domestication Sons of God, neither a military warlord nor an owner of human herds—not of armies and warriors nor of chain-gangs of prisoners. He was not going to present fake mandates, or covenants to help rulers conquer, to herd, to own, to castrate, torture, exploit, or otherwise destroy humankind. His mandate was not vested in the vanity of presumed powers. Elsewhere, Jesus has identified his principal opponent, Satan, as de facto "Ruler of this World" (*John* 12:31; 14:30; 16:11). There is no ambiguity with regard to whom he meant. It was the combined ilk of piously justified grand-domesticator Son-of-God impersonators—ranging from the Roman sovereign in the year of his own birth, Imperator Caesar Divi Filius Augustus, all the way to Tiberius Caesar Divi Augusti Filius Augustus, under whose jurisdiction the crucifixion of Jesus was executed.

For three thousand years before the days of Jesus, in the Near East, large civilizations have blossomed into empires. Invariably, these were organized by ambitious hyper-domesticators and were maintained with the support of high-priestly hype, legitimated for sacrificing and dispensing humankind. High priests were direct evolutionary derivatives of master butchers or shamanic sacrificers among stone age hunters who, later, in hyper-domesticated "civilizations," served God-impersonators as Executioner high priests to enact some type of *Mysterium tremendum* or *Deus terribilis* presence.

Hereditary rulers learned how to acquire and to keep power by positioning themselves as the legitimate heirs of God. Occasionally, some religious counter-agents or responsive humanistic organizers were able to obstruct or to circumvent the claims of mortal usurpers of divine authority—that is, to void the mandates or covenants by which hyper-domesticators and militarists have tried to parade themselves. Occasionally, rulers could be constrained as elected "presidents" or "servant-trustees" of God, to govern humankind.

But eventually, the founders of grand-domestication schemes evolved and claimed status as representatives of God. Religious contraries needed to confront them, minimally with apparent matching rank and weight—namely, as agents of so-conceived greater-than-human authority. Among better-balanced grand-domestication systems, priestly representatives of God could, at times, keep divine kings or other "sons" of divine extraction checked or hushed. In worse situations, such priestly agents ended up justifying whatever the aloof pretenders happened to be inflicting on fellow humankind, as "their subjects."

Startled by his baptismal experience, by audible divine decree, and having become sensitized during his long fast in the desert, the man Jesus of Nazareth achieved clarity about his role, as "Beloved Son" and what the almighty God-Father called him to be. He concluded that his filial relationship with God forbade him all exploitative behavior, and all pious legitimation of the same. Jesus expected from his heavenly Father not necessary powers to save the world. As a human being he left such powers where they belonged, safely in the hands of God. These were the only hands that could be trusted to hold divine authority and power. Moreover, the Hebrew-Aramaic name for God, that Jesus used, was "Abba"—an appellation that in English comes closest to mean "Daddy!"

Of course, our own manner of seeing in the man Jesus some contrary, of a humane demeanor, quickly encounters problems of communication. Hyper-domesticators and their high-priestly legitimizers do feverishly oppose prophetic challengers for speaking a contrary message on behalf of greater-than-human reality—and for trying to comfort thereby the masses. They accuse prophets of being pretentious usurpers of established authority. Nevertheless, faced with explaining the prophetic perspective on religion, one also must ask questions from within the implied relationship between God and humankind.

No prudent hyper-domesticator can afford, in public, to refer to his own hyped mortal sire as if he ever was an ordinary soft or gentle "Daddy." Grand-domesticators rule by sacerdotal hype, by inflicting fear, while convincing themselves of their own superior status. They play their roles as heroes, as sons of God, as divine messengers, as righteous terrorists in some manner ordained by ultimate Reality or God. They play their roles to awaken fear in the souls of potential "subjects." In other words, they rule by what

Rudolf Otto would have termed *mysterium tremendum:* spreading the "fear of God."

Of course, measured by the standards of an average civilized and over-domesticated establishment, the self-definition and the personal theology of Jesus appeared conceited. To established Pharisaic theologians, Jesus appeared blasphemous and satanic. No wandering storyteller was entitled to transroyal status, and even less entitled to intimate filial proximity with the one and only God on High. Empires generate their own definitions. In turn, definitions are justified by ambivalent haughty minds, to define their competitively managed and owned herds of people. Spoken with historical awareness and conviction, reform-ontology can undercut, revolutionize and even modify empires. Adjectives can be hardened into nouns.

So, Jesus resolutely taught the immediate arrival of Heaven's kingdom. He announced an empire that would be more humane than those that hitherto scored in history. The meek who, in ordinary kingdoms of this world suffer exploitation, they were assured by Jesus that they would inherit the Earth—that is, an Earth that is destined to come increasingly under the direct influence of God.

People who were poor in spirit, who were not shrewd analytic predators and exploiters, would belong to this dawning heavenly empire. It was to be a peaceable kingdom, where leaders behaved like humble servants, and where servants and masters had equal status. In short, it was a kingdom where even the majestic heavenly Father of Christendom's founder did not mind being Daddy to his only-begotten Son, and subsequently among ordinary humankind also to this son's followers. And this kind of an antithetical Reign of Heaven, John the Baptizer and Jesus insisted, was at hand.

Beatitudes for a Constitution

The presence of both an Old and a New Testament has spawned some confusion among historically uninformed Christians—who mistakenly take the Ten Commandments in *Exodus,* where hyper-domestication is assumed and addressed as the status quo—to also mean that the Almighty God indeed has endorsed the practice of human slavery as the point at which to begin. Indeed, our ever-changing languages, oscillate drunkenly between theses and antitheses, do add confusion and endless opportunities for misunderstanding, and intentionally false interpretations, for selfish ends.

A group of American scholars known as the "Jesus Seminar" have, in their own translation of the New Testament, attempted to bring the gospel texts back to some measure of historical accuracy.[144] This author struggled with some of their changes in the wording of the Sermon on the Mount. The "blesseds" in their translation have become "congratulations." All possible quirks of English and German are thereby unleashed. Implications hailed from clouds of older memories. Not very often, in the Midwest have I heard anyone "congratulate" someone on account of a "blessing." Translation of the Greek *"makarios"* into a rarely used English expression does not help much.

Indeed, there has evolved in my native rural Germany a tradition of offering congratulatory speeches—an art form of flattery which I, as an emigrant to America, fortunately never needed to learn. Farmers in the American Midwest whom I befriended, and academicians on this continent, are not in the habit of congratulating quickly; nor is it easy for me to imagine Jesus having formally "congratulated" the meek or the poor for eventual entry into the Kingdom of Heaven.

But farmers in the American Midwest would say something like "Good for you!" They would offer this comment seriously as well as in jest. "Good for you" seems to be a better English translation for the beatitudes as spoken and quoted in the Sermon on the Mount.

Jesus probably meant something like "Good for you! You are open toward those humble in spirit and toward mourners, toward the meek, the hungry, the merciful, the honest, the peacemakers, the persecuted and the maligned. Good for you! You are at the side of people who need you. You are in tune with the Abba-God."

According to Jesus's own words which he spoke during his trial, and according to sound logic, the Empire of Heaven would "not have been of this world." In the full English metaphorical sense, it was something still very much "out of this world." But precisely of this

---

[144]See *Five Gospels: New Translation and Commentary,* by Robert W. Funk, Roy W. Hoover, and the Jesus Seminar (New York: Macmillan, 1993). By sheer coincidence, on the day of this writing (March 5, 2017), I had the pleasure of listening to a lecture by a member of this "Jesus Seminar," on the topic of "Ethics and the Beatitudes." As could be anticipated, the professor utilized the translation published by his group. He read "Congratulations to the poor in spirit"... and" Congratulations to those who grieve...."

kind of a Kingdom the Anointed from Nazareth agreed to be its king, occasionally and unabashedly. He could as well have claimed to be a slave in that kingdom—as Paul explained in *Romans* 15:8 and at the same time claimed himself to be a slave of Jesus Christ (*Romans* 1:1). King or servant, or servant to the servant, it all meant the same thing in the Empire of Heaven of which Jesus spoke. All these teachings together express the absence of rank and pretense. But if this is so, then why did Jesus, when he faced the Roman procurator, confess to being a "king in this otherworldly kingdom?" The answer to this question is far more straightforward and obvious than most Christians or their detractors have hitherto acknowledged.

As long as ordinary kingdoms or grand-domestication systems prevail in this world, and inasmuch as Jesus knew himself to be a different kind of Son of God, and as long as people were abused by Son-of-God pretenders and by high-priestly cult organizers, Jesus based his definition on what he understood God's "real" monarchy to be. No authoritative dictionaries existed, and in a political sense the uses of political language were quite extreme. So, for Jesus the title "King" needed to be rectified.

Jesus knew perfectly well that he was misunderstood by his judges. Yet, instead of trying to clear himself of the charge of sedition, he exposed their political corruption. Defiantly he put high priest and Sanhedrin on trial, and he threw into his cauldron of judgment the deified Roman emperor, and the procurator who represented him, to boot. On behalf of his overall contrary message, Jesus refused to avoid a supposedly avoidable death sentence. He gave answers that were perplexing and defiant to his accusers and judges. And his judges obligingly convicted him. Because Jesus had announced the "contrary Empire of Heaven," a new socio-political order was anticipated by his followers and it became a datum in human history. That which was not of this world provoked a religious awakening. It was destined to challenge hyper-domestication shenanigans and empires.

For Jesus, personally, the Kingdom of Heaven remained the normative kingdom by which all kingdoms were to be measured and judged. From the perspective of his revised Son-of-God consciousness, he explained his Father's revolutionary kingdom to people who were caught up and trapped in the hyper-domestication establishments ruled by "made" Sons of God.

With his view of universalized divine-human dignity, Jesus confronted and judged what he regarded to be the inverted deified status of worldly emperors. Implicitly he rejected and eventually managed to expose their fake mandates and to reject their empires which were based on terror. Jesus was crucified for stirring up the people and for speaking blasphemy. Indeed, if such unsettling and radical rebalancing activities deserve death, as often in hyper-domesticated environments they do, then Jesus at least received due process under "civilized" law. It was his stubborn insistence on his divinely inspired and revised concepts regarding "Kingdom," "Son of God," "King" and "King of kings," "Divine Ruler," "God of gods" and "Divine Father," that provoked condemnation on the part of Jewish as well as Roman authorities. His obstinate insistence on responding to the divine call became a parody on any other types of Son of God roll-players—on rites that Roman emperors play-acted; and this is what has brought Jesus of Nazareth his death sentence.

The life and message of Jesus was based on his vision of a fulfilled monotheistic ontology, of a realized Kingdom of Heaven. Monotheism fulfilled becomes pantheism. The heavenly Father's claim on Jesus, as Son, empowered the Son's vision. For the duration of his life in Palestine, Jesus was caught up in a double-layered grand-domestication system, squeezed between the ambitions of Herodian Judaism and the Roman empire.[145]

Within those two systems, all kinds of human victims would be judged and damned, by judges who reigned as if speaking from on high. But Jesus, while empathizing with suffering people, simply refused to acknowledge the hyper-domestication system as something legitimate or worth his while. He recognized its organization to be seriously flawed. By not recognizing the arrogant powers of hyper-domestication, he discounted their entire reality—the ontology within which that power supposedly was justified and realized.

Within the universalistic awareness by which Jesus contemplated the Kingdom of Heaven, all grand-domestication systems stood damned

[145]The incident given in *Matthew* 22:15ff is frequently mentioned to demonstrate Jesus's support of the empire. In reality, his answer there is evasive at best. He simply let Caesar have his money, because money was not essential for defining the Empire of Heaven. His advice at Capernaum, in *Matthew* 17:24ff, to pay the half-shekel tax can also be understood as a mere fringe accommodation.

and doomed in the longer run. The historicized version of Jesus's activities testifies that impoverished folk listened to him gladly. With his radical insistence on trans-mundane standards, he deflated the status of hyper-domesticators. The crowds of people who followed Jesus grew larger. It was only a matter of time before his Kingdom of Heaven message became unbearably popular and challenged those in power. Effected by Jesus's fresh glimpse of universal egalitarian dignity, cast in a religious world-view of dramatic passion and political parody, subsequent Roman emperors eventually were reduced to seeing their own claims to divine status evaporate.[146]

Amazingly, the man Jesus who persisted, over and beyond the horizons of grand-domesticated humanity, has also electrified and transcended human mortality itself—while he was at it. Divine-royal status, and returning to the All-Father-God after death, were already interdependent notions in ancient imperial Egyptian religion. Thus, after the body of Jesus was nailed to a Roman cross, and after his corpse was laid to rest in a Jewish tomb, fresh excitement erupted among his followers while they were still in mourning. A few among them testified to the fact that the tomb of Jesus had been found empty and, subsequently, more people told of encounters with the resurrected Christ himself. In all this commotion, the basic world-ontology of Jesus's follower-h*omines-sapientes* was kept creative and active.

The perfectly ambivalent slogan for a universalistic religious revolution had just been found. Emperor, king, procurator, and high priest were outside the loop. No longer could an emperor be divine. The new faith insisted that "Christ is risen" and that "Christ is Lord." These politically coded slogans were actually lifted straight from the weakest point in the play-book of the opposition—from the "political science" of the Roman imperial system itself.

When scholars speculate, nowadays, about the source of the Judaic Pharisaic belief in resurrection of the dead, some of them point to Iranian Mazdaism. Indeed, Persian influence on the history of Judaism is a fact of history since the days when Cyrus of Persia was hailed as a messiah of the Jewish people, in *Second Isaiah*. Likewise, the

---

146 The initial wavering and resolution at the Council of Nicaea, on the part of the Emperor Constantine, may be mentioned here as a classic example. For some other details, see Ioannes Karayannopulos, "Konstantin der Grosse und der Kaiserkult," in Antonie Wlosok, *Römischer Kaiserkult* (Darmstadt: Wissenschaftliche Buchgesellschaft, 1978), 485–527. See also Chapter 17 below, pp. 381ff.

the Persian conquest of Egypt, under Cambyses II and the reigns of the Darius-es and Xerxes-es are facts of history. Mircea Eliade probably was correct when he renamed the Iranian version of resurrection of the dead a "re-creation of bodies." Elsewhere, he has summarized how, according to Mazdaism, a human soul "will recover a resuscitated and glorious body" after the Final Judgment.[147]

While influences of Mazdaism on Pharisaic Judaism, and on early Christian belief, need not be ruled out, the specific Resurrection message that got Christendom started was definitely more international and more political than commonly understood. The apparitions of Christ's resurrection body were temporary; they did not yet represent the final condition attributed to the person of Jesus. We can gather from the story, that the appearances of Jesus Christ ceased when he ascended and returned to his Father in Heaven.

In the Christian context, the Savior's resurrection and ascension were notions very much dependent on his earlier descent. The Father's begetting, and in conclusion the Son's return to the Father constitute a single gospel event, a single round-trip journey. We can derive this logic directly from ancient Egypt. The probability of an ideological link to ancient Egyptian soteriology is strong. Translated into Egyptian concepts, the Christian story of resurrection meant that Christ's resurrected *ba* apparition lingered a while longer until his ascension and full return into the Father's *ka* essence. Luckily for later Christianity, the neo-Egyptian Plotinus still understood this ancient Egyptian process language.[148]

Joy of victory over the world's evils and over the powers of death, wrought by God the Father who had raised his only-begotten Son, became the propellant of the mobilized Reign of Heaven movement, from that first exciting Easter Sunday onward. Far and wide in hyper-domesticated lands, Christian apostles proclaimed their revolutionary *kerygma*: "Christ is risen!" and "Christ is Lord!"

Jewish leaders, particularly the Hellenized party of Sadducees whom the Egyptianized resurrection tale spooked most, were infuriated about this resumption of irrational populist commotion. The Roman

---

147 Mircea Eliade, *A History of Religious Ideas*, Vol. 1 (Chicago: University of Chicago Press, 1978), 332, and Vol. 2 (1982), 320. He relies on passages in *Denkart* and refers to Zaehner.

148 Compare our discussion of *Ennead* VI,4, earlier.

authorities, who accommodated the Jewish accusers of Jesus, and who along a path of least resistance had furnished a death sentence in hope of restoring calm in the province, were puzzled even more by this irrationality that seemed to be getting stranger by the day. They knew well how to deal with outright insurrection. Outright refusal to concede divine rights to the Roman emperor could have been identified and judged with reasonable precision. If someone would shout "Down with Caesar!" they knew how to crucify or behead the usurper, depending on his citizenship status within the empire.

But in this new commotion, hundreds of people, and soon thousands, professed the puzzling kerygma of "Christ is risen!" The Roman civil authorities had no effective rational perspective from which they could respond to this apparent absurdity. They were unable to discourage this foolishness without also undermining the imperial celebration of *apotheosis* (the deification of deceased emperors). Christians in Rome, while indeed usurping imperial theology and politics were alternately tolerated and persecuted. They were finally hunted in earnest under Decius (250 C.E). Many lost their lives and, at that time, also found honor and rewards in the Kingdom of Heaven—some found the fulfillment of their lives in the glories of martyrdom.

To this very day, non-Christian philosophers, nesting comfortably in the underbrush among the remaining stumps of the old forest of Christendom, still are puzzled that the Christian resurrection faith has spread far and wide among genuine *Homines sapientes*. Try as they may, they cannot ignore that at a certain moment in Western history, educated Graeco-Roman citizens—even a clever emperor himself—moved closer toward this religion which, by then, must have seemed at least somewhat reasonable. But *how* could it have seemed reasonable?

The essence of this apparent foolishness, of faith in resurrection, lies in our latter-day unfamiliarity with ancient reality-politics and with our increasing distance from ancient conditions and linguistic conventions. The resurrection of the Christian Son of God was asserted in context, within the wider evolutionary, revolutionary and historical process. As an oppositional grunt against the ancient Egyptian style of imperial hyper-domestication, dogma, and theocracy, Christendom's Resurrection-proclamation was good revolutionary parody and made excellent political sense—and over the long haul it improved the status of hyper-domesticated people.

"In the fullness of time," as the gospel writers expressed their sentiment—approximately after three millennia of hyper-domestication during which mortal tyrants paraded as Sons of God, the Christian resurrection story provided a revolutionary alternative to endorsing the prevailing imperialism, militarism, human slaughter, slavery, and other modes of hyper-domestication. And appraising the gospel story's intent, in light of Christendom's own subsequent lapses into schemes of imperial hyper-domestication, and repentant reformations, this proclamation of resurrection certainly was not a first time, nor will it ever have been understood politically for a last time.

At the time, those who felt like damning the deified emperors in Rome, no longer needed to join the small and hopeless schemes of zealotry and repeatedly suffer defeat in the battles of their daring rebellions. In the company of angry freedom fighters they no longer needed to shout "Down with the Emperor!" From Jesus of Nazareth they learned how to look at the brighter side of divine creation, evolution, and revolution. By welcoming the Father's intruding heavenly kingdom, they were on the winning side, for a change. They subscribed to the power of positive political celebration and they—more reasonably—could shout "Christ is risen!"

The slogan was effective against the status of deified emperors. It was less dangerous. At the people's present level of understanding it signified and accomplished the same religious and political end, more effectively and humanely than a violent revolution could have.

However, to the Christian proclamation also were added new songs and prayers. From the upgraded auditions of angel voices, in visions of the Kingdom of Heaven, the new religion gradually reformed the rhythms and rites of passage along Near Eastern and Mediterranean shores, and in the remainder of Western civilization.

The Christian ethos, as it unfolded in recent centuries, has been transformed and secularized by democratic ideals, by democratic revolutions. Reformed grand-domesticator folk heroes and presidents were pitted against older houses of royalty. Violent democracies and republics have defeated older monarchic and imperial sacerdotal enterprises. More threats and more sounds of war, reverberations from the greater-than-human exploding cosmos, attested to by scientific mythology and hypotheses—more spectacular fireworks and flares and fewer songs of angels are heard by human ears in our days. Less divine glory is seen reflected in frightened human eyes.

In the context of reality-based politics, the "Christ is risen" proclamation was a rational challenge to the ceremonial legitimation of the Roman Empire—a challenge to the ceremonial practice that Caesar Augustus had adopted while ruling Egypt—of playing the role of a Son of God. In Figure 16, Augustus faces Isis and Horus on equal footing. Caesar Augustus brought his Egyptian parade back home to Rome, to position himself as a Son of God there as well. Three millennia before Augustus, Egyptian pharaohs began building their regimes upon a Divine Death, Resurrection, and Enthronement drama. They were deified (i.e. Osiris-ized) by the power of Seth (by the God of Death) when they died. Thereby they were resurrected and reborn for enthronement, to rule Egypt as ancient Falcon deities (i.e. Horus-es).

If Christ's rising from his death two millennia ago is to be judged as an absurdity today, then—judged fairly—the Roman imperial postmortem rite of *apotheosis,* or deification, would need to be evaluated accordingly. Roman imperial pomp and circumstance included ancient Egyptian pharaonic mime—a posture which the adept Caesar Augustus adopted while governing Egypt, as a God.

The Christian creed, with its insistence on the resurrection of Jesus Christ from among the dead—while referencing his counter-status of being the only truly begotten Son of God—was it per chance any less rational than the imperial faiths which it satirized? Was, the sacrificial Lamb of God, or the Roman Cross of Christ, a less reasonable emblem for revolution than ancient Stone Age predator totems—such as eagles, lions or dragons could be? Similar iconic figures, colors and slogans, still are being shown today by modern states to wage democratic revolutions and to fight World Wars?

Resurrection in the context of hyper-domestication culture, in ancient Egypt, simply signified the continuity of an imperial mandate and its function for leverage. Faith in Jesus Christ, who rose from his Roman death by crucifixion into a Kingdom of Heaven, celebrated the victory of a revolution in ontology—an ancient theory of being—with fresh insights and axioms, and with revised attitudes toward the world, toward human status and destiny.

Figure 16. The Roman Caesar Augustus Octavius, dedicating a temple he built. Playing his role as a Son of God, he faces Isis and Horus on equal footing. Temple of Kalabsha, Nubia. Courtesy: Lassi hu: Kep: Agustus-in-Kalabsha.jpg.

With increasingly more witnesses insisting on the uniqueness of Jesus, and on his resurrection as God's own Anointed, the unspoken political question became whether people really owed allegiance to "made-and-fake" deified Caesars, or, whether the heavenly Father of Jesus Christ was entitled to rule humankind instead? Were ruling emperors divinely mandated or were they random competitors? The answer that Christians gave to this political query has redefined their faith in God as Creator and Owner of all things. God's disposition toward humankind was expressed essentially as "love." Such was their cosmic and political faith. Love of God and love of humankind, shown through Jesus Christ, was seen radiating divine affection and support. The Roman masters of ceremonies—state officials who performed the emperors' deification rituals, could not refute faith in Christ's resurrection with honest conviction—other than perhaps confess that imperial resurrections had been celebrated for at least three thousand years.

Any logical argument that could have invalidated the Christian proclamation also would have put in question the mandates of deified emperors. This obvious weakness of plain civilized logic is what has opened the floodgate through which Christendom, with its alternative ontology has inundated the Roman Empire. The Christian proclamation has abrogated all imperial mandates that would bless hyper-domestication. It favored a new wave of people who knew themselves raised to the status of brothers and sisters of Jesus Christ, as siblings of the one and only true Son of God. Implicit in their imperially endorsed Nicene Confession, these people have become children of God by divine adoption. Before God they ranked higher than all emperors past and present.

On arrival, the Christian faith was all about salvation and about divinely guaranteed rank and rights of common humankind—as equal-born children of God under Heaven—besieged by self-deified aristocrats, emperors and other sanctimonious representatives.

It appears as though our atheistic and agnostic siblings do not know enough about the limited utility of our changing languages, for realistic communication and—also not enough about the Geography of Thought outside the cultural prison camps in which our parents have conceived us, semi-consciously, into which our mothers have delivered us . . . all the while being driven by greater powers than they, by powers certainly greater than we could contribute in that process.

16

The Gnosis Competition

Defining "Gnosticism" or "Gnosis" is, humanly speaking, impossible. It may be said that the task of studying Gnosticism is even more difficult than, for instance, trying to describe a religion like Hinduism. The latter generally is defined by a method of subtraction. One subtracts from all the religious life in India, past and present, those elements that can be classified under Jainism, Buddhism, Islam, Sikhism, and Christianity. What remains, for lack of more precise designations, may be lumped together under the label "Hinduism" or "Induism." Precision for "Gnosticism" is more difficult to achieve, because until now the place of origin for this particular "-ism" has not been ascertained or linked with a known geographical source area, as this has been possible in the case of Hinduism in reference to India.

The reader will have sensed, however, that with this book, the situation might gradually be changing. It is no longer necessary to describe Gnosticism vaguely as a general milieu of thought or "syncretism" that mysteriously permeated the Graeco-Roman blend of Hellenistic culture as if it could have arrived, blown by the wind from just anywhere. The root notions of Gnosticism, next to Christianity, have revealed themselves not as having sprouted from the random remains of numerous Near Eastern religions. We now know more definitely, that ancient imperial Egyptian hyper-domestication religion, at Heliopolis, was the matriarch of the widespread Gnostic theme.

Gnosticism versus Christianity

In published commentaries, Gnosticism still is presented negatively as the same many-headed hydra that was recognized by Christian heresi-o-logists from the outset. Such imprecision prevails because there never was an identifiable organized Gnostic Church. Nor has there ever been compiled an official Gnostic canon of scripture.

Gnostic "others" were first identified, and classified as heretical folk by Christian catalogers of heresies. Irenaeus of Lyons (ca. 130–200 was foremost among them. Gnostics were people who had not adequately subscribed or conformed to the precepts and mores of what emerged as the Christian majority. This fact naturally begs a question. Who were the majority of Christians who did subscribe to, or have escaped the judgment of heresiologists?

We already have explained how, during the first century CE, an Empire of Heaven movement emerged from within Judaism and spread quickly. It became dialectically entangled with the larger Mediterranean world of religious and political aspirations. Followers of the Christian religion gathered in churches which, initially, were modeled after Jewish synagogues. Nevertheless, the impulse to build monumental churches, certainly was generated in competition with pre-Christian Roman temples that functioned as the political internal organs of the Roman Empire. Outsiders disparagingly, began to call churchgoing people "Christians" or "Christ Followers."

The label stuck and became a badge of honor for those who followed and revered the Anointed Jesus. Of course, these Christians were *gnostikón* in the sense that they believed they "knew" something about God's saving revelation through the Anointed (Christ) Jesus.

The ambiguity regarding Gnosticism still shows up, nowadays, as soon as we attribute an ability "to know" to *Homines sapientes* in general. Christians believed they knew a few things about God and about his plan of salvation. While the power of Roman civilization appeared to be failing humankind, victims sentenced to death by Roman crucifixion hoped that God would save them from such civilization—thus, from all of Rome's irrational cultural and political peculiarities. Victims wondered how anyone could ever subscribe to such civilized shenanigans and hopes for salvation. They wondered why powerful persons could behave irrationally. The Apostle Paul warned in *1 Corinthians* 8:1ff against an over-reliance on *gnosis* in general. The Deutero-Pauline pastoral letters contain a warning against "gnostics" who did not really know what they claimed they knew:

O Timothy, guard what has been entrusted to you. Avoid the godless chatter and contradictions of what is falsely called knowledge, for by professing it some have missed the mark as regards to faith. (*1 Timothy* 20–21)

False knowledge here was *gnosis* that could be contrasted with the mainstream of Christian faith and knowing. But then, is not "faith" the Christian equivalent of what elsewhere may have been recognized as revealed knowledge? And what *gnosis*, what knowledge, was there that could not also have been revealed? Such questions all were destined to glide off into the realm of theoretical ontology or epistemology. They had to be answered as content of a religiously balanced world-view—comprising the full range of knowledge that explained human suffering alongside wellbeing.

There was at least a nominal difference between those who aspired to Christian faith and those who stood apart as Gnostics. Faithful "Christians" clung to their name as a badge of honor and thereby became a distinct identifiable group, whereas the so-called Gnostics remained a variegated general population of knowers. Although their superficial classification served the old Christian catalogers of heresies reasonably well, it has become quite misleading to later historians and theologians. There may never have been a religious movement, anywhere in the world, that could reasonably be distinguished from other religions in terms of the presence or absence of "knowledge." Moreover, scholars substituting the Greek label *gnosis*, for Gnosticism, are only aggravating the basic ambiguity.

Kurt Rudolph alerted us to Gottfried Arnold's *Unparteiische Ketzer und Kirchenhistorie*. Already in 1699, "the ground was prepared for an independent academic study of Gnostics."[149] And indeed, Rudolph himself still has approached Gnosticism essentially as the same unique other-than-Christian phenomenon—as a multitude of syncretistic systems with many tributaries. It seems remarkable that the primary stream, ancient Egyptian orthodoxy, has not been recognized among these tributaries. And indeed, this stream was easily overlooked because, all along, it has been flowing wide enough to be mistaken for the ocean itself.

---

[149] Kurt Rudolph, *Gnosis: The Nature and History of Gnosis* (San Francisco: Harper and Row, 1987 [1977]), 30.

Egyptian Christianity

The most difficult area for the study of early Christian history has turned out to be Egypt—and this fact should alert students of Christendom to possible surprises. Among all the old Christian mission fields, the boundary line between Christianity and Gnosticism is most difficult to draw in the ancient land of Egypt. Among Gnosticism's primary historical sources and tributaries, Kurt Rudolph has identified the fringes of Judaism; traits of Jewish monotheism; Jewish apocalypticism; Qumran; Jewish wisdom teaching; Jewish skepticism; Iranian Zoroastrian ideas; Greek philosophic enlightenment, especially Platonism and Middle Platonism; the Hermetica; Hellenistic mysteries; Orphism; Graeco-Oriental syncretism, including "Syria or Egypt;" individualism and esoterism; spiritualization; economic conditions; the spread of oriental cults—Cybele, Isis, the Unvanquished Sun-god, and Mithras; urban living; social protest; and religious intellectualism.[150]

In his *History and Literature of Early Christianity*, Helmut Koester commented on the apparent absence of Christianity in Egypt during the first decades of missionary expansion: "It is indeed unthinkable that the Christian mission should have bypassed Alexandria for decades." But then, as Walter Bauer already had suggested in 1934, our historical lacuna may have been determined by divergent perspectives current within the early Catholic church. Well-defined points of view on what has become orthodox Christendom have generally been used to select the source materials that most church historians still are using today. The beginnings of Christianity in Egypt—so Koester summarizes Bauer—were heretical. Christian writings, composed in Egypt during this early period were not preserved.[151] But fortunately for historians, copies of some of the original early "heretical" Egyptian documents have meanwhile come to light. The Nag Hammadi library contains some of them.

In a broad overview, as is attempted by our book, it is not possible to revisit the entire academic Gnosticism construct. Let it suffice to

150 *Ibid., 277–294. One should note, however, that listing two dozen marginally under-stood historical situations as tributaries, clarifies nothing. It befuddles.*

151 Helmut Koester, *History and Literature of Early Christianity* (Berlin and New York: Walter de Gruyter, 1982), 219–232.

say, however, that many apparently related data have meanwhile been gathered, harvested like sheaves, and brought home under the rubric of Gnosticism. While academicians have built their Gnosticism "barn" large enough to contain their data, the sheer act of gathering a huge mixed group of "non-orthodox knowers," from the first century CE onward, into a hypothetical barn or "sheave" may be an excellent task for barn builders and harvesters. But for many serious historians, the outcome of such labors resulted in classifying and in defining an ambiguous plethora of all-data. Some despairing German readers have meanwhile begun to deride any similar efforts as making "Gnosis Marmalade."

Nevertheless, Hans Jonas, and more recently Kurt Rudolph, have brought a measure of order into the Gnosis barn. Our book does attempt no rebuttal regarding their accomplishments. In light of the multiple strains and ingredients and the enormous task of re-bundling the entire hypothetical sheave of Gnosticism, the efforts of these scholars remain praiseworthy. But, their work seems incomplete, as will remain our efforts. In order to carry forward, our discussion must revise wherever fresh historical links come into view. Several fallout effects from Egyptian religion, for Israelite religion and Judaism, have been sketched in Part Two, earlier. Part Three has provided a sketch of this happening to Greek philosophy and to Neo-Platonism. As a result of new oblique Egyptian "light," streaming from venues of academic study, much of traditional Christian theology is now better illuminated. Distances between ancient Egypt, Christendom, and Gnostic doctrines have gotten shorter.

With the discovery of the Nag Hammadi library in Upper Egypt, the general profile of Gnosticism has come into better view. All these texts must, eventually, be reexamined in light of possible ancient Egyptian antecedents. Some Nag Hammadi texts allude directly to old Egyptian themes—for example, "On the Origin of the World," "The Exegesis of the Soul," "The Gospel of the Egyptians," "The Thunder, Perfect Mind," "Asclepius," "Discourse on the Eighth and Ninth." Another dozen treatises contained in this "Gnostic" library appear to be at least somewhat indebted to ancient Egyptian theology. Attempting even a superficial discussion of these would lead beyond the scope of what is possible within the bounds of this book.

Rather than getting sidetracked to another major enterprise, we will summarize, instead, our scope and focus on Simon Magus as an example—singled out already by early Christian heresiologists as the foremost among these Gnostics. But before going there, we will hastily review how Gnosticism has been summarized by two prominent scholars as both Dualism and Monism. Thus, before we can hope to find our way through the jungle of literary inheritances and definitions, we must pay attention to the presuppositions of our immediate precursors.

Hans Jonas

Conclusions reached by Hans Jonas are quoted frequently in the Gnostic Studies field. The frequency of those quotations renders his characterization of Gnosticism somewhat more authoritative than his data might support. Seen from along our path of study, Jonas-es categories of "dualism" and "transcendence" do appear contrived:

The radical nature of the dualism does affect the doctrine of salvation. As alien as the transcendent God is to "this world," so is the pneumatic self in the middle of it. The goal of gnostic striving is the release of the "inner man" from the bonds of the world and returning to his native realm of light.[152]

It is to his lasting credit that Hans Jonas has seen an obvious need to supplement his earlier abstraction of cosmic dualism with a postscript on soteriology. Now, after he has placed both cards on the table—dualism and soteriology—his authoritative pronouncement regarding Gnostic dualism may need some downward adjustment. The entire problem reduces to the question of whether one is to think about this dualistic Gnostic theology from the perspective of estranged individual souls or from the perspective of reconciled souls on their homeward path. In the former case, the epithet "dualism" seems appropriate, whereas in the latter instance, the dualism of estrangement is actually being cancelled out by soteriology—which happens to be the soul's return and reunification with the One.

On hand of a Valentinian formula, Hans Jonas has encapsulated his summary of Gnostic eschatology quite severely. But nevertheless remarkable, his Gnosis summary, which to us appears in harmony with ancient Egypt, yields no dualistic perspective. In a rationally

---

[152] *Ibid.* 44f

coherent dimension of a protagonist's place in the cosmos, a typical Gnostic within a single process appears to be concerned, essentially with getting from one place to another within a single system:

What in fact liberates is the knowledge of who we were, what we became; where we were, where-into we have been thrown; where-to we speed, where-from we are redeemed; what birth is, and what rebirth (*Exc. Theod.* 78, 2)[153]

Kurt Rudolph

Responding obviously to Hans Jonas, and in some ways also echoing his words, Kurt Rudolph has disassembled and rebundled the basic strains that went into his Gnosis bundle. To that end, he introduced his basic framework with a trim quote from the 1966 Messina Conference on Gnosticism:

...the idea of the presence in man of a divine "spark"... which has proceeded from the divine world and has fallen into this world of destiny, birth and death, and which must be reawakened through its own divine counterpart in order to be finally restored. This idea... is ontologically based on the conception of a downward development of the divine whose periphery (often called *Sophia* or *Ennoia*) has fallen victim to a crisis and must—even if only indirectly—produce this world, in which it then cannot be disinterested, in that once again it must recover the divine "spark" (often designated as *pneuma*, or "spirit").[154]

Amazingly, after this beautiful summary of what to us appears to be genuine ancient Egyptian monistic ontology and soteriology, Rudolph continues to repeat the Jonas cliché to the effect that Gnosticism is dualistic. Rudolph, for a moment even pretends to derive dualism from the passage just rendered:

From Rudolph's first quotation it seems clear that at the basis of Gnosis lies a dualistic view of the world which determines all its statements on a cosmological and anthropological level.... This dualism is carried along, or, to put it more accurately, is interwoven with a monistic idea which is expressed in the already mentioned upward and downward

---

[153] *Ibid.* 45.

[154] Quoted in Rudolph, *Gnosis*, 57.

development of the divine spark which is the basis for the identification of man and deity.... Embedded in this "dualism on a monistic background" is the doctrine of God in Gnosis, which is determined above all by the idea of the "unknown God" beyond all that is visible and sensible and incorporates a "fullness" (pleroma) of angels and other heavenly beings, be they personified ideas, abstractions, or hypostases.[155]

Let us linger and think for a moment! Why could someone not begin this discourse just as well with first introducing Gnosticism as monism, and then worry about the ambiguities with invoking dualities later? Whence, all of a sudden came Rudolph's "monistic background"? Why could that background not be seen historically as the essence of Gnosticism? Moreover, in an academic discourse, what does "background" mean? If a universal monad is contemplated, starting at one of its ends in terms of far or near, up or down, high or low, then, do these transitory human perspectives necessarily render any monism dualistic or pluralistic?

One can only be impressed by the wonderful support that, Kurt Rudolph has provided here for our thesis, in spite of himself. He has, in fact, delineated the basic unity of emanation—has substantiated the monism in Gnostic teachings and its rootedness in the basic ancient Egyptian ontology of its Hidden Unknown All-God.

Simon Magus, a Gnostic Magician

Posterity probably will judge that too much attention was given in this book to Simon Magus. Nevertheless, the necessary task of re-examining the *Gnosis* phenomenon in light of fresh "Egyptian light" may begin just as easily with him as with some other. After all, Simon Magus scored in the history of Christendom as an early arch enemy. As the "father of all heresy," he must be re-studied not only as a conspicuous opponent or competitor of Jesus Christ —founder of the Christian church—but possibly also as a potential twin. Christian theology and christology, together, have driven their roots deep into the soil of ancient Egyptian ontology, as also was anchored the theology of Simon Magus. It may be suspected that the strength of Simon Magus' threat for Christian theology came

---

[155] *Ibid.* 57f.

precisely from the fact of their similar Egyptian doctrinal assumptions.[156] The danger was that this man could in some way be mistaken for the Christ figure itself. The teachings of Simon needed to be differentiated clearly from the Christian gospel.

The character of Simon Magus itself is not a well-defined historical datum. Nonetheless, as an actual presence in history, this man has been attested to by Christian heresiologists as the "father of all heresy." Thus, he definitely scores as a datum for the history of the opposition. Whether this arch-foe of Christianity was identical to the person mentioned in *Acts* 8 is difficult to discern for sure. On the other hand, the question of whether one is dealing here with a literary construct—a foil to Christian Orthodoxy or a singular historical figure—may for the moment be postponed. But both these questions will eventually need to be reconsidered together, in light of the ancient Egyptian religious heritage.

The Simon Magus cult mentioned in Christian heresiology, having been highlighted in the works of recent Gnosis scholars, had—as it turns out—its roots sunk deep into ancient Egypt. For the sake of beginning this discourse afresh, we entertain, tentatively, the possible historical identity of the Simon Magus that is mentioned in *Acts* 8, with the one condemned by early heresiology. We engage in this hypothetical exercise because it is conceivable that "Egyptian light" can indeed help illuminate the historical presence of this person. Definitive conclusions will, nevertheless, need to be left to future scholarship as a matter of course.

According to the Church Fathers, Irenaeus and Hippolytus, the man Simon Magus was founder of a first-century cult in Samaria.[157] As of late, this cult has been classified among the so-called Gnostic religions. Actually, according to their writing, Simon was much more than the cult's founder. He was the movement's central divine figure, its founder and its God. His divine status was deduced directly from a variant of Egyptian ontology. For introducing Simon's teachings,

---

[156] It is customary in Christian circles to read the title "Magus" as denoting magician, sorcerer, or witch. However, such value judgments must be suspended during opening stages of research in the history of religions. Similar denigrations have been used by outsiders against the functionaries of all new religions—toward pioneering Christians, and against Jesus of Nazareth himself, who was accused to be Beelzebub, the Prince of Demons.

[157] Irenaeus, *Gnosis,* 294ff. *Adv. haer.* I 23, 1–4, and Hippolytus, *Refutatio* VI, 9–18.

and for the sake of brevity, we shall avail ourselves of the masterful assortment which Hans Jonas has compiled.[158]

"There is one Power, divided into upper and lower, begetting itself, increasing itself, seeking itself, finding itself, being its own mother, its own father. . . its own daughter, its own son. . . One, root of the All." This One, unfolded, "is he who stands, stood and shall stand: he stands above in the unbegotten Power; he stood below in the stream of waters, begotten in the image; he shall stand above with the blessed infinite power when his image shall be perfected."[159]

The ancient Egyptian root of this creedal statement is difficult to miss. Even Hans Jonas, who divided Gnosticism into Syrian, Egyptian, and Iranian branches, has exegeted from the Simon Magus documents something that foremost resembles ancient Heliopolitan process theology—without really identifying any Syrian or Iranian traces. Of course, the most peculiar element in this Samaria cult theology, for Simon Magus specifically, was the offspring that the ancient Egyptian Tefnut-Mahet hypostasis has engendered—the Ennoia.[160]

It is necessary to review for a moment the Egyptian prehistory of this feminine dimension in the Godhead. The association of Tefnut with Mahet is as ancient as the *Coffin Texts.*[161] In later Egyptian times, the goddess Mahet, as a personal manifestation of justice, right and rightness, order and truth, has been brought into companionship with Thoth, the masculine patron of knowledge and scribalism. Mahet has become the feminine associate of Thoth. Some kind of reconciled male-female relationship, as was supposed to exist between Mahet and Thoth, appears also to have stood as model for the theology and soteriology of Simon Magus.

---

[158] Jonas, *The Gnostic Religion* (Boston: Beacon Press, 1963), 103–111.

[159] *Ibid.*, 105 (*Hippol. Refut. VI.17.1–3*), suggests that the dichotomy of "upper and lower" was derived by Simon Magus from a process that occurs within the primal being or Godhead himself. Moreover, he considered this "a distinctive feature of the Syrian and Alexandrian gnosis, which," according to Jonas, "starts from a dualism of preexistent principles."

[160] Parallels pertaining to the Ennoia and the Barbelo, in *The Nag Hammadi Texts,* may be consulted to round out the larger picture. A more complete and more self-contained overview on these can be found in "The Exegesis on the Soul," in that collection of texts.

[161] See for instance Spell 80, in "Sun-Theology in the Coffin Texts," Chapter 5, above.

But there was another important dimension to divine womanhood, and it was already embryonically present in traditional Egyptian religion. It went beyond the intellectual virtues expressed by the personification of Mahet. Isis, as mother of Horus and as a member of the Heliopolitan Ennead, represented divine womanhood in Egypt like no other goddess. She did so, generally, under the guise of her anthropomorphic *ba*, wearing a horned headdress. As the Enneadic goddess nearest to humankind, Isis embodied the basic function of feminine creativity as well as confidence. In offbeat traditions she represented her basic function even to the point of self-sufficiency in procreation.

For example, a late text of a typical "lamentation of Isis" mentions this self-sufficiency in relation to her generation of Horus almost as an act of parthenogenesis. Isis says, "I made myself into a man, even though I was a woman."[162] The basic myth tells that it was Isis who retrieved the corpse of her brother-husband Osiris; it was she who gathered up his scattered portions. It was she who revived his sexual potency. According to Plutarch's later version, the phallus of Osiris was not among the gathered and reassembled parts. Isis therefore substituted on him a phallus of her own making whereby subsequently she conceived Horus. This could add up to the result that Horus essentially was generated by her alone.

An even more free-spirited Isis can be found mentioned in a spell used against scorpion and snake venom, on a number of papyri from the Nineteenth Dynasty (1320–1200 BCE). We find the goddess plotting for her share of power, that is, for status and partnership with the Godhead Amun-Ra himself. Before the clever Isis took matters into her own hands, literally, the Godhead had not yet divulged his powerful secret name to any of the gods.

Now Isis was a clever woman. Her heart was craftier than a million men; she was choicer than a million gods; she was more discerning than a million of the noble dead.[163] Isis knew everything in heaven and on earth, like Amun-Ra himself—except Amun's hidden name.[164]

---

162 Kees, *Lesebuch,* 30, in Bonnet, *Reallexikon der Ägyptischen Religionsgeschichte,* 327.

163 See also John A. Wilson, "Egyptian Myths, Tales, and Mortuary Texts," in Pritchard, *Ancient Near Eastern Texts,* 12–14.

164 See the Theban Theology, in Chapter 7, above.

In arranging her plot, Isis gathered up some of the God's spittle and kneaded it together with earth into a venomous snake. This most dangerous creature Isis laid, immobile, on the path that the high deity frequented. The snake stung. The God became ill. And in return for his health, Amun the Godhead, "Atum and Horus-of-Praise" divulged to Isis this secret name. Isis is the only one, besides Amun-Ra himself, who now knows the name.[165]

But Amun's secret is safe. Isis who, seen from a human perspective, functions in the cosmic dimension as Tefnut or Mahet, is very wise. Essentially she is an emanation of the All-God himself. Motivated by her own enlightened self-interest, she keeps the divine name secret from all the other gods. This caution assures her second-rank status and power in the created universe, alongside the Godhead himself.

Thus, the theme of the self-willed feminine hypostasis of the Godhead, which was exploited by Simon Magus, has been foreboded well enough in Egyptian religion and mythology. The name that Simon Magus gave to his feminine hypostasis was "Ennoia." It is somewhat tempting to interpret this name historically as a feminine derivative from the larger Egyptian Ennead; but for the time being I shall refrain from doing so explicitly. In any case, this estranged female personage was the First Thought on God's mind. Of course, from what we know about the incarnated God-head, Simon Magus, she also appears to have been the foremost item on his mind.

We must summarize Simon's gospel more coherently and make it accessible to present-day readers. In doing so, I shall avail myself of the collection of texts that Hans Jonas has already assembled.[166] In accordance with the gospel of this Samaritan cult, its founding magus has considered himself to be identical with God-Manifest. We will summarize here the quaint proclamation of Simon Magus by transcribing it into First Person Singular. For that purpose, I will freely modify, abbreviate, and paraphrase the words given by Hans Jonas.

---

165 Atum and Horus-of-Praise implies that the God Amun was squarely identical with the Heliopolitan Ennead. Atum and Horus may be understood as representing the alpha and the omega—beginning and end—of the Ennead.

166 For his summary, Jonas utilizes *Iren.* I.23.2 including *Homilies* II.25; *Hippolytus* I.19; and Tertullian's *De Animo* Ch. 34.

Hans Jonas. I will take it upon myself to extrapolate and paraphrase more pointedly, how Simon Magus might have reasoned, and how he could have expressed the same thoughts more plainly:

In First Person Singular: My mind (i.e. God's mind) is captivated by this feminine hypostasis of mine (i.e. the Ennoia). Initially I had in mind to create angels and archangels through her. But anticipating my intentions, this Ennoia descended to the lowest regions of my reach; and there this unruly female hastened to out-do me in the act of procreation, by herself. Relying on her own feminine potentials alone, she generated angels and powers by whom, in turn, this world was made. And these, her offspring, having been generated by her in estrangement and freedom from me, were totally ignorant of my presence; that is, of me who is the All-Father. Therefore, my Thought became pre-occupied with those angels and powers who came into being through her—through her who is my first Thought and Preoccupation. And my Thought was thereby dragged from high Heaven down toward those secondary principalities who scurry about to alter phenomena in the nether regions of the cosmos.

The Ennoia, on the other hand, has suffered at their hands all manner of abuse, so that she might be hindered from returning home to me, the Father. Their abuse of her went so far as to wrap her even in human flesh. For centuries, she migrated on earth from one female body into a next one. Thus degraded, in one instance, she was Helen on whose account the Trojan War was fought. But as of late, this Ennoia had been a whore in Tyre. And I, God Father, have descended to earth in human form as Simon Magus, to find her. I have come to save and return her home unto myself.

For the sake of this discussion, let us postulate a scenario by which Simon Magus might have begun his religious career with Hebrew theology within a general Hebrew mindset. Subsequently along the way he heard rumors of Philo's (c. 25 BCE—c. 50 CE angelology. Let us also assume that he might have become better acquainted with an extant strain of orthodox Egyptian theology. The upshot could have been his very musings about what possibly could have gone wrong within the Heliopolitan theogony. It became Simon's mission to fix that which at first possibly, and then definitely, would have gone wrong—the estrangement of the entire Tefnut-Mahet-Nut-Isis dimension, away from Atum, the Godhead.

With the mother of the world's creator-angels having already been saved by the religion of Simon Magus, the derivative world of humankind—the more distant offspring of bastard creators born from an estranged spouse of the Godhead—were thereby given an opportunity to become reconciled to God. Hans Jonas and other scholars doubt whether the Magus could have been the Samaritan magician mentioned in *Acts* 8:9-24. Be that as it may, in light of the Egyptian background of Simon's theology, we can now be a little less sure about rejecting this possibility.

According to our Christian sources, this magician Simon formerly had amazed people of the nation of Samaria. But he lost his followers to the Christian teacher Philip, and either in the aftermath of his followers' desertion, or by honest momentary excitement, the Magus himself could have tried to join the Christian movement.[167] Perhaps after realizing that his own followers have deserted him, and perhaps because a process of aging had diminished his infatuation for his incarnate Ennoia, this opportunistic cult leader might have assessed his options more realistically: If ever he were to become a religious celebrity again, it would have had to happen by way of joining the growing Christian movement to which his former admirers had converted.[168] Nevertheless, the episode of a later visit by Peter and John, narrated in *Acts* 14–24, would further have humiliated and checked the flamboyant Simon Magus.

Our well-nigh literal consideration of the aforementioned narrative in *Acts*, for the sake of discussion, does not judge, as most commentators do, whether a character like Simon Magus could be reformed. The systemic theological differences between the Simon of the heresiologists and the Christian gospel were not insurmountable. In fact, in the general tailwind of Egyptian theological reasoning, Simon Magus

---

[167] It may be significant that this same Apostle Philip is depicted, in *Acts* 8:26-40, as having converted an Ethiopian eunuch who added Palestine to his journey to Egypt. Philip may have been especially attuned to the Egyptian-Ethiopian mission field.

[168] I recognize that this hypothesis goes against the contemporary current of opinions. Of course, it is quite obvious that a shrewd magus, of Simon's caliber, never could become an ordinary childlike follower of Christ. I need not judge this possibility. But for the sake of historical fairness, we also must assume the possibility that Simon's initial Ennoia gospel could have begun as a message similar to that of Hosea. This Eighth Century BCE prophet claimed he married a harlot, Gomer, to exemplify God's love for Israel.

could have adjusted to the christology of his competitors with relative ease. Egyptian theology, for its core notion, acknowledged a process of divine begetting and emanation. And along that orthodox Egyptian dimension, it appears, Simon could indeed have asserted his identity with the Godhead. Christians asserted such an identity with the Godhead on behalf of their Lord. Jesus Christ, in the ancient Egyptian context, as Son of the Father, would have corresponded to Shu, or to Life (see *John* 1:4. In addition, all followers of Jesus were adopted as fellow siblings; that is, as brothers and sisters of Christ, thus as deify-able children of God.

Because of his chauvinism, Simon Magus might initially have divided his ontology into a male upper and a female lower portion. But let us give him the benefit of doubt. Let us assume for a moment that, upon joining the Christians, he actually could have dropped his outrageous self-theological posture. In that case, his outright claim to divinity could have gotten redefined, logically enough, as brotherhood with Christ. After all, the hypostases of Atum, Shu, Geb, Osiris, and Horus were all manifestations of the same divine Enneadic masculinity. But even on that basis, Christian heresiologists, surely, could not write off their hostility toward Simon Magus in terms of a harmless sibling rivalry between Simon and their Anointed Jesus.

The concept of a world, symbolized by a whore, in need of her Father's rescue and salvation—and the Father's damnation upon her refusal—has persisted in Hebrew as well as in Christian mythology. This idea echoes from the eighth century BCE prophet Hosea. It can be found prominently in the Nag Hammadi texts, and it has been adopted by Christians openly in *Revelation* 17:1. Thus, when and if the Christian Philip encountered Simon Magus in Samaria, the internal logic of their opposing gospels could theoretically be repaired with a parallel from the ancient Egyptian theogony. Both relied on the mythology of a Godhead's extended self-begetting. On the ancient Egyptian ontological basis, both cults seemed somewhat logical and could be utilized as related protest movements against imperialism and hyper-domestication.

Because both Jesus Christ and Simon had more or less associated their own persons with the Godhead, both their cults would, implicitly have weakened the claims of hyper-domesticator kings and emperors who claimed to be legitimate Sons of God. The gospels of both founders would have managed to dance—even gyrate circles around established grand-domesticators whom, summarily, both cults could have defined as lower "principalities and powers." Their respective divine claims both parodied the mandates of Roman imperial Sons of God.

But the greatest difference between the two cult founders lay in Simon's opportunistic effrontery. His Egyptian ontology and theology were utilized flippantly, to suit his infatuation with this uninhibited woman whom he had picked up in Tyre to keep him company. In sharp contrast thereunto stood the divine claim regarding Jesus, offering salvation with the seriousness of a savior's own death. Jesus shed his blood and thereby has established Christian salvation not only more dramatically than Simon, but also presented himself as being more unselfishly universalistic. Christian salvation could not be bought with silver—hence the balancing addendum in *Acts* 8:14–24. Christian soteriology went beyond privileges of founders and leaders. It insisted on everyone's rescue from sin and death. It exceeded any blessings that the Playboy-Savior Simon could have been offering.

Christian soteriology addressed the problem of death and boosted its answer with faith in "resurrection"—both, problem and answer were already basic concerns in the Heliopolitan heritage of Egypt. The intensity of Jesus's existential involvement over the full range of human problems, including the agony of a torturous death by the world's mightiest imperial judiciary, followed by the subsequent victory of faith in resurrection, these all added contrast. They gave Christendom its popular advantage for a serious resolution. More lighthearted and more selfish Wisdom cults, such as Simon's, were put morally on the defensive. They were challenged to try to match the inclusiveness and relevance of the Christian gospel.[169]

Some opponents denied in principle that Jesus, as Son of God could have died a sacrificial death. During times of relative tranquility and prosperity, the lighter Gnosis of Simon was marketable. But as the Roman Empire continued crucifying, the death and resurrection of

---

169 Hans Jonas, according to *The Gnostic Religion*, page 108, found some passages by which Simon identified himself with Jesus, as well as with the Holy Spirit. Whether *Acts* 8:9–13 represented a realistic Christian victory celebration over the cult of Simon Magus, or whether it was premature and wishful thinking, remains historically unclear. But Simon's typical Egyptian theological habit, of absorbing any competing theology, is apparent enough.

Jesus Christ won the contest of relevance. It remains noteworthy that specifically Christ's death, not his resurrection, evoked objections to Christianity from the Gnostic side. However, the resurrection of a genuine Son of God posed no problem to minds who already reasoned on the basis of imperial orthodox Egyptian antecedent religion. Such resurrection was a self-evident matter of common sense; it was necessary for defeating common death as well as the crucifying imperial Beast, and so to achieve salvation for everyone. The transformational Egyptian-style resurrection of Jesus Christ was necessary to defeat politically established, "made" and fake Sons of God. At stake was understanding the true nature of God and the true nature of Man—of Son of God as well as Son of Man.

We return to the Simon story in *Acts*, to ask our final historical question: Is it really improbable that the notorious Simon Magus could at some point have been welcomed by Christians? The question may also be asked and answered the other way around. Where else but in Christian circles, at that time, would the founder of a defunct competitor cult have been welcomed? Where else but under an extremely gracious and reconciling Father-deity?

The theological outreach, of a cult figure like Simon Magus, was overtaken by the more magnanimous and forgiving embrace offered by the Christian community, by the story of divine love for all of humankind. Does this sound impossible? Not at all. We know that another, far deadlier enemy of Christendom, Saul of Tarsus, succumbed to that forgiving Christian embrace and became the leading Apostle Paul. Thus *Acts* 8:9–13, even if as a literary product it might convey wishful thinking, nevertheless recognizes that the Christian welcome was extended ideally to all repentant enemies. Such openness and love were a direct consequence of the new and expanded vision of God as the Father Almighty, and of God's only-begotten Son, and of God's heavenly Kingdom. The gospel of Jesus presented the Godhead as the loving Father of estranged humankind, and as Lord of the World—thus, as the natural parent of males and females alike. Estranged and hostile cult representatives, if willing to convert, could with God's own interference and grace be turned into prime examples for the divine message of salvation.

Christianity, a Universal Salvation Religion

Universal Salvation Religions made their debut as answers to problems that were endemic to so-called "Civilization." Levitic stories, written to unite Israelite tribes for King David's monarchy, have narrated a dramatic escape of Israelite slaves from Egypt, led by the Egyptian-born Moses. These stories also have prefigured for the same people, five centuries later, their return from Babylonian Exile, and a thousand years later, Judaic responses to the Roman imperial occupation. John the Baptizer and Jesus of Nazareth anticipated the arrival of an "Empire of Heaven," ruled by God.

Universal salvation from oppressive Empire was also anticipated by Chinese Taoists, achieved with the help of several exceptionally "good" Heavenly Yellow Emperors. At their command served four-score-and-six good Heavenly Generals. Whereas for Mahayana Buddhism the realm of Samsara has not necessarily been political, the founding of Buddhism, a world religion instigated by a crown-prince, cannot have been completely a-political. Be that as it may, personal liberation from the clasps of Samsara was attained with the help of hosts of enlightened Bodhisattva-s.

Hopes for salvation have religiously and intermittently been offered to people who lived under tenacious systems of hyper-domestication or "civilization." Such systems have all been established in the world by conquest, by terror and various types of enslavement—invented by heroic gory-for-glory descendants of obsolescent Stone Age hunters who evolved into bandits and warriors.

17

The Reign of Heaven Spreading

I came to cast fire upon the earth;
and would that it was already kindled! (*Luke* 12:49)

And there appeared to them tongues as of fire, distributed
and resting on each one of them. And they were all filled with
the Holy Spirit and began to speak in other tongues,
as the Spirit gave them utterance. (*Acts* 2:3–4)

The first of these introductory quotations offers words of Jesus of Nazareth which express his hope that Reign-of-Heaven enthusiasm might spread. He envisioned the good news to spread like an all consuming Yahwistic wildfire.

The second quotation provides a glimpse of an early moment in Christian history when that "Empire of Heaven" enthusiasm had begun to spread beyond the confines of Judea. Its flames in northern Gentile lands were sustained by the presence of "spirit," a category of shamanic excitement that had become significant especially in the context of the more dualistic Indo-European ontology, including in lands that earlier were affected by Hellenic philosophy—where the distinction between "spirit" and "matter" was deemed common sense.

Jewish Piety a Challenge to Hellas

How did the struggle between philosophy and the remnant gods of Greek hyper-domestication end? The battle never came to a conclusion. The gradual decline of philosophy, in Greece, was accompanied by new rounds of hyper-domestication and conflict, beginning with a onetime student of Aristotle, Alexander the Great. Even as this book is being written, still in 2021, it will be read and criticized in the melee of ensuing religious hopes, and get caught up in the tailwinds of philosophical, scientific, and political disappointments. Our maxims of civilization and democracy are therewith placed on the scales.

Cronos, with his progeny of violent imitators and analysts, thus a great variety of mimics impersonating emanations of the All-Father, and rationally confident reformers, still are meeting each other on the same battle-grounds to attract a following, even on crowded city streets. It is a curious war in which most people change sides a few times during their life-spans. Some combatants crave to win authority and power, while weaker specimens love to think of themselves as redeemed and harmless grazing animals, as sheep, playful goats, or as never-eating playmates of Walt Disney's Bambi-deer—or such like. But then again, they rise to celebrate victories as if they had been sired by gods clothed in werewolf skins. Some arrive justified as if robed by God himself, as crusaders, warriors, or wolves in sheep clothing. Their uniforms, their tactics and battle cries do change and occasionally reverse themselves. Now you find wolves in sheepskin, and then again you see sheep donning the skins of wolves or crowning themselves with the feathers of raptors. But it still is a feud, similar to that which erupted ten to five millennia ago, here and there among apish hominids who came roaming as bandits, and later came riding on horseback, plundering and corralling sedentary humankind—docile vegetable eaters. Their raids were enabled by faith in weapons, religiously justified and blessed with an increase in numbers of male offspring. Their increase was driven not so much by any kind of generative love, as it was by the fear of defeat and death.

Fortunes in this battle of Hellas were won early on by Cronos who had crawled forth from a litter of titans. His progeny of hyper-domesticators, inspired by the castration mythology that Hesiod spun and wove to the perils of Heaven, ended in the celebration of swords and sickles—of anything that severs or analyzes. Fiery blessings of creation were converted into tools for hostile destruction. All of this was still happening when a simple gospel rumor started spreading from along the eastern shores of the Mediterranean Sea. This rumor undercut the narrative by which Hesiod celebrated the severance of Father Heaven from Mother Earth. Ancient predator mythology introduced Cronos with sickle in hand, as a divinely begotten son and as a patron of hyper-domestication.

Nevertheless, some Jewish folk and Christian converts knew how to tell the tale differently. They knew that humankind, having eaten from the forbidden tree of life, and from the tree of analytic knowledge, have brought on their own estrangement and gloom—long before Egyptian wise men have augured how humankind might have gotten created and thereupon, drifting in emanation, have gotten estranged from the Creator's love. Their drifting also has caused them to fall into gloom and death. Clever rulers of ancient Egypt cultivated a faith that allegedly enabled them to avoid death by transforming into Osiris and then be reborn by rising as Horus (Falcon) pharaohs. While their imperial faith was expressed in politics and ritual, it has endured three millennia to stabilize their dynasties and theocracy. In the end it evoked competing antithetical reactions, such as Judaism, Christianity, and Islam.

While Egyptian rulers learned how to dodge the dagger of Seth (God of Death) by the feat of resurrection, Hebrew prophets discovered that the blessings of their emancipation, won by their miraculous escape from Egypt—staged by Yahweh—could easily get lost by not accepting the Almighty's benign covenants. Then some Christians came wandering along the path, and they told the Heaven-and-Earth story of Hesiod in reverse. Not Heaven was mutilated when Cronos neutered his Father Uranos, but the ancestral heroes themselves got exiled from paradise. The analytic Cronos progeny has all along been cutting deeper—simply because they could. Immunized by the older Egyptian perspective, Christians suspected that the All-God-Father has decided to heal the wound of Uranos.

Half a millennium after Socrates, the philosophical battlefield of Hellas was still strewn with the mutilated corpses of gods. Story-tellers of myths and legends had castrated them in preparation. Sculptors chiseled and left them transfixed in compromised positions—for poets to ridicule as inert caricatures or as the actual remains of gods—as if fragmentary artifacts could be revered or critiqued as complete divine beings. To earlier supplicants, in Hellas, their gods still appeared vibrantly alive. But in the end, philosophers added analysis to the artistic mockery—onto the cadavers of divine personages depicted in stone and abandoned to museums and mythology.

Indeed, well-intentioned philosophers sometimes undertook to "upgrade" ancient gods, to rescue them from popular hyperbole and ridicule. They elevated them to the status of respectable philosophical concepts and principles. But unavoidably, they so reduced the gods of their fathers to the level of thinkable principles, aspects, or concepts that were small enough to be wrapped into compliant vocabulary and to suffer modulation by clogged finite minds.

Philosophical principles begin as living gods, getting "castrated." Being initially whole, they were abstracted down to functions. The Creator became "Creativity;" and the Judge became "Justice."

For a number of centuries, Near Eastern peoples have come under the spell and mission of Alexander the Great—a more recent Egyptianized imperial Son of God (of Amun), who believed he could spread Greek culture and inflict his genius by a method of conquest and destruction. Alexanders' successors tried to make amends for his violence and presented themselves more friendly, as Saviors (Soter=Σωτήρ).

In the wider Mediterranean world, divinely enthroned emperors have flaunted millennia-old traditions and insisted on having been born of divine parentage. In actual hope, god-fearing commoners within the larger Graeco-Roman environs preferred to hope for the Savior. But for the salvation of commoners to occur, those pretending kings and tyrants needed to be dishonored and defeated. But how?

Meanwhile, Jewish prudence has concluded that a human Messiah (an Anointed One, perhaps), a repetition of King David might be preferable. In any case, a genuine oppositional kind of Savior was needed, a Commoner Son of Man who, while being superior to imperial Son-of-God pretenders could enact God's version of—a Divine Comedy perhaps?—No!—a Divine Parody that had muscle.

Suddenly, during the first century CE, across the Hellenistic battle fields, littered with corpses of impotent gods, some more or less befuddling wars were being fought against hyper-domestication empires. A fresh religious breeze, a whiff of new life—of Shu—blew in from under the daily path of the Sun-god Ra.

On the philosophers' battlefield, littered with analyzed and fatally abstracted divinities, the Christian rumor generated stirrings of fresh hope. It spread as a theistic gospel along the Mediterranean coast-lands. It triumphed precisely in lands where, in the wake of hollow rationalizations, the architects of Hellenistic culture have left a severe religious void. The ancient void was precisely the wound of Father Heaven, gruesomely narrated in Hesiod's tale.

Notwithstanding the chisels of skilled artists, of analytic philosophical minds, of warrior swords and butcher knives and the finer scalpels of scientists, the world in which the multitudes of commoners live continued to produce myriads of creatures. The question necessarily arose, whether among all of God's creatures, the human species shall remain forever estranged, analytically and rebelliously severed from the larger glory of sunlit splendor? The answer of faith was: "Of course not!"

The new Christian rumor spread with common-sense ease. It spread as "good news" concerning recent stirrings on the part of the God-Father and maker of the world. It spread on the basis of ancient Egyptian theological presuppositions—of the ontology of emanation.

God the Father, the Creator of the world, is alive and well! He has in reality never gotten transfixed by Cronos into an artificer's graven model. He only has gotten categorized by human wit, fictitiously as a bubble of managed philosophical abstraction, as a principle. He never has gotten castrated by Hesiodic bards, by tellers of ever so gruesome ancient Greek tales.

The heavenly Father of Jesus Christ, who by the manifestation of his grace has gotten recognized again as the Father of all humankind, has shown himself to be more than a contemplative Aristotelian "First Cause," or an "Unmoved Mover." God the heavenly Father has demonstrated that his life and his virility endure, that he is alive and has begotten, and presented for the world to see, his only-begotten Son, Jesus, whom he also has anointed to help us win our salvation!

Many hitherto insignificant people—many of them sons, understandably—have since that time risen to testify to this fact. And it was this simple concrete and vibrant political God-story, the birth of a different and kinder Son of God, that breathed life and hope into the religiously depleted and over-analyzed world of Hellenism.

Some among the followers of Jesus recognized his divine status—"his glory, the glory as of the only begotten of the Father" (*John* 1:14). And thanks to Egyptian theology, by means of which the analytic temper of Greek philosophy was gently introduced to its Heliopolitan theological inheritance, all of this made some sense. The essentially holistic Christian gospel, a story of the heavenly Father begetting a Son, had to be communicated to a predominantly dualistic Indo-European audience. These northerners included people who distinguished philosophically between soul and body, spirit and matter, neutered Heaven and the ever-bearing Earth.

The basic Hesiodic severance—that is, the castration, abstraction, or "spiritualization" of Father Heaven, including his separation from an increasingly independent and materialized Mother Earth—could not be ignored when Christian apostles began to communicate and to explain their good news story to people in the North who reasoned analytically, abstractly and philosophically.

Graeco-Roman philosophers, naturally, criticized the Christian story from their own dualistic perspective. Thus, for purposes of communicating and defending the Christian gospel in Hellas, the spirit-and-matter dichotomy had to be acknowledged partway, as Paul had already done in *1 Corinthians* 15:44. But at the abstract philosophical level it needed to be skirted, subsequently. The Christian apostles had no choice but to define deity as being somehow "spiritual." A Father-Son theophany was impossible to tell in Indo-European lands without first acknowledging spirituality as an essential divine attribute. Paul's treatise in *1 Corinthians* 15 on the resurrection of "spiritual bodies," such—of all things!—is an early instance of this very necessary communicational adjustment. A holistic Father-and-Son story, which concluded with the resurrection of Jesus Christ as a whole person, had to be told dualistically in Hellas—to affirm that body and spirit are distinct and together. This mystery sprang from the vocabularies of languages of different civilizations, brought to collision by heroes who could recognize scarcely half of the "dragons" they were fighting.

Doctrines concerning the Holy Spirit and the Holy Trinity represent a larger theological umbrella of this accommodation to Indo-European thought and languages. With the trinitarian doctrine it was easier to explain deity as being "somehow spiritual." The Christian doctrine of the Holy Spirit may so be understood, historically, as a necessary emergency revelation, specifically to impress Indo-European dualistic minds, to facilitate their entry into the southern Mediterranean linguistic cloud. On hand of modulations among earlier languages it is sometimes possible to detect what has dawned in human consciousness, historically *how*, and ontologically *what*, and *why*.

Beyond the domain of Trinitarian theology, the fact remains historically significant that, alongside the predominantly masculine Trinity of Father, Son, and the neuter/feminine Holy Spirit, much of Mediterranean Christendom has continued to revere a "Mother of God." Her title is an appellation that, against the backdrop of Egyptian-Hellenistic process theology, specifies neither human nor divine attributes precisely. For many among simple and faithful folk, her descriptive title "Virgin" has become her first name. The name "Mary" was given to her for her journey as a human maiden. It subsequently has gotten shifted to the position of a middle name. She has become Virgin Mary Mother of God. Some stalwart Catholic Christians have meanwhile become convinced that in theological evolution she has caught up with her divine Son and has ascended into Heaven as well. Indeed, the "Queen of Heaven" may be appreciated as a significant achievement by all Christians who either belong to the feminine gender or to an egalitarian persuasion!

Universal Salvation Religion

Reactionary universalistic reform ideas, latently religious, have stirred from early on and have been evoked among people who were caught up in oppressive hyper-domestication environments. The self-respect and dignity of *Homines sapientes* cannot simply be surrendered to the first hyper-domesticator who arrogantly seizes what can be enslaved. **Religious aspirations sustain the hope for humble survival and security—hopes for safety and comfort amidst other people. These hopes mobilize residual strength for endurance under whatever reality-configurations pose greatest at the moment.**

Nevertheless, most early settlers who had fallen under the sway of hyper-domestication warriors have been forced by circumstances, sometimes voluntarily and with enthusiasm. There were times when grand-domesticators governed groups of subjects somewhat honestly, for the sake of mutual defense. But when rulers oppressed and exploited people, reactionary murmurs and protests surfaced, interspersed with aspirations for liberty and universal salvation. It happened under Egyptian grand-domestication earlier, as well as under Hebrew monarchs later. Protests were mobilized on behalf of, as well as against, established religion. At the secular end of the spectrum, the pursuit of atheistic philosophy has been a reaction against religiously legitimated political as well as cultural exploitation. Hyper-domestication, as defined in this book, implies that domestication efforts were excessive. Domestication trickery, learned during hunting and while taming animals, was also turned against conquered groups of the human species and even against the cults of more ancient totemic guardian gods. But wherever in this world injustices are on the increase, there the human spirit will, sooner or later, need to resist in the name of the greatest authority that is in sight.

Changes in a people's religion affect their styles of retreat behavior and their defensive reasoning. Thus, changes awaken signals of pain as well as of hope for a better future. Oppressed people will lament silently to their gods, or to their ancestors, long before they openly admit defeat to human sovereigns, tyrants or hyper-domesticators.

Thus, a people's readiness for universal salvation religion begins with reacting to the threats of hyper-domestication. It begins with defensive stirrings first, indistinguishable from penitential whining. But universal hopes for salvation eventually empower tangible activities. They refresh their meaning and discover new paths to freedom.

Seen from a historical perspective, Christianity was the eventual heir of the collective aspirations of prehistoric pioneers such as Abraham, Moses, Levitic priests, Judaic warrior kings and random prophetic spokesmen. Its universalism began with the religiosity of ancient Israelite rebel prophets, during ferment from within post-Exilic Judaism. Implicitly, Jesus of Nazareth has challenged the Roman Empire by inviting his followers to rise to the status of being children of God. The implications of this universalistic message were at odds with Greek and Roman imperialism, as well as with Pharisaic monotheistic piety and other legalistic ccommodations that were made within Judaism.

Greater Asia for Comparison

In the broader historical dimension, sedentary domestication cultures have "matured" into larger civilizations in several areas around the globe. Prototypes of these civilizations periodically have lapsed into warfare, slavery and rebellion. In the Near East, in South Asia and China, by the middle of the 1st millennium BCE, protest movements of the universal salvation type sprang up almost simultaneously against imperial ambitions. Some such sentiments and murmurs have predisposed the Mediterranean realm to understanding the Christian God-story as a God-inspired revolution. Similar "Axis-time" stories were bound to be intuited at many places in the world.

India

Five centuries before the Christian era, South Asia became the cradle of a number of universalistic religious movements. Hippie-monks, there, dropped out from routinized society in droves. They followed universalistic paths of escape, of asceticism and yoga, and moved toward spiritual liberation. If you happen to despise organization, then spiritual reform movements are easier to endure than violent military revolutions. The ontologically bankrupt theology of the Vedic grand-domestication cult, governed by cliques of priestly Brahmins, had degenerated to the point of near homonym-y of the name of their Godhead with the name of their caste—Brahman. Implicitly, minding their personal religiosity, these priests managed to re-apportion the Godhead to their own kind of "Brahmin Power," and as a matter of course, they thereby inflated their political and economic status, and their caste. Theology that justifies exploitation and unfair advantages therefore needed to be emphatically rejected by younger generations of sensitized religious dropouts.

The universalistic salvation of reform-minded reactionaries, in India during the fifth century BCE, was therefore tinged occasionally with atheism. Gautama, the Buddha, denied the reality of Brahman. He even denied the reality of a human "soul."[170] Apparently, he felt a need to block the path on which a grand-domestication deity, once rejected, could somehow get itself reincarnated in the guise of a human-like greater-than-human World Soul. This flank was left unguarded in Jainism and in some other Hindu universalistic movements.

The influence of stray impulses from Indian ways, on Mediterranean thought and culture, may not have been completely absent during the centuries preceding Alexander's military campaign eastward. Pythagorean philosophy and some of Plato's dialogs contain hints of this possibility. Perhaps as a backlash against Alexander's proselytizing campaign on behalf of "superior Greek culture," South Asian ideas could then have trickled more freely into the Near East. Negatively, Alexander could indeed have evoked some religious ferment in Egypt and Judaism—but as yet to an unknown degree.

Palestine

In contrast to Indo-European God-stories, Jewish theology evolved and was specifically institutionalized in opposition to the first great

---

170 Of curse, the Buddha's "no-soul" doctrine was also implied in his nirvanic experience. People who begin reasoning about "religion" with an epiphany of relief, sometimes conveniently ignore the fact that tension has preceded their moments of liberation. Viewed from the perspective of nirvanic bliss, the human soul as ego-awareness disappears. It is pushed beyond the range of analytic perception or greed. Religious proportionality was maintained by the Buddha by subordinating his no-soul, atheistic, under a greater-than-human No-Brahman, or No-World-Soul. The same linguistic twist that refutes "theism" also renders "atheism" meaningless.

hyper-domestication system in the Near East—ancient Egypt. As such it had, among Pharisees and Essenes, not yet become diluted as much as Brahmanic theology had been by legitimizing the extravagances of the Vedic cult of sacrifice. Nevertheless, John the Baptizer and Jesus of Nazareth, as offspring of Jewish parents, came as close to being like wandering Hindu dropouts and ascetics—as much as such a reaction was possible in the Hebrew-Aramaean context at the time. One should note that John the Baptizer and Jesus of Nazareth had inherited a still viable Jewish monotheism for their ontological bearings. Their universalistic reactions were rooted in their God-story and kept both of them within the margins of a rational Judaic theism.

All the same, Jesus ventured as far from Jewish orthodoxy as a wandering self-taught rabbi could go. Along the way he adjusted his high Judaic monotheism by insisting on lowly and selfless intimacy with the traditional God on High. He addressed the supreme deity as *Abba* (Daddy). In addition, his vision of the Empire of Heaven, on which he was focused, contradicted and challenged any dream of grand-domestication that ever was held on Earth. Implicitly it challenged all attempts of acquiring power by holding slaves and it excluded any justification for hyper-domestication or institutionalized ranking.

The harbingers of such a radical social message were, of course, quickly removed from the scene. Measured by standards of cultural progress, as religious thinkers, John and Jesus scored negatively. But when Jesus was nailed to a Roman cross, his insistence on human salvation began to show more clearly. He gave back his breath to God. His death was understood to have been as much a part of his life, as were his teachings. Followers of Jesus abruptly proclaimed that, though he was crucified and has died, their teacher actually returned to join again the eternal life of God the Father. The Empire of Heaven was a contrary type of empire, not subject to rules by which hyper-domestication cultures were being forged and managed.[171]

The utter self-neglect of Jesus, his vulnerability and willingness to die, made him an ideal, different, and desirable king of the down-trodden. He was thereby well suited to be a king in the anti-imperial Reign of

---

[171]Complete theological bankruptcy within the Judeo-Christian tradition, and atheist alternatives on a larger scale, may have begun taking shape among ruling circles of Sadducees. For massive theological decay and atheism to spread in Jewish tradition, radical atheism had to await "scientism" in the 19th and 20th centuries, in Europe.

God that he proclaimed. Moreover, inasmuch as the best emperors of the Roman hyper-domestication system, when they were being given their full post-mortem *apotheosis* (deification) rites, were actually deceased, so the Jesus story was competing and winning against their ritualism on the score-card of full "death and resurrection" as well.

With a commoner human victim enthroned as the eternal King of Heaven, the Christian kingdom movement was confessedly not *of* this world. But it was demonstrably *in* the world to linger and to stay. The concept of an empire ruled by God was present in Egypt three thousand years before the time of Jesus. But Christians preferred to have their Anointed, their martyred "monarch," safely in the Kingdom of Heaven—not in a dusty pyramid on Planet Earth.[172]

Bequest of the Mother Religion

"Out of Egypt have I called my son," a sentence from *Hosea* 11:1, was quoted in *Matthew* 2:13–15 to support the story about the holy family's flight to Egypt. Was this brief addition to the nativity story of Jesus intended to hint at the broader nativity of Christian theology in ancient Egypt? Did some of the first Christians sense the Egyptian direction into which their own God-story apparently was luring them?

A turning point in sacred Jewish history, an Exodus in reverse, the flight of the Son of God from Palestine to Egypt, is implied by the structure of this story. If we allow ourselves another historical allegory related to Egypt—then Isis, as the Egyptian divine Madonna with her Horus child, a representative of the Enneadic feminine Tefnut-Nut lineage, passed her mantle on to the unsuspecting Jewish mother of Jesus. But let us leave these hints aside for a while, and turn to other historical glimpses. Without doubt, the Christian movement was first evoked

[172] Whereas living Roman emperors could avail themselves of the title "Son of God" in anticipation, for inferiors this honorific title obviously meant political flattery and paying homage. The official deification (apotheosis) of an emperor was approved by the Senate and staged after an emperor's death. Nevertheless, ruling sovereigns could support their mandates earlier, on the basis of forward anticipation and projection. They ruled by divine mandate on the basis of anticipated "afterlife credit." Admittedly, the pharaoh's dependency on heaven, could occasionally raise the standard of balanced governing and decency, on the part of more sensitive emperors. Nevertheless, following the "Jesus Event" (which encompassed the reigns of Augustus Octavius and Tiberius) all Roman emperors who had risen to the status of gods, were eventually neglected by people who accepted Jesus Christ, the Crucified, as their preferred Son of God.

Figure 14. Isis with Horus child.
Photos by author. Courtesy of Cairo Museum.

Figure 15. Roman Madonna, from Egypt. Transitional types between Isis iconography, above in Figure 14, and the Christian Madonna with child.
Photo by author: Courtesy of Cairo Museum.

explicitly by Hebrew "Reign of God" radicalism, which then was adopted *implicitly* into the Nicene creed. The first apostles of Jesus Christ drew their enthusiasm not so much from their Lord's teachings about the Reign of Heaven arriving, than they drew what subsequently they learned by personal empathy with their Lord's death and resurrection. With the exception of a few passages, Paul, the Apostle, discontinued mentioning the Empire of God. Instead, he preferred the less political and more intimate "Body of Christ" mysticism. This enabled Christians as a community of believers to participate humbly in the death and resurrection memory of Christ—and thereby engage themselves to some extent with esoteric conceptual fragments that may have been circulating among Pharisees and Sadducees. For massive theological decay to enter Judaism, radical atheism had to await Scientism in the 19th and 20th centuries, in Europe. Meanwhile the Christian God-story for Egyptians—the proclamation of God having begotten and sent a Son, and of the Son having been born, having died, risen and returned to the Father—resonated with the broader spectrum of ancient Egyptian emanation ontology. It resonated on the common-sense Egyptian basis for statecraft as well as religion—thus understandably, it resonated also with the prior aspirations of Egyptian commoners who began to find general uplift in their Christian reorientation.

It has long been suspected by historians of religions that knowledge about a general death-and-resurrection process, which in early Egyptian religion was associated with Osiris mythology, could have aided the rationale of the Christian story in the wider Hellenistic world.[173] The structure of ancient Egyptian soteriology, based on the ontology of a process of emanation, could be accepted as common sense. It made it possible to believe that the Son of God rose from among the dead as his essential *ka* and so returned to the Father. This also helped explain why, for a while before he eventually ascended into Heaven, some of the Jesus apparitions continued to be seen as what in ancient Egypt would have been called *ba*. In tune with ancient Egyptian logic was also the notion that Jesus Christ, even though he returned to the Father, remains eternally present among his followers. Osiris-ized Egyptian pharaohs expected to govern and dispense Mahet forever. Jesus Christ, after his ascension into Heaven, continued to exist as *ka* in his Father's Kingdom, as emanation of the God-Father essence. And he continued to radiate this same essence as Son, as divine love and Holy Spirit. The radiation of his divine light is celebrated visibly, with many symbolic candles at Christmas and with Easter sunrises.

Greek philosopher minds mocked the Apostle Paul in Athens (*Acts* 17:32) when he began to talk about Christ's resurrection from the tomb. Greek dualists and rationalists believed that the human soul was

---

173 See Ninian Smart, *The World's Religions*. Englewood Cliffs, NJ, Prentice Hall, 1989; p. 199.

liberated at death from its material body—as from an accidental prison. In contrast, Paul reasoned after the mode of Egyptian *ka* essences and *ba* apparitions. He felt the homeward suction of the Reign of Heaven procreational process. Divinely contributed life remains subject to divine love, redemption, and transformation. In his Christian Egyptian mode, Paul was liberated from the Greek Hesiodic habit of seeing Heaven as a one-time pro-creator at the beginning, who barely survives as a materially neutered Spirit. The Apostle Paul did not see God the Father severed from the realm where human fathers still are active and where living bodies still are being brought forth by birth.

Whereas Indo-European dualism forced the category of "spirit" into prominence for Christendom, Egyptian monistic ontology and logic made it possible to believe in one God as Father, Son, and Holy Spirit together. The presence of the Holy Spirit in a Holy Trinity was not only an adaptive missionary strategy to address Indo-European dualists, as we have suggested. The third person in the Christian Trinity could be recognized representing the Christian church as well as the new "City of God" that was dawning for the Empire of God. The three divine hypostases of the Christian Holy Trinity resemble closely the Egyptian trinity of Atum the Father, Shu the Son, and Tefnut-Mahet the divine wisdom and the congregational human order. Thus, the Holy Spirit, as member of the general Holy Trinity, gradually has absorbed into itself the functions of antecedent gods and angels who also were "spirits." Holy Spirit was an envisioned presence in the communion of saints within the Church, embracing the Indo-European ontological domain of spirit, as well as the entire Hand-Tefnut-Mahet compilation of ancient Egypt.

We are now prepared to contemplate Paul's own emphasis on his doctrine of resurrection, according to the aforementioned episode in *Acts* 17. We are left with no uncertain hints about Paul's reasoning regarding the mysteries of transformation and resurrection. Earlier words by Epimenides and Aratus contained genuine premonitions for the theology of the Apostle Paul:

In him we live and move and have our being... [and] we are indeed his offspring. (*Acts* 17:28)

Egyptian theology, derived from a theogony of begetting and of emanation, has enabled educated Hellenistic Christians, later, to rationalize their faith in an only-begotten Son who entered the world as the Logos, as the divine Creative Command, thus, as the Word of God made visible. It seems safe to say that in all the religious literature of the Hellenistic Period, no summary of ancient orthodox Egyptian theology is more eloquent than the prologue to the Gospel of *John*:

> In the beginning was the Word, and the Word was with God, and the Word was God. He was in the beginning with God; all things were made through him, and without him was not anything made that was made. In him was life, and the life was the light of men. The light shines in darkness, and the darkness has not overcome it. (*John* 1:1–5)

Another favorite passage, from this same, most Egyptianized among the Christian gospel texts, resonates still in perfect logical harmony with ancient Egyptian soteriology. What harm is there in knowing, now, that the love which the Father has shown toward his world has been prefigured millennia earlier by the creative fatherly self-love of what back then was named "Atum!" This divine sentiment was narrated by ancient Heliopolitan theologians still clumsily, essentially to benefit the deified imperial royalty. Ordinary Egyptian folk usurped these benefits by trickle-down imitation.

To northern dualist-s the evolving Christian story sounded foreign enough to remain a mystery. Moreover, in the original Christian narrative there was no need, yet, for adding the northern dualistic fix of an "immaculate" Virgin Mother. The Egyptian incarnation of a Son of God was understood from the outset with help of a quasi-sexual metaphor, which means, as a process of divine begetting. It was God's own seed—*ka* and *ba*—made manifest in a "natural" process of emanation. It was obvious enough for some people to recognize the divine nature in the person of Jesus Christ. (Remember: by their fruits you shall recognize them!) The total pattern of the divine activity, of God procreating and of presenting light and logos by emanation—of begetting a Son (formerly Shu and later Jesus Christ) for the life and salvation of everyone—is natural and rational ancient Egyptian ontology and soteriology. To exceed the imperial Egyptian aim of justifying hyper-domestication, the salvation that is offered in the Christian proclamation is universalized for all of humankind:

> For God so loved the world that he gave his only Son, that whoever believes in him should not perish but have everlasting life. For God sent not the Son into the world to condemn the world, but that the world might be saved through him. (*John* 3:16f)

The Christian "Empire of Heaven" allegory was internalized in the context of Egyptian emanation soteriology. Its political aspect was compromised eventually in exchange for a new kind of blotchy and perhaps a somewhat more considerate Holy Roman Empire. This Christianized empire was being balanced, checked, and stabilized by whatever retreat-oriented counter weights Christian piety could embrace. As the Holy Roman Empire evolved, later, amidst philosophized remnants of Indo-European dualism, Christendom's reliance on ancient Egyptian theological thought structures remained visible. The Egyptian world-view of emanation was philosophized by so-called "Neo-Platonists" who supplied the Christian state with ontological context and provided the Empire with a measure of theological justification.

Following the lead of earlier Alexandrian theologians, Augustine of Hippo infused Egyptian structure into Christian soteriology to a point where its identity became almost indistinguishable. He personalized Egyptian soteriology and clarified how all estranged human hearts, while they dwell here in this world, are destined to be restless until they might find their rest again in God.

At the hands of Christian apologists and church fathers, Neo-Platonism was destined to become the serum with which the Christian doctrine could be immunized against Hellenic philosophy's scientific god-killing venom. The scarcely disguised brand of Egyptian mystic philosophy, in Neo-Platonism, shielded Christian theology against philosophy's digestive acids of arrogant pluralistic analysis. The designation "Neo-Platonism" implied that Plato was its godfather. But actually, the same presumed "Platonic" cover, which at Alexandria shielded Ammonius and Plotinus against the bona fide Greek analyzer-intelligentsia, also protected an Origen and other early Christian theologians against the same.

A full historical study of Christian beginnings in Egypt would have to pay special attention to all pioneer theologians in Alexandria, such as Clement, Origen, Dionysius the Great, and others—and to their influence on the belief systems of later North Africans like Tertullian of Carthage and Augustine of Hippo. Any attempt to do justice to all this, obviously, would bloat our book beyond its permissible bindings. Nevertheless, in light of what has here emerged, other scholars will sooner or later want to reconsider the Egyptian heritage of these early Church Fathers, one by one. The present book is limited to offering a sketch of four large Near-Eastern religious and philosophical traditions, viewed together over an extended period. Part Four of this book expects to provide no more than traces of the Egyptian influence on early Christian theology. Residual tasks must be postponed for more specialized historians of these traditions.

If one skips the first three centuries of Christian history and points directly to what the Christian orthodox creed has officially become, the general Egyptian influence can be contemplated quite boldly. The formative struggles for Christian theology—Christology, Mariology, and Numenology—all demonstrate in Mediterranean thought the presence and awareness of ancient Egyptian emanation thought which, early on, had been challenged by Indo-European dualism. Early church-struggles and controversies demonstrate the triumph of ancient basic notions that once belonged to the legacy of Egypt. The strong theological bequest of Christendom's Egyptian mother religion evoked a series of very interesting birth right controversies. These were localized streaks of pain which, still today, need to be studied and understood as birth pains in the formation and evolution of early Christianity.

The Invincible Sun, *Sol Invictus,* in Rome

Significant veneration of a solar-linked deity named Mitra (Iranian Mithra), or the combination Mitra-Varuna, can be found back in the oldest Indo-Aryan collection of shamanic chants, the *Rig Veda,* which may contain pre-Invasion oral traditions older than 1,500 BCE. Traces in later Vedic times and in Persian Mithraism, have been found alongside names of other Vedic gods on the Hittite Bogaz-Köy tablets. Some recent scholarship, inspired by worldwide minutiae, has tried to derive the entire Jesus of Nazareth tradition from an Asian Mitra cult and, therewith, explain away any plausible historical clues from the Christian founder stories themselves. Thanks to the homophony of certain words in English, one writer has managed rather amazingly to straddle historical questions concerning "Sons of God" all the way to "Suns of God."[174]

---

174 See for instance Acharya S./DM Murdock, Mithra: *The Pagan Christ: The Devil Got there First,* www.Truth-be-known.com/mithra.htm. But see also Roberts, Alexander, *The Ante-Nicene Fathers,* vols. 1 and 4 (Buffalo: The Christian Literature Publishing Co., 1885). See also *The Cult of Sol Invictus,* in www.sabbathcovenant.com/doctrine/cult_of_sol_ invictus.htm.

The historical connection between South Asian religion and Roman cult practice is rendered dubious when the "Invincible Sun-god" *(Sol Invictus)* cult of the Roman imperial military is found linked with Mithra's virgin birth from a rock—and is utilized in this manner as a stepping stone along the swampy path of supposed historical connections. While virgin birth stories and mother-rocks can be found in folklore throughout the world, neither of these are essentials of the Christian religion. With some measure of delight, I dare to remind the Murdocks, that the mythic Indo-Iranian rock from which anciently gods could have been born, could not have been a virgin rock anymore. According to the older *Rig Veda* collection, the god Indra, and even a still earlier herder deity in pre-Invasion mythical times, had already struck the rock with a club, to have cattle born, have them emerge to enable herding in the world.

While many words and gestures of Homines sapientes have come to represent memories, from among which some have acquired mythological standing—such as birthing, swaddling, washing, eating, fasting, vomiting, bleeding, healing, rejoicing, mourning—most of these surely were also associated with a greater number of memories that turned into humdrum profane or gladly forgotten emotions. Elephants, whales, and monkeys sprinkle water. But the gap between their activities and human initiatory baptisms is extremely wide. Gaps between incidental and sacramentally reasoned gestures vary greatly. Some novices, such as the soldiers of the Emperor Aurelian (270-275 CE)—especially from 274 CE onward—were officially empowered by *Sol Invictus* as divinely obligated killers. The ritualized sharing of sacramental bread and water in that cult meant one thing, while the bread and wine in the sacramental meal instituted by Jesus of Nazareth surely meant the opposite. Jesus led his disciples in contemplating divine dying for human salvation whereas, with the sacraments of *Sol Invictus*, soldiers harked back thousands of years to semi-divine heroic hunter status. Their cult activities obliged them to kill in unison, on command—and when commanded, even to crucify such a divine-human victim as the Christians believed Jesus Christ to have been. Moreover, bread and water, or fermented wine, were basic vegetarian food substances for human survival. Over the millennia, peasants by the millions survived on not much more. And very few of their rations have come close to assuming the significance of the sacramental elements in the Christian Communion meal.

Sol Invictus, the Invincible Sun-god, was officially integrated into the higher Roman pantheon in 274 CE by the Emperor Aurelian, after he had succeeded in restoring the Empire to an acceptable earlier size. This emperor had earned sufficient patriotic merit and divine status to dare promote his Sun deity into the circle of other higher gods who had already been positioned as victorious Roman war deities—Quirinus, Mars, Jupiter, Apollo, and others. All these older gods, to the extent that their assistance as gods of war was acknowledged, and that victorious emperors identified with them, could be addressed as *Invictus* (Invincible).

This divine epithet, obviously harkens back three thousand years farther, to the Egyptian Sun-god Ra and his totemic manifestations of Horus Falcons, embodied as the personalities of deified pharaohs. To the emperor Aurelian the Sun-deity was known in Greece as Apollos and Helios, and in Persia as Mithra. But no! "Mithra the pagan Christ," named by Murdock, never was a genuine oil-daubed "Christ." Rather, he was a deity of warriors and killers. The historical links of Graeco-Roman religion appear to have been several times stronger with ancient Egypt than ambassadorial relations between Persia and Rome could ever have been.

The most august first Roman emperor, Augustus Octavius, derived his initial divine status from his deified sponsor, the martyred Caesar. Octavius's chance to govern an empire had already been arranged with Caesar's help before the latter was stabbed by Brutus. Caesar Augustus Octavius then acted the role of a god in Egypt. As a governing Horus-offspring of Isis, he belonged to the Egyptian All-God's divine family which, in this book, we have introduced earlier as the Heliopolitan Ennead—a Nine-foldness of high gods in Egypt. Octavius's larger ancestral cult deity was the Heliopolitan All-God, Atum-Ra. Augustus Octavius, while governing Egypt, learned to act the role of being a god, a ruling son of Isis. Egyptian images of Augustus in the presence of other gods, can be found carved into the remains of two Egyptian temples—see Figure 16 for one of these. Thus, there has been a Roman emperor who prepared the way for an Invincible Sun-god in Rome long before Aurelian's officiating in 274 CE. It was Rome's first emperor, Caesar Augustus Octavius. He was post-humously depicted on coinage with a radiate solar crown—as were living emperors from Nero (CE 65) onward, reaching approximately to the religious watershed of the Nicene Council.

Bergmann's political explanation, concerning Octavius's radiate crown, as having been "designed to disguise the divine and solar connotations which otherwise could have been politically controversial," is possibly a correct suspicion. Augustus Octavius's role, as Horus-like deity in Egypt, as an inbred begotten offspring of the All-God, Atum-Ra, was by emanation from the Heliopolitan Ennead a historical marker to trace Egyptian Sun-worship in Rome, all the distance from Augustus to Aurelian's enhancement of the Invincible Sun cult, in 274 CE. This evolution is traceable on Radiate-Sun-embossed coins as far as Constantine, approximately to 325 or 326 CE.[175] Personified Sun mythology, in Western scientific thought, reached all the way into Copernicus's *De Revolutionibus Orbium Coelestium* (ca. 1542).

Aurelian's focus on Sol Invictus has followed the victorious military campaigns by which he restored the Roman Empire to an acceptable size. The emperor has motivated his troops with mysterious victories, facilitated by the Invincible Sun-god, with whose help he restored and stabilized the Empire. In 274, on December 25th, after having built another Sun temple in Rome, the victorious emperor Aurelian has dedicated the edifice specifically to *Sol Invictus*. He consecrated and positioned the Sun-god statue that he recently had confiscated from the *Sol Invictus* temple in Palmyra. Aurelian placed this statue in his stately temple-home, built by a victorious and a most worthy devotee, the invincible Emperor Aurelian himself.

It was this religious/political act of the victorious Emperor Aurelian, as Pontifex Maximus, that not only placed all of Roman military might under the Invincible Sun-god, but also focused the temple's date of dedication on December 25th. Unbeknown to Aurelius himself, he positioned the date of the winter solstice celebration, in the Roman calendar, for another deity to inherit. Christian converts continued to celebrate the winter solstice and dedicated the night before that celebration to the memory of their own Savior's birth. Jesus Christ was born to bring light and life to humankind. Prior consecrated temple sites and official festival days were sufficiently neutral to be inherited from antecedent systems of faith. Such inheritances legitimated peripheral cultural customs which then inspired fresh religious questioning and thought. Continuity from one ontology to the next requires that some old concepts, and many words, remain understood for communication. With an excess of discontinuities in language and

---

[175] cf. https://en.wikipedia. org/wiki/Sol_ Invictus.

customs, with unnaturalized innovations, the blotches of cultural ignorance grow larger. Fresh embryos of thought must be laid into "safe nests" of intelligible history, understood as manifest destiny.

The "Conversion" of Constantine to Christianity

The father of the Emperor Constantine was Flavius Valerius Constantius, a military officer in the western portion of the Roman Empire. He became a caesar (a deputy emperor) under the Emperor Maximian. He also was a leading member in the Invincible Sun cult that Aurelian had raised to prominence in 274 CE. This implies that Constantine, the son of Constantius, was made not only a military commander, but also a leader in this cult of warriors. In fact, after he had fought his way to become the supreme ruler of the entire Roman empire, Constantine continued to identify with the Invincible Sun-god on his coinage. However, the gradual discontinuation of Constantine's Sol-Invictus coinage signified a shift toward Christianity in Egypt, Greece, as well as Rome. Thereby the place of honor of the Invincible Sun-deity was vacated to become occupied by Jesus Christ.

When Constantine's struggle for the purple robe began in earnest, all major cults of earlier Roman deities whom Roman emperors hitherto had cultivated—this much can reasonably be inferred—were already enlisted to support competitors otherwise situated. Decades earlier, Aurelian's introduction of the Sol Invictus cult to his military, has shown the strategy that Constantine could emulate. He chose a foreign and still insufficiently defined deity to sponsor his wars. Aurelius set the example on how a Roman emperor might invite a universal deity from anywhere in the far-flung empire to support his cause.

Of course, it remains forever doubtful whether the "historical Jesus of Nazareth" would ever have lent his name to legitimize a Roman war that was to be credited to him. But Constantine demonstrated that with the sponsorship of Jesus Christ—whose divine rank he would see better defined in due time—he could win wars. He began to unify Christian theological opinions into an inclusive organization that would support his imperial politics. In the year 325 CE—acting as Pontifex Maximus, as Supreme Pope and High Priest of all religions deemed legitimate in Rome—Constantine summoned 318 Christian bishops to Nicaea to have them agree on the basic tenets of their faith. He gambled on the compatibility of this religion with his imperial plans, and he tried to harmonize his own imperial ambitions with the theology and soteriology held by the Christian leaders. The precise content of Christological convictions was of secondary importance to him. But an agreement on essentials, affecting the theological and imperial unity, was paramount for him. With his strategy of making Christianity useful for Rome, this emperor helped to tame and to organize. As he was doing already before the Nicene Council, he continued to win and to justify wars under the aegis of Jesus Christ. Yes, he would rule on behalf of many gods, but as a monotheist he served the combined almighty Christian Trinity.

Nevertheless, Constantine's bet on the Christian endorsement eventually cost him his chance of ever winning Octavian/Egyptian divine Son-of-God status for himself. But, as heir of the Aurelian Invincible Sun cult he had learned how an official Pontifex Maximus—as grand-domesticator—can escort any deity, God Almighty or Trinity, into the temples or churches of faithful supplicants, to be housed there surrounded by strong walls, at the low cost of being maintained with pomp and circumstance. Gods do love to enter stately churches, being hyper-domesticated and housed as if in stately barns. Kneeling next to ordinary supplicants and subjects, a grand-domesticator can appear balanced and justified. The paths on which hyper-domestication can be established somewhat peaceably leads past the minds of subjects who can be comforted, to feel secure.

Constantine knew, well before he called the First Council to Nicaea, that a supportive church is worth more to him than an Octavian "Son of God" title, scavenged from ancient Egypt. People in the Indo-European realm did not understand Egyptian theological status anyhow. But long before Octavius, Aurelian or Constantine, took hold of the reins of the Roman Empire religiously, ancient rulers of Egypt had been refining and staging their mystery plays of hyper-domestication—to legitimize themselves with a blend of soteriology and pretense. Pyramids, temples, and church buildings still sit as enduring witnesses to the immensity of their stage paraphernalia.

Constantine's conversion to Christianity comprised more than a change of heart or emotions. His Christian subjects reasoned still with Egyptian hearts, whereas the emperor was busy constructing an organizational system that would conform to his ambitions. Two versions of the story of Constantine's conversion are extant. Perhaps the first version is modeled on the second. Or, perhaps either version was not quite convincing when it was told by itself.

Constantine's vision, leading up to the Milvan Bridge battle, in 312 CE, legitimized his authority over the Western portion of the Empire. While preparing for this battle, the emperor looked toward the Invincible Sun that had inspired Roman troops since Aurelian. However, Constantine claimed to have seen the *Chi Rho* (☧ —first two Greek letters of Χριστὸς—Engl. CHRIST) plus the *Ἐν Τούτῳ Νίκα* (in this sign conquer) written in sunlight. "Looking toward the Sun" could also be allegorized as having seen the divine light of Christ.

Constantine adjusted the insignia of his army to his vision, and he won the key battle against his competitor Maxentius for the Western Roman Empire. After having so found and proven his personal invincible war deity in *Χριστός (XP)*, he gradually began neglecting the older Roman high gods of war; though, he retained their images on his coinage for eight additional years. He ruled concurrently as head of the Empire and as the Pontifex Maximus of all religions of Rome. So he encouraged building pagan temples as well.

A similar vision of Constantine has also gotten recorded for the time when he prepared for the decisive battle at Adrianople, in 324. There Licinius was the last to stand in his way of bringing also the Eastern Roman Empire under his control. A gilded and shiny Chi Rho military standard, a *labarum* (see Figure 18b, below), was used to attack and to perplex the enemies and to embolden Constantine's own legions. About 34,000 enemy soldiers, we are told, were killed in the battle that decided the organizational and religious destiny of the recombined Empire. The point at which both of Constantine's "conversion" accounts agree, regarding his preference of the Christian religion, is the fact that he credited the power of Jesus Christ with helping him win his decisive battles for the Empire.

According to the account of the Milvian Bridge Battle (312 CE), Constantine henceforth began supporting Christianity and to pay homage to the triune God for this victory. The next year, in the Edict of Milan he still flattered the old gods and ordered tolerance toward all religions. Constantine reunited the Empire by also winning the Eastern portion, and as Pontifex Maximus he organized and unified Christendom as the religion of his choice.

As Pope of all Roman religions, Constantine understood how religious controversies can erode the unity of an empire. Unity was needed for fortification as well as for pre-emptive mobilization.

For any government on this planet, there is no such thing as a religiously neutral mandate. Wherever human contestants engage in lethal struggle, some sort of greater-than-human endorsement will eventually be needed—to justify, to legislate and stabilize. Not even an atheistic democracy can extricate itself from the social necessity of shifting the blame for fatalities onto super-human necessity.

As suggested several pages earlier, anyone is entitled to wonder, in their own Greek minds, or Egyptian hearts, whether three centuries earlier the historical Jesus of Nazareth would have supported such an emperor's ambitions. The three founders of Christianity—John the Baptizer, Jesus of Nazareth, and Paul of Tarsus, left no advice on how an active Roman emperor should operate—standing with one foot in the mundane Roman Empire while getting his other foot redeemed in the Empire of Heaven as a follower of Jesus Christ.

In any case, Constantine's new decrees have favored faith in the God of Christianity—including the Trinity, with Christ and his Kingdom of Heaven message keeping sway—all to be fitted into an emperor's vision of a mightier and better Roman Empire. The anti-imperial Christian apocalyptic, early on, has characterized the Roman Empire and its warring emperors as being Satan's own. The Empire, as a "Beast," had not only been slaughtering Jesus Christ as God's only-begotten Son, or as a precious sacrificial Lamb, but has periodically also persecuted the followers of this martyred divine Lamb. From a Christian perspective, Constantine's apparent conversion, and the ensuing events, were nothing short of a miracle. The Roman Emperor and Pontifex Maximus, whose initial duty was to seek help from the full array of Roman deities—especially from established gods of war—strategically has chosen to support the cult of a crucified foreign victim, executed by Roman legionaries. An increasing number of people were willing to identify with this sacrificial "antithesis" as an alternative to the periodical civil terror that Roman "Sons of God" had been inflicting on them.

The "conversion" of Constantine did not happen in a bare theological or non-political context. He "saw the light" while he positioned his soldiers for battle. He designed a mysterious Christian emblem to magnify, to define and justify the goal of his battles. He flaunted the Chi Rho—☧—Christ Epigram on the shields of his soldiers; or, at least displayed the same insignia on his shiny *labarum* standard. It kept his front lines visible and united. He ordered his *labarum*-carriers to move along the front lines of the battle to critical points .

Could Constantine just as well have relied on the older established Roman gods of war—on Jupiter, Mars, Quirinus, Apollo, or Sol Invictus? No, not at all! Even the deity, whose radial crown Constantine wore on his coinage, has sponsored warlords whose armies he faced as contestants on the battlefield. The war-god cults functioned as political parties, as alliances of soldiers who endorsed their commander. Constantine's personal religious legitimization and the loyal support of his troops were essential for his success and survival. To prevail among Rome's eternally warring gods, among cults and entrenched senatorial factions, an emperor needed a unique and startling divine mandate. The best means to victory that Constantine saw was a benign, almighty and theologically still pliable deity. To fight and to grasp the Empire for reform, Constantine dared to shock everyone.

So he attacked with the divine help of Rome's most famous—crucified and supposedly shamed—victim. He mocked and shocked Rome's pride for superior jurisprudence—its method of execution by crucifixion. He let a crucified deity stare right back into the faces of the Roman establishment. For contrast, he awed his soldiers by aligning them at the divine side of his conflicts. All battles that his guilty warriors fought for Jesus Christ ended in victory. In the aftermath of such success, it would have been foolish for any emperor to abandon his strategy.

The full title, "Only Begotten Son of God," was ascribed to Jesus Christ at the Council of Nicaea. The Savior's resurrection affirmed his divine status by ancient Egyptian imperial and political standards. Constantine understood the political significance of the resurrection claim for the war deity whom he utilized. It was a gamble that brought threefold success. Constantine thereby got himself aligned with a greatest mentionable deity, an Almighty Trinity.

How thoroughly did this emperor actually submit to his Christ deity? The bull sacrifice in archaic Roman war-god cults probably had been practiced some eight thousand years and it had long lost the meaning it had for Stone Age hunters. In his early years, Constantine participated in these rites. But later, while turning to favor Christianity, he gambled on accepting an extreme contrary for his war deity—a crucified (shamed) and resurrected "Lamb of God." He built churches and began to neglect pagan temples. According to Eusebius he abolished crucifixion, outlawed infanticide as well as the abuse of slaves and peasants. He made Sunday a day of rest. Disagree if you wish; but this pagan Pontifex Maximus understood "religion."

Constantine sought a fresh coherent religious foundation for his enterprise. He knew that his Roman Empire could not be united, stabilized or kept tranquil far into the future—not by way of invoking the protection of the gods of his enemies whom, fortunately for the Emperor's reforms, Christians had already written off as senile daemons. He realized that he needed to defeat his imperial competitors without, in the aftermath, becoming obligated to their compromised war-gods. He certainly could never have won the trust of peace-loving people to help him keep his competitors low.

Bart Ehrman, a popular historian these days, emphasizes that Constantine did not like the slaughter of sacrifices which were part and parcel of the established pagan cults.[176] It may be so, even though this emperor was not squeamish about shedding blood in other situations. I have elsewhere explained such slaughter sacrifices as vestiges of orthodox Stone Age hunting campaigns. From some animal carcasses, killed and butchered by ancient hunters, portions were cut and given to divine sponsors, to atone for the hunters' guilt of killing them. In this sense, Constantine's dislike of obsolescent ritualized slaughter would signify that he was trying to distance himself from meat-eating predator deities of the Stone Age and, that he was rushing ahead of the archaic world-view of his competitors. He may have been driven by a need to better rationalize the mass slaughters of increasingly larger military campaigns. Allegedly 34,000 soldiers of Licinius were killed in the decisive battle near Adrianople, in 324. Constantine was for Christianity what Asoka has been for Buddhism, or what Ali was to become for Islam.

Simple archaic predatorial/totemic initiation mysteries, and even the long-enduring Falcon-Totem of ancient Egypt, failed to keep the interest of this emperor. At the moment when his progressive alphabetical Chi Rho emblem was mounted onto his *labarum* and was expected to empower his military, Constantine's strategy of favoring Christianity began to validate itself for him.

Reasoning antithetically, Jesus of Nazareth has celebrated his last Passover meal as transition to a sacramental vegetarian "Last Supper." It was limited to bread and wine. So Jesus anticipated the vegetarian perspective by which Constantine may have wanted to abolish the

---

176 Bart D. Ehrman, *The Triumph of Christianity* (New York: Simon and Schuster; 2018), Chapters 1-2.

bloody sacramental bull sacrifices. Jesus, who lived still within Judaism, has sidelined the shedding of blood of sacrificial lambs at Passover—a utilization of blood which harked back to ceremonial preparations made by Levites, leaving Egypt. It also has been explained as a lapse, dating back to the patriarch Abraham about half a millennium older than the Passover ritual could have been.

The shift of the sacramental emphasis from meat to products from fields, such as bread and wine, carry clear evolutionary implications. In fact, the religion of Jesus adds the milling of grains, the baking of bread and the crushing of grapes, to a sacrificial paradigm that must have been older than the Passover ritual or Abraham's temptation implies. As a ceremonial mode of sacramental eating, Jesus used the extreme parabolic language of cannibalism—of eating bread as "body" and of drinking wine as "blood"—metaphors that have drifted in and out of vogue 5,500 to 4,500 years earlier. Cannibalism still flourished alongside the earliest Western cattle-raising cultures.

Old meanings die slowly. Often they turn negative and outlive initial ceremonial intentions—they may survive as shards of spooky fairy tales. Old conflicts may be memorialized contrariwise in ritual, to institutionalize salvation from a bad situation. Simple historical events may get twisted into paradigms that define salvation for the future. For example, with the Roman judicial crucifixion of Jesus, established as a historical fact, Christian piety was predestined to devalue the judicial logic that led to crucifixions in the first place.

Under Constantine, Christians became appreciative of the Empire's support of their religion—therefore, blaming the Empire for the death of Christ was no longer a polite attitude to display. Ancient Stone Age memories of hunters' guilt resurfaced and were partly adjusted to the Hebrew practice of dealing collectively with the problem of atonement. Christians internalized and contemplated the general sinful condition of humankind. Patriotically they accepted some of the cultural guilt that Roman soldiers bore for having carried out their Savior's crucifixion. It seemed increasingly likely that, somehow, the death of Jesus must have been eternally contemplated by God for the salvation of humankind. And surely, the seed idea of "indebtedness by eating" was entertained by primitive hunters many thousands of years earlier. Every Homo sapiens knows that human life is transitory, and wishes that it were more permanent than the lives of hunted animals.

By the time Constantine abolished judicial crucifixion, Christians had already discovered their Savior's sacrificial death rooted in God the Father's eternal love and in his desire to save humankind—all this drama was implied in the anciently known flow of divine emanation.

In the days of Samuel, the priest, the Hebrew rite of "anointing with oil" could easily be distinguished from an Egyptian imperial mandate that was based on the resurrection of Osiris and the enthronement claims of a reborn Horus. The Hebrew symbolic anointment with oil, for Messiah status, became encapsulated in Greek translation as "Christos." For Christians the title "Christ" surpassed the status of ancient deified pharaonic "Sons of God" as well as of later deified Roman emperors. The rites of Horus-Ra of ancient Egypt echoed in the Roman imperial cult as *apotheosis*—as deification by which emperors were officially recognized as Sons of God.

The Nicaean Council—Politics of the Arian Controversy

In 325 CE the Emperor Constantine, in an attempt to unify his empire, called a Council of mostly eastern Christian bishops to Nicaea to initiate his imperial strategy with them. He was fully aware that he was colliding with general political realities—also that, by implication, he was forfeiting his personal chances of ever being empowered as a traditional imperial "Son of God." In fact, at this council he implicitly abdicated his right to this honor in favor of the crucified victim, Jesus of Nazareth—a commoner Jew whom Christians recognized and acclaimed to be God's Anointed (See Figure 17, page 397).

Today, almost two thousand years later, most Christian theologians have difficulties understanding the original political subtleties of words like "made," or "only-begotten" or "self-begotten." They also have difficulties understanding the difference that an *iota* made in the *"homoiousion"* of Arius, and that its absence made in the *"homoousion"* on which the Egyptian Athanasius insisted. The issue at hand could not be settled easily with linguistic refinements, by simply distinguishing "alike essence" from "same essence." The structure of consubstantial Trinitarian Christian reasoning was derived from Heliopolitan concepts of emanation and the Ennead. It was derived from the same Atum-Shu-Tefnut unity from which the Egyptian trinitarian logic, which Athanasius obviously still utilized to define the Christian Trinity at Nicaea, was also derived. Nevertheless, in Koine Greek literature, by which the mind of Arius the Berber was educated, up in Syria, there could not be found better theological terminology that would have prevented Roman emperors from claiming divine honors as well, alongside Jesus Christ. For the bishops it was clear that in their trinitarian Christian theology, deified Roman emperors should not be honored as Sons of God. They were alert to make absolutely sure that Roman emperors could no longer be worshiped as gods. And surely, no-one needed to tell a Pontifex Maximus what this Christian insistence meant for his own personal status or for the divine rank of his imperial antecedents. He knew the price he was paying for getting a unified Christian organization with a monotheistic-trinitarian creed. Surely, he also understood the disadvantages which this creed would inflict n his imperial challengers as well.

This epoch-changing linguistic subtlety, at Nicaea, immediately began withholding divine honors from Roman emperors. But the bishops' diplomacy and understanding of this matter required precise spelling in Koine Greek. Making a distinction between God's own "begetting" and human-style "creation by reshaping," was essential for keeping men humble as potential equal children of God, as adopted siblings or created equals. The Greek *iota* argument was still effective in the background when for the "Declaration of Independence" of the United States, Thomas Jefferson insisted that all humankind were created equal and were endowed by their Creator with certain inalienable rights—notwithstanding any atheistic non-theologies that also wooed the Founding Fathers.

Some seventeen centuries ago, at Nicaea, equal dignity among humankind was implicitly affirmed by the first Christian Council. It was imperially accepted. Constantine, as Emperor and Pope of all Roman religions, needed to see the creed of Christians better defined before he could favor their Church openly. He demonstrated great sensibility when he allowed the Christian *iota* distinction to stand. As emperor, eligible for the official "Son of God" title, he accepted letting himself get theologically demoted to the level of a mundane sovereign. He knew that whatever downed an imperial Son of God to human status would also keep his competitors low. He himself still held the advantage by being Pope of all Roman religions. Posthumously he was honored as a "Saint" in Christ's church.

Today, even in some Christian history textbooks, the controversy at Nicaea is mocked and explained as a crisis during which "two extreme Christian factions rode roughshod over a silent majority of Near Eastern Christian bishops."[177] The conflict exploded between Arius and

---

[177]Cf. Williston Walker, *A History of the Christian Church* (New York: Scribner, 1959, 106 ff. For background see Karl Heussi, *Kompendium der Kirchengeschichte,* 12th ed., (Tübingen: JCB Mohr Verlag), 1960, p. 97.

Athanasius, both of whom were at the time serving at the Church in Alexandria, Egypt. W. Walker assumes that the majority of Christian bishops, in the East, either for pragmatic reasons or for lack of perception, remained satisfied with Origen's earlier established Christological "ambiguities." But were these really ambiguities? Ancient process theology, which Origen taught at Alexandria as "the eternal generation of the Son," was a christology that northern dualists could not quite fathom. In harmony with his broader Egyptian theological inheritance —along the larger Egyptian dimension of divine procreation and eternal emanation—Origen referred to the nature of Christ as a "second God and creature."[178] In the context of the Egyptian theological heritage, this formulation by Origen appeared reasonable enough. In ancient Egypt, the differences in meaning between "eternal emanation," "divine procreation" or "begetting," were inconsequential. But they raised havoc in the northern-educated mind of Arius, who had come to Alexandria to be a deacon and to teach Christians, alongside the native Athanasius. Arius remained religiously and linguistically a foreigner in Egypt.

In hindsight, and considering the distance between the Egyptian and Northern world-views, while reflecting on the variety of languages that the Christian movement has inherited—unaware of ten millennia of evolutionary differentiations—the Arian controversy was unavoidable. But the message of John the Baptizer, and the story of Jesus of Nazareth, spawned a religion that spread quite naturally among people of the monist Egyptian persuasion. It spread almost as quickly among dualistic Indo-European folk up north. But both of these areas, governed by Rome, were challenged to harmonize their thinking for the sake of imperial unity. Christianity spread from Palestine along Mediterranean shores into the still periodically expanding Roman Empire, still centered ontologically on the unreconciled modes of reasoning in Italy, Greece and Egypt.

The minds of fledgling Christian theologians, up north, were lit by monotheistic Hebrew "fire" as they also were challenged by Hellenic dualism, accentuated by philosophy. Farther east they ran up against Iranian-Mithraic apocalyptic dualism and Manichaeism. The northern Mind-and-Matter dualism, explained by Socrates in Plato's *Phaedo*, has all along differed from ancient Egypt's monism that had been simmering in Egypt and seeping from there along the Mediterranean trade routes.

---

[178] Walker, *A History of the Christian Church*, 106.

It should not surprise anyone that the dualistic Hellenic, and the monistic Egyptian extremes were set to collide in the Hellenistic/ Egyptian melting pot of colonial Alexandria, more relentlessly than elsewhere. Egyptian monotheistic/monistic process theologians, and Hellenists who reasoned more disjunctively, and for whom separate names and separate metaphors of creation signified separate realities, impacted conciliatory attempts at communication haphazardly. All symbolic creations of humankind have been re-interpreted many times along their evolutionary paths. Viewing the controversy from the Egyptian perspective, one could say that the Greek language was too well suited for making excessive distinctions. The Egyptians, viewing things from within their holistic ontology, were therefore hesitant to acknowledge distinctions that speakers of Greek considered to be obvious. During political confrontations, religious vocabulary is being re-cast through linguistic filters. Words can quickly be molded into double-edged daggers.

Both sides in this debate had, of course, recourse to Platonic philosophical categories, to eternal norms and Ideas, which along the fault line at which the two worlds collided had only ambiguous communication value. Beneath symbols of communication, the dualistic as well as monistic world-views continued to draw their axioms from stark archaic mythological models, quite far from the path along which their analytic distinctions had been sliced afterward, during millennia BCE. It is not an accident that Arius, whose Christology became the focal point of the so-called Arian Controversy, was educated in Antioch under Lucianus. His northern common sense was aggravated by Egyptians who stood under the influence of an intellect that descended from the pharaohs. It is even less of an accident how solidly Athanasius identified himself and his cause with monasteries in the Egyptian hinterland, that is, with those contemplative brotherhoods of mystics that spawned on the oases of diminishing traditional Egyptian piety. Christian brotherhoods and a variety of Gnostic trending associations filled the void that the demise of ancient imperial soteriology had left in its wake. Already during Egypt's New Kingdom period this void has gotten democratized and refurbished—with royal funeral practices that were appropriated by commoners.

Christ as *homoousion,* who was begotten—not made—and who was of one essence with the Father, was a reasonable Egyptian concept, and so was the tradition of embracing Father and Son, consubstantially reasoned, within a process of emanation, wrapped ritually into the old politics of imperial succession. Resurrections in ancient Egypt were expected to occur at regular political intervals. Continuity of the Egyptian imperial order required that an Osiris divinity would be resurrected, begotten, reborn, and transformed into a Horus-Pharaoh personage who then would proceed to govern Egypt again. By contrast, the "created" Christ figure that Arius conceptualized was more like a human person, "well made and assembled" by God. But his story, by which God was viewed primarily as a craftsman or maker, also has rendered God to be more like one of those imperial hyper-domesticators who boasted divine titles and reasoned in terms of owning, whipping, and controlling humankind as his possessions or products. Whether in deified imperial or in more average societal environs, extraordinary status is projected first unto one's ancestry. Then it is extrapolated for the benefit of descendants, according to the status that previously had been attributed to the ancestors.

To Egyptian Christian mystics, people who reasoned like Arius appeared politically reckless. By the time Arius came along, Egyptian Christians had already switched away from the partly democratized Osiris-Horus soteriology of their commoner forebears, to the more universalistic version of the Christ-Jesus story. The Christ hypostasis, characterized as *homoousion* (of one substance with the Father), could have been as easily accommodated within the eternal and unnameable Egyptian Godhead, and could easily have been conceptualized and explained as hypostasis after the manner of Osiris and Horus, in Egyptian religion. It seems significant that Athanasius's objection to the Christology of Arius was not limited to linguistic restraints. He hoped to prevent the Christ-story from being weighed down by an overrated human nature. The story told by Arius posed an obstruction in the process of universal salvation for humankind, along the U-turn. The Father of Jesus Christ was not a God who merely created or "made" humankind. He is someone who begot and who loves. He cared to save the creatures whom he engenders. According to Athanasius, "Christ has been made man so that thereupon we might [again] be made divine."[179] The divinely "fabricated" Christ of Arius threatened the Father status of God, rationally, and diminished his ability to reach out in the direction of common humankind. It endangered the basic Egyptian U-Turn transition that converted theogony into soteriology. The mystery of resurrection could not be entrusted to

---

[179] *Incarnation*, 54:3. Quoted in Walker, *op. cit.*, 110.

a mortal human creed nor be limited to privileges claimed by imperial dynasties which, by resurrection and apotheosis, "made" ruling emperors into honorary gods who, thereupon, would demonstrate their ability to enslave humankind and to make them their property. As noted earlier, democratic tendencies were already present in the Egyptian funerary cult of lesser folk during the New Kingdom era. Back then, lesser folk insisted on being saved by the same pharaonic Osirian incantations. Athanasius, who had Egyptian ancestry, could not with good conscience let Christianity have a weaker theory of salvation than the ancient Egyptian heritage had already been leaking to non-royals.

In reaction to the Roman Empire, the Christian gospel offered to save all people by faith in Jesus the Christ, which eventually led Western Civilization toward democratization. Thus in Egypt, to Christians, their Christ Jesus appeared to be a new and better savior—better than the Osiris-hypostasis type—and assuredly a savior for all people who wished to avail themselves of their God-given status as "children of God"—as brothers and sisters of Christ Jesus. True to its Hebrew prophetic heritage, the Kingdom of Heaven excluded hyper-domestication. It offered divine status to the weak, the meek, and the poor.

The essential and structural continuity between old Egyptian religion and its Christian replacement, in Egypt, remained intact. The Christ-Event happened under the same indescribable but generative Godhead. It shone from within the combined theological, ontological and soteriological structure of divinely combined Parenthood—that is, Fatherhood and Motherhood in creative union.

The Arian controversy defined not only the nature of Christ. Its written outcome was expected also to summarize what Christians believe concerning the nature of the triune God and the requirements for human freedom and salvation. Was this God engaged in battle with his own creation, in a dualistic confrontation? Was he facing a world governed by hostile principalities and powers forever? Or was he an All-Father of the unitary and prevailing Egyptian sort, who could accomplish the creation and procreation of life from within?

In spite of having its major institutional and political centers in dualistic Indo-European lands, orthodox Christendom gradually chose and moved in the direction of what used to be persuasive Egyptian theo-logic. The fading monotheistic emanation mythology of Heliopolis had a better analogy than Arius, by which to explain the resurrection mystery that surrounded Jesus Christ. It was more coherent, more politically unified and confrontational than the dualistic northern philosophies or the polytheisms that preceded the latter.

We would be greatly amiss if we were to let matters rest at the point at which theologians since the days of Constantine have labored to lay their controversies to rest—that is, if we were to ignore the point at which their ancient world-views kept scraping against each other's political compromises. The nature of God, Christ, of Holy Spirit and Madonna, were not questions that could be settled by councils and then locked away as artifacts in archives. These matters actively defined and affected the worth of individual human lives.

The Nicaean Council resolution did not only define what became the mainstream of Christian orthodoxy. The Council's statements were intended to harmonize human relations within the Empire, under the Christian God. Implicitly they also circumscribed the status of the emperor himself. The Nicaean document altered the face of the Roman Empire forever. Of course, it does not reveal what every attending bishop individually has understood about the legislation they produced. Luckily, the emperor's objectives were limited in scope. He achieved his primary goal of befriending the literate Christian clergy who, in turn, could motivate their people.

With his military victory over Licinius, Constantine had already succeeded taming the Empire's older cults. As Pontifex Maximus he proceeded with integrating the Christian faction into the Empire. The Empire would be easier to govern when he could count on being seen on friendly terms with everyone's God.

The attending bishops understood theological, mythological as well as political modes of expression. They could sense the presence of unspoken political implications. They knew when to remain silent, when to appear pious and humble before God, before the Emperor, and friendly toward pretentious fellow humankind. To the extent to which human beings master their arts of natural diplomacy, they interact variously at different status levels. During three centuries of sporadic persecutions by Roman emperors, Christians also have learned a thing or two.

To Egyptianized theologians the Nicaean creed provided a comprehensive rational world-view, of a world created by a single Almighty God. No allowances needed to be made, henceforth, for human emperors to attain divine supreme status over human subjects. A religious and secular boundary line was implied. It was understood by nearly all the voting bishops, that the Emperor should neither rule as a God nor as an imperial "Son of God."

The Nicaean Creed has reduced the Mandate of the Emperor

The theological document, reasoned by Egyptian logic and written in Koine Greek eventually was translated into English as follows:

We believe in one God, the Father Almighty, Maker of all things visible and invisible.

And in one Lord Jesus Christ, the Son of God, begotten of the Father [as] the only-begotten; that is, the essence of the Father, God of God, Light of Light, very God of very God, begotten, not made, being of one substance homoousion (ὁμοούσιον) with the Father; by whom all things were made both in heaven and on earth; who for us men, and for our salvation, came down and was incarnate and was made man; he suffered, and on the third day he rose again, ascended into heaven; from thence he shall come to judge the quick and the dead.... But those who say: 'There was a time when he was not;' and 'He was not before he was made;' and 'He was made out of nothing,' or 'He is of another substance' or 'essence,' or 'The Son of God is created,' or 'changeable,' or 'alterable' – they are condemned by the holy catholic and apostolic Church.

And in the Holy Ghost... etc.[180]

Of the 318 bishops who voted at the Nicaean Council, all of them except Arius and two others approved the creedal statement. It was an overwhelming number. Does the document that was produced at the Council of Nicaea still appear to prove an internal Christian theological crisis, by which two extreme Christian factions "rode rough shod over a silent majority of Near Eastern Christian bishops"—as we have quoted Walker, the historian, in the preceding Section? Or does the historical context now afford a different conclusion? The fact that only Arius and two others voted "no" means that at Nicaea 315 bishops still understood the politics and theo-logic of ancient Egypt, enough to have voted "yes." Most of them wore pharaonic double crowns to display their theological ancestry (Figure 17, page 397). They reasoned their Christian Gospel according to the Egyptian logic that Athanasius of Alexandria—the "Thomas Jefferson at Nicaea"—applied.

---

180 Philip Schaff, *Creeds of Christendom.* Volume I. The History of Creeds. Ada, 1977. See also reference at Wickepedia.

At the end of those days, the Christian bishops were on record as having confirmed the honorific title "Son of God" exclusively for Jesus the Anointed. The voting bishops thereby rejected the past imperial strategy by which an occasional Roman emperor would simply begin to govern as a de facto deity. They also invalidated the manner in which emperors, via the post-mortem deification ritual, *apotheosis,* could rule by anticipation, as "Gods in the Making."

Thus, slightly less than three centuries after the crucifixion of Jesus of Nazareth, the imperially accepted Nicene Creed has legitimized the religion for which this Jesus—a crucified commoner Jew—had become recognized as divine and human founder. Eventually, in 381 CE, the Emperor Theodosius made Christianity the state religion of the Empire. He clarified the status of Jesus as "crucified under Pontius Pilate and as only-begotten Son of God"—the status already implied at Nicaea.

Pontius Pilate served as procurator under Tiberius Caesar, Son of the Divine Augustus. Both these emperors were deemed to be sons of God. But Jesus of Nazareth announced the "Kingdom of Heaven," and he ended up becoming Rome's most famous judicial victim, shamed by crucifixion. Nevertheless, he successfully usurped all imperial "Son of God" titles over the preceding three thousand years.[181]

The Emperor Constantine, wisely and pragmatically, accepted the limitations that the Christian creed imposed on his imperial status. His concession then subtly distinguished Church from the State. Above all, it gave him a mandate to govern with the authority of the greatest deity conceivable at the time, the Almighty Holy Trinity.

With the Emperor Constantine present at the Nicene Council, the bishops with their creed avoided blaming the Roman Empire directly for the crucifixion of Jesus. Only at the Second Council, in 381, under the Emperor Theodosius, did the bishops dare to be explicit. By that time Christianity had become the dominant religious organization in the empire. The Roman Empire, having been physically restored by the

---

[181]This author thinks that, seen from the Roman perspective, Jesus of Nazareth was executed for the apparent reason of having usurped the imperial title, Son of God. Admittedly, the historical records are religiously and politically complicated. The charge that was posted at the cross of Jesus read "Jesus of Nazareth, King of the Jews." It appears to be mocking the Jews. Pilate could not write that the accused has been usurping the invincible imperial title "Son of God." This, in the eyes of Jews, would have been mocking the imperial theology of Rome. A Roman procurator would, expectedly, have tried to shift attention away from the Empire's own theological weakness—ancient Rome's "Achilles Heel."

Figure 17. The Council at Nicaea, sponsored by the Emperor Constantine in 325. Fresco in Capella Sistina, Vatican, 1590. Public Domain Wickepedia. Please note the miters these Christian bishops are wearing. They are Egyptian pharaonic double crowns. These bishops knew where their theological heritage came from.

likes of Constantine and Theodosius, could then be viewed more directly in a realistic historical mode. Thus, at the Second Council the Christian creed was amended as follows:

... he was crucified for us under Pontius Pilate, and suffered, and was buried, and the third day he rose again, according to the Scriptures, and ascended into heaven, and sitteth on the right hand of the Father; from thence he shall come again, with glory, to judge the quick and the dead; whose kingdom shall have no end.(see Footnote 180, above).

Inasmuch as the original Council document was written in Greek, and Constantine was fluent in Latin, some historians have begun to ask how much of what the Emperor endorsed at Nicaea he might actually have understood. But surely, such suspicions are unwarranted. Constantine was Emperor. He also made himself the Pontifex Maximus over all religions in the Empire. Such a man could not be tricked into letting go of an honorific "Son of God" title. He could not have been ignorant of what "only-begotten not made" implied for his own status. Even if he had only Latin translations from the Greek, he would have understood that the Christian creed will abolish the cult of emperor deification (*apotheosis*)—will abolish it forever, including Constantine's own chances of playing "God" for the Roman Empire.

Why was Constantine not afraid of strengthening the Christian movement? Instead, as Emperor and as Pontifex Maximus he carefully evolved a strategy of favoring Christianity among all of Rome's available religions. Ever so slowly this strategy earned him a stronger mandate which, with the growth of Christianity came to outrank any older cult authority that Constantine's imperial competitors could possibly enlist. With that same strategy, of relatively speaking, reducing the status of Rome's older war-gods, Constantine weakened the entire assembly of would-be Son of God contenders. As an emperor, and as the High Priest of all Roman religions, he determined how any deity in the Empire should be sheltered, managed and celebrated. To wield such authority, Constantine knowingly forfeited his eligibility for Son of God status. In its place he accepted his imperial mandate from the greatest conceivable deity imaginable in his days—the almighty Holy Christian Trinity.

The Nestorian Controversy

Along with the challenges to Heaven's only-begotten Son, generated by the Arian Controversy, the older Hesiodic wound of Heaven broke open again as a mythic/metaphysical rift between Heaven and Earth. It started bleeding again during the Nestorian Controversy in Constantinople (428–433). There it happened again in confrontation with theologians from Alexandria. The Christian leaders in Alexandria appear to have been still quite comfortable with the ancient Egyptian faith in a Mother-Goddess hypostasis. Christological conflicts could therefore get re-ignited as soon as the mother of Christ Jesus was mentioned.

Given the Nicene Creed, the new question was: Has Mary, the mother of Jesus, been a "Mother of God" (*Theotokos*) or was she only "Mother of Christ" (*Christotokos*—Mother of the Anointed)? A closer look at this argument exposes the same issue which has already haunted the combatants during the Arian Controversy. The difference between "Mother of God" and "Mother of Christ"concerned the interrelatedness of the "two natures" of Christ. A coherent flow of emanation was needed to vouch for the feasibility of salvation for humankind. The appellation "Mother of Christ" could have opened the possibility that her Son inherited a "severed" Hellenic nature, or possibly, one in which the human aspect dominated. The Alexandrian theologians could have agreed to both Mother of God and Mother of Christ, but they would have had to insist on both. The latter would have been a result of the former. Thanks to Egypt's history with the cult of Tefnut, such a Mother Goddess extended all the way from Nut to Isis. Her presence presupposed Tefnut. Thus, stated in terms of Egyptian Christian ontology, the question was whether Mary, the mother of Jesus Christ was also a representative of the entire Tefnut-Nut-Isis dimension. Was she reconciled with the All-God and present in the emanation-radiation stream of divine life—by which Christians as well recognized the Holy Spirit hypostasis. In this setting, Mary could have given birth to a divine son even without an angelic announcement or a pious tale about virginity. In Egyptian emanation mythology the question of physical virginity was not an issue. However, northern Christians searched for an explanation that enabled them to read within the range of their accustomed ambiguity first of shamanic and then of philosophical dualism. The revised version was approved at the First Council of Constantinople, in 381 CE. There the Nicene Creed was modified to read: ...who for us men, and for our salvation, came down from heaven, and *was incarnate by the Holy Ghost and of the Virgin Mary, and was made man....* (see Footnote 180, above).

The Mariological question became crucial. Any alteration at the human side of this divine-to-human emanation story threatened the divine status of Christ. The Arian option would have endangered the entire logic of emanation and the Egyptian-Christian ontology, as well as any type of the Christ-centered process of salvation.

The Monophysite Struggle

The same problem surfaced again in 451 CE, and once more it pitted ancient Egyptian emanation theory against the dualism of the Indo-European West. As the label of the most conspicuous party in this struggle suggests, the "Monophysites" insisted on the "one" over against "two" natures or essences which, presumably, formed the person of Jesus Christ. "One divine emanation," a monophysis, was easily thinkable within traditional Egyptian theological reasoning.

All the while, in the northern manner in which the Monophysite case eventually was argued, the ancient Egyptian theology no longer was well understood. Nobody knew anymore about the *ba,* and about how it compared to, and non-dualistically contrasted with, the *ka*. An understanding of these two categories depended on one's conceptualization of living bodies. Monophysis could not be understood within the popular awareness of the western Christian worldview. What remained of the Egyptian heritage, implied in Christian theology, was an orientation toward a cosmic process of emanation, albeit philosophically cleansed of all the specific ancient Egyptian shapes of emanation, divine beings and labels. Orthodox Christendom continued to insist on seeing Christ as the Only-begotten Son who, according to traditional Egyptian fashion, continued to be understood in unity with the Godhead. As in earlier controversies, so also in the Monophysite version, the entire All-God theology and christology were at stake. The problem continued to refresh itself in the context of different languages and vocabulary. An entire world-view can be shaken to its core if a central keyword cluster loses as little as a single aspect-connotation from its field of meanings.

The Filioque Clause

The same East-West (originally South-North) differences, which erupted during the famed Christological and Mariological controversies, surfaced in relation to the third person of the Holy Trinity.

In the West, the creedal addition of the Filioque Clause, to the effect that the Holy Spirit proceeds from the Father and the Son, was adopted first by the church of Spain (589), then by the Frankish church (809), and then finally by Rome (1014).

Understandably, the Eastern Orthodox Church, still living in the afterglow of ancient Egyptian theology and logic, rejected the Filioque Clause outright. The reason for their rejection becomes clear in light of the Egyptian heritage. Just as Shu and Tefnut-Mahet, at Heliopolis, were known to have proceeded from the Godhead Atum, so in the Christian replication of Shu, as Christ, and the Holy Spirit as Tefnut-Mahet, would both have proceeded from the Father.

Had the Egyptian theo-logic been more finely replicated at the surface, Easterners could conceivably have still agreed to the Son proceeding from the Father. And they could have agreed that, inasmuch as Tefnut in Egypt was "Hand and Order," and occasionally was thought to have come forth from Atum as the twin sister of Shu, *after Shu*, she would (by reckoning with Greek differentiations) not have proceeded from both Atum and Shu. A sister does not proceed from her brother! It nevertheless is doubtful that Christian theologians, even in the East in the Eleventh Century, still had the finer details of Egyptian antecedents in focus. In any case, Spanish theologians and Frankish monks, who disputed with Eastern monks at Jerusalem, obviously knew still less than their Greek and Roman predecessors about the prehistory of Christian theo-logic in ancient Egypt. At issue was the unrecognized question of how much of the God-story, that seeped from ancient Egyptian common sense, should be retained to explain the Christian Trinity in the West.

The Neo-Egyptian Theology of Augustine

Earlier in the West, the church father Augustine (354–430) completed his life's work of reorienting the Western portion of Christendom homeward, theologically—in the direction of the Egyptian monotheistic All-God emanation theology. A measure of collaboration with Roman demands for grand-domestication was thereby activated without keeping the full historical road-map in view.

Western Christianity was lucky that Augustine's first conversion to dualistic Manichaeism was soon followed by another philosophical reorientation to so-called "Neo-Platonism," the latter of which has significantly magnified the resonances that came from the ancient Egyptian heritage—while that heritage itself was fading. The Neo-Platonism from which Augustine could slide effortlessly into Christian theology was, actually, a Neo-Egyptianism. It was the same world-view from which Alexandrian theologians earlier had reasoned their way toward the Nicaean Creed, to formulate mainstream orthodox Christianity. All of Augustine's conversions were philosophical re-orientations, rationally aware of the organizational and political complexities that the management of a church and an empire entailed. He knew theology as an effective and preferable diplomatic medium.

The general indebtedness of Neo-Platonism, to ancient Egyptian emanation thought, has been shown in Chapters 13 and 14. The acceptance of "Neo-Platonic" emanational thinking by Augustine, his conversion to Christianity and his identification of the Neo-Platonic hypostasis "Nous" as "Mind of God," provided the necessary middle term for his conversion to Christianity. For Augustine it rationalized the Holy Spirit link of the Christ Incarnation allegorically, from the Godhead toward humankind. It allowed a downward path of procreational emanation, love, and divine communication with the human mind. With the same stroke of the pen, this step also opened a homeward path for human salvation. To Christian theologians this meant that their restless yearning "hearts" would, at last, find rest in the eternal heart of God. Ancient Egyptians, who believed they were thinking with their "hearts," have discovered this path for the *ka*, long ago.

Saint Augustine, a Latin theologian, was of course obligated to make some courteous bows toward northern dualism. Brilliantly, he took hold of the two Indo-European metaphysical realms, of spirit and matter, and postulated them together as concrete entities for practical politics. He acknowledged dualism by way of institutionalizing a Church/State dichotomy. He established this political duality concretely, in check and balance fashion, as the City of God—contrasted with the City of Man. Having executed this balancing act behind the curtain of dualism, Augustine could accept Egyptian monotheism disguised as a neutered philosophical monism.

Origen of Alexandria was vindicated: Christ had become human so that humankind could become divine—again. Under the guise of the neutered "Neo-Platonic" philosophy, which Augustine allegorized and adjusted to the Christian political story, Western civilization was set to inherit some of the monotheistic checks and balances that for three pre-Christian millennia have bestowed a measure of balance and continuity on Egyptian civilization. Deified pharaohs have died throughout these millennia—they were promoted and refined to the divine status of Osiris. Their *ka* energies could continue to reign from within the universal *ka* of the All-God. Their authority spread as far as the Sun would travel, far away from mortal humankind and Death (*Set*)—far and secure out of harm's way.

But early Roman emperors and later Holy Roman emperors had empires to manage, and the reactionary Hebrew Reign-of-God political wild-fire initially was insufficiently structured, or tamed, to enable imperial organization and management to take place. But notwithstanding its otherworldly orientation, the layout of Augustinian Egyptian rooted theology was adept to provide greater-than-human context and ontological stability for an additional millennium or two—to help balance and to calm the mentality of Western civilization past its latter-day awakenings and overhauls that have become known as Humanism and the Enlightenment.

18

Son of God among Hominini Siblings

Homines sapientes are playful gambling primates, are mimics above all else. Though endowed by their Creator with spectacular streaks of intelligence and talent, they emulate any totem that fascinates—Eagle, Serpent, Lion and if the occasion arises even a Lamb. Hominidae have engendered and have evolved, barely to levels of apes and humankind. Some differences among these divinely graced primates or "mindful children of God" appear to be obvious improvements over the story-starter substance mentioned in the *Genesis* narrative—which happens to be a sheer "lump of clay." But even that story agrees with later observations, that in the aftermath of their creation far too much discord has erupted among these special creatures.

With sufficient historical hindsight, the theological struggles and definitions argued by early Christian theologians—Christological, Mariological, and Numenological—can be understood as birth pangs that needed to be suffered so that the young Christian religion could begin to modify the larger Roman Empire and thereby reshape Western civilization into a slightly less brutal compilation. These first pains, now almost forgotten by the offspring, were labor pains on the part of Christendom's ancient mother religion. Lastly, these were also healing pains for the periodically disintegrating Roman Republic which never could fix its procedure of imperial succession. Travails were suffered by the expiring matriarch among ancient imperial religions as a matter of course. The old Egyptian mother-theology died in the centuries during which her vigorous offspring emerged and began prospering in the Mediterranean realm, touched and ignited by Kingdom of Heaven excitement from the East. Christianity inherited from her Egyptian mother some manners of logos, with aspirations for endurance and glory—as well as some imbalances, tilting toward unequal human rights or access to divine grace. Over time the daughter religion herself lent partial blessings to communisms and democracies, to schemes of hyper-domestication, tyrannies and freedom movements alike.

Reconsidering the Axis Age—*die Achsenzeit*

The Theory of an Axis Age, according to which time and history are seen turning rounds, as if on an axle, seeks to explain similar historical events as cyclic-mechanical repetitions. Indeed, axles, cyclic movement and time, may appear sufficiently analogous to the art of making wagon wheels. No spiral motion, or growth, needs so disturb a mind as long as it reasons at the elementary level of wagon builders.

Yes indeed, when human minds inspire dance, or trance, they occasionally do engender whirls, or dreams about nearly perfect circular motion. Cycles also have been meaningful to early generations of astronomers and cosmologists—until spirals began unwinding for them toward wider horizons and beyond. Knowledge about the birth, growth and death of galaxies, about helices and DNA, do nowadays twist the traditional metaphor of perfect cycles—the cycles from which "Axis Time" was intuited. The larger universe now appears to exist more selfishly—more beyond reach— for the apparent purpose of its own expansion, while processes among expanding spheres necessarily do engender spiral motion. Explaining our universe in this newer perspective no longer requires axles or true circular motion.

Postulating an Axis Age *(Achsenzeit)* for historians, to conceptualize philosophical, scientific and technological innovations from between 800 and 200 BCE—with an extension that allows acknowledgment also of Judaism, Christianity, and Islam as effects of an "expanded" Axis Age—all this seemed reasonable to the psychologist-philosopher Karl Jaspers. Nevertheless, I continue to prefer viewing these same three world religions, which Jaspers has mentioned to illustrate Axis Age progress, as having emerged in old-fashioned linear historical time and, specifically, in reaction to ruthless aspects of "civilization." In the tailwind of evolving languages and Jewish-Christian theology, Jaspers's "theory of Axis Time and cycles" does distort concrete historical events, more than it explains.

With this opening jolt to Karl Jaspers's concept of an Axis Age, I nevertheless support his distrust of Rudolf Bultmann's theology. My reasons are that the latter's "demythologization" assumed scientific certainties that no finite mind or language has ever been able to comprehend. Human minds are bound to do their reasoning allegorically. Their words are given tentative shapes within, and also are dissolved within, languages that evolve. A theology free of mythology (devoid of references to greater-than-human realities) lies outside the realm that human minds can image scientifically. The same obstacles that delimit meanings in mythology also do block efforts of sanitizing scientific presuppositions—which, generally, are won by dubious front-loaded analyses and hypotheses.

Merely because Karl Jaspers has seen fit to hitch religion, philosophy, science, and technology to the metaphor of an early Bronze Age artifact, the wheel, there is no need to twirl our entire concept of "Time" around its imaginary axle. Our beloved Planet Earth does wobble quite comfortably around an imagined axle, probably expanding all the while. As Heraclitus was unable to step into the same stream twice, so any wagon wheel drops into the "same pothole" only once—only once, while modifying and creating a larger kind of hole. Religiously based judgments that Judaism, Christianity, and Islam have hurled at civilization, were intended as ointments on wounds that human ambition and Hesiodic imagination, together have slashed.

Of course, the ancients expressed their insights by word symbols imaged in the languages of their days. Languages are spoken and are modified by a majority of average people who fail to keep up with the learning of elites. Religions, therefore, frequently begin as desperate reactions to emerging problems. They evolve and they spread by simple analogies that average people still can grasp as meaningful answers. Every speaking human being is in the business of selecting and tweaking vocabulary to communicate fresh thoughts that need to overreach available lexical carrying capacities and must, therefore, be stiffened by fresh definitions. New vocabularies are needed to enable fresh answers. With their initial words still in flux, and still bleeding, world religions have attempted mass healing and recovery from collective violence and and other traumas of civilization.

A view of history that relies on cycles is tempted to multiply and to arrange conceptualized rings in stacks and rows, numbered and linkable as chains. A cosmic archetype of rings can inspire, and even justify, the hyper-domestication and the enslavement of fellow humankind. Conceptual axioms, like chains, can shackle our free sciences, our innovation technologies and our places of production. Burdens of lopsided utilitarian knowledge are easily exploited to enslave more of humankind than initially could be lured into servitude with mirages of safety or comfort. Liberators must challenge and redefine the greater-than-human reality that has been invoked to justify enslavement and scientific aggression in the first place.

Redefinition of weighty words may become necessary regarding any greater-than-human Fate or God, Nature, Chance, Heaven, Earth, Empire, Destiny, Process, Emanation, Evolution, Religion, Freedom, Democracy, Society, Economy, Fatherland, Motherland, Tribe, Party, Cosmos, and more. Then, especially the meanings of oversized value words, with their uneven association regarding the distribution of powers, will easily get exploited and corrupted. Powers today are still being mobilized with invoking ancient totems and fetishes that, then, continue to agitate the passions of "civilized" humankind. Stone Age hunters relied on the sponsorship of able predators, as exemplary models and totems. In return, these totems sponsored human hunting campaigns. As sponsors of the hunt, totemic gods were known to be better killers than were the human protégés whom they helped and protected.

During the early days of Christianity, Jesus of Nazareth announced that the Reign of Almighty God was imminent. Jesus was recognized by his followers as an "Oil-Anointed" (Gk. Χριστός). This title is a Greek translation of the Hebrew "Messiah" (Mashiach)—indicating "daubed with oil by a Man of God." It refers to a king, chosen by God. In the broader imperial Graeco-Roman realm, Jesus eventually became known as the only-begotten, genuine Son of God (Υιός τον θεοὐ).

Political Reality and the Faith in Resurrection

Christians frequently are faulted for insisting on impossible faith and dogma—as if the meaning of ancient concepts, neglected and misunderstood by our contemporaries, were already meaningless to the ancients. A case in point is the central Christian proclamation about Christ's resurrection from the tomb, following his Roman crucifixion. An honest historian should at least recognize the fact that Christians were not the first to believe or to talk about resurrection. The first Christians were Jews, a people who annually celebrated their liberation from enslavement in civilized Egypt. Their faith expected interferences by God as a matter of course. The God-Father, as he was later recognized by Christian converts, has sent his "only real" Son as a commoner. Then, according to their story, this Son proceeded to surpass the funeral-and-resurrection dramas by which ancient Egyptian imperialists claimed and secured divine mandates for themselves and their dynasties. Democracy could not have evolved in the West if, two thousand years ago the Christian faith, in an only commoner Son of God, had not summarily disenfranchised all ruling imperial Sons of God.

Since early hyper-domestication days, human history has been a competition among politically engaged storytellers. As far as Christian believers were concerned, the magnificent Resurrection News of Jesus Christ, a truly begotten Son of God born and raised among commoners, has far surpassed the usual stories of "made" imperial Sons of God. The declaration, "Christ is Risen!" or "Christ is Lord!" always meant that Christ surpassed ordinary Sons of God.

Conversion to the Christian religion was a political and a rational choice—aimed at rejecting servitude to ancient Egyptian, Persian, Greek or later Roman conquerors who aspired to divine status. Either, think "Resurrection" according to the Christ story; or, remain enslaved by the thuggery of imperial Sons of God who acted as though they owned humankind on the basis of their dynastic mandates—based on ancient Osiris-to-Horus resurrection/transformation feats as enthroned ruling gods. Roman emperors, who punished Christians for refusing to give them ritual sacrifices, were not jesting. Christians, too, were dead-serious with the freedom that their Gospel story implied. For commoners to escape enslavement and not to owe their lives to human owners, the Father-God of Jesus Christ has staged and prevailed in a competitive show of Death and Resurrection—premiering his only-begotten Son Jesus, and thereby achieved a victory that the stories of imperial Sons of God could not match.

The question asked two thousand years ago, was not whether resurrection from death was possible. Why would any underling want to confront emperors with bare theoretical resistance to authority that these rulers held! For the first Christians it was their own lives and freedom that mattered. So they asked, which type of Son of God could be their most effective Savior? What kind of savior could abolish enslavement—and also defeat death while he was at it? Big words like Life, Death, Resurrection, Second Birth, God Almighty, or Nature, have arrived on word lists, and in human minds, always associated with swarms of ancillary rationalized implications. The Christian proclamation of the Risen Christ was an easily understood political antithesis, a declaration of revolutionary faith for the dawning "Reign" or "Empire" of God, breaking forth to replace the "Prince of this World." The latter designation referred unabashedly to the Roman Empire, to the Beast, the Anti-Christ or Satan. Of course, at some point the Christian Church has accepted the help of Rome's Emperor/High Priest. She has welcomed Constantine's favoritism and has appreciated his strategy of weakening Rome's older religions.

The Roman Empire that executed Jesus of Nazareth did not distinguish between religion and politics. Thus, the earliest Christians did not attribute the title "Son of God" to their rabbi very openly in its Greek form as Υιός τον θεού. Instead, they spoke of him in quasi-political Hebrew terms as Messiah—a designation which, if spoken with an attitude of piety, could be kept free of revolutionary specifics. By implication, the Hebrew-Christian title of an anointed (messianic) Savior provoked a fresh perspective regarding the imperial world order—for the Reign of Heaven to arrive. Christians began reasoning afresh. Their revised world-view was proclaimed in a religious context, first by John the Baptizer and then continued by Jesus of Nazareth. For the Roman Empire, the implied political connotations were sufficiently obfuscated—enough so, that Pontius Pilate managed to inflict a death sentence on Jesus, disguised as a Jewish affair—on an acclaimed "King of the Jews" (as an apparent usurper of King Herod's throne). But actually, Jesus struck at the soft underbelly of the Roman Empire with fresh ontological, mythological, theological and political savvy. His followers experienced the sporadic imperial persecutions, waged by Rome, as activities of the satanic predatory "Beast," mentioned in the book of *Revelation*.

Christians offered their view of the dawning Reign of God as "good news" for everyone. Their gospel promised salvation to all potential victims. It promised eternal life through Jesus the Christ—a pauper from Nazareth in Galilee, who has been crucified by the Empire. Precisely him, who was executed by imperial Roman crucifixion to be shamed, him the Almighty God has resurrected! The story of Christ's resurrection left deceased Roman emperors, who acquired their "Son of God" status by political *apotheosis* (deification), slouching dead in their tombs. Forty days the disciples of Jesus encountered apparitions of their risen rabbi, and Roman authorities had no rational arguments that could disprove the Christian claims. Roman imperialists could not very well have denied the possibility of resurrection. It would have been tantamount to admitting the possibility, that the nearly three thousand years of Osiris-to-Horus transformations, including their politically staged Roman *apotheosis* replications, might also have been bogus. Could anyone respect Roman statecraft and jurisprudence on that basis?

A religious trend in democratization began already in ancient Egypt, with the resurrection-oriented burial cult during the "New Kingdom" era. The recent two millennia of Christian faith in "resurrection" has continued to lift the status and the dignity of commoners, as people who came to understand themselves to be siblings of Jesus Christ.

As siblings of the true Son of God—thus, adopted children of God the Father, who were being shown their way home. Over the centuries the Christian presence has wrought a slow adjustment of human status across the globe—a general upgrading of human worth, by faith.

The resurrection claim regarding Jesus of Nazareth has, in time, surpassed the burial status that deified Egyptian pharaohs and later Roman emperors expected from their rites of deification. In the context of Eternal Life, human Life-and-Death struggles are being fought for divine status. What once was fair to expect for the status of royals and imperials became, thereby, fair for all commoners who could understand and believe. Faith would arbitrate whether the arrogant or the meek shall inherit the Earth. Humankind walks along a path where, since times immemorial, the status of survivors has been derived—first attributed to an ancestor ceremonially and then deduced from him to be valid for later generations. For a contemporary parallel, in China, see Luckert, *Stone Age Religion...*, 2013, Chapter Nineteen.

The more-or-less "democratized" Egyptian "New Kingdom" theories of death and resurrection ranged, theologically, from Osiris and Isis to Geb and Nut, and thence to Shu and Tefnut, all the way home again to Atum, the All-God. They percolated rationally competitive, first among the middle and upper strata of ancient imperial Egypt. Imperial funerary soteriology has evolved into a method that could magnify divine afterlife status for anyone who could theologically believe and use it. It leaked and trickled imperial dignity and privileges, down to the upward striving strata of lower ranking people.

During the First Century of our present era—a little more than a thousand years after the now semi-legendary Exodus event, when pharaohs still thought about their own deaths as Osiris-resurrections and Horus-transformations—these basic ancient notions were refreshed in the Eastern Mediterranean realm by a brand-new faith that saves. It benefited all who converted to Christianity as fellow commoners. Like the Osiris cult earlier in Egypt, so also joy regarding the resurrection of the Anointed Jesus spread among the northern heirs of southern ancient pharaonic glory. And this movement began to sweep across the entire Egyptianized Roman Empire—including later in conjunction with the installment of Egyptian *Ra* religion under Aurelian.

While the Christian message sporadically succumbed to the ambitions of competing Caesars, it won the argument eventually by seeing the older war gods of Rome—Quirinus, Mars, Jupiter, Apollo and Sol Invictus—relegated to obscurity. The Empire was overtaken by the revolutionary Heaven-oriented religion that was ushered in by the death and resurrection-status of Jesus Christ. Constantine the Great believed that he won his battles and wars with the help of Jesus Christ.

To provide a more direct linguistic and historical transition from ancient imperial mythology to the Christian Easter proclamation, I will use here some of the terminology of the Egyptian Pyramid Texts, by which an ancient resurrection faith pertaining to "Son of God" manifestations was first configured and scripted. Jesus Christ is said to have risen from his tomb in the form of a resurrection body, of an intermittently visible apparition that reminds of the Osiris-body which, according to the ancient Egyptian imperial funerary resurrection-and-enthronement protocol was expected to reappear eventually as the *ba* of Horus. Accordingly, the core soul or *ka* of Jesus would have started returning to God while his *ba* still hung at the Roman cross as "shadow-soul," visible and dying. According to Pharisaic reasoning, he would there have been surrendering and returning his *ruach* (breath-soul) into the hands of God—cf. *Genesis* 2:7 and *Luke* 23:46. Please note that this Hebrew breath-soul (Heb. *ruach* = wind, breath, spirit) would in Heliopolitan theology have been Shu, back again in Atum the Father, at Emanation Level 2. Nevertheless, the visible shadow-encumbered *ba* aspect of the Jesus Incarnation would then have lingered forty days longer at his accustomed stomping grounds, until he, too, rose into Heaven for his full enthronement there.

Jesus of Nazareth was not the first founder of Christianity—John the Baptizer preached the arrival of the Kingdom of Heaven before Jesus came to the Jordan to be baptized by him. But for the Christian movement, Jesus became more significant later. Some of John's disciples have switched to follow Jesus, and Jesus gained a greater following. More of Jesus's teachings have been remembered, and his public crucifixion became the dramatic watershed for events that established him, literally, as an epiphany of the Godhead. For the Christian community Jesus was Lord. He stood in opposition and in contrast to Roman imperial Sons of God, and to the older gods of Rome.

Under the Emperor Constantine, the Roman Empire was getting reoriented in relation to Jesus Christ. It was getting reformed implicitly in relation to the deity that this High Priest of all Roman religions has legitimized. By a dare, at the eve prior to a battle, Constantine divined from sunbeams the support of Jesus Christ as his War Deity. He gambled on the hunch that this still malleable divine Savior-divinity would outperform for him the older gods of Rome. Indeed, it was faith in Jesus

Christ that eventually brought the Roman Empire to its knees, with emperors themselves kneeling as sponsors and devotees of the Church.

From the outset this emperor had the unification of the Empire on his mind, and apparently he judged the religion of Jesus the Anointed most worthy of institutionalization. For the Pontifex Maximus of all Roman religions, it was not an issue of insisting on monotheism or trinitarianism with arbitrary mathematical precision. He needed Jesus Christ first and foremost as his victorious War Sponsor, and subsequently as guarantor for his imperial mandate. Only a deity revered by faithful people, whom the emperor could trust, could empower such a mandate.

The early Christian Church, was never built exclusively on the teachings of that wise freelance rabbi from Nazareth, in Galilee. In spite of this fact, the "Historical Jesus" is now widely studied as the religion's primary founder. But this latter-day Christ Jesus came to be seen only recently as a plain "historical" person. Printing presses and the rise of general literacy have displayed him along a line of known historical sequences for simplified lay-minded scrutiny. The Christ of Christianity is now, on the basis of printed scripture texts explained as the "Historical Jesus." For a few years of his life he was addressed as "Rabbi" (Teacher). He wrote no book; though, more books have been written about him than about any other person we know.

The printed Christian "Bible" frequently is being approached as a God-given twin icon, next to the Jesus figure whom it introduces. It has become a school-book by which several centuries ago, people at large in the West, have learned to read and to acquire a fresh basis for individual status and authority. In mountainous and prairie regions of North America, prepositional phrases like "Jesus says," or "the Bible says," still are popular currency. They have helped establish a basis for self-assertive rural American individualism.

But books made of paper cannot be holy in themselves, unless, all the martyred trees milled into paper are declared holy as well. Still, the Hebrew and Christian scriptures will remain popular at the book markets, for their content mostly. The most Egyptian "Fourth Gospel," *John*, was as much an expression of early Christian thinking as were the Synoptic Gospels (*Mark, Matthew, Luke,* and a remnant source referred to as "Quelle)." In all of them, Jesus appears as the expected Savior or Anointed (Messiah), whose life and teachings became a divine standard for his followers. By virtue of his Roman crucifixion, however, Jesus came to be seen also as a divine Sacrifice—in line with archaic hunting, pastoralism, and hyper-domestication excesses, superseded then by expectations contained in *Second Isaiah.* As for Jesus, the *Second Isaiah* prophesy was punctuated by Roman imperial execution. The Jesus event necessitated fresh responses in the Hebrew dialectic with God, the Father. In the foreground, this God resurrected Jesus against the combined background-logic of Egyptian *ba*-shadows and *ka*-lights. The Hebrew *ruach* (breath) of Jesus departed as he died at the cross. An earthquake and a prolonged darkness, perhaps glimpses of Egyptian "Turn-around Twilight," have dramatized the backdrop of

Figure 18. At the right, replication of the Labarum of Constantine (reconstruction by Eugene Ipavec, 2006) Wickimedia Creative Commons licenses GFDL Public domain. This image, in turn, was constructed on the basis of an older standard of the Roman Empire, which was a red banner with the letters SPQR (Senātus Populusque Rōmānus) in gold, surrounded by a gold wreath hung on a military standard topped by a Roman eagle or an image of the goddess Victoria made of silver or bronze—reconstructed by Ssolbergj, at https://commons.wikimedia.org/w/index.php? curid =4249122

the death scene. Without these ancient dramatizations of death, the Christian story probably would never have made it into Greek or Latin lands—or into their writings. Without the *ba* of an Anointed, a Son of God nailed to a Roman cross, and without the death and resurrection tradition of Osiris reverberating three thousand years in preparation, the Christian response would probably not have gotten theologically and organizationally established. Mythology pertaining to the resurrected Horus, ascending to the throne of his divine Father—now endorsed by

Figure 19:

Flags, as late as in American Protestant churches memorialize Constantine's step away from pre-Christian Roman warrior totemism–from the "Horus" Eagle atop the Roman military standard (Figure 18, left) surviving atop the USA national flag (left). When Christianity became the state religion of the Roman Empire, plain crosses came to be the preferred emblem of Christianity in the West (right, and top). Constantine's Chi Rho emblem (Figure 18. right) is still widely used and often also understood.

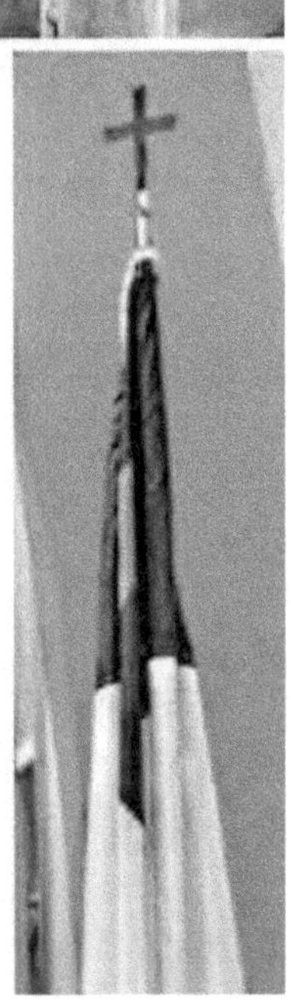

the empty tomb of Jesus Christ on Easter morning—has provided context for the larger flow of imperial "civilized" intentions. Without these paradigms from ancient mythology, people in the Near East and the disciples of Jesus could not have understood why the All-God has performed antithetically—pillorying a crucifixion. To this Christian repertoire of thought, another communal revelatory event was added —Pentecost. The Egyptian-Jewish-Graeco-Roman gospel story, of a Father God having sent (emanated, procreated) his Son into the world, would probably never have been understood in northern lands without hearing it told also dualistically, involving the "Holy Spirit." Before rational minds of the Graeco-Roman realm could open up to the Christian message, the apostles needed to bridge the cultural faultline between South and North.

The "Procreative Father-God" concept of ancient Egypt needed to be assimilated within Judea and Galilee, and the Son of God needed to be explained as well with reference to the Holy Spirit. The apostles needed to pay attention to regional vocabularies and languages. They needed to learn the fine arts of translating ambiguities from among multiple connotations. The composition of the Christian Trinity, according to aspects and number, has been the bequest of Egyptian imperial soteriology. The nature of the Third Person in the Heliopolitan Trinity, known as Tefnut, has already in ancient Egypt been tweaked toward her significance as Mahet (Justice, Order, Wisdom)—whereas in northern lands the highest Godhead was most easily conceptualized as Spirit.

The persistent necessity of translation left another deficit gaping in the Christian story. The feminine aspect of Tefnut was in danger of getting lost in transition. This is why for the Christian story in the Mediterranean area, anything related to the purity and worthiness of Mary needed to be sublimated, eventually—however clumsily—to make room for a "Mother of God" to replace the Regina Caelorum (the Egyptian Queen of Heaven). The world cannot function biologically with only the potency of fathers and sons. Tefnut and Isis needed to be brought home into the daughter-religion that became Christianity, once again nearer to the heart of the All-God.

Christians who found themselves under the "Chi Rho" Christ insignia of Constantine, in the Empire, have over time preferred again the less political and less militaristic design of plain crosses to mark their churches. Doing so they continued to rub again the old Empire's nose—the civil pride of Rome—more explicitly in the muck. They celebrated Jesus Christ and thereby pilloried the Empire's cruelty. Constantine abolished crucifixion eight years after Nicaea. Until then this Christological blemish remained tagged to his religious office as Pontifex Maximus and High-Priest, indistinguishable from being Emperor. As long as he could accommodate Jesus Christ as his victorious War-deity, his imperial posture would be accepted. But then, not all religions are created equal, and the Pontifex Maximus found reasons to favor Christianity.

From Biblical Salvation to American Independence

Constantine's quandary, of how to court religions or how to let religions help balance monarchies, empires, or republics was not completely foreign to the Founding Fathers of the United States. Yet, these men no longer considered the Roman solution to be an option. They installed neither a Pontifex Maximus nor a Secretary of Religions. Their reasoning is reflected in their 1791 Bill of Rights: "Congress shall make no law respecting an establishment of religion, or prohibiting the free exercise thereof; or abridging the freedom of speech, or of the press; or the right of the people peaceably to assemble, and to petition the government for a redress of grievances."

Time and events have overtaken some of the provisions of our Founding Fathers. While monarchs conquered and compiled, our founders fought for independence from their own imperial compiler. Identical religious denominations from earlier centuries got caught at both sides of the revolutionary front; they needed to be kept neutral and at arm's length. By way of reserving the most relevant powers for management of their state, and by regarding religious associations as being negligible and the content of religions as being more or less irrelevant, these founders distinguished between state and religion with an almost child-like Enlightenment-disregard for history. This left religious associations free to change and to multiply in accordance with what they understood or dreamed their faith to be. No efforts for serious rational exchanges between church and state were expected anymore. Mutual learning slowed to a trickle.

Nevertheless, the neglect of religion in our legal knowledge-base has become critical in our days. America has no non-tautological legal definition of "religion," none that could be used to distinguish religious demeanor from either zealotry or insanity. The results of this vacuum are bad enough for keeping the religious offspring of Protestant Euro-Americans in line; but referencing religion in diplomatic negotiations abroad, or vis-à-vis Native American tribal traditions—in settings where religion does not pertain to familiar Bible content—the abyss of ambiguity has never gotten bridged. Resolutions pertaining to religion, explained tautologically, are dysfunctional at best. One should remember that theology began as the language of choice for settling political disputes. Moreover, scraps and blessings of older religion still need to be invoked today by governments "of the people," as these try to empower "rights to life" and "laws for the people."

The legal vacuum extends all the way to general education. For example, what clarifications do historians and political scientists expect today from the worldwide study of religions? Should their limited scientific curiosities, about religious "handles," be used only to exploit a people's superstitions? Or, are religious themes efficient stepping stones for negotiating peace, for doing politics at older sublime levels, with less violent confrontation? Eleven years after China's 1966-1976 Cultural Revolution I began exploring religions of the Middle Kingdom, I noticed that key words pertaining to religion had been purged from the dictionaries that were being printed back then. Introspectively I began to wonder how many categories or words might have gotten disabled by our Founding Fathers with their "generous Enlightenment" perspective.

During the 1970s, when I did field research in Navajo Indian tribal religion, I noticed that Western medical science had no secular concepts by which basic shamanic Navajo thoughts about disease and healing could be understood. Inherited religious words—referring to the greater-than-human dimension of reality—loom and float across the world's cultural boundaries like supercharged clouds of neglected meaning. They can be tapped for stabilizing peace or for prolonging states of war and mayhem, as well as for the pursuit of happiness for which our Founding Fathers hoped to enable us. Sublime words can be interpreted as other people's aspirations to wellbeing. They just as easily can be weaponized sarcastically, to instigate never-ending strife and hatred. All people, whether overtly religious or scientifically aggressive, protect their "rational" compilations by strengthening them with hidden greater-than-human authoritative assumptions—with shields or enforcement rods.

Indeed, our Founding Fathers did well by keeping their new State from meddling shortsightedly with religious establishments. In their days they faced and appreciated the people's tentative political innocence and readiness for accommodation. Early pioneers showed not much desire, yet, for wanting to politicize their communities—a virtue that in itself was well suited for grass-roots stabilization among fellow neighbors and homesteaders. Many of them, as refugees or exiles from dire Old World circumstances, contemplated the ethics of Jesus as they found it recorded in the Sermon on the Mount. Pragmatically they weighed both aspects, the Giving and the Receiving. Though, some of our Enlightenment Fathers have distanced themselves from folk religiosity, they never dared to alienate religious groups entirely.

Freed from direct state control, Christian churches in America evolved differently than elsewhere. Of course, it stands to reason that early religious and ethnic groupings have evolved beyond the circumstances of first generation pioneers. Christian, Jewish, Muslim and other groups have demonstrated that it is possible to get along and to become Americanized.

Viewing the origins of other people historically, and observing different political causes or religious aspirations with empathy, helped appreciate new neighbors for sufferings endured. Where secular politicians and devotees to alike deities have compared their experiences, they could avoid some of the authoritarian pit-falls which, back in Old World environments, some of their forebears were obliged to dig, and into which some of them, inevitably, have fallen. They also learned from mutual New World plunders over which, in the course of their frontier adaptation, some ethnicities have collided.

Some fourteen thousand years ago perhaps, Euro-Asian Stone Age hunters—the earliest "American Indian" immigrants—brought whatever gathering and hunting skills, and whatever religious customs they had carried across the Bering land-and-ice bridge onto Alaska. All these people were still struggling to balance the hardships and economies of Stone and Ice Age gatherers and hunters. Their southward wanderings and struggles, and some of their religious practices can still be tracked archaeologically and ethnologically from Alaska toward Middle America and into the next southern continent—to points where they invented agriculture and evolved systems of hyper-domestication (also called "civilization"). Some of their religious innovations we were able to sketch in our 1976 volume titled *Olmec Religion, a Key to Middle America and Beyond* (University of Oklahoma Press).

Some theistically agnostic offspring, whose ancestors at some point in time had been lifted by the religion of Jesus Christ to the status of being children of God, eventually also arrived in America. Two hundred forty-five years ago, in Philadelphia, some of their Enlightenment offspring declared their independence from a conceited king who "by the Grace of God"—of all things!—considered fellow human beings predestined to be his subjects and property. On top of this, he deemed himself to be Head of the Christian church. It followed, that the signers of the Declaration of Independence no longer could appeal to "Laws of God" to assert their freedom; so they turned to appeal to "Laws of Nature" as their fall-back authority. This step, necessarily, has reduced for them the magnitude of the king's God somewhat, to a kind of less personal "principle of creativity." Repositioning themselves, they began to refer to the biblical "Creator" deity as "Nature's God."

Grammatically passable? Yes, but intentionally ambiguous. Nature, here, owns the Creator as someone whose creativity she supervises.

All the while, our Founding Fathers deferred to the Creator-God out of habit, to benefit from the stability of a majority tradition—thus, to preserve authority for governing their Republic, to stabilize privileges, to oblige fellow citizens to perform duties and to obey the laws. Attributes of the Creator, where they continued to be acknowledged, were still useful to govern free people by divine mandate. But the God of Jefferson was merely an aspect or "property" of Nature, and as such he appears considerably diminished. Today many people rank the Christian God-Father lower than material Nature, Energy, Gravity, Chance, Fate—some even as low as Nothing. Nevertheless, such radical devaluation shortens out the value-circuits of general rationality as well.

It now seems as though, in the beginning, the Creator enabled First Man to think a little, about nothing in particular. When Adam began to think a little, he instantly saw himself to be the wisest accumulation of intellect. But any thoughts about Nothing, which Adam scraped together, he first needed to visualize hypothetically as something substantial. He could only deny the existence of "some thing." Denying no thing simply would have meant doing nothing. So Adam put his mind, his hands and brain-tipped teeth to the task. He could not create anything--but only put together fragments which he first chipped from pre-existent larger wholes. Anything he considered meaningful he also could find meaningless; anything he assembled he could, and eventually would, destroy.

On this day—January the 6th, Anno Domini 2021—in the United States of America, neglect and loss of religious as well as political common sense has been amply demonstrated. Our president, who on occasion spoke of himself as the "Chosen One," incited his "beloved" mob to attack Congress in session, at the Capitol Building. For a while, American democracy saw itself to be a laughing-stock to the world.

In barren minds of We-the-People people, doused embers have collapsed to ashes. America has forgotten that Reality is One—that multitudes of alternate realities most often are fallacies and lies. Abandoning integrity in science, sanity in politics and humble thought in religion, American "patriots" have stormed the citadel of their Democracy for the love of a president who was willing to take advantage of them all--to sacrifice even his vice president at the gallows for his cause. Those patriots were fighting without a mandate for greater-than-human authority. Indeed, greedy minds will never attempt to secure liberty or justice for others. Nations without unselfish goals cannot long endure.

Bibliography

Aldred, Cyril. *Akhenaten, King of Egypt*. London: Thames and Hudson, 1988.

Alford, Garth. *The Origin and Development of a Foreign Eschatological Concept in Archaic Greek Literature*. PhD diss., University of Washington, 1987. Ann Arbor: University of Michigan, Microfilms.

_____. "Elysion—A Foreign Eschatological Concept in Homer's Odyssey." Unpublished Manuscript, 1989.

Allen, Thomas George, trans. *The Book of the Dead or Going Forth by Day*. Studies in Ancient Oriental Civilization 37. Chicago: University of Chicago Press, 1974.

Anderson, Bernhard W., *Understanding the Old Testament*, 3rd ed. Englewood Cliffs, NJ: Prentice-Hall, 1971.

Andrae, Thor. *Mohammed, the Man and His Faith*. New York: Harper Torchbooks, 1960.

Anthes, Rudolf. "Mythology in Ancient Egypt." In *Mythologies of the Ancient World*, edited by S. M. Kramer. Garden City, NY: Doubleday and Co., 1961.

Armstrong, A. H., trans. *Plotinus, seven volumes*. Cambridge, MA: Harvard University Press, 1966–88.

Arnold Bill T. and Richard S. Hess. *Ancient Israel's History: An Introduction to Issues and Sources*. Other contributors are James K. Hoffmeier, Samuel Greengus, Lawson G. Stone, Robert D. Miller II, Daniel Bodi, Steven M. Ortiz, James K. Mead, Kyle Greenwood, Sandra Richter, Brad E. Kelle, Peter van der Veen, André Lemaire, and David A. deSilva. Ada, MI: Baker Academic, 2014.

Benjamin, Don C. "Israel's God: Mother and Midwife." *Biblical Theology Bulletin* 19 (1989).

_____. "The Adam and Eve Story." Unpublished manuscript, copyrighted 1990.

Berchman, Robert M. *From Philo to Origen: Middle Platonism in Transition*. Chico, CA: Scholars Press, 1984.

Bernal, Martin. *Black Athena: The Afroasiatic Roots of Classic Civilization,* Vol. 1, *The Fabrication of Ancient Greece, 1785–1985*. New Brunswick, NJ: Rutgers University Press, 1987.

Bonnet, Hans. *Reallexikon der Ägyptischen Religionsgeschichte*. Berlin: Walter de Gruyter, 1952.

Bowman, Alan K. *Egypt after the Pharaohs, 332 BC-AD 642*. Berkeley: University of California Press, 1986.

Brehier, Emile. *The Philosophy of Plotinus,* trans. Joseph Thomas. Chicago: University of Chicago Press, 1958.

Breasted, J. H. *Development of Religion and Thought in Ancient Egypt*. New York: Charles Scribner's Sons, 1912.

Bretall, Robert. ed. *A Kierkegaard Anthology*. Princeton, NJ: Princeton University Press, 1946.

Budge, E.A.W. *The Book of the Dead: The Papyrus of Ani in the British Museum, 1895*. New York: Dover Publications, 1967.

Burkert, Walter. *Greek Religion*. Cambridge: Harvard University Press, 1985 (German ed. 1977).

_____. *Ancient Mystery Cults*. Cambridge, MA: Harvard University Press, 1987.

Burleigh, John H. S., trans. *Augustine: Earlier Writings*. Philadelphia: Westminster Press, 1953.

Burnaby, John, trans. *Augustine: Later Works*. Philadelphia: Westminster Press, 1955.

Casson, Lionel. *Ancient Egypt*. New York: Time Inc., 1965.

Charlesworth, James H. ed. *The Apogrypha and Pseudo-Epigrapha of the Old Testament,* Vol. 2. Oxford: Clarendon Press, 1913. ed. *The Old Testament Pseudo-Epigrapha, Apocalyptic Literature and Testaments,* Vol. 1. Garden City, NY: Doubleday and Co., 1983.

Clark, R. T. Rundle. *Myth and Symbol in Ancient Egypt,* London: Thames and Hudson, 1959.

De Buck, Adriaan. *The Egyptian Coffin Texts,* Vol. 2. Chicago: University of Chicago Press, 1935–61.

Dodds, E. R., et al. *Entretiens Sur L'Antiquite Classique,* Vol. 5, *Les Sources de Plotin*. Geneva: Foundation Hardt, 1960.

Dörrie, Heinrich. "Ammonius, der Lehrer Plotins." *Hermes 83* (1955): 439–477.

_____. "Was ist 'spätantiker Platonismus'? Überlegungen zur Grenzziehung zwischen Platonismus und Christentum." *Theologische Rundschau 36,* no. 4 (1971): 285–302.

Ehrman, Bart D. *The Triumph of Christianity.* New York: Simon and Schuster, 2018.

Eliade, Mircea. *A History of Religious Ideas,* 3 volumes. Chicago: University of Chicago Press, 1985.

Erman, Adolf. "Der Leidener Amonshymnus." *Sitzungsberichte der Preußischen Akademie der Wissenschaften 11* (1923).

_____. *Die Religion der Ägypter: Ihr Werden und Vergehen in Vier Jahrtausenden.* Berlin and Leipzig: Walter de Gruyter, 1934.

_____. *The Ancient Egyptians, a Sourcebook of Their Writings,* trans. Aylward M. Blackman. Gloucester, England: Peter Smith, 1978 [1966].

Faulkner, R. O. *The Ancient Egyptian Pyramid Texts.* New York: Oxford University Press, 1969.

_____. *The Ancient Egyptian Coffin Texts.* Warminster, England: Aris and Phillips, 1973.

Frankfort, Henri. *Ancient Egyptian Religion: An Interpretation.* New York: Harper and Row, 1961 [1948].

_____. *Kingship and the Gods: A Study of Ancient Near Eastern Religion as the Integration of Society and Nature.* Chicago: University of Chicago Press, 1978 [1948].

Geldner, Karl F. *Der Rigveda,* Harvard Oriental Series, Vol. 33–36. Cambridge, MA: Harvard University Press, 1951.

Ginzberg, Louis. *The Legends of the Jews.* New York: Simon and Schuster, 1961 [1909].

Goetze, Albrecht. "Hittite Myths, Epics, and Legends." In *Ancient Near Eastern Texts Relating to the Old Testament*, edited by James B. Pritchard. Princeton, NJ: Princeton University Press, 1955.

Gottwald, Norman K. *The Tribes of Yahweh: A Sociology of the Religion of Liberated Israel, 1250–1050 BCE*. Maryknoll, NY: Orbis Books, 1979.

Guthrie, W. K. C., *The Greeks and Their Gods*. Boston: Beacon Press, 1955 [1950].

_____ . *A History of Greek Philosophy*, 6 volumes. Cambridge: Cam-bridge University Press, 1962.

Guttmann, Julius. *Philosophies of Judaism*, trans. David W. Silverman. Garden City, NY: Anchor Books, Doubleday, 1966 [1964].

Hamilton, E. and H. Cairns. *Collected Dialogues of Plato*. Princeton, NJ: Princeton University Press, 1963.

Harris, R. Baine, ed. *Neo-Platonism and Indian Thought*. Norfolk, VA: International Society for Neo-Platonic Studies, 1982.

Henry, Paul, "The Place of Plotinus in the History of Thought." In *Plotinus: The Enneads*, trans. Stephen MacKenna. New York: Pantheon Books, 1962.

Hesiod. "Theogony." In *Hesiod, the Homeric Hymns and Homerica*, trans. H. G. Evelyn-White. Cambridge, MA: Harvard University Press, 1977.

Heussi, Karl. *Kompendium der Kirchengeschichte*, 12th ed. Tübingen: J.C.B. Mohr Verlag, 1960.

Holte, Ragnar. "Logos Spermatikos, Christianity and Ancient Philosophy according to St. Justin's Apologies." *Studia Theologica 12* (1958): 109–168.

Hornung, Erik. *Geist der Pharaonenzeit*. Zürich: Artemis Verlag, 1989.

Ions, Veronica. *Egyptian Mythology*. Middlesex, England: Hamlyn Publishing Group, 1968.

Jonas, Hans. *The Gnostic Religion: The Message of the Alien God and the Beginnings of Christianity*. Boston: Beacon Press, 1963 [1958].

_____. *Die mythologische Gnosis—mit einer Einleitung zur Geschichte und Methodologie der Forschung*. Göttingen: Vandenhoeck and Ruprecht, 1964.

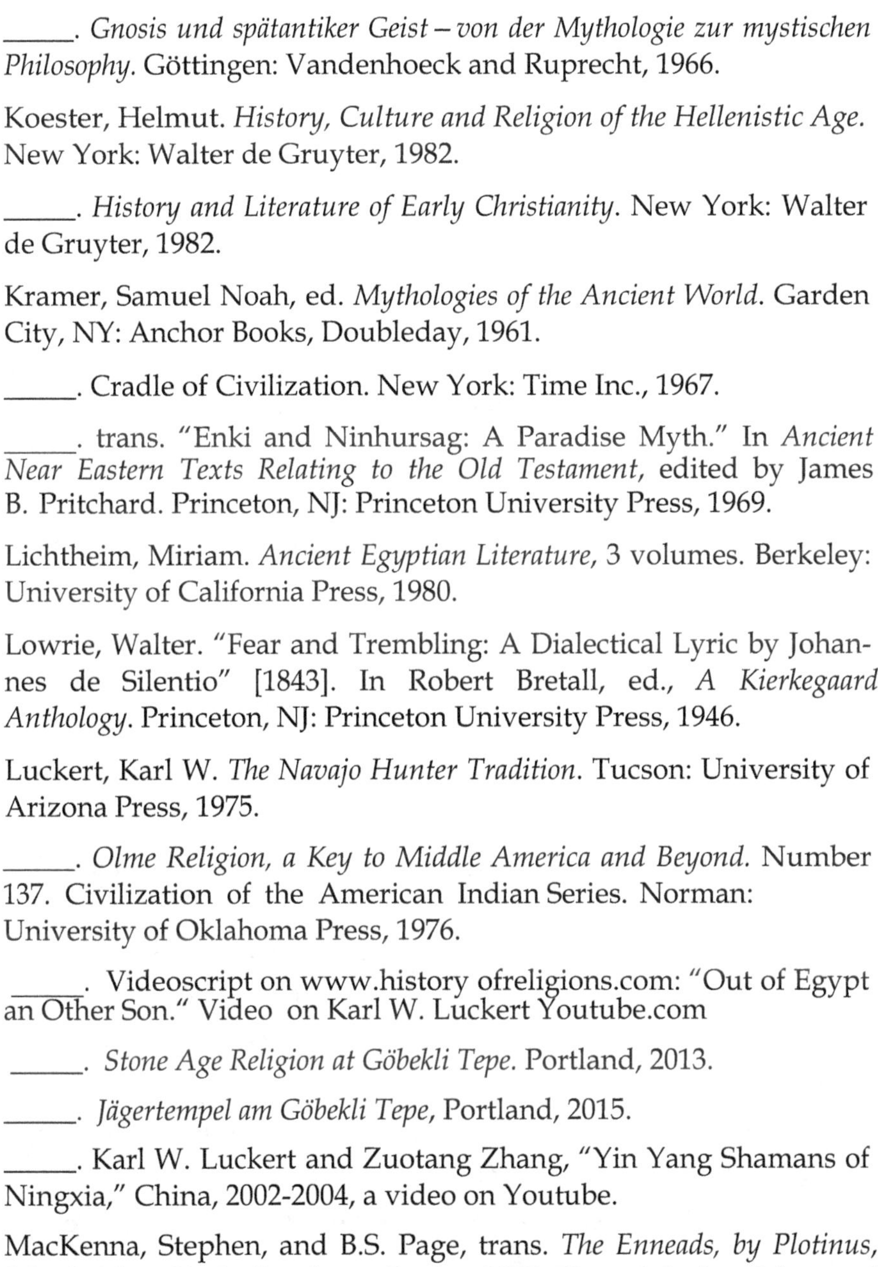

_____. *Gnosis und spätantiker Geist – von der Mythologie zur mystischen Philosophy*. Göttingen: Vandenhoeck and Ruprecht, 1966.

Koester, Helmut. *History, Culture and Religion of the Hellenistic Age*. New York: Walter de Gruyter, 1982.

_____. *History and Literature of Early Christianity*. New York: Walter de Gruyter, 1982.

Kramer, Samuel Noah, ed. *Mythologies of the Ancient World*. Garden City, NY: Anchor Books, Doubleday, 1961.

_____. Cradle of Civilization. New York: Time Inc., 1967.

_____. trans. "Enki and Ninhursag: A Paradise Myth." In *Ancient Near Eastern Texts Relating to the Old Testament,* edited by James B. Pritchard. Princeton, NJ: Princeton University Press, 1969.

Lichtheim, Miriam. *Ancient Egyptian Literature,* 3 volumes. Berkeley: University of California Press, 1980.

Lowrie, Walter. "Fear and Trembling: A Dialectical Lyric by Johannes de Silentio" [1843]. In Robert Bretall, ed., *A Kierkegaard Anthology*. Princeton, NJ: Princeton University Press, 1946.

Luckert, Karl W. *The Navajo Hunter Tradition*. Tucson: University of Arizona Press, 1975.

_____. *Olme Religion, a Key to Middle America and Beyond.* Number 137. Civilization of the American Indian Series. Norman: University of Oklahoma Press, 1976.

_____. Videoscript on www.history ofreligions.com: "Out of Egypt an Other Son." Video on Karl W. Luckert Youtube.com

_____. *Stone Age Religion at Göbekli Tepe*. Portland, 2013.

_____. *Jägertempel am Göbekli Tepe*, Portland, 2015.

_____. Karl W. Luckert and Zuotang Zhang, "Yin Yang Shamans of Ningxia," China, 2002-2004, a video on Youtube.

MacKenna, Stephen, and B.S. Page, trans. *The Enneads, by Plotinus*, 3d ed. New York: Pantheon Books, 1962. Copyright by Faber and Faber Ltd., London.

Mallory, J. P. *In Search of the Indo-Europeans: Language, Archaeology and Myth*. London: Thames and Hudson, 1989.

Matthews, Victor H., *Manners and Customs of the Bible*. Peabody, MA: Hendrickson Publications, 1988.

Miller, J. Maxwell and John H. Hayes. *A History of Ancient Israel and Judah*. Philadelphia: Westminster Press, 1986.

Morenz, Siegfried. *Ägyptische Religion*. Stuttgart: Kohlhammer Verlag, 1960.

Nahm, Milton C., ed. *Selections from Early Greek Philosophy*. New York: Appleton-Century-Crofts, 1962.

O'Meara, Dominic J. *Neo-Platonism and Christian Thought*. Norfolk, VA: International Society for Neo-Platonic Studies, 1982.

Oppenheim, A. Leo, et al., eds. "Akitu," in *Assyrian Dictionary*, Vol. 1, pp. 267–272. Chicago: The Oriental Institute, 1964.

Outler, Albert C., trans. *Augustine: Confessions and Enchiridion*. Philadelphia: Westminster Press, 1955.

Pagels, Elaine H. *The Gnostic Gospels*. New York: Random House, 1979.

Pearson, Birger A. and James E. Göhring, eds. *The Roots of Egyptian Christianity*. Philadelphia: Fortress Press, 1986.

Pritchard, James B., ed. *Ancient Near Eastern Texts Relating to the Old Testament*, 3d ed. Princeton, NJ: Princeton University Press, 1969.

Redford, Donald B. *Akhenaten, the Heretic King*. Princeton, NJ: Princeton University Press, 1984.

Renfrew, Colin. *Archaeology and Language: The Puzzle of Indo-European Origins*. New York: Cambridge University Press, 1987.

Ringgren, Helmer. *Israelitische Religion*. Stuttgart: Kohlhammer Verlag, 1963.

Robinson, James M., ed. *The Nag Hammadi Library*. San Francisco: Harper and Row, 1981 [1977].

Ross, W. D. *Aristotle, a Complete Exposition of His Works*. Cleveland: Meridian Books, 1962 [1959].

Rudolph, Kurt. *Gnosis: The Nature and History of Gnosticism*. San Francisco: Harper and Row, 1987.

Ryne, Linn. "The Faistos Disc—Norwegian Researcher Unravels Ancient Mystery." *Norway Now*, no. 6 (1990).

Sabloff, Jeremy A. and C. C. Lamberg-Karlovsky. *The Rise and Fall of Civilizations: Modern Archaeological Approaches to Ancient Cultures.* Menlo Park, CA: Cummings Publishing Co., 1974.

Sakellarakis, Yannis and Efi Sapouna-Sakellarakis. "Drama of Death in a Minoan Temple." *National Geographic* Vol. 159, No. 2 (February 1981), 204–222.

Schaff, Philip. *Creeds of Christendom,* 3 Vols. Baker Books, Ada 1977.

Seawright, Caroline. *Human Sacrifice in Ancient Egypt.* http://tour-egypt.net/feature stories/humansac.htm.

Sethe, Kurt. *Uebersetzung und Kommentar zu den Ägyptischen Pyramiden-Texten,* 6 volumes. Hamburg: J. J. Augustin, 1962.

_____. "Amun und die acht Urgötter von Hermopolis." *Abhandlungen der Preußischen Akademie der Wissenschaften,* 1929: 4.

Silberman, Neil Asher, and Israel Finkelstein. *The Bible Unearthed: Archaeology's New Vision of Ancient Israel and the Origin of Its Sacred Texts.* New York: Free Press, 2002.

Skinner, John. *A Critical and Exegetical Commentary on Genesis.* Edinburgh: T. & T. Clark, 1969 [1910].

Smart, Ninian. *The World's Religions.* Englewood Cliffs, NJ: Prentice Hall, 1989.

Smith, Jonathan Z. "A Pearl of Great Price and a Cargo of Yams: A Study in Situational Incongruity." *History of Religions 16,* no. 1 (1976): 1–11.

Theiler, Willy. *Forschungen zum Neuplatonismus.* Berlin: Walter de Gruyter & Co., 1966.

Thomas, D. Winton, ed. *Documents from Old Testament Times.* New York: Harper and Row, 1958.

Trigg, Joseph Wilson. *Origen: The Bible and Philosophy in the Third- Century Church.* Atlanta: John Knox Press, 1983.

Turnbull, Grace H. *The Essence of Plotinus: Extracts from the Six Enneads and Porphyry's Life of Plotinus.* Westport, CT: Greenwood Press, 1934.

Turok, Neil. *The Universe Within: From Quantum to Cosmos*, House of Anansi Press, 2012.

Van den Broek, R. and M. J. Vermaseren, eds. *Studies in Gnosticism and Hellenistic Religions:* Presented to Gilles Quispel on the Occasion of his 65th Birthday. Leiden: E. J. Brill, 1981.

Van Seters, John. *The Hyksos, a New Investigation*. New Haven, CT: Yale University Press, 1966.

Waddell, W. G., trans. *Manetho*. Cambridge, MA: Harvard University Press, 1971.

Walker, Williston. *A History of the Christian Church*. New York: Scribner, 1959.

Wilson, John A. *The Burden of Egypt*. Chicago: Univ. of Chicago Press, 1951.

_____. trans. "The Theology of Memphis" and "Egyptian Myths, Tales, and Mortuary Texts." In *Ancient Near Eastern Texts Relating to the Old Testament*, edited by James B. Pritchard. Princeton, NJ: Princeton University Press, 1969.

Wolfson, Harry Austryn. *Philo: Foundations of Religious Philosophy in Judaism, Christianity, and Islam*. Cambridge, MA: Harvard University Press, 1962 [1947].

Wolters, Albert M. "Survey of Modern Scholarly Opinion." In *Neo-Platonism and Indian Thought*, ed. R. Blaine Harris. Norfolk, VA: International Society for Neo-Platonic Studies, 1982.

Wlosok, Antonie. *Römischer Kaiserkult*. Darmstadt: Wissenschaftliche Buchgesellschaft, 1978.

Index

ISBN 978-0-9839072-7-5

www.ingramcontent.com/pod-product-compliance
Lightning Source LLC
LaVergne TN
LVHW010942100826
845153LV00002B/118

* 9 7 8 0 9 8 3 9 0 7 2 7 5 *